More Advance Praise for

Armies of Heaven

"Rubenstein's book is a thrill to the casual reader and to the scholar alike. His prose carries the reader along with the extraordinary events of the First Crusade, effortlessly integrating the bloody realities of the battlefield, astute portraits of the leaders, and a convincing historical argument about the nature of the First Crusade. *Armies of Heaven* shows how easily piety, violence, and political scheming intermesh, but also warns against facile comparisons of medieval crusades to contemporary conflicts, the rhetoric of al-Qaeda notwithstanding. Steven Runciman's account of the First Crusade provided a standard of eloquence for the last fifty years; Jay Rubenstein's matches Runciman for style, and surpasses with a discerning eye and a sly but scathing wit."

—Christopher MacEvitt, author of *Crusades and the Christian World of the East: Rough Tolerance*

"The First Crusade has been a source of fascination from the late eleventh century down to the present. Recent historians have analyzed this epochal event in terms of demography, economics, secular politics, ecclesiastical politics, and ecclesiastical theory. Jay Rubenstein asks a refreshing question: How did the thousands and tens of thousands who joined the sacred undertaking view it? His fascinating answer is that most of these crusaders were convinced that they were living at the cusp of the end of days, at the point in time when the world order would change dramatically. Rubenstein's insights will profoundly enrich our understanding of the First Crusade, its glories, and its horrors."

—Robert Chazan, New York University

ARMIES OF HEAVEN

The FIRST CRUSADE *and the* QUEST
for APOCALYPSE

JAY RUBENSTEIN

BASIC BOOKS
A Member of the Perseus Books Group
New York

Designed by Jeff Williams

Maps courtesy of the University of Tennessee Cartographic Services Laboratory, Will Fontanez, cartographer.

Library of Congress Cataloging-in-Publication Data
Rubenstein, Jay, 1967–
    Armies of heaven : the first crusade and the quest for apocalypse / Jay Rubenstein. — 1st ed,
        p. cm.
    Includes bibliographical references and index.
    ISBN 978-0-465-01929-8 (hardcover : alk. paper) — ISBN 978-0-465-02748-4 (e-book) 1. Crusades—First, 1096–1099. 2. Military history, Medieval. I. Title.

D161.2.R73 2011
940.1'8—dc22

                                                                    2011004195

10 9 8 7 6 5 4 3 2 1

This book is for Meredith

Contents

The world of the First Crusade

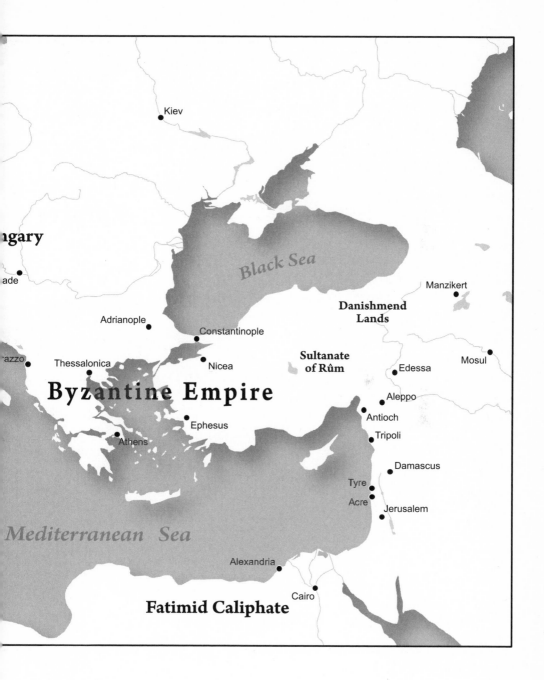

Kiev

Hungary

ade

Black Sea

Manzikert

Danishmend
Lands

Adrianople

Constantinople

azzo

Thessalonica

Nicea

Sultanate
of Rûm

Edessa

Mosul

Byzantine Empire

Aleppo

Ephesus

Antioch

Tripoli

Athens

Damascus

Tyre

Acre

Jerusalem

Mediterranean Sea

Alexandria

Cairo

Fatimid Caliphate

Introduction

In 1096 approximately 100,000 people—warriors, priests, women, poor folk, bishops, prophets, and a few children—left homes in France, Italy, and Germany and marched to Jerusalem. They intended to worship at Christ's tomb and, in the process, to reclaim the city for the Christian world. Three years later, on July 15, 1099, a fraction of that group broke through Jerusalem's defenses, killed the city's garrison and residents, and transformed the ancient Middle Eastern city into the capital of a European principality. This long campaign became known as the First Crusade. Contemporaries, not realizing that it would be the first of several such expeditions and not yet having invented the word "crusade," simply called it "the pilgrimage" or "the movement." Sensing its importance, they began documenting it almost immediately, in part to celebrate the army's achievement but also to try to understand it. Something profoundly important had happened, not just in the history of Europe or even in the history of the world. It was a new phase in God's plan. At the very least, the armies had set in motion events prophesied for centuries. The work begun with Christ's crucifixion a millennium earlier might now be drawing to a close, the apocalyptic clock started due to the actions of modern men.[1]

Even with centuries of hindsight, this sense of cataclysmic upheaval seems appropriate. Most immediately, the crusade led to the creation of French-speaking settlements in the Middle East, governments that would endure in some form for nearly two centuries. Because of the crusade, Western Europeans grew more familiar with Greek civilization and came into closer contact with Arab civilization than ever before. The crusade also fostered the development of military technology, such that war at home and abroad occurred on a scale previously unimaginable. War also became an honorable profession. Prior to the crusade, violence on the battlefield was a sinful act, as it would be in any other setting. Now warriors had the option of practicing their art while adding to their store of virtues—not in spite of their brutality but because of it.

More fundamentally, the crusade helped to fashion a broader sense of Christian identity in an otherwise divided European homeland. Pilgrims came from different cultures and spoke different languages—German, Flemish, Norman, French, Provençal, and Italian—but their shared experiences instilled in them a common identity: Now all were Franks. The most frequent title for contemporary histories of the era celebrated this new sense of brotherhood: *Deeds of the Franks* or, as one historian preferred, *God's Deeds Through the Franks*. It would be no exaggeration to say that the economy, spirituality, technology, and morality—the foundations of Western culture—would be remade because of the First Crusade.

But even this list of historical transformations fails to capture how precisely apocalyptic the First Crusade was, both for the people who marched to Jerusalem and for those who stayed home and celebrated. In the 1090s, as far as anyone could tell, God (or Satan) had loosed Antichrist on the world. The armies of Gog and Magog had broken through the gates behind which Alexander the Great had imprisoned them. And Christian armies were preparing to make a stand at Jerusalem, to fight around Mount Calvary, where Christ had died, and before the Mount of Olives, where He would soon return—not merely to follow in the footsteps of saints but to wield swords alongside them in battles against a demonic foe. When Jerusalem fell to the Franks and when Christ did not appear, apocalyptic enthusiasm did not die. Rather, historians in Europe and in the Middle East continued to write books about the crusade for decades, asking not just whether the end of the world was nigh. They wondered instead, had the Apocalypse already happened?

This book will retell these tales of Jerusalem's conquest and the apocalypse that accompanied it. The former story, the military history, has been written often and well. But it has not been told in a way that engages the grand ideas behind the First Crusade—the beliefs that helped to create it and that helped to drive the armies forward toward their goal.

On a fundamental level, the First Crusade was a holy war, a style of combat that was, in the 1090s, altogether new: a war fought on behalf of God and in fulfillment of His plan. It did not just provide soldiers with a new path to salvation, a way to use martial prowess to perform good deeds. It also enabled them to fight in battles longer and bloodier than any they had ever imagined. So full of pageantry and gore were the sieges of Nicea (May–June 1097), Antioch (October 1097–June 1098), Ma'arra (November–December 1098), and Jerusalem (June–July 1099) that they surpassed earthly conflict, pointing soldiers toward heaven as well as giving them some experience of hell. When the survivors returned to Europe and relived their memories, cooler and more educated heads could only agree: They had witnessed the Apocalypse.[2]

Despite an abundance of evidence, the apocalyptic crusade has not received its due, in part because historians mistrust our best and most abundant evidence for it: a collection of chronicles written by churchmen in France and Germany starting around the year 1107. Apocalyptic language permeates these books, but among all the available evidence, they have usually held a position of secondary importance. The normal goal of history is to peel away myths that accumulate with the passage of time and focus on whatever nuggets of authenticity remain—hence our preference for "eyewitness" evidence and for the more staid and sedate passages in certain eyewitness texts—particularly in *Deeds of the Franks*. For the crusade, however, this intellectual winnowing, sifting through myth and prejudice to focus on the small grains of demonstrable truth, has distracted us from the war's original meaning. Through the efforts of modern, eleventh-century men, an event of apocalyptic proportions, if not the Apocalypse itself, had just occurred.

An examination of this imaginative world will help explain why 100,000 people charged recklessly into a conflict fought nearly 2,000 miles from their homes and why their victory inspired such intense celebration and speculation. The typical aspects of medieval piety—a desire to undertake pilgrimages to Jerusalem, the need to perform penance acutely felt among warriors, and a simple longing for adventure—take us a long way toward answering this question, but they do not go far enough. There was nothing typical about the First Crusade. To understand this extraordinary event, we must take seriously those passages that are most extraordinary, for what is most unusual (and ubiquitous) in First Crusade histories is the belief that men were living in prophetic time, their every deed advancing God's designs.

Woven into this history, then, more thoroughly than in any previous telling of the First Crusade saga, are all of the dreams, visions, and miracles that occurred during the expedition. As often as possible, I have placed the progress of the army alongside the apparent progress of the Apocalypse. The further crusaders descended into their journey, the more detached from earthly reality they seemed to become. The closer they got to Jerusalem, the more in tune their activity seemed to be with the plans of God and the movements of angels. Fundamentally, this is what an apocalyptic event is—a sudden leap forward in salvation history, when the story of man as written by God approaches its climax.

The First Crusade was neither the first time nor the last that Christians would believe themselves on the verge of Armageddon. But in all other cases (and for obvious reasons), these moments of expectation ended in disillusionment. What is remarkable about the First Crusade is that observers on the ground, even with twenty years' hindsight, continued to see in it signs not of an imminent apocalypse, but of an apocalypse fulfilled.

1

Jerusalem, on Earth as It Is in Heaven

(1009, 1064–1065, and 1095–1096)

Jerusalem. Anyone who reads history books, even just a little, anyone who, avid for learning, pays attention to men who calculate the passages of years knows Jerusalem, capital of all Judea, a city of no small nobility and no small fame, raised to the heights of royal dignity as often as it has suffered the conquests of tyrants, razed to the earth and deprived of her own children, led off into captivity, suffering so many historic upheavals until the coming of the Savior.

—BAUDRY OF BOURGUEIL, 1107

In 1095 Jerusalem was the center of the earth, the site of Christ's death and resurrection, where God had trumped the devil and worked salvation for humanity. Men and women across Europe dreamed of visiting that city, of praying before the tomb of Christ, of catching, if only for a moment, a direct glimpse of heaven. Out of such dreams and desires the First Crusade was born. It seemed the most natural thing, barely in need of explanation. "There was a great movement throughout all parts of France," wrote one anonymous historian around 1100, "so that if anyone truly wished to follow God, with a pure heart and mind, and wanted faithfully to carry his Cross, he did not hesitate to take the fastest road to the Holy Sepulcher."[1] [Plate 1]

Whatever Christians believed in 1095, there was no rational explanation or single event that triggered this sudden desire to possess Jerusalem. Various Muslim factions had held it for over four hundred years. The few pilgrims capable of undertaking such an ambitious journey did so, with varying degrees of difficulty and success. The urge to incorporate a far-flung Middle Eastern city into the Christian world was thus a wholly new ambition. It was also an idea with little theological justification. As any second-rate preacher would have known, Christianity had made the physical trappings of Judaism and the Old Testament—the sacrifices, the legal code, and, yes, the city of Jerusalem—irrelevant. The journey to salvation was a journey of the heart, a story that could be lived anywhere: Jerusalem in a nearby cathedral or parish church, the River Jordan in a baptistery. But by the end of the eleventh century, European Christians were not content with these allegorical Jerusalems. They wanted the real city, too.

This is the story of that transformation and its consequences—the war that was to become the First Crusade and the Apocalypse that it unleashed.

The First Thousand Years

Jerusalem, the city of Christ, had ceased to exist by 1095. Roman legions sacked it in 70 AD while suppressing a Jewish revolt. In the process they destroyed most of the important religious monuments and left the city as a whole in ruins.

In 135 AD, during another rebellion, the Emperor Hadrian ordered Jerusalem destroyed completely, building in its place a Roman outpost called Aelia Capitolina (taken from Aelius, Hadrian's own family name). The traditional site of the crucifixion, called "Golgotha," or "place of the Skull," Hadrian had covered in earth and concrete and then built on top of it a temple to Venus. The city thus disappeared for nearly two hundred years.

The Emperor Constantine, newly converted to Christianity, took a sudden interest in the city in 325. He dispatched—at the risk of anachronism—a crack team of archaeologists to recover the sites where Christ had died, had been buried, and had risen from the grave. By 327 his men had made significant progress: The temple of Venus had been destroyed, and the sites of the crucifixion and of the Holy Sepulcher had been located (or else chosen, since no real evidence would have, or could have, survived). On Constantine's order, construction work also began on a magnificent new basilica that would incorporate both places into its architectural scheme.

A little later Constantine's mother, Helena, visited the city. According to some traditions, Helena engaged in some archaeological work of her own, discovering the remains of the True Cross—some of which she took back to Constantinople, some of which she left in the Holy Land. For the next three centuries, thousands of Latin Christians would follow in her footsteps, traveling as pilgrims to Jerusalem, now a thoroughly Christian city, to pray at the tomb of Christ and to venerate the relics of His Passion.[2]

But not everyone celebrated these developments, including the Roman Christians who decided to live there. St. Jerome, writing in 395 from his hermitage in Bethlehem, famously argued that there was no special benefit to be gained in the Holy Land. Sacred places by themselves—even Jerusalem—had no real virtue. "What is praiseworthy," he wrote, "is not to have been to Jerusalem, but to have lived a good life while there." The heavenly court was no more accessible in the city where Christ had lived, he went on, than it was in, say, Britain, since the true kingdom of God lies in the heart of every believer.

This lesson formed one of the fundamental tenets of Christianity. Literally speaking, Jerusalem was a city on earth. But in the structures of medieval Christian thought, such literal meanings were inconsequential. The earthly city in the Middle East is just that: a city. Read allegorically, Jerusalem is God's church. Spiritually, it is a soul at peace. Prophetically, it is the kingdom of God that shall appear at the end of time. Higher truths are in the mind and in the soul, not in a pilgrimage destination.[3]

By the seventh century, however, Western Christians had more practical reasons to lose interest. Travel into the old province of Judaea was becoming dangerous. In 614 Jerusalem fell to the Persian ruler Khosrau II, who took the True Cross back to his capital city of Ctesiphon, near Baghdad, as plunder. According to a later version of the story, Khosrau then declared himself a god and kept the cross in a throne room atop a bronze tower. The cross sat on his right; to his left he kept a statue of a golden rooster. Encircling the throne were models of the sun, moon, and stars, and he had further rigged up the tower with a secret irrigation system that enabled him to pretend to be a rain god.

Fifteen years later the Emperor Heraclius managed to recapture Jerusalem and the True Cross, but this second era of Christian Jerusalem lasted less than a decade. In 638 the city fell again, this time to Muslim armies. In the face of Islam's astonishingly rapid expansion, the frontiers of the Eastern Roman Empire collapsed. The Western Roman Empire was already in ruins. Jerusalem, a Muslim city, had become for Latin Christians a dangerous, out-of-the-way destination. In the centuries that followed, there seemed little reason to go.[4]

The rediscovery of this tangible, earthly city seemed to happen suddenly around 1000, owing to changes in both piety and politics. In terms of the former, European Christians began to look for Jerusalem at home, within their own churches, not within their own souls, as St. Jerome had encouraged them to do. That is to say, in the 900s ordinary believers developed an enthusiasm for "local pilgrimages," visits to nearby churches where they might pray before saints' shrines and seek forgiveness for sins, healing for a disease, or release from chains. It was the beginning of a golden age in pilgrimage. But there are obviously differences between visiting the Cloak of Our Lady of Chartres or the reliquary of Sainte Foy at Conques or the shrine of St. Léonard of Noblat, on the one hand, and attempting the long and arduous pilgrimage to Jerusalem, on the other. The latter was infinitely more holy, just as it was almost inaccessible.

Around the year 1000, however, as this new enthusiasm for pilgrimage was reaching a sort of zenith, a new road to the Holy Land became suddenly traversable. The land route through Hungary opened after Stephen I established himself as that country's first Christian king. Intrepid pilgrims who wished to attempt this most dangerous and glamorous devotional act now had a viable opportunity to do so.[5]

The timing was fortuitous, or perhaps portentous, since it occurred at the end of the first millennium, a time of increased apocalyptic expectation. Just as pilgrims started looking more and more toward earthly Jerusalem, so did Christian thinkers and theologians begin searching the stars and their libraries for signs of the advent of Antichrist and the eventual return of Christ in majesty. The roads to the heavenly and earthly Jerusalems were opening all at once.

What pilgrims saw when they visited the earthly city was disturbing: Barbarous, unbelieving tribes governed Jerusalem and controlled access to the holy sites. To the pilgrims, these were a people whose language, culture, and religion were entirely incomprehensible. Christian travelers brought back from the Middle East, with an ever-increasing frequency and shrillness, tales of shoddy and profane treatment meted out to Christians and their shrines by these enemies whom their own faulty grasp of history and prophecy could not fully explain. The situation required a violent, if not apocalyptic, response.

The Sacking of the Holy Sepulcher in 1009

The first major confrontation—the first near crusade, or the first mini-apocalypse—occurred in the year 1009. At that time the caliph of Egypt, al-Hakim bi Amr Allah, who also controlled Jerusalem, ordered his followers to destroy the Holy Sepulcher. He may have done so out of simple irritation at the crowds of Christians flocking to Jerusalem during the Easter season, or maybe he was angry about what the Christians were doing once they reached Jerusalem. According to a later Arab historian, when al-Hakim asked an advisor named Qutekin al-Adudi why the Christians bothered with their pilgrimages, he learned about the miracle of the Holy Fire. The lamps in the Aedicule—the small building inside the Church of the Holy Sepulcher that actually contained the tomb—were all extinguished on Good Friday and then miraculously relit themselves the next day and burned with a remarkably pure white light. But the miracle was a fake: Through the mixing of particular types of oil, the advisor explained, the lamps became especially combustible and burned with an unusual intensity. News of such fakery so infuriated al-Hakim that he ordered the entire church knocked to the ground.

How important the Easter services were in triggering this reaction we cannot be sure. But an outraged sense of piety does seem to have played a part in al-Hakim's decision. The destruction of the Holy Sepulcher fit into a larger program of persecution aimed at both Jews and Christians, who in normal times were regarded as *dhimmi*, inheritors of the early stages of the divine revelation of which Islam represented the final chapter. As such, they were considered protected religious minorities, subject to certain taxes and restrictions but otherwise free from direct persecution.

Al-Hakim reversed this policy of tolerance. Besides the Holy Sepulcher, he ordered many other churches and synagogues destroyed, outlawed Christian ceremony, had Torah scrolls desecrated, and required Christians and Jews to identify themselves with special clothing on the streets and badges when visiting the baths.

This drive to create a pure space for the practice of Islam points to a deeper eccentricity in al-Hakim's character. Agitated by dissenters and heretics within his own faith, by the end of his life he began actively promoting a belief in his own divinity. Not all of his followers were willing to follow him on this path. One February night in 1021, while riding alone on a donkey in the hills outside of Cairo, as he often did, al-Hakim disappeared. His bloody clothes were discovered, but his body had vanished. Though he was probably murdered, loyal followers remained hopeful that he had been taken up to heaven, his mysterious disappearance apparently evidence of his messianic status. A solar eclipse the next day lent some credence to the belief.[6]

Regardless of the facts on the ground in Egypt and Palestine, Christians in southern France had a remarkable and peculiar reaction to the destruction of the church. They blamed the Jews, particularly French Jews. "There were a great many of that race at Orléans, the royal city of Gaul," contemporary historian Rodulfus Glaber wrote, "and they are notorious for being even more arrogant, envious, and insolent than the rest of their brethren." Rumor spread that these Jews, inspired by the devil, had hired a serf to travel to Cairo and to deliver to al-Hakim a letter written in Hebrew and hidden inside his staff. The letter warned the caliph— in what was, in hindsight, a startlingly accurate prediction—that the Christians wished to inhabit all his lands and would do so if he did not immediately destroy the Church of the Holy Sepulcher, thus robbing them of any reason to travel to Jerusalem. Enraged and a little frightened, the caliph ordered his followers to tear down that building and all other Christian holy places throughout Palestine.[7]

French Christians rose up in anger against the Jews. "They became objects of universal hatred; they were driven from their cities, some were put to the sword, others were drowned in rivers, and many found other deaths." Given the option of death or baptism, a few "preferred to slit their own throats" rather than receive the sacrament. The man accused of carrying the secret Hebrew message to the caliph in Cairo was burned at the stake. Those Jews who escaped Christian fury went into hiding for five years and then, little by little, returned to their old lives in the cities. Some Jews who had converted subsequently renounced their faith. Their apostasy disappointed Rodulfus Glaber, our source for these events, but he found it nonetheless fitting that a few Jews would survive, bearing witness to their own wickedness and continuing guilt for having shed Christ's blood.[8]

It is remarkable how easily contemporary observers associated Islamic violence in the Middle East with Jewish perfidy at home. Indeed, the whole incident seems, at first glance, just another dismal chapter in the long saga of Christian violence against Jews. But it is not another chapter in a story. It is instead the first chapter—the first of the medieval pogroms against the Jews, inspired by rumors of events in Jerusalem. The second pogrom would occur some eighty-five years later as a result of the preaching inspiring the First Crusade, with sequels to follow at the calling of the Second and the Third Crusades. For medieval Christians there existed some profound historical and psychological connection between Christian concerns for the Holy Land and Christian hatred for the Jews, even though the more obvious villains in this story were Muslims, who, after all, controlled Jerusalem and who had in fact destroyed the church.

In the Middle East, the events in 1009 were not as momentous as they had first appeared. A new modus vivendi was established between Christians and Egyptians, and repairs to the Church of the Holy Sepulcher began almost immediately. A more ambitious program of reconstruction would commence in 1037, although the final product would be on a much smaller scale than the first basilica of Constantine. The pilgrims who visited this church seem to have been blissfully unaware that it was not the original. One well-informed historian writing in the early twelfth century even claimed that the structure had never suffered any damage since Constantine the Great had first overseen its building.

In the East and the West, the events of 1009 all but vanished from memory. A pattern, however, had been set—a combination of apocalyptic expectation, anti-Jewish violence, and terrors inspired by news from

Jerusalem—that would repeat itself at the time of the First Crusade, though no one alive in 1095 knew they were following precedents.[9]

Pilgrims' Progress, 1064–1065

Reconstruction of the Holy Sepulcher began, and pilgrimages resumed. To judge from the historical record, most were relatively peaceful—or at least not eventful enough to be of interest to historians. Only if a celebrity happened to go to Jerusalem would someone think it worth taking note. Count Fulk Nerra of Anjou, for example, made at least three pilgrimages to Jerusalem, two before and one after the Sepulcher's destruction. Duke Robert I of Normandy would go as a penitent to Jerusalem in 1034 and die on his way home, leaving a bastard son named William (later, "the Conqueror") as heir to his duchy. Some of the pilgrimages comprised large groups. These numbered into the hundreds and possibly thousands and included great pilgrimages in 1026 and 1033 as well as the failed pilgrimage of Bishop Lietbert of Cambrai in 1054. The largest and most famous of these expeditions commenced in 1064, when thousands of Germans gathered together to visit the Holy Land, many of them expecting, apparently, to arrive just in time for the Apocalypse.[10]

A lot would have changed along the land route to Jerusalem in the 1050s. Pilgrims might have recognized the differences, but they would have had difficulty identifying the causes. From the Christian traveler's perspective, the roadways had grown more dangerous. The behavior of the Muslim lords had become more erratic, for reasons that seemed inexplicable in the eyes of the pilgrims. The reality was that the cultural and political frontiers of the Islamic world were shifting as the tenuous peace of the previous half-century was undermined by the arrival of Seljuk Turks. A nomadic tribal group from Central Asia, they had begun to settle in on the lands of the Abbasid caliphs in the 1030s, eventually establishing themselves as the dominant political power and seizing the capital city of Baghdad in 1055. The Turks had readily adopted the Abbasids' practices of Sunni Islam, indeed adhering to a more orthodox line than had their predecessors. They also adopted a policy of expansion, at the expense of both the Greek Christians and the Fatimid caliphate in Egypt. This program was still in its infancy in 1064, as German pilgrims by the hundreds prepared to travel to Jerusalem. But the Turks had begun to make incursions into enemy territories through a series of small-scale raids, with independent amirs seeking to establish lordships for themselves along the frontiers of the Islamic and Byzantine worlds.

Rumor of this increased level of danger would have reached the German pilgrims, but it did not discourage them. Contemporaries estimated that somewhere between 7,000 and 12,000 people participated in the 1064 journey—likely an exaggeration, though not an outrageous one. All levels of society were represented: commoners, lords, soldiers, clerics, and a handful of bishops in full episcopal regalia, including Siegfried of Mainz and the formidable Gunther of Bamberg. Such a disparate group would have left with a variety of motives, including a simple desire to visit Christ's tomb. But many of them had a specific reason for going: They expected the world to end on Easter the following year, and they wanted to be in Jerusalem to see it.

The year 1065 had no obvious chronological significance, as did, for example, the year 1000. These pilgrims were responding instead to a somewhat obscure tradition according to which the Apocalypse would occur on Easter during a year when two important religious celebrations fell on the same day: the Annunciation and Good Friday. The former, marking the day when Mary learned that she would give birth to Christ, always occurred on March 25. The latter, commemorating the day Christ died, varied according to the Easter calendar. It was a relatively rare occurrence for the two anniversaries to coincide. The last time it would have happened before 1064 was seventy-two years earlier in 992, though it would occur again relatively quickly, in 1076.

How many of the German pilgrims accepted this idea, and how fervently they believed it, we cannot know, but the liturgical anomaly does help to explain why such a large number of pilgrims decided to go to Jerusalem during an otherwise unremarkable and even unpropitious year. All of them would have speculated about the likelihood of portentous events occurring on March 25. As the day grew nearer and as the journey grew harder, more and more of them must have begun to think that they were indeed living in apocalyptic times, that this pilgrimage would be unlike any other that had gone before.[11]

About this last point, at least, they were correct. For as the pilgrims neared their destination, apparently on Maundy Thursday—three days before the predicted end of the world on Easter—an army of Turks suddenly came upon them, riding quickly, firing arrows, and screaming bloody murder in the terrifying and unfamiliar Turkish style. The pilgrims had likely stumbled onto one of the small Seljuk armies seeking to make inroads against Fatimid power, but far as the Germans could tell, this was just another band of pagans, apparently attracted by the bishops' finery and showy wealth. Whatever the case, the Turks had caught the Christians completely off-guard. Many of them had not bothered to carry weapons. Indeed, as pilgrims they were supposed to travel unarmed—though it is difficult to believe that the bishops and nobles accompanying this pilgrimage had not hired a band of retainers to keep them safe, whatever religious etiquette might dictate.

The Christians who had weapons fought back. Others resisted as best they could, perhaps fighting with rocks or branches or whatever else happened to be on hand, thus preventing an immediate massacre. The Turks could easily encircle the Germans, but as long as the latter maintained discipline and stuck close together, they stood some chance of survival. Acting quickly, a significant number of the pilgrims managed to make their way to an abandoned town to hide behind its walls.[12]

A makeshift siege began. The Turks surrounded the city and tried to starve the Christians into submission. According to one particularly lurid account, the Turks tried to break the pilgrims' will by bringing forth "a most noble abbess" whom they had captured during the fight and raping her repeatedly just within sight of the walls but out of the range of any archers. They eventually killed her, but the pilgrims maintained their discipline, holding out, perhaps hoping to catch a glimpse of Christ in the sky as that ominous Easter Day, March 27, approached. They were living through the Last Days, many surely believed, trapped in a destroyed city set against an endless desert, besieged by the servants of Antichrist.

By Easter Sunday, with the end of the world no longer offering a potential escape, some of the priests suggested an alternative route. Rather than continue to fight, they should instead offer the Turks money and thus buy their safety. This counsel pleased everyone.[13]

The pilgrims extended an offer of surrender, and an "Arab duke," along with seventeen of his most important advisors, agreed to meet with them. They entered the city, eight of them separating from the other ten and climbing a ladder to an upper room. There, the bishops of Mainz and Bamberg waited. But the Turks did not intend to negotiate. Their leader instead boasted that he would take as plunder everything the Christians had and "eat their flesh and drink their blood." To add visual insult, he unwound his turban and tied it, as if a chain, around the bishop of Bamberg's neck. Normally a restrained man, Gunther threw one punch and knocked the duke unconscious. Before his followers could react, the Germans wrestled them all to the ground and tied them up so tightly that their wrists bled, doing the same to the seven others in the upper room and to the ten down below. The pilgrims then boldly paraded their captives along the city's ramparts in clear view of the enemy camp, for a time discouraging any fresh assaults.

Escape remained impossible until, miraculously, a small Egyptian army attacked the Turks and rescued the Christians. The prince of Babylon was grateful to those who had inflicted such a wound against his enemies. To the Germans, unfamiliar with the confessional differences of Islam, it seemed a miracle: "Satan had cast out Satan."[14]

The story as it reaches us is part epic adventure and part yellow journalism, the facts lost to repeated retellings and inevitable exaggeration. Even so, such a story would have provided useful imaginative fodder for preachers hoping to inflame Christian passion. The Turks, or, more generally, the Saracens, were money-crazed killers, blood-drinking cannibals, who preyed upon pilgrims, men of God, ordinary women and children, not to mention nuns. A war was already occurring in the Holy Land, incited by the "enemies of Christ." The Church of the Holy Sepulcher was in danger. Pilgrims were being molested, in some cases literally. If something were not done soon, no right-thinking person would ever be able to visit Jerusalem again. A few preachers, recalling the echoes of pogroms past, even claimed that the Saracens had already tried to destroy Christ's tomb and had nearly succeeded.[15]

That the disaster of 1065 had occurred against a background of apocalyptic expectation would have sharpened the general sense of anger at home. Untroubled by Christ's failure to return, audiences would have been more excited by the fact that it had almost happened. Thirty years before the First Crusade formally began, the dream of a journey to the East, a pilgrimage of vengeance, would have been alive in the Christian imagination.

The Sermons of Peter the Hermit, 1095–1096

The man who exploited these emotions and stories most effectively was a priest named Peter. Once a hermit, he may have been a pilgrim to Jerusalem in the early 1090s, or he may have simply invented stories after listening to other pilgrims' tales. Among modern historians, Peter has not enjoyed an enthusiastic reception, on the basis of either integrity, courage, or importance. From the perspective of some contemporary writers, however, particularly those who lived in German-speaking lands, Peter was the inventor of the crusade.

According to a highly respected historian named Albert of Aachen, writing around 1108, Peter was inspired to preach the crusade because of his own experience in the Holy Land. While visiting the Lord's Sepulcher for the sake of prayer, "he saw with a sad heart things wicked and unmentionable, and trembled in spirit, and called down on these sights God the avenger." Peter took his complaints to the spiritual leader of Jerusalem, the patriarch, who lamented his own powerlessness in the face of the Turks, saying that the strength of the Christians in that city was "to be reckoned as no more than that of a tiny ant, against the pride of so many."

Help had to come from the West. The patriarch instructed Peter to carry home news of Jerusalem's plight and beg for help. No less a figure than Christ Himself reiterated this message, appearing to Peter in a vision at His own Sepulcher and ordering Peter to obtain patriarchal letters sealed with the sign of the cross. It was not Peter's personal calling, Christ said, but rather "our mission," and He enjoined Peter to hurry home and lift the hearts of the faithful "for cleansing the holy places of Jerusalem." Peter then went to Rome and informed the pope of the situation in the Holy Land and of Christ's instructions for the liberation of His tomb. The pope had no choice but to obey these heaven-sent commands.[16]

Peter probably never met with Pope Urban II, and he may never have gone to the Holy Land. But in 1095 and 1096, he did begin traveling around France, Normandy, and Germany, telling of the horrors being perpetrated in Jerusalem and describing the desperate need there for military aid from the West. Not just a preacher of war, he adapted the persona of an ascetic hermit, drawing on many of the burgeoning religious ideals of his day. He sometimes rode a mule, always traveled barefoot, and avoided eating bread and meat, though he did, strangely, drink wine and eat fish, "thus seeking in the midst of delicacy a reputation for abstinence," according to one twelfth-century critic.

His mission attracted numerous followers. Some were impressed by his unusual approach to the eremitical life, by his forceful calls to repentance, and by the liberality with which he redeemed prostitutes. These once fallen women must have formed a substantial part of Peter's retinue, no doubt causing scandal for many. But others would have recognized something more fundamentally pious in his demeanor. His ragged clothing, his connection to Jerusalem, the redeemed sinners in his entourage, perhaps even his preference for fish—all of these signs together would have shown how Peter followed the example of Christ, who had also walked barefoot, avoided handling money, and taken as companions one prostitute and at least two fishermen.

Peter's message made ecclesiastical authorities nervous, but they could not deny its effectiveness. He was "greatly esteemed by those who know worldly things," said one writer, "and he was raised above even bishops and abbots in the practice of religion, because he ate no bread or meat." "I don't remember anyone ever being so honored," observed another one, who saw Peter preach in person. With wondrous authority he could bring warring parties together and force them to make peace. His followers, or perhaps simply his fans, would pathetically pluck hairs from the mule that he rode, preserving them as if they were holy relics.[17]

While preaching forgiveness and poverty, Peter also told stories about Jerusalem, reaffirming what veterans of the 1064 German pilgrimage and their friends would have long known: Jerusalem was in the hands of pagans who every day were preventing Christians from worshipping at the tomb of their Lord. If the Christians there did not get help, and soon, their religion and Jerusalem itself might not long survive. Already the pagans had transformed the "Temple of the Lord" into a "Mahomerie," or, as we might say, a mosque (he was specifically referring to the Dome of the Rock). It would clearly be a good and righteous service to God if those warring knights, whose conflicts had at last achieved some sort of resolution through Peter's oratory and his very demeanor, would now turn their weapons against a real enemy, against the unbelievers who every day were defiling the sacred sanctuaries of Jerusalem.

But Peter added just a little bit more incendiary material to his message of peace and war. Based on what Albert of Aachen said, he must have carried with him a sealed letter from the patriarch of Jerusalem. By itself that document would have proved a powerful talisman. But at some point in his itinerary, he turned it into something else altogether—a charter that had fallen from heaven. On it was a mandate that "instructed all Christendom from all parts of the world to take up arms and journey to Jerusalem to fight against the pagans and to claim eternal possession of the city with all its pertinent lands." He added a line of prophecy: "Jerusalem will be downtrodden by gentiles until the times of nations are fulfilled." This line was the conclusion of Christ's instruction to His disciples about how to recognize the Last Days.[18]

The nuances of Peter's message are lost, but its general tenor is clear: The Last Days were at hand, and Jerusalem needed to be conquered. Peter's followers were to create peace at home, to follow the literal examples of Christ, and to journey to Jerusalem in anticipation of the Last Days. Simple as it was, the message was powerful. Armies of believers assembled in response, some of them departing with Peter as early as March 1096. Many of the men who had heard Peter's message and answered his challenge reached conclusions similar to those drawn by the French in 1009, when they, too, heard of crises in Jerusalem. "Do we need to travel to distant lands in the East to attack the enemies of God, when there are Jews right before our eyes, a race that is the greatest enemy of God? We've got it all backwards!"[19]

Thus did the First Crusade begin, at least in the eyes of many contemporaries. It was the result of the highly combustible ideas and images proclaimed by one extremely charismatic hermit. To others, the crusade seemed simply to come from nowhere, a heaven-sent miracle. About the formation of Peter's armies in 1096 one writer recalled, "And then from every part of the earth, but especially from the western kingdoms, infinite crowds of kings and nobles and of commoners, of either sex, came together in armed bands to seek out Jerusalem, roused into a fervor by the many reports about the suffering of the Holy Sepulcher and the destruction of all the churches that the Turks, a most vicious people, had subjected to their lordship and laid low for many years with unimaginable hardships."[20]

But as the same writer noted elsewhere, this sudden uprising was inevitable. Indeed, long foretold, it should have been obvious. Four years earlier, "there were seen through many territories small worms previously unknown. They flew not far from the ground, that is, you could have touched them with a hand or a staff. In width they were about the same size as flies, but a bit longer. Their numberless armies were so great that one of them was almost a mile wide and two or three miles long. They were so dense that they truly blocked sunlight from the earth. Some people interpreted this portent to signify the ones who took the road to Jerusalem, just four years later." In such a fashion did the crusade appear to those who witnessed its call and felt its draw.

It was a plague of flying worms, like something out of the Book of Exodus, one of the supernatural disasters sent to punish the Egyptians, wreaking destruction on behalf of God's chosen people. The crusade defied nature, came from nowhere, and moved apparently without guidance, though it always headed relentlessly toward the East.[21]

2

The Pope's Plan

(November 1095)

Urban II would publicly preach the crusade on November 27, 1095, at a church council held in the French city of Clermont. He had been considering the idea of a great war in the East for at least eight months, and he must have had some sense of the Jerusalem-based madness that he was tapping into. The sermon, he knew, would receive an enthusiastic response, but the plan was still risky. He was in effect staking the prestige of his office on a highly improbable military expedition. And in 1095 his ability to preserve even his own hold on power was no sure thing. He was one of two men claiming to be pope, the result of a war that had begun in 1075 and showed no signs of ending any time soon. As Urban considered an attack on Jerusalem, it was not even safe for him to enter Rome. Whether he saw war in the East as a way to solve his problems at home is unclear. What is certain is that the imprimatur of a papal approval transformed the movement of Peter the Hermit from being, at best, a somewhat grander reenactment of the German pilgrimage of 1064 into a real military campaign.

Urban had no word for "crusade." It would take a century before Latin writers felt the need to invent a term to describe this phenomenon. What he would urge upon warriors at Clermont was simply to follow the *iter*, or "the road"—a bland description of a war that would transform Europe and spark an apocalypse.

The Pope's Problems: War with Germany,
an Oversexed French King, and Greeks in Crisis

The pope's main problem, as he pondered the fate of Jerusalem, was his war against the German emperor Henry IV (1056–1106). At stake was the question of who had the right to invest bishops with their offices—secular rulers or churchmen, kings or popes. Hence, the most common name for this struggle was the "Investiture Contest."

Early on Henry IV had responded to the policies of Urban's predecessor, Gregory VII (1073–1085), by appointing his own pope, Wibert, Archbishop of Ravenna, or, as he is better known to history, the Antipope Clement III, or, as he was known to one of the crusaders, "that blockheaded pope." Clement was still alive in 1095 (he would outlive Urban by a year), and he still enjoyed significant support. His followers and Urban's had literally divided the Vatican between them, with Clement's men occupying the main body of the church and Urban's supporters holed up inside a tower. The building remained open for prayer, but Clement's men were known to hide in the rafters and throw rocks on any of Urban's friends who dared enter. No one could say in 1095 which pope would prevail, let alone whether the reform papacy, in the person of Urban II, could raise an army and carry out an impossible mission some 2,000 miles from home.[1]

Urban's problems were not confined to Italy and Germany. He faced serious political difficulties in France, too, where he was engaged in a battle of wills with King Philip I (1060–1108). One year earlier Philip had been excommunicated at a synod in Autun owing to irregularities in his recent marriage. In 1092 he had repudiated his first wife, Bertha of Holland, in order to marry Bertrada of Montfort, who was herself already married to Count Fulk of Anjou. Neither Philip nor Bertrada could secure a divorce, and neither marriage offered sufficient grounds for annulment. Their union was therefore bigamous on two counts. Part of Urban's urgent business at Clermont was to reaffirm this excommunication, a move unlikely to endear him to either the French king or any of the nobles loyal to him.

The dispute, however, did not cut the pope off from all, or even most, French-speaking territories. In the 1090s French kings exercised direct control over only a small collection of lands around Paris known as the

Île-de-France, allowing Urban some freedom of movement. Still, apart from a brief sojourn in Anjou, ruled by the jilted Count Fulk, Urban was effectively stuck south of the River Loire. Any recruiting to the north (the eventual source of most of the crusading armies) would have to occur through letters and envoys.[2]

There was one other significant problem for the pope that he perhaps hoped to address: the schism between the two great branches of the Christian faith. The Greek Orthodox and Latin Catholic churches, based in Constantinople and Rome, respectively, had for centuries taken different spiritual and liturgical paths. Only recently had they formalized their separation, when a papal mission sent by Pope Leo IX to Constantinople in 1054 ended in mutual recriminations and anathemas. Leo's successors dreamed of ending this schism between Greek and Latin Christianity, and in the 1090s, during the papacy of Urban II, reunification suddenly became a real possibility.

This diplomatic opening grew out of a military threat. At almost exactly same time that the Great Schism of 1054 occurred, armies of Seljuk Turks began to encroach upon Byzantine territories in Syria and Asia Minor. Their military advance reached something of a crescendo in 1071 when the Greeks, fighting against the armies of the Sultan Alp Arslan, suffered a catastrophic defeat at the battle of Manzikert. The Emperor Romanus Diogenes, who had been present at the battle, was captured and imprisoned. Though the emperor was released quickly, and under generous terms, later tradition held that Alp Arslan forced him to grovel before him and pretend to be a footstool. "Hearing these things, the princes of the empire put someone else over themselves, judging unworthy to hold the scepter and to exercise the Augustan honor him who had allowed so many indignities to be inflicted on his body; and they removed his eyes." An era of civil war in the Byzantine Empire ensued, as the frontier of Asia Minor collapsed.[3]

Within three years of Manzikert, at Rome the newly elected Pope Gregory VII began crafting a response to the Greek crisis, one that would establish precedents for Urban II's later call to crusade. In a series of letters written in 1074, Gregory outlined plans for an expedition to the East aimed at saving Constantinople. The pope himself would raise the armies and act as their leader and general. These Christians, Gregory explained, "have been laid low by the pagans with unheard of destruction and slaughtered daily like cattle." Elsewhere he wrote of Muslims killing Christians with a "pitiable savagery" and a "tyrannical violence" outside the walls of Constantinople. Gregory's armies would bring this reign of terror to an end, and after saving Byzantium, he all but boasted, his troops would march to Jerusalem and liberate the Holy Sepulcher. It was an audacious plan, its ambitions comparable to the dreams of Urban II in 1095 (and perhaps those of Peter the Hermit, too). If successful, the pope would transform the world: He would not only rescue Byzantium but also settle differences between Latin and Greek Christians and at the same time guide other sects—Syrian and Armenian Christians—back into the Catholic fold.[4]

Unknown to Gregory, his imperial rival Henry IV was toying with similar ideas. Or at least one his counselors, Bishop Benzo of Alba, was doing so. Under Benzo's plan, Henry would first conquer Rome. With the papacy brought to heel, he could then go to Constantinople, there to claim the Eastern Empire from the increasingly feeble Byzantine rulers. Finally, as ruler of the Eastern and Western worlds, he would march to Jerusalem, where, it seems, the Muslims would offer him no opposition. "An awestruck Babylon will come into Zion, *wishing to lick the dust of his feet.* Then shall be fulfilled what is written: *And his sepulcher will be made glorious!* O, Caesar, why do you wonder at these things?"[5]

None of these plans, in the 1070s and 1080s, would come to fruition. Reports of Byzantium's imminent downfall proved to be exaggerated. The Turks' expansion toward Constantinople slowed after the victory at Manzikert—they would not get there until 1453—and the Greeks got back to politics as usual, with backstabbings, palace coups, and confinement in monasteries of formerly prominent leaders.

Yet the Turks remained a persistent threat. They had successfully claimed much of Asia Minor, taking Nicea as one of their capitals in 1078. The Emperor Alexius Comnenus (1081–1118) enjoyed some initial military success against them, but he was unable to achieve anything like a secure victory. For this reason, in the late 1080s the emperor turned west for assistance. He first solicited help from Count Robert of Flanders, who visited Constantinople while returning from a pilgrimage to Jerusalem around 1089. Robert agreed to provide aid, and the following year he sent five hundred mercenaries to fight for Byzantium.

About five years later, Alexius sent a delegation to speak before Urban II, asking for help in organizing a military response to the Turks. The delegates made a formal plea before a church council held in Piacenza in 1095, and it was probably at that point that Urban began seriously to contemplate calling for a military expedition to the East.[6]

War with Germany, conflict in France, a rival pope, and Christians in the East under siege: Remarkably, the crusade could solve all of these problems. If the initial rallying cry were successful, it would unite behind Urban II a significant portion of Christian Europe. At the very least, the creation of such an army would represent a real propaganda coup against Henry IV and his servant Clement III. If the crusade succeeded and Jerusalem fell, then even the most skeptical observer would have to admit that God was on Urban's side. Clement III would lose his support. Henry IV's stature would diminish. And Philip I would have to start taking papal excommunications more seriously. Finally, a grateful Byzantium would owe its survival to Rome and would undoubtedly offer appropriate submission in matters political and spiritual. After less than half a century, the schism would come to an end. The advantages of the crusade, in retrospect, seem obvious.[7]

There was only one problem, and Urban II was educated enough to recognize it: The plan was insane. A military expedition from Europe would have to attract sufficient manpower, travel all the way to Jerusalem, consistently turn back armies along the way—armies that had already proved too powerful and skilled for the Greek Empire and its well-paid mercenaries—save Constantinople, and in the end take possession of Jerusalem, a city that had been under Muslim rule for over four hundred years. It was impossible. The most Urban could hope for was some sort of muted success. Western Christians at his behest might fight alongside the Greeks and create some sort of alliance that could eventually lead to the accomplishment of some of Rome's larger goals: a new spirit of détente with Constantinople and perhaps an eventual attack on Jerusalem. But from an immediate and practical standpoint, Urban was setting himself up for failure.

And things got off to a bad start. If the pope believed in signs—and he most likely did—the prospects for success would have looked bleak once the Council of Clermont, where he would proclaim the crusade, had begun. For just before the opening ceremonies, Bishop Durand of Clermont, the host for the gathering of "107 bishops and an even greater number of abbots," unexpectedly died. He had been healthy enough to welcome Urban II to his city, but then he passed away the day before the council began.

The news must have cast a pall over the gathering. One of the abbots in attendance, named Baudry—who would later write a history of the crusade—left Clermont thinking that the main thing people would remember about it was not Urban II's sermon but rather the sight of Durand's body, blanching before the eyes of all the assembled dignitaries. Baudry wrote two epitaphs for Durand, saying that the council served as a kind of triumph for the newly deceased bishop, a man who had created in his city a veritable golden age after a time of mud.[8]

Even so, ten days later, on November 27, 1095, with due solemnity and determination, in an open field near the church where Durand, the host, had been freshly laid to rest, Pope Urban II announced his plan to remake Christendom.

The Lost Sermon

Unfortunately, we don't know what he said. No one kept a copy. A few years after the fact, several historians composed versions of the speech, but none of them made any particular claim to accuracy. One of them, a participant at the Council of Clermont, blandly observed, "The apostolic lord gave his sermon in these words—or in others like them." Another writer, not an eyewitness, said his sermon captured the pope's intentions, not his language. That is inevitable, he further explained, since most of those in attendance forgot what the pope said. We have, then, only echoes of the first call to crusade. We can only speak about what Urban II likely said and not what he actually proposed.[9]

Setting aside the details, we can say that the sermon largely concerned Jerusalem. The very name "Jerusalem" inspired passion and poetic flights of fancy. Urban II understood the word's power and would have wanted to exploit it. All of the crusader chroniclers expressed that theme as well. Jerusalem was the center of the earth—"the navel of the world, a land fertile beyond all others, like another paradise of delights." It was "a desirable place, an incomparable place," the city where Christ had suffered, died, and been resurrected, and a place where the ground had since drunk up the blood of martyrs. In a culture that placed extraordinary value on relics—including objects touched by saints and the actual bodies of saints—the entire city of Jerusalem was a holy artifact. It radiated spiritual energy. A traveler to Jerusalem could not take a step without touching a spot made sacred through contact with the Savior's body or His mother's or else their shadows. More than a relic, the earthly Jerusalem was "the image of the heavenly Jerusalem. This city is the form of that city for which we long." Just as the bread and wine consecrated by a priest contained deeper heavenly realities, disguised by otherwise drab earthly forms, so did the physical city of Jerusalem connect to deeper, hidden truths.[10]

As an image of the heavenly city, Jerusalem was also a byword for peace. If the "r" changed to an "s," the name would become "Jesusalem," or "peaceful salvation." And that name, counterintuitively, points to a crucial aspect of the crusade and of Urban II's message at Clermont: the need for peace. It was, by 1095, a long-standing plea and aspiration among churchmen. For a century they had been trying to impose on warriors a code of conduct, known variously as "the Peace" or "the Truce of God," to compel them to limit their aggressive impulses. The unarmed—monks, clerics, and women—were to be kept safe from bloodshed at all times, and for four days out of the week, Thursday through Sunday, no one was to strike a blow against anyone at all.

The renewed proclamation of this code was the opening decree at Clermont. The goal was to create peace for its own sake, to be sure, but this peace also related to the crusade. Peace was, in fact, the precondition for a war in Jerusalem. For only peace at home would allow large armies to abandon their families and properties, leaving everything they valued unprotected for months and even years, all in the name of fighting abroad for the survival and expansion of Christendom but with no tangible benefit for themselves.[11]

The creation of peace did not come easily. Simply stated, knights wanted to fight—with one another, with peasants, with all and sundry. It was their calling, part of the job description. Quiet amity, even with a promise of salvation attached, could not compete with the pleasure of war. Urban II realized as much. That's why the call to peace in 1095 came with a proviso: Knights could continue to fight and loot and plunder so long as they did so against a foreign, unbelieving enemy. In that case, not only would their violence be tolerated, as it had been from time to time in the past in so-called just wars, but it also would be positively laudable. In previous wars, to kill an adversary was, at best, a morally neutral act, an unfortunate necessity created by political circumstance. To kill a Muslim, by contrast, increased a warrior's store of virtue, giving him some security as he contemplated the fearsome stakes of Judgment Day. This novel (if not entirely unprecedented) proposal surely formed one of the key elements behind the crusade's popularity, its specific terms constituting the one authentic sentence about the crusade that survives from the Council of Clermont: *Whoever might set forth to Jerusalem to liberate the church of God, can substitute that journey for all penance.*[12]

This is a fairly guarded promise and a deceptively complicated one as well. The process of applying it to crusade warriors would have required a small army of well-educated clerics and confessors. What is most striking about this crusade indulgence is what it is not. It is not, for example, a guarantee that anyone who fights for Jerusalem will have his sins forgiven. It is not even a promise of martyrdom—that anyone who dies while fighting for Jerusalem will receive an immediate welcome into heaven. It instead establishes a sort of procedure allowing knights, under the right circumstances, to exchange the performance of their job (making war) for the forgiveness of sins already confessed. That is, a military expedition to Jerusalem would function essentially like a common devotional rite: the penitential pilgrimage. Pilgrims, too, like crusaders, could confess their sins and then, in exchange for a journey to a holy site, receive an indulgence for those sins.

The addition of warfare into the mix made the crusade an inspired, galvanizing idea. Urban's audience loved it, bursting out with shouts of "God wills it! God wills it!" At such an apparently miraculous show of unity, the pope raised his eyes up to heaven as if to offer silent, humble thanks.[13]

The lure of Jerusalem and the chance to obtain forgiveness for sins were two of the key components behind the crusade's appeal. For many historians, they are sufficient by themselves. I am more skeptical. The indulgence, as just described, was deliberately cautious. If warriors found it exciting and inspiring, that was only because they willfully misunderstood the indulgence's terms—they believed themselves eligible for more forgiveness than Urban II had in fact promised. The argument that the indulgence and pilgrimage alone explain the crusade's popularity also presumes that eleventh-century knights lived in continual terror of the afterlife, overcome with awe at the sacramental authority of the church. There is some truth to this caricature. But it remains a caricature.

Our best evidence that knights felt burdened by an unbearable weight of sin comes not from knights but from monks—that is, from men who had devoted their lives to the idea of expunging their own sins. It is inevitable that they would project similar ideals onto the warriors whom they saw setting out to perform God's work. Not every warrior, including those who had embraced the crusade, would have felt so timorous. The French could take as an example their own king, Philip. Fearless in the face of damnation, he preferred to live as an excommunicate condemned to hell rather than give up his bigamous marriage.

To make the idea of a penitential war compelling, to give this message teeth, Urban II would have needed to do more than frighten knights with stories of hellfire or to entice them with promises of heaven. He needed to sell the crusade as a heroic battle, a grand adventure comparable to the deeds being celebrated in the new epic poetry, or *chansons de geste*, of the eleventh century, as a great war against a worthy, fearsome adversary: Muslims, or as they were more commonly known in eleventh-century Europe, "Saracens."[14]

To make this case, Urban II had a number of horrific images to draw upon. He may have even called on volunteers from the audience, veterans of the Jerusalem pilgrimage, to share their stories. The poet and abbot Baudry attributed these words to the pope: "How many injuries pilgrims have endured, you know best, you who are here and who have returned from there, who have sacrificed your possessions and your blood for God." Baudry may not have remembered exactly what the pope said, but he did at least remember veterans of the Jerusalem pilgrimage, spreading their tales of horror and Muslim atrocities. "Sometimes," Baudry wrote elsewhere, "we saw among us citizens of Jerusalem, poor and exiled men, as well as beggars from Antioch, lamenting the state of the holy places and begging for some sort of public relief for their own poverty."[15]

At Clermont Urban II gave at least tacit endorsement to their complaints (whether he made arrangements to relieve their poverty as well, we don't know; Peter the Hermit likely did so). In the hands of a skilled preacher, these pilgrims' tales of woe could become the stuff of nightmares. Consider how another crusade chronicler called Robert the Monk reimagined Urban II's sermon:

"From the land of Jerusalem and the city of Constantinople, troubling news has arisen and many times has now come to our attention—namely, that the people of the kingdom of Persia, a foreign people, a people entirely hostile to God, *a generation whose heart was not steadfast and whose spirit has not kept faith with God*, has attacked Christian lands and devastated them with sword, plunder, and fire. Some of the captives they have led into their own land, while others they have laid low with a wretched death. The churches of God they have altogether overthrown or enslaved to their own cult. The altars they have wrecked, polluted with their filth; for they circumcise Christians and either pour the blood from the circumcision over the altars or else use it to fill baptismal vessels. And if it amuses them to punish someone with a truly foul death, they puncture his navel and pull out the ends of his intestines. These they bind to a pole, and then by whipping their victim, they force him to run around and around until his intestines have all come out and he falls dead to the ground. Some they tie to poles and shoot with arrows; others they force to stretch out their bare necks so that with their swords they can cut off their heads in a single blow. What can I say about the wicked violations of women? To speak of it is worse than to keep silent."[16]

Such charges sound incredible. But the images were carefully chosen. Consider, for example, the idea of "forced circumcisions." Most obviously it tapped into fears of castration, which in the eleventh century was not a psychological anxiety but was instead a common judicial penalty. More subtly, circumcision—though associated with Islam—was a Jewish rite. By forcing it on Christians, the Saracens were effectively compelling them to undergo a Jewish initiation and thus, on a ritual and physical level, to renounce their faith. The Saracens were also making a mockery of baptism, filling baptisteries with Christian blood. Baptismal water washed away sins. This Christian blood, shed into baptisteries, polluted churches and robbed fonts of their efficacy. Pouring this same blood onto altars, moreover, made a mockery of the Eucharist—where priests regularly created a more potable manifestation of Christ's blood.

Fear of pollution was the essential theme in the eleventh-century Christian depiction of Islam. Abbot Baudry, who, again, attended Clermont, rhymed the name "Turk" with the Latin word for "filthy": *Turci spurci*. The same writer dwelt at length on how Saracens tried to spoil all Christian ceremonies in the East. The Turks, he said, drove worshippers from the altars of God, even as they robbed churches of their money. In the very Temple of Solomon (or al-Aqsa Mosque), they set up idols to worship. What the Saracens were doing to the Holy Sepulcher, he preferred not to say. As with the rumored violation of Christian women, readers were left to use their imaginations.[17]

These missing details can be found elsewhere—at least in regard to women. The Turks, so listeners were told, had raped mothers in front of their daughters, forcing the children to watch, sing obscene songs, and dance as their parents were violated. Wearied with the mothers, the Saracens turned their attention to the daughters, whom they now raped, ordering the mothers to sing and dance in turn. So boundless were Saracen appetites that they also raped men, violating the laws of nature and humanity. Their targets were mainly poor folk, but according to rumor they had also raped and killed a bishop.[18]

Did Urban II actually use rhetoric such as this in framing his case for the crusade? There is no reason to think that he did not, but without a record of the sermon, we cannot be certain. In a letter written shortly after Clermont to Christians in Flanders, however, Urban did draw attention in a very general way to these charges: "We believe, brothers, that you have already heard through the report of many different people about the savage barbarism that has devastated God's churches in the East with wretched destruction, including the holy city of Christ, made famous through his suffering and resurrection, now disgracefully reduced to slavery along with the rest of churches, shameful to say!"[19]

Less certain is whether the pope used another type of rhetoric likely to motivate an army of Christian soldiers—the apocalypticism that had helped inspire the great pilgrimages of 1033 and 1064, among others. Did he describe Saracens as harbingers, or even servants, of Antichrist? To some extent, again, it would be surprising if he did not. Urban had been an active presence in the papal court since 1080, during the worst years of the Investiture Contest, the wars between popes and emperors, when charges of being in league with Antichrist were thrown back and forth with some regularity. On the other hand, Urban II himself used the word "Antichrist" rarely. It can be found only once, in one of his letters, where he described Bishop Otbert of Liège, a supporter of Henry IV's, as "the standard-bearer of Antichrist and the beast of Satan."[20]

Still, it was an effective and easy ploy, and at least one version of Urban II's Clermont speech made heavy, if eccentric, use of it. Imagine what would happen, Urban II asks his audience, if Jerusalem, "the mother church of all churches," were to return to Christianity and, more particularly, if God "might not wish some parts of the East to be restored to the faith, in opposition to the times of Antichrist looming on the horizon." Antichrist would then arise to fight—not against pagans or Jews but, as his name implies, against Christians. As was known from the Book of Daniel, he would also overthrow the kings of Egypt, Africa, and Ethiopia. Logically speaking, Antichrist could accomplish none of these things unless Christianity had first taken root in those three places, where, in 1095, paganism still thrived.

Jerusalem, this literary pope adds, would be downtrodden until "the time of nations" was fulfilled. This expression, "the time of nations," taken from Luke 21:24 (and used, as we have already noted, by Peter the Hermit), refers to a point in the future when many unbelievers will finally accept Christianity.

The apocalyptic program outlined here is a convoluted one: Essentially, the crusade had to establish Christianity in the Holy Land so that Antichrist could reverse that gain. But, as we shall see, the language may point toward a more authentic apocalyptic tradition that did play a part in motivating crusaders and in helping them to understand what they were fighting for.[21]

The Crowd Roars

Though we don't know exactly what Urban II said, we do know what happened after he finished talking. As the crowd roared its approval, one of the local bishops, Adhémar, from the nearby city of le Puy-en-Vélay, stepped forward and knelt before the pope, the first person to pledge to take up the cross and go to Jerusalem.

Adhémar had been bishop of le Puy since 1089. Its cathedral, dedicated to Notre Dame, sits atop a steep hill but is itself dominated by the tiny church of Saint-Michel d'Aguilhe, or St. Michael of the Needle, an architectural wonder, built in the tenth century atop a steep, sheer volcanic rock nearly three hundred feet high. By the time of Adhémar's episcopacy, it was attracting copious crowds of Christian pilgrims, many of them on their way to or from the famous shrine of St. James in Compostela. As bishop of le Puy, Adhémar thus understood the power and the magic of pilgrimage. He had reportedly made the journey to Jerusalem himself around 1086. Nothing is known about his trip, however, except that he seems to have gone. Adhémar also understood warfare, coming from a noble family and having been trained as a knight. At the time of the crusade, he was still considered an excellent horseman. And he had been involved with the planning of the crusade for at least three months before Clermont, when Urban II had consulted with him at le Puy in August 1095. It was probably then that they together choreographed this scene, to be performed on November 27.

In any case, before a rapturous audience, Adhémar asked permission to become the first warrior-pilgrim pledged to travel to the Holy Land, promising to depart by August 15, 1096. Urban not only readily assented but also appointed Adhémar to be his legate, to offer judgments and counsel about matters spiritual and military throughout the course of the campaign, speaking as if with the voice of the pope.[22]

At this point Urban apparently quoted Scripture: "If anyone does not take up his cross and follow me, he is not able to be my disciple." It was a metaphorical exhortation from the gospel, referring to a moment where Christ urged His followers to be ready to suffer on His account. But Urban and Adhémar interpreted it in a dully literal fashion. For as Adhémar knelt before the pope, a seamstress stepped forward, needle at the ready, and sewed a premade cross onto the right shoulder of Adhémar's cloak. The audience again roared in approval. Laymen and clerics together shouted their willingness to go to Jerusalem, to battle against the Saracens, and to liberate Christ's sepulcher. As they did, a small army of seamstresses rushed into their midst, carrying hundreds of cloth crosses in hand, ready to stitch them onto the shoulders of cloaks as quickly as vows were made.

Not wishing to underplay the theatrics, Urban and Adhémar had also arranged for representatives of the count of Toulouse, Raymond of Saint-Gilles, to arrive at precisely that moment and announce that their lord, along with countless of his followers, had already received the cross and vowed to go to Jerusalem. A wealthy and powerful lord, Raymond's comital authority stretched roughly across what is today southern France, known in the Middle Ages as "Occitania" because of the dialect of French spoken there. Raymond was also, like Adhémar, an experienced pilgrim, who (according to a highly suspect rumor) had lost his eye on an earlier trip to Jerusalem. The bold count ever afterward carried the eye with him, a reminder of what Christ's enemies were capable of doing and a prod to think always on Jerusalem. In 1095 he would have been in his mid-fifties. He had fought Muslims in Spain, and he had for decades been counted among the pope's special warriors, "The Faithful Men of St. Peter." The crusade represented for him a capstone to his career and his life.[23]

At news of Raymond's decision (news with which Adhémar and Urban had long been familiar), the pope broke into another rapturous oration. Upon seeing Bishop Adhémar alongside envoys of Count Raymond, he all but proclaimed an end to the war between church and empire: "Behold! Thanks to God! Now for the Christians about to depart there will be two outstanding leaders to the fore! Behold! Priesthood and kingdom—the clerical order and the lay order brought to concord to lead the army of God. Bishop and count, Moses and Aaron envisioned anew before us!"[24]

The furor to go to Jerusalem grew still more heated, and the oath taking and the cross sewing continued, possibly for hours. But once an appropriate sense of calm began to fall over the assembly, in a final bit of stagecraft a cardinal named Gregory stepped forward and cast himself down on the ground before the pope, begging absolution for his sins. All of those in attendance followed his example, beating their chests and crying for forgiveness for every wrong they had done. Pope Urban obligingly granted them their indulgence, at the same time encouraging all of the bishops and abbots and priests to spread the word among the laypeople about his new project. He urged his clerical listeners to tell everyone about the dangers faced by Christians in the East, about the threats to the Holy Sepulcher, about how pagans were corrupting the altars of God and torturing Christians, and about how wicked knights could now make peace at home and win honor for themselves abroad and in heaven. He commanded all the recognized preachers to spread this message. But he also encouraged anyone who had accepted a cross onto his shoulder to use it as a prop and to make known the same message to his family and friends. An ill-prepared army of lay preachers was thus added to the mix of papal plans and crusading passions stirred up by the likes of Peter the Hermit.[25]

With this sudden, public rollout, and with no official record of council proceedings to fall back on, Urban II essentially surrendered control of his message. He would try to take it back and even hone it during the next several months, as his preaching itinerary around the south of France continued. But soon after November 27, there were as many ideas about the crusade as there were people wearing crosses sewn onto their cloaks (and, eventually, tattooed onto their bodies). Whatever the pope may have chosen to emphasize at Clermont, the crusade over the next several months would become an aggressive and apocalyptic institution, one with eyes focused simultaneously on earth and on heaven, on Islam and on Antichrist, embracing far more wide-open possibilities of forgiveness and redemption than Urban II ever intended. The stakes of the battles would stretch beyond anyone's previous experience or imaginings.

3

The Response:
The Princes, the Prophets, the People
(December 1096–May 1097)

Two calls to crusade spread across Europe, one in the north and one in the south. The northern crusade was Peter the Hermit's, a violent, apocalyptic, somewhat acephalous movement rooted in an expectation of the end times and of an imminent battle with Antichrist, likely to occur in Jerusalem. In the south Urban II's crusade was a more tightly organized affair. It depended on the participation of the princes and the recruitment of men from their households and from among their immediate entourage of knights. Like Peter the Hermit's crusade, Urban II's emphasized the need to liberate Jerusalem, and whatever his exact words, the message tapped into similar prophetic emotions and expectations.

But Peter and the pope were not the only ones who gave shape to the crusade idea. Other preachers, pilgrims, prophets, zealots, and crackpots delivered sermons infused with their own particular apocalyptic and feral sensibilities. Urban II may have preached a sermon at Clermont that stressed the need to create peace and the opportunity to attain salvation, but these themes would not be the dominant ones of the crusade. The expedition would not happen in the name of a papal indulgence. It would be a campaign aimed at the transformation of the entire world, and perhaps of heaven and hell, too.

Papal Failures

As for the pope, his recruitment campaign did not end at Clermont. He continued to preach, stopping at monasteries, pilgrimage sites, and cathedrals. A month after Clermont, in December 1095, he celebrated a memorable Christmas at Limoges. As at Clermont, a large crowd gathered to hear him preach. It filled the entire city such that if one looked down on it from above, the buildings would have appeared to be islands surrounded by seas of faces.

The masses had come to celebrate Christmas, to witness the dedication of the two recently rebuilt churches, and to experience the pageantry of the papal court. The congregants may also have heard rumors of the pope's plans for Jerusalem. At Limoges that day, they certainly heard him preach about the Holy Land in tones similar to the ones used at Clermont. "The special cause of his visit was this: that the church of Christ and the Christian people in the East were suffering greatly under the heavy persecution from the Saracen nation and its spreading wickedness." Urban II declared that it was now the duty of the Frankish people to liberate Christians on the other side of the world, "to go to the East and drive that heinous people away from Christ's inheritance." Like the Council of Clermont, all of the events were highly choreographed and intended to inspire. What we cannot say is whether the gathering at Limoges, or any of the subsequent ones, actually worked.[1]

Consider the best documented of these rallies: the pope's visit about six weeks later to Anjou, where in February 1096 he recruited Count Fulk for the expedition. Fulk was an obvious candidate. As a wealthy, influential, and cultured lord, credited with writing a short history of his county, he would have brought real clout to any military campaign. More to the point, his family had strong connections to the Holy Land. One of his predecessors, Count Fulk Nerra, had made three separate pilgrimages to Jerusalem. Closer to home, Fulk Nerra had dedicated the church of Beaulieu in honor of the Holy Sepulcher and was buried there in 1040.

The pope worked aggressively to recruit the new Count Fulk. As Fulk himself described the courtship, "Around the time of Lent, Pope Urban II came to Angers and admonished our people that they ought to go to

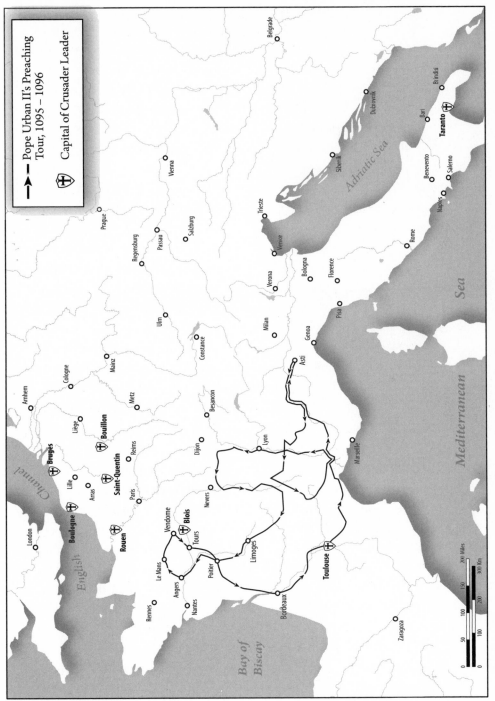

Urban II's preaching itinerary in 1095–1096 and the capitals of crusade leaders

Jerusalem to fight against the gentiles, for they had occupied that city and all the lands right up to Constantinople." The pope lavished great signs of favor on Fulk and his followers. To the count he offered a golden flower, "which I, in order to remember this event and because of the pope's love, have passed on as a sign of praise for me and my heirs." It is possibly the earliest recorded instance of a papal practice common in the later Middle Ages—distributing golden roses of remarkable craftsmanship to deserving Christian princes. [Plate 2]

Fulk liked the flower, but it left him unmoved. While some of his retainers took up the cross, the count preferred to stay at home and look after his own people, struggling with the consequences of a protracted famine.[2]

There is little evidence that Urban was any more successful as a recruiter anywhere else. After Clermont he drew crowds but did not necessarily win hearts. His biggest success remained the wealthy and respected Count Raymond of Saint-Gilles, whom he had convinced to take the cross before the Council of Clermont. Raymond's decision, in turn, depended less on papal razzle-dazzle and eloquence and more on back-room negotiations with the pope and Bishop Adhémar of le Puy. What these two churchmen promised Raymond in exchange for his service we cannot say, but he seems to have left home thinking that he would be the leader of the crusade and perhaps eventually the king of Jerusalem, too.

Most of the men and women who took the cross, however, never heard Urban II preach a word, for the very simple reason that they lived north of the Loire and hence outside the papal itinerary. So why did they bother going?

In the case of the princes, we can sometimes re-create their social circumstances enough to speculate as to the motives behind their decisions. But it is not so easy to say why the great mass of ordinary people decided to join the crusade. They left no writings and exist only as shadowy background players in the major historical narratives. By reconstructing the social world around them, however, we can begin to see (if not hear) the preachers and prophets who inspired them. Only a consideration of all these groups—princes, prophets, and ordinary people—can allow us to recognize the full range of beliefs and passions that together inspired Christians across Europe in 1096 to turn their gaze toward Jerusalem.

Accidental Successes: The Princes Respond

Although Europe in 1095 was on the verge of a sudden and unprecedented economic expansion, in the eleventh century conditions were fairly straitened. The Franks' homeland—to quote one crusade sermon—was too narrow, surrounded on all sides by either sea or mountain, overburdened with people, and barely able to produce enough food to feed the farmers who grew it. The Holy Land, on the other hand, was flowing with milk and honey, or at least it had been at the time of Moses and the Exodus. Most Christian preachers would have understood this promise of abundance allegorically, but anyone who had heard stories about the incredible wealth of Constantinople (and of the Islamic kingdoms beyond it) might have been inclined to read God's words to the Israelites literally. For these reasons, we cannot entirely dismiss greed or simple worldly ambition from the list of possible reasons for joining the crusade.[3]

The crusade leader whose motives have always seemed the most worldly was a giant—indeed, one of the tallest men in the world. His name was Mark, but at an early age his father, Robert Guiscard, or Robert "the Cunning," had taken to calling him "Bohemond," drawn apparently from a folktale about a giant. Robert Guiscard had come to Italy from Normandy as a simple mercenary, but by 1059 he had established himself as duke of Puglia and Calabria. For reasons of politics and marriage, Robert had named Bohemond's younger half-brother Roger Borsa as heir to his Italian lands, but Bohemond still seemed destined for great things. Robert Guiscard was engaged through the first half of the 1080s in a series of wars against Byzantium, causing the Greeks' western frontier to collapse at the same time that the Seljuk Turks were making inroads from the east. It was these Greek lands, if not the Greek empire itself, that Bohemond seemed fated to rule.

By the time of the crusade, however, fame and fortune had passed Bohemond by. Guiscard's Greek holdings were lost back to Constantinople shortly after his death in 1085. By 1096 Bohemond was merely a second-tier lord in southern Italy helping his uncle, Count Roger of Sicily, lay siege to the city of Amalfi. At some point during the fight, however, probably around July 1, 1096, Bohemond heard rumor of an army of pilgrims marching to the Holy Land to fight Muslims. His curiosity piqued, Bohemond made further inquiries. These pilgrims were, as reported, well armed. But each of them wore a cross on his right shoulder as a symbol of faith and of his higher calling, and they shouted as their war cry "God wills it! God wills it!"

The news ignited Bohemond's imagination. In Jerusalem he saw at last a goal worthy of his prodigious and frustrated ambitions. Perhaps it offered him the chance to make untold fortunes or else to establish a new principality outside of Italy, a country that had not been kind to him. Maybe, as Greek princess Anna Comnena suspected, Bohemond saw in the campaign an opportunity to renew his father's war against Byzantium and perhaps to place himself on the throne of Constantinople. Whatever the case, he called his armies together and announced his intention to take the cross. Not content to do so by himself, he tore off his own costly and oversized garment and had it cut into crosses for his men on the spot. The gesture proved spectacularly effective. Manically enthusiastic warriors surged forward, hoping to grab a "cross of Bohemond" for themselves, and then by the hundreds they abandoned Amalfi and the surer money of Roger of Sicily for the uncertain prospects of Syria, Palestine, and Jerusalem.[4]

Bohemond's case was probably unique. He had nothing to lose by going to Jerusalem. The princes and wealthy knights who took the cross, by contrast, were abandoning their homes and their estates, and by doing so, they were putting at risk their wealth, their property, the safety of their families—in short, everything upon which their social status depended. Anyone who decided to travel to Jerusalem because of practical considerations almost certainly did so to escape troubles at home rather than to find tangible rewards in the Holy Land.

Robert, Duke of Normandy, is a case in point. By virtue of office and inheritance, he controlled one of the wealthiest, best-governed principalities in Europe. As the son of William the Conqueror, he also had acquired significant military experience. (Robert is depicted in the Bayeux Tapestry sitting beside his father and preparing to draw his sword to fight at the Battle of Hastings.) Yet despite this impressive pedigree, Robert's hold on the ducal throne in the 1090s was tenuous. Ever since the death of his celebrated father in 1087, he had been at war with his younger brother, King William II of England. His youngest brother, Henry, rootless but ruthless and ambitious, represented another serious threat to Robert's

*Robert of Normandy, sitting to his father's left, depicted on the
Bayeux Tapestry* (Scala/Art Resource, NY)

authority. By 1096, after nearly a decade of interminable conflict, Robert's
barons were beginning to desert him for his rivals.

In the midst of this ongoing crisis, he heard rumors of the march on
Jerusalem, relayed by emissaries of Pope Urban II. At least one of them,
Abbot Jarento of the monastery of Saint-Bénigne in Dijon, offered to bro-
ker a peace between the duke and his brother William, without which
Robert never would have dared leave his home. Nor could he have afforded
to: Under the terms of the treaty, Robert ceded to William temporary control of the duchy in exchange for 10,000 marks of silver. It was still a risky

maneuver for Robert. There was no guarantee William would ever give up Normandy on his brother's return—if Robert did return. The thought must have occurred to Robert. He had only to remember that his grandfather, also named Robert, had abandoned Normandy at a time of similar upheaval to travel to Jerusalem and then died on the way back. He was originally buried in Nicea, though his remains had since been transferred to southern Italy. The crusade did at least offer Robert an immediate monetary payoff and the chance to escape a nearly impossible situation at home. If he did make it back alive, the prestige of the journey might add just enough luster to his name so that he could regain his duchy and even strengthen his hold against his calculating and formidable brothers.[5]

Another Robert, Count of Flanders (also Robert of Normandy's cousin), took the cross at the same time. His motives are easier to divine. In 1089 his father, Robert the Frisian, had gone as a pilgrim to the Holy Land, where he experienced firsthand the erratic governance of the Seljuk Turks. On his return, he stopped at Constantinople and upon meeting with the Emperor Alexius II agreed to send five hundred Flemish warriors to fight for the Greeks. Through his father's experiences, the younger Robert would have been well acquainted with the needs of both Byzantium and Jerusalem. Urban II would have known about these connections, and in December 1096 he sent Robert a letter describing the plans he had outlined at Clermont and exhorting Robert to allow his subjects, if they so desired, to take the cross. Robert answered with more enthusiasm than expected and vowed to join the crusade himself. Perhaps he had already caught Jerusalem fever from Peter the Hermit or else from memories of his father's stories.

As near as we can tell, Robert was not driven by any unusual fears about his own salvation. On the contrary, he was proud of his track record of good and charitable deeds. If pressed for a motive, he departed because of a general "Christian rage burning against the perfidious Persians, who, in their pride, attacked the church of Jerusalem and laid low Christian worship everywhere." Not just about Jerusalem or salvation, the crusade was about historical mission—about the need to put the world right, starting with the Church of the Holy Sepulcher and then, possibly, working back toward Europe.[6]

Another, more intriguing case is that of Godfrey of Bouillon, who would complete the crusade and become ruler of Jerusalem. Godfrey was the younger brother of Eustace, Count of Boulogne (who also went to Jerusalem, but in the retinue of Robert of Flanders). As a younger son, Godfrey enjoyed no claim to his family's holdings. Fortunately for him, at the age of fifteen he had inherited the estates and title of his uncle, Godfrey the Hunchback, Duke of Lower Lotharingia. The hunchbacked Godfrey was a loyal ally of Henry IV in his wars against Pope Gregory VII (despite the fact that his wife, Mathilda of Tuscany, was Gregory's staunchest supporter). While on campaign in the Low Countries and encamped near Antwerp, Godfrey the Hunchback arose in the middle of the night "to answer the call of nature. An assassin waited outside his resting place, and stabbed him hard between the buttocks. Leaving the sword in the wound, he hurried away." So the Hunchback was found, blade in rectum, bleeding profusely, and, one would think, almost certainly dead. But he lingered for a week, and in his last moments named his teenage nephew Godfrey as heir. The man behind the assassination was rumored to be none other than Robert the Frisian, Count of Flanders, who ten years after the murder would make a pilgrimage to Jerusalem in penance for his many crimes, this one among them, and who would inspire his son Robert to join the hunchback's nephew Godfrey on crusade.[7]

The young Godfrey's fortune, however, proved fleeting. Henry IV of Germany confiscated his ducal title and the lands that went with it and granted them instead to his own two-year-old son, Conrad. Godfrey had to content himself with the less significant title of Marquis of Antwerp. But he does not seem to have held a grudge. Rather, Godfrey continued his uncle's policies and fought alongside the German king against the pope. The two of them eventually took the war to Gregory VII's doorstep and laid siege to Rome in 1083–1084, ultimately placing the blockheaded antipope, Clement III, on the throne. After this campaign Henry declared himself Roman emperor and, as such, promoted his son Conrad to the kingship of Germany. Perhaps in recognition of loyal service, he restored Godfrey to the title of Duke of Lower Lotharingia.

After ten years, then, Godfrey had finally returned to the office that he had briefly held as a teenager. In doing so, he must have recognized that his status as duke would never be secure. Like Robert of Normandy, he had little reason to stay at home.

Still, as a German magnate who had never heard Urban II preach and who had fought against Urban's predecessor, he does not seem a likely candidate for the crusade—unless, like Peter the Hermit, Godfrey did not see the crusade as a papal expedition. Modern observers naturally imagine that Rome and its pope lay at the spiritual center of the medieval world. But for actual medieval Christians, piety happened at home, on a local level. The most important church for Godfrey was not the Vatican or the Church of the Lateran at Rome but the abbey of Saint-Hubert in modern-day Belgium, located about twenty-five miles northeast of Godfrey's famous castle of Bouillon. St. Hubert was a legendary figure in Lotharingia—the first bishop of Liège and the man credited with evangelizing dangerous pagan tribes who lived in the forests of the Ardennes. Later known as a patron of hunters, Hubert enjoyed in Godfrey's day a reputation for being especially adept at curing rabies. Godfrey acted as "advocate" for Hubert's monastery—that is, he was its patron and protector, offering military muscle when the community's spiritual weapons proved inadequate. During the performance of these duties, Godfrey must have worshipped before the altar of St. Hubert—receiving the Eucharist, giving thanks, taking oaths, praying for the souls of his dead relatives. Especially striking to Godfrey would have been a round chapel—an increasingly familiar architectural form in eleventh-century Europe, but still unusual enough to be noteworthy—modeled on the Church of the Holy Sepulcher in Jerusalem. The monks of Saint-Hubert called it "To Holy Jerusalem," meaning that Jerusalem and the tomb of Christ had been an important part of Godfrey's spiritual outlook for most of his adult life.[8]

At the time when Peter was preaching near Lotharingia, Godfrey had entered into a convoluted political fight between the monks of Saint-Hubert and their bishop, Otbert of Liège, over the abbey's leadership. Otbert had exiled Abbot Thierry, whom the monks had elected, and replaced him with his own candidate. Urban II became involved in the dispute, too, firing off a blistering letter in which he described Otbert as the standard-bearer of Antichrist and Satan's mule. Godfrey vacillated for a time about what to do, but he ultimately sided against the bishop and with the monks, helping to maneuver Thierry back into office.

Perhaps in the midst of this wrangling, which involved some sort of contact with papal emissaries, Duke Godfrey would have heard rumor of the call to liberate Jerusalem. It is equally likely that he had heard descriptions of Peter the Hermit's thrilling sermons. Whatever the case, as soon as the dispute with Otbert was settled, Godfrey decided that he ought to visit the real Holy Sepulcher in Jerusalem and give to it the same kind of service he had so long offered to its model in Belgium.

To pay for this hugely expensive endeavor, he turned to none other than the same Bishop Otbert. In an arrangement similar to the treaty struck between Robert of Normandy and his brother William, Godfrey gave Otbert the lordship of his castle of Bouillon in exchange for 1,300 pounds of silver. Thus, the only man whom Urban II would formally label as "a servant of Antichrist" was also the man who made possible the crusade of the future king of Jerusalem, Godfrey of Bouillon. For the church Saint-Hubert, the irony cut closer still. To help pay for his new castle, Otbert sent men to plunder the church, strip its altars, and tear the jewels from its gold crosses. Saint-Hubert thus lost a great deal of its wealth because of its patron's sudden and impulsive commitment to Jerusalem. (And within a year, Abbot Thierry would be forced into exile again, his position made untenable by Godfrey's absence.) Before leaving, however, Godfrey made one final gift to Saint-Hubert, offering to its saint a fine set of crystal dice. Perhaps he was symbolically giving up games of chance—one of the aristocratic pastimes that came under heavy ecclesiastical criticism. Or perhaps, like Caesar at the Rubicon, Godfrey was recognizing that there could be no turning back: The die had been cast, and he would never return home.[9]

In 1099 Godfrey would take charge of the crusade. But in 1096 the man who seemed most likely to do so was Hugh of Vermandois, usually called "Hugh the Great," the younger brother of King Philip of France. Despite the bad blood between king and pope, Hugh caught crusading fever immediately after the Council of Clermont. He must have been making tentative plans to participate during the 1095 Christmas court, for two months later, in February 1096, he was leading a council in Paris to discuss the logistics and goals of the mission. Imbued with the sacred blood of kingship, Hugh was a logical choice to take over the expedition. Though not as wealthy as Raymond of Saint-Gilles, he was royalty nonetheless, and that counted for a lot. His followers believed so: Many decided to accompany him, expecting that, at journey's end, Hugh would be crowned king and in return for their support would grant them lands and lordships around Jerusalem—a point of business likely discussed at Paris that February.

But it was a ludicrous idea: a handful of two-bit warriors spinning fantasies of world domination when in reality their own king's authority barely extended fifteen miles beyond the walls of Paris. Some of those in attendance must have expressed such skepticism, the excommunicate king among them. On the night of Tuesday, February 11, however, God intervened.

That night the moon went slowly into eclipse, and what little remained gradually took on a soft red glow. As Hugh and the others watched with fascination, and perhaps fear, the moon turned into a steadily darker, richer color until finally, terrifyingly, it had become the color of blood. The gathered knights and clerics stayed up all night and watched the skies, wondering at the meaning of it all and then marveling even more at dawn, as the moon, now restored to its proper color and shape, suddenly wore a ring of bright light, as if crowned with a heavenly diadem. That morning nobles lined up to join Hugh on the road to Jerusalem, with Philip's blessing.

We can easily imagine the excited hum among the knights and clerics. In Christian prophecy the moon would turn blood-red during the Last Days, after the angel of the Lord had opened the sixth seal: "The sun became black as sackcloth, the full moon became like blood, and the stars of the sky fell to the earth as the fig tree drops its winter fruit when shaken by a gale." This passage in turn grew out of the language of Old Testament prophet Joel: "And I will give portents in the heavens and on the earth, blood and fire and columns of smoke. The sun shall be turned to darkness, and the moon to blood, before the great and terrible day of the Lord comes. And it shall come to pass that all who call upon the name of the Lord shall be delivered; for in Mount Zion and in Jerusalem there shall be those who escape, as the Lord has said, and among the survivors shall be those whom the Lord calls." Eclipses, a bloody moon, cries to the Lord from Mount Zion, and destruction to be wrought at Jerusalem—the words of prophecy had become the language of current events.[10]

Bloody Moons and Blazing Stars:
The People Respond

Outside Paris the day of the Lord was truly at hand. Regardless of the careful plans and schemes of the princes, their followers had worked themselves into a frenzy. Stories of atrocity in Jerusalem shocked them. Mysterious signs in the sky and on earth filled them with terror. And they responded to these fears, as had Christians in 1009 when they heard of al-Hakim's destruction of the Holy Sepulcher, by killing Jews.

To take a few examples of the signs: A comet whose tail looked like a sword blazed through the skies. Clouds the color of blood rolled in from both the east and west and then clashed together in the heavens. A priest called Siggerius saw two celestial horsemen charge at one another to do battle; one of the warriors carried an enormous cross with which he beat his opponent to death. Another priest and two of his friends, while walking in the woods, saw a sword of wondrous length raised into the air by an unknown hand until it disappeared in the heavens. Others still, as they cared for horses, saw the shape of a city in the sky, and diverse, ethereal crowds from various directions, on horseback and on foot, strove to enter it. A woman, pregnant for two years, finally gave birth, and to a talking baby. Another baby was born with twice the usual number of limbs, and still another with two heads. Some people said that the Holy Roman Emperor Charlemagne, after nearly three hundred years, had come back from the dead, ready to lead his people into Jerusalem. "According to the prediction in the gospel, people everywhere rose up against people, and kingdom against kingdom. There were great earthquakes in all places, and plague and famine, terrors from the sky, and great signs. For because at that time the gospel trumpet sounded the arrival of the just judge, and behold! Everywhere the universal church could see the world bringing forth portents and prophetic signs."[11]

These phenomena were "apocalyptic" in the most technical sense: the enactment of events foretold in the book of the Apocalypse, the last book in the Bible, normally called "Revelation" in English. Not just fire and brimstone, though it contains plenty of both, the Apocalypse was the revelation of history's end, the culmination of mankind's endeavors on earth.

Scene from the apocalyptic tympanum at Conques. Such images, reminders of the horrors of the Last Days, were ubiquitous in the crusader-era Christian world. (Erich Lessing/Art Resource, NY)

As such, the study of the apocalypse was inseparable from the study of history. In the same way that some modern historians have seen all events as leading toward the triumph of a social or economic philosophy (communism or democratic capitalism, for example) and tried to locate evidence for their beliefs in historical narrative, so historians in the Middle Ages used history to isolate evidence of the divine plan at work. And the climax of the divine plan, illustrated in frescoes and sculptures in churches all across Europe, was the Apocalypse.

Throughout the early Middle Ages, people inevitably lived with an awareness of their world's fragility and the certainty of its end. But at particular times, this sense of inevitability turned into imminence. With the right conjunction of unusual events and unscrupulous leaders, the eyes of ordinary people could begin to see in even the most workaday circumstances indications of divine or diabolical wrath. The previous list of apocalyptic signs, for example, ends with the rather bland, yet somehow sinister observation that in 1096 horses were born with really large teeth—"so large that they ought to have appeared only on three-year-old stallions."

Omens, like this last one, exist in the eye of the beholder, and in 1096 people everywhere beheld omens. On an overcast day in Beauvais—when the clouds, to a level-headed observer, might look like a crane or a stork—an unruly and anxious mob, primed by their own priests and their bishop, began to buzz with the revelation that a cross had appeared in the clouds, sent from heaven to call or guide them to Jerusalem. They wanted to go to the Holy Land, not to redeem their sins or to perform penance but to carry out God's work—or, rather, to carry out his orders.[12]

Sometimes God even spoke directly. As word of the crusade spread, men and women by the hundreds claimed that Christ had branded their bodies with crosses, including at least one man who said that he had received a cross on his eyeball. Some people recognized these signs for what they were: bodily disfigurements or else pitiful tattoos made in haste in green or red ink and intended to raise money. But faked or not, the miracles were widespread and popular, even providing entrée into polite society and high office. One man named Baldwin, for example, who had received a cross on his forehead, or more likely cut one into it, survived the journey to the East and became archbishop of Caesarea, even though years later the scar on his head continued to ooze pus.[13]

If miraculous crosses failed to stir audiences, preachers, fund-raisers, and con artists turned to animals. Some venerated a she-goat supposedly infused with the Holy Spirit. Others paid reverence to a goose whose owner claimed that the bird was leading her to Jerusalem. Owner and pet made their public debut in Cambrai when the goose followed its lady to the cathedral's high altar. There she announced that the bird understood her desire to go east and that it intended to accompany her. A solemn request for donations likely followed. "Lo and behold!" the contemporary historian Guibert of Nogent observed, "The rumor flew as if on the wings of Pegasus and filled castles and cities with the story that God was sending geese to free Jerusalem!" The goat and goose may have been "detestable to the Lord and unthinkable to the faithful," but many "stupid people" believed them.

Ridiculous as these preachers sound, they had a discernible impact. The woman with the goose, for example, appears in both Christian and

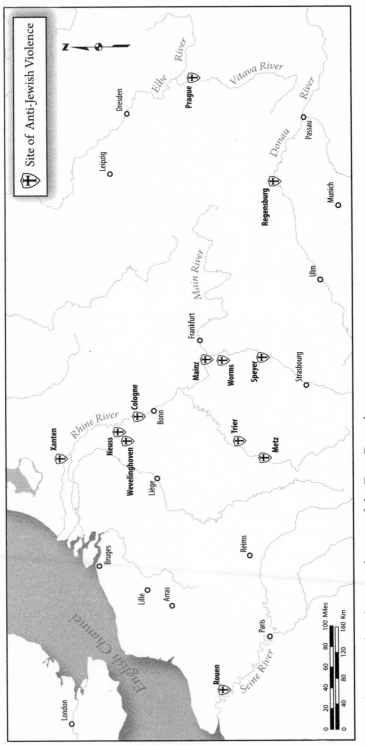

Site of Anti-Jewish Violence

London

English Channel

Bruges

Lille
Arras

Rouen
Seine River

Paris

Reims

Liège

Wevelinghoven
Neuss
Xanten

Cologne
Bonn

Rhine River

Trier

Metz

Mainz
Worms
Speyer
Strasbourg

Frankfurt

Main River

Regensburg

Ulm

Munich

Passau

Donau River

Prague

Vitava River

Elbe River

Dresden

Leipzig

20 40 60 80 100 Miles
40 80 120 160 Km

Sites of anti-Jewish violence at the time of the First Crusade

Jewish chronicles. The Christian writers were content with simple ridicule. A Jewish writer, however, added one important detail: In Mainz, a city along the Rhine, the woman's presentation agitated some of her audience members. Enraged, but probably unsure why, they cornered a group of Jews and asked, "How will you be saved? Behold the wonders that the Crucified does for us!" They all then charged at the Jews and tried to kill them.[14]

Little seems to have come of this individual attack, but shortly thereafter, on May 25, 1096, an army of crusaders, composed mainly of foot soldiers and a handful of knights, arrived at Mainz and demanded that the Jews accept baptism or death. The Jews tried to buy the pilgrims off with bribes, as they had done in the past, but this army's enigmatic and fanatical leader, Emicho of Flonheim, "a most noble man and in that region a most powerful one, too," refused their offer.

At first the burghers at Mainz seemed to rally around the Jews, but after two days of a minor siege, some of them decided to throw open the gates. The pilgrims viewed the burghers' surrender as a miracle. They said to one another, "Behold the gates have been opened by themselves. All this the Crucified has done for us, so that we might avenge his blood on the Jews." And a general slaughter began.

Many Jews opted to kill themselves rather than suffer death at their enemies' hands: "They fell upon one another, brothers and sons, women, mothers and sisters, and died amidst mutual slaughter. Mothers with sons nursing at their breasts cut their throats with knives, horrible to say, and others they threw from the walls." By one reckoning, 1,014 Jewish men, women, and children died in one day. And the pogrom at Mainz was only one of several outbreaks of anti-Jewish violence, committed mainly along the Rhine in the spring of 1096. Similar incidents occurred at Speyer, Worms, and Cologne. There are also records of pogroms connected to the crusade occurring as far west as Rouen and as far east as Prague.[15]

Peter the Hermit seems to have played an important role in inspiring these attacks. He may not have directly encouraged pilgrims to kill Jews, but he stirred up their passions about Jerusalem and turned the thoughts of ordinary men and women to the need to avenge the sufferings of Christ. He also threatened Jews in order to get supplies and, presumably, money from them. At the city of Trier, for example, Peter arrived on April 10, 1096, with a letter from French Jews suggesting that all German Jews would find it in their interest to give his armies full support in their expedition. The "or else" clause of the letter was left to the imagination. But like John the Baptist, Peter prepared the way. Other preachers and knights bore most of the direct responsibility for the massacres. Some of them we can name (Folkmar, Gottschalk, Emicho—whom we will meet again in the next chapter); most of them we will never know.[16]

Contrary to popular stereotype, most of the leaders of these pogroms were only secondarily interested in extorting money from the Jews. They were mainly concerned with striking a blow for Christianity, and they were willing to spare the Jews who accepted baptism. For example, outbreaks of anti-Jewish violence in Regensburg on May 23, 1096, and in Trier around June 1, 1096 (about two months after Peter had extorted supplies from them), led to mass conversions rather than mass murder. In the case of Trier, the bishop's followers apparently imprisoned the Jews and kept a close watch on them lest another series of heroic suicides and martyrdoms occur before they could be converted. The next day the bishop's followers led the Jews to the churches and forcibly baptized them. In Regensburg the Jews, by this point having heard news of the other pogroms in Germany, resignedly accepted baptism, with no casualties.[17]

The primary goal in all these pogroms was thus not the confiscation of funds but the destruction of Judaism. For most of the crusaders—or perhaps we should say simply "for most of the Christians" because many of the attackers would not have been pilgrims to Jerusalem but simple believers caught up in the spirit of the age—the spur to violence would have been a simple desire for revenge. The Jews had killed Christ, they believed, and ought to be punished accordingly.

For Emicho of Flonheim and his followers, the motive was subtler. More than military, his mission was messianic. According to a Jewish chronicler, Emicho "concocted a story that an emissary of the Crucified had come to him and had given him a sign in his flesh"—presumably a cross (one suspects that Emicho's tattoo must have been elaborate and detailed to have inspired such fanatical devotion)—"indicating that, when he would reach Byzantium, then He [Jesus] would come to him [Emicho] himself and crown him with the royal diadem and that he would overcome his enemies." This passage is rife with prophetic meaning. In popular medieval legend, during the Last Days a Christian leader, sometimes called the Last World Emperor, would unite his people in the Eastern and Western worlds before going to Jerusalem to wear his crown. It was this same legend that had inspired Henry IV to consider conquering not just Rome but Byzantium and Jerusalem, too. The Last Emperor legend also caused the unnamed false prophets in 1095 and 1096 to declare that the Emperor Charlemagne had returned from the dead. Perhaps Emicho himself was one of these prophets. Perhaps, more simply, Emicho believed that he himself was Charlemagne. Whatever the case, he told his followers that God had chosen him to liberate and rule Jerusalem, and they responded most immediately by killing Jews.[18]

As for the Jews who converted and survived, the outcome was predictable: "In 1096, the Jews of many provinces became Christians, and then walked away from their Christianity." "Some [converts] later returned to Judaism," another chronicler observed with palpable regret. This sort of surprise or disappointment is difficult for a modern observer to fathom. If Jews were forced to renounce their faith and accept baptism at swordpoint, they most certainly would return to Judaism at the first possible opportunity.

One explanation for such disappointment is that the writers believed that the legal system had failed them. Church law—although it forbade the use of force to convert Jews—held that baptism was permanent: once a Christian, always a Christian, however conversion came about. But after the fires of 1096 had burned out and the crusaders had left to meet their fates in the East, the Emperor Henry IV overruled custom and law, permitting Jews to abandon Christianity and return to their faith (as the Jews had also done after the pogroms in 1009).[19]

But more than a failure in justice, these relapses also represented a failure in prophecy, and in history, too. The Jews *had* to convert. There was no other fate imaginable for this stubborn remnant of what seemed to eleventh-century Christians an outmoded religion. History, logic, and the Apocalypse dictated it. After all, at the beginning of the Last Days (and surely in 1096 the Last Days had begun) the Jews would finally recognize their error and embrace Christianity. The Last Emperor legend made this point with especial clarity. In the Last Days, the "King of the Greeks and Romans" will arise to conquer all of the kingdoms of the

Christians, before taking his fight to the pagans. He will devastate their cities "and destroy the idols in their temples and call all the pagans to baptism, and in all their temples the cross of Jesus Christ will be raised. Whoever does not adore the cross will be punished with the sword, and after 120 years all the Jews will convert to the Lord, and his sepulcher will be made glorious." Just as predicted, Christ's anointed king had ridden through Germany, slaughtering the enemies of the faith and leading the Jews to conversion, all in the name of making glorious the tomb of Christ.

Yet unaccountably, history had failed. The scourge of God had passed, and the Jews had quietly returned to the anachronism that was their religion. And they had done so with the active connivance of a Christian emperor who himself imagined on occasion that he might fulfill the same prophecies.[20]

In the summer of 1096, however, there seemed to have been no failure. Quite the contrary, German crusaders left their homelands believing that they had made significant progress toward solving the Jewish problem. In retrospect, twelfth-century historians viewed these pogroms as mistakes and wanted to separate them from the serious, and more successful, business of crusading. They decided, by and large, to blame the killings on commoners, who "had a zeal for God, not founded in knowledge."

We must wonder, however, if some of the princes—the respectable crusaders, as it were—were involved as well. Godfrey of Bouillon did threaten to take revenge on the Jews of Mainz and Cologne for their ancestors' murder of Christ, but the Jews successfully bought him with one thousand marks of silver. He also received a reprimand from Henry IV for his actions. It would be surprising if Godfrey had been the only prince to have tried this ploy. Evidence for pogroms in central and southern France is slight, but not altogether lacking. Count Fulk of Anjou, the man who preferred to stay at home rather than seek Jerusalem, did associate pogroms with his fellow aristocrats and on the model practiced by Emicho of Flonheim. About Godfrey, Raymond, Robert of Flanders, Robert of Normandy, and the rest, he wrote, "In the beginning of such a great journey they compelled whatever Jews they found either to accept baptism or to die a sudden death." Perhaps if the conversions had proved more enduring, we would now have more evidence celebrating princely attempts to bring an end to Judaism. The future leaders of the crusade would in that case have worked alongside Folkmar, Gottschalk, and Emicho rather than standing to one side and watching with mild distaste as their social inferiors surrendered to these base instincts and brutal prejudices.[21]

However widely or narrowly we distribute the blame for the pogroms, the anti-Jewish violence in 1096 was an integral part of the call to crusade. Remaking the world and avenging the crimes against Christ and Christians required a general attack against every possible spiritual enemy, not just Muslims. Removing the perceived stain of Judaism from the earth was thus, in the eyes of many, a necessary first step to reclaiming the rightful inheritance of Jerusalem.

No one, however, seems to have put much thought into how these same armies might respond to another apparent enemy of Latin Christendom, a people whom Urban II had intended his armies to assist rather than oppose: the schismatic Byzantine Greeks. Before reaching Jerusalem, the pilgrim masses, all of them on different roads to Constantinople, would have to engage with this other spiritual rival—wealthy, powerful, and cultured enough to be contemptuous of this latest hoard of barbarians to arrive at their gates.

4

The Road to Constantinople

(June 1096–April 1097)

The plan was to meet at Constantinople. All of the armies seemed to know it, no matter when they departed or where they started or how closely they were connected to the pope. Each aimed for Constantinople.

All of the armies, too, faced similar challenges in balancing their members' needs and desires. The various leaders—Raymond, Godfrey, Hugh, and even the more eccentric ones like Peter the Hermit and Emicho of Flonheim—would have had to channel their followers' apocalyptic enthusiasm and energy into more earthly directions. A successful military campaign needed organization and discipline. Soldiers covered in crosses and Jewish blood expected something apocalyptic at the end of the road, but a successful march to Jerusalem demanded that the armies maintain at least a toehold on earth.

The first armies to depart were those led or at least inspired by Peter the Hermit, who had begun their pilgrimage by massacring Jews, and they had the most difficulty maintaining a balance between this world and the next.

The Hermit's Armies

The official date of departure for Jerusalem, as far as the pope was concerned, was August 15. But Peter the Hermit's followers could not wait so long. Or perhaps they had never heard about an official departure date.

Many of them had likely been preparing to leave, as we have seen, since well before the Council of Clermont.

The vanguard arrived with Peter in Cologne in early April 1096. Peter spent a week there preaching, but the French nobles who had accompanied him, notably Walter of Sansavoir and his kinsman Walter of Poissy, could not brook further delay—or else Peter sent them forward to clear a path for him. Whatever the case, the two Walters set forth on the pilgrims' route to Hungary with a handful of knights, several thousand foot soldiers, and an unknown number of pious and unarmed pilgrims.[1]

Because of his name, Walter of Sansavoir—which translates roughly as "without possession"—has often been referred to as "Walter the Penniless." As such, he seemed an exemplary standard-bearer for the early crusading spirit: a poor man who, drawing inspiration from Peter the Hermit, ascended to a position of great authority and led a massive army. Unfortunately, "Sansavoir" is a toponym, derived from Walter's homeland in France. Walter himself was an aristocratic warrior. Geography and timing make it likely that his followers were involved in the pogroms in Normandy, but once they left Cologne, Walter seems to have done an effective job reining in the soldiers' passions. Some time in early May 1096, they crossed over from Germany into Hungary, where they appear to have received a cordial reception from Coloman, the Hungarian king.

Even at this early stage of the march, there were likely problems with supplies. Unlike in modern warfare, medieval armies did not bring food with them. Rather, they were dependent on markets, hospitality, and their own foraging. The appearance of as many as 15,000 soldiers and pilgrims would have certainly put an unusual strain on local supplies. Hungarians were by this time accustomed to large groups of pilgrims from the West, but serious troubles started near the beginning of June. At that time the crusaders approached the Sava River, which separated the cities of Zemun and Belgrade. It was also the border between Hungary and Bulgaria, at the heart of the frontier region between Latin and Greek Christianity, between Europe and Byzantium.[2]

The details of what went wrong are elusive. Apparently, as Walter's armies prepared to cross the Sava, sixteen of his men decided to barter for weapons with a few local dealers. Then, as now, shopping for arms in a border town could end badly. Words were exchanged, and certain "evil-minded"

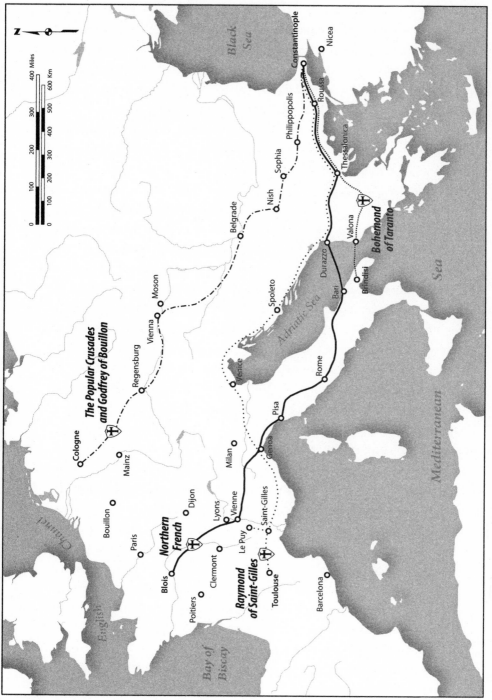

Routes taken by the main crusading armies

Hungarians attacked the pilgrims; stripped them of their clothes, money, and valuables; and sent them wandering naked back to Walter's camp. At the same time, on the other side of the river, the governor of Belgrade refused to give supplies or to open markets for the crusaders.

Walter responded in typical warrior fashion—by plundering the countryside and trying to round up as much Bulgarian cattle as possible. Several mêlées between Franks and Bulgarians ensued, and in the midst of the fighting about 140 of Walter's followers sought refuge in a chapel. Churches in Western Europe provided a right of sanctuary to fugitives, although lords and princes did not always respect it. The Bulgarians in this case did not. They set fire to the church, killing about half of the Franks inside and injuring many more. Those who survived somehow found their way back to the main army, and Walter led them all into the woods outside of Belgrade, continuing on to Constantinople.

At the city of Nish, Walter received a more sympathetic hearing. The Byzantine governor there granted him gifts of weapons and supplies and, more important, letters of safe passage and promises of open markets all the way to Constantinople. Departing Nish and making it about halfway to Constantinople, the army stopped in early July at the city of Philippopolis, named for Alexander the Great's father, Philip of Macedon, who had conquered this territory in 342 BC. The citizens were willing to extend to the army the courtesy of a market but apparently did not want to have any dealings with particular soldiers.

As Walter tried to negotiate more favorable terms, his kinsman Walter of Poissy fell ill and died. The cause of death is unknown, but as the army planned a makeshift funeral for him, those preparing his body discovered on it a spectacular cross, apparently painted there recently by the hand of God. The bishop of Nish heard about the miracle and came out of the city to inspect the body himself. So impressive did he find this cross that he ordered Walter carried into the city to receive an honorable burial, the citizens crowding the streets to gaze at the wondrous portent on Walter's flesh. They also gladly welcomed the rest of the soldiers into the city so that they might purchase supplies as they wished.

Despite some difficulties and lost lives, Walter of Sansavoir had held his men together for the roughly 1,200-mile journey between Cologne and Constantinople. God was very much on the pilgrims' side.[3]

PETER THE HERMIT was just a few days behind. He had left Germany around April 20 with an army estimated by twelfth-century German historian Albert of Aachen as having 40,000 men. He described it as "countless as the sands of the sea"—an echo of the promise that God had made to the Jewish patriarch Abraham five millennia before: "I will make your descendants as numerous as the stars in the sky and the sand on the seashore. Your descendants will take possession of the cities of their enemies." With these words, God had assured Abraham that his children would inherit the land of Canaan, the same land toward which the Franks now journeyed. As if leading the new Children of Israel, Peter the Hermit sought to collect on that promise.

Peter's army included men and women, rich and poor, taken from all parts of northern Germany and France, all drawn by the charismatic hermit's message of redemption and divine mission. Like Walter of Sansavoir's troops, they seem to have met with relatively little difficulty for the first several weeks of their march, including their crossing into Hungary in late May. Yet King Coloman no doubt was beginning to weary of incursions from the West. Even though he agreed to allow Peter into the kingdom, he required him to swear that he would maintain peace and keep his followers from pillaging the countryside. Peter rejoiced at his good fortune and for a time succeeded in keeping control over his army. Though a prophet, Peter the Hermit had a better grasp of military discipline and organization than historians have often credited him with.[4]

But problems began again around Zemun and the Sava. This time rumor reached the Franks that the Bulgarians and Hungarians were conspiring to wipe them out just as they were about to enter Byzantine territory. The plot was part of an agreement between a local Hungarian warlord named Guz and the Byzantine governor of Belgrade, named Nicetas. Peter the Hermit refused to accept the story. As a true warrior of God, he could not believe that a Christian people would oppose his great spiritual work. But as he neared Zemun, or so the story goes, he saw hanging from the city walls the armor and possessions of the sixteen men from Walter's army whom the Hungarian weapons dealers had robbed and humiliated. Outraged, Peter instructed his captains to attack the city.

That was Peter's side of the story. Not all contemporary historians were sympathetic. One of them, Guibert of Nogent, claimed that the Frankish army, consisting of Germans and "the leftover shit of our own people," brought disaster on itself. On the way to Zemun, they behaved like prisoners or serfs. When the Hungarians, like good Christians, offered to sell them grain and meat at generous prices, the crusaders responded belligerently. They expected to take what they wanted, and they did not anticipate that the locals would resist. Like madmen, they burned down the Hungarians' granaries, "raped virgins, dishonored marriage beds by carrying away women, and ripped out or burned the beards of their hosts."

Such behavior, on the face of it shocking, was not unheard of among eleventh-century Europe's warrior class. If a knight felt that his honor had been impugned, he was likely to respond in violent and sometimes imaginative ways. In this case, Peter's troops had expected the Hungarians to treat them as pilgrims and offer charity as they set about their religious-military endeavors. Instead, their hosts tried to cut business deals as if Peter's men were ordinary soldiers, or even merchants. By the time this band of crusaders had reached Zemun around June 5, nerves on both sides were frayed, and the frontier lords could certainly have decided to hang some confiscated weapons and armor from the city walls as a scornful sign of welcome.[5]

Peter the Hermit's response was swift, brutal, and effective. On June 22 he unleashed a ferocious attack against the city, instructing his archers to locate watchmen atop the ramparts and to fire at their eyes. The initial assault cleared the way for Godfrey Burel, one of Peter's infantry captains, to place a siege ladder against a fortified wall. Within a short time, crusaders were pouring into Zemun and massacring the defenders, unleashing upon them all the wrath of warriors whose mission God had sanctioned. According to one probably exaggerated estimate, 4,000 Hungarians were killed, compared to only 100 crusaders. Whatever the precise numbers, it was an impressive victory, and Peter occupied Zemun for five days, allowing the Sava River to carry severed limbs past the walls of Belgrade, lest its defenders make the same mistake as their fellow conspirators. The governor Nicetas abandoned Belgrade altogether, traveling on to Nish, where Walter Sansavoir had received such a pleasant welcome, there to rethink his strategy in response to what was a new phenomenon: a zealous army of pilgrim warriors.[6]

After a six-day rest at Zemun, Peter received word that King Coloman of Hungary, enraged at the Franks' behavior, was gathering his own army to attack. The crusaders needed to cross the Sava River quickly, but only 150 ships were available—not nearly enough to carry all of Peter's followers and his supplies. They moved as swiftly as they could, with some of Peter's army forming makeshift rafts from timber and rope. At some point during the crossing, seven small boats filled with Hungarian archers (specifically, "Pechenegs," Turkish settlers in Hungary) opened fire on the pilgrims, killing them by the dozen. Peter, however, managed to dispatch an ad hoc Frankish navy to challenge the Hungarians, and the Franks sank all seven of the attacking vessels. The river crossing thus finished with some semblance of order, but it was a slightly depleted and somewhat humbled army that continued on past Belgrade to Nish.[7]

Upon their arrival there about two weeks later, the Franks received a surprisingly civilized reception from their former enemy Nicetas. He quickly agreed to open the city markets to Peter, and Peter in turn agreed to hand over hostages as pledges of his army's good conduct. But at this point, either Peter had begun to lose control of his followers or perhaps the Bulgarians had begun to weary of the Franks. This was, after all, the second major army in less than two weeks to have stopped at Nish in order to replenish its supplies. Whatever the case, haggling between some soldiers and a merchant turned ugly, and the soldiers set fire to several mills and a handful of houses outside the city. The citizens immediately took complaints to Nicetas, observing to him, with admirable understatement, that "Peter and all his followers were false Christians—thieves, even—and not peaceful men." The governor ordered a punitive raid against the back of Peter's slow-moving forces, where the weak and unarmed were concentrated, walking alongside the wagons and the supplies. The Bulgarians seized whatever food and cattle they could find, killed and beheaded the old and the infirm, and enslaved some of the women and children.

By the time Peter had heard of the troubles, the attack had ended. Perhaps he should have pushed on at this point, but a Frankish sense of honor demanded either that they retaliate against Nicetas or else that they seek some other form of justice from him. Peter therefore turned the army around, and negotiations began anew. Some of his followers, however, had no patience for further talk. Around 2,000 "hard-headed and thought-less young men, a wild and undisciplined sort of people," attacked the city in the hopes of undermining any potential peace talks. Then once negotiations had begun, they started loading up their wagons to press the crusade back into motion, hoping to force Peter to abandon what seemed pointless debate and deliberation.

Their activity did not pass unnoticed. When Nicetas saw what must have seemed inexplicable movements within Peter's armies, he ordered a full-fledged assault. The crusaders panicked. Men and women fell into the river and drowned. They were shot down with arrows fired from the ramparts of the city walls. They were cut down or imprisoned. All of their money and supplies, including a wagon full of gold and silver, were captured. Peter himself with only a few companions ran into the woods that surrounded Nish. They wandered without direction on the thickly forested hills. As far as they knew, all of their companions had been killed, their crusade ended in disaster.[8]

Peter himself managed to work his way up a mountain near the city, and by the time he had reached the top, he had gathered together about fifty of his followers, including Godfrey Burel and Walter of Breteuil, both of whom had been offered as hostages to Nicetas. Unsure how many, if any, of their companions, once as numerous as the sands of the sea, had survived, Peter ordered his men to sound trumpets and to make as great a noise as possible. By the time the sun had set, as Albert of Aachen told it, 7,000 pilgrims, dazed and groggy, emerged from the forest. They marched to a nearby deserted town (its citizens had probably left out of fear of what Peter might do to them) and camped outside its walls, living on whatever grains they could scavenge, waiting to see how many more of their companions had escaped and might yet return to them. Miraculously, a full three-quarters of the army found their way to Peter's camp.

In the meantime, unknown to Peter, Nicetas had written to the Emperor Alexius II to warn him about the latest Frankish army and to ask for advice. The emperor, who now would have known about Walter's army as well, took the situation in hand, sending envoys to Peter. They found him near the city of Sophia, a little over one hundred miles from Nish, and brought both a stern message and welcome news. Alexius, they informed

Peter, was displeased because "your army has plundered and created chaos throughout his territory." Nonetheless, Alexius forgave Peter his trespasses and instructed the governors in all his cities to open their markets to him provided that Peter did not disturb any one place for more than three days, kept the peace, and made his way to Constantinople as quickly as possible. Once more, and for the first time since Zemun, Peter rejoiced at his good fortune.[9]

It was a remarkable achievement. A charismatic hermit, who had embraced poverty and believed that God had sent him a message from heaven, had raised an army of several thousand Christians and had managed to hold it together on a long and dangerous march. That discipline broke down outside of Nish, after more than two months and one thousand miles of marching, is less remarkable than that the apocalyptic doctrine Peter had espoused was powerful enough to keep his followers so focused and organized that most of them safely reached Constantinople.

Five days after leaving Sophia, Peter stopped at Philippopolis, where Walter's army had been just ten days earlier. There, Peter, "insignificant in stature but great in voice and in heart," told crowds of locals about his sufferings and his adventures. Though he undoubtedly needed to speak through an interpreter, many were moved to tears, and listeners lined up to give him and his followers money, food, horses, and mules. No doubt a few listeners pledged themselves to his cause, too. Peter also would have taken a moment to visit the grave of the cross-decorated Walter of Poissy, whom he had recruited just to the north of Paris while traveling with his entourage of beggars and redeemed prostitutes.[10]

IN THE MEANTIME, three other armies, organized by preachers and at least one prophet, were closely following Peter's footsteps. All of them seem to have departed around the end of April 1096. One, estimated at over 10,000 men and women, was led by a monk named Folkmar, who had given up his vows and abandoned his monastery to pursue dreams of Jerusalem. Folkmar chose a slightly different path from Walter and Peter, leading his followers into Bavaria and, apparently, through Prague. There, around June 1, his message inspired yet another pogrom against the Jews. His army also seemed to have had fewer aristocrats among its leaders; an observer in Prague wrote that, in the wake of the army's departure, "hardly any farmers remained in the towns and villages in German lands, particularly in East Francia."

Folkmar had the misfortune to enter Hungary shortly after King Coloman had ordered his attack against Peter the Hermit at Zemun. Coloman had by now repeatedly given the Frankish armies the benefit of the doubt. For Folkmar's warrior band, composed largely of agricultural laborers, neither the king nor his subjects had any patience. During negotiations for markets at the city of Nitra, "trouble was stirred up." The locals responded swiftly: They put part of Folkmar's army to the sword and enslaved many of the rest. A few crusaders managed to escape and make their way back to Europe. To save face for having abandoned the cause, they explained that a cross had appeared in the sky to guide them away from Nitra and save them from immediate destruction.[11]

FURTHER DETAILS on Folkmar's experiences in Hungary are vague. The story of another army, led by a priest called Gottschalk, might help fill some of the gaps.

Gottschalk heard Peter the Hermit preach the liberation of Jerusalem and took inspiration from his message to raise his own army. According to Albert of Aachen, it numbered around 15,000 people, who, like Peter's army, took the land route into Hungary toward the end of April. They arrived at Moson, Coloman's capital, around June 20, just about the time Coloman began to hear rumors of trouble all along the pilgrimage route and involving all three of the Frankish armies that he had welcomed into his kingdom. Perhaps this is why Coloman held Gottschalk's men up a little longer around Moson. Or perhaps Coloman was just beginning to recognize what an economic crisis the pilgrims might represent. In any case, the delays led to restlessness among the pilgrims, who began to plunder wine, grain, and livestock for their own use. One market deal turned particularly sour, and a group of pilgrims—to express their displeasure as vividly as possible—drove a spear through a young Hungarian man's anus. Word traveled back to the king, and he ordered all the pilgrims slaughtered to a man. It is probably then that Coloman ordered similar attacks against Peter's armies at Zemun and Folkmar's at Nitra.

Battle lines were drawn near a church dedicated to St. Martin about thirty miles southeast of Moson. But neither side was terribly anxious to engage the other. The pilgrims must have recognized that they were outnumbered and outarmed. The Hungarian generals suspected that the pilgrims were willing to fight to the very end—they were far from home and desperate and as soldiers of God believed that death in this alien land would ensure them a welcome into heaven.

The Hungarians therefore proposed a truce. King Coloman, they announced, would restore the pilgrims to favor and freely open his markets to them provided that the pilgrims temporarily surrendered their weapons. "If, indeed, you surrender them to the king with all the money you have, you might soothe his anger and find grace in his eyes. But if you do otherwise, not one of you will stand before his face or go on living, since you have committed such contumacy and calumny in his kingdom." Gottschalk agreed to this proposition, likely recognizing it as his only hope of survival. He would have been inclined to give the benefit of the doubt to Coloman. The pilgrims turned over their weapons and money.

As soon as pilgrims had been disarmed, the royal army killed almost all of them in a merciless slaughter. A few crusaders escaped the chaos and made their way back to Germany. The field outside of St. Martin's, they swore to anyone who would listen, was left covered "with dead and butchered bodies and blood"—newly crowned martyrs of Christ, though their killers were fellow Catholics whom the pilgrims themselves had persecuted.[12]

By THE TIME THAT Emicho of Flonhcim and his army arrived in Hungary, Coloman had lost any inclination to cooperate with the crusade. Like the citizens at Nish, he had learned to see the pilgrims as false Christians, thieves, and violent men. With Emicho, this analysis was appropriate.

Emicho had led the most brutal pogroms against the Jews in the Rhine Valley, stirring up such a frenzy that the killings continued well into the summer, after his own men had turned toward Hungary. The size of his army is difficult to gauge. Albert of Aachen gave the outlandish figure of 200,000 soldiers, including 3,000 knights (another contemporary offered the more likely figure of 12,000 soldiers). It would have been well financed, not only because of the plunder Emicho had taken but also because he counted several prominent nobles among his followers. These included Thomas of Marle, Drogo of Nesle, Clarembald of Vendeuil, and William of Melun, nicknamed "the Carpenter" because of the way he hewed his enemies in two as if they were lumber. Albert characterized Emicho's men as a frivolous group, given to revelry and fornication. But as their ruthless treatment of the German Jews demonstrates, they were dangerously fanatical, their leader proclaiming himself an apocalyptic emperor intent upon wiping Judaism from the face of the earth and making himself king of all true Christians.

When Emicho and his band arrived at Moson, Coloman refused to deal with them: His kingdom was now closed to the Franks. The last battle with Gottschalk was recent enough that the neighboring fields were still littered with stinking corpses. Emicho, the mad emperor, consulted with his leading men about how to respond, and together they chose to lay siege to Moson and to devastate the Hungarian kingdom.[13]

The siege lasted for several weeks. Emicho's armies tried to seize control of the region by building bridges that would allow them to cross the River Leitha outside of Moson and to traverse the swamps in the area more easily as well. The Hungarians did their best to disrupt these maneuvers, resulting in several minor skirmishes. In one encounter, William the Carpenter, earning his nickname, cleaved off the head of one of Coloman's chief advisors. The pilgrims celebrated around his severed head that evening, admiring in particular its long and flowing gray hair. But eventually food began to run short, and Emicho realized that more aggressive measures were called for.

On August 15, 1096, in a final push again Moson, his men moved two catapults close to the city and broke through the walls in two separate places. As the Franks poured through the breach, the Hungarians offered one last desperate defense (King Coloman, however, was preparing to flee into Russia along a secret network of bridges he had had constructed in the swamps around the city). Victory was seemingly within Emicho's grasp. Perhaps he might have crowned himself king of Hungary—presumably asserting his right as Last World Emperor. We shall never know because just as quickly as his men had penetrated the city, they turned around and retreated in a fright. Why they did so is unclear. Albert of

Aachen reckoned it a judgment of God, and it must have looked like one since according to eyewitnesses the Danube and Leitha rivers both ran red with blood. The better-equipped knights with faster horses managed to escape. All others presumably perished or were enslaved. The crusade's first great acts of slaughter thus occurred in battles that pitted Catholic Christians against other Catholic Christians.

As for Emicho, he was one of the fortunate few who escaped. But his credibility had been badly damaged, and rather than continue the crusade, he thought it best to return to Flonheim. But some of his companions—including Thomas of Marle, Drogo of Nesle, Clarembald of Vendeuil, and William the Carpenter—were not ready to give up. Rumor had it that other pilgrims were gathering in Italy to cross the sea and thus avoid Hungary altogether, entering the Byzantine Empire directly. These few survivors therefore broke away from the pilgrims' land route and met up with another potential king of Jerusalem in September: Hugh of Vermandois, called "Hugh the Great," brother of King Philip of France, leading a small but wealthy army of knights confidently toward the center of the earth.[14]

The Princes on the March

Hugh's army was one of the first of the better-organized princely forces to depart, probably leaving France sometime near Urban II's proposed date of August 15, 1096. Eschewing the roads through Hungary, the army aimed instead for Bari in southeastern Italy, intending to sail from there to Durazzo (Durrës, in modern Albania).

As Hugh's followers set about putting their moral and financial houses in order, Hugh himself wrote a letter to the Emperor Alexius, warning him of his imminent arrival. The letter does not survive. Instead, we have a satirical paraphrase written in the biography of Alexius by his daughter Anna Comnena. Hugh, according to Anna, proclaimed himself "the King of Kings, the greatest of all beneath the heavens," and warned Alexius that he expected to be received in Constantinople with all the pomp suited to his great station. The language, though a bit over the top, does accord with what we know about Hugh and his followers—namely, that they expected him to become king of Jerusalem. We also know that most Latin observers found Greek court ceremonial more than a little overbearing.

It is easy to imagine, then, the brother of the French king firing off a pompous and high-handed missive to the Greek emperor before departing for the East.

Alexius must have viewed Hugh's letter not so much as a sign of Frankish pretension but as part of an ongoing crisis. By the time it arrived, he had already received the armies of Walter and Peter at Constantinople. He would have also had to deal with the crises created by Peter's followers near Belgrade and afterward at Nish. Finally, Alexius would have heard how King Coloman, because of the Franks' boorish and brutal conduct, had decided to forbid them from entering his domain. Alexius's own subjects, already overburdened with the massive armies of Peter and Walter and equally aware of the chaos engulfing Hungary, were likely ready to take a similar stand against Hugh—even without knowing that while passing through Italy, Hugh had welcomed into his army some of the most erratic and violent members of Emicho's following.

As soon as Hugh reached Bari in early October, he sent ahead a party of envoys to the Byzantine port of Durazzo to announce his imminent arrival. Accompanying this diplomatic group, unaccountably, was William the Carpenter. At Durazzo, according to Anna Comnena, the Franks repeated the veiled threats of Hugh's earlier letter, backed up this time by Urban II's endorsement: "Be it known to you, Duke, that our Lord Hugh is almost here. He brings with him from Rome the golden standard of St. Peter. Understand, moreover, that he is supreme commander of the Frankish army. See to it then that he is accorded a reception worthy of his rank and yourself prepare to meet him."

Hugh arrived at Durazzo a few days later, after, according to one source, his ship nearly sank during a treacherous crossing of the Adriatic. Envoys from Durazzo's Byzantine governor met up with him, on the beach and still reeling from the voyage, and escorted him into the city. There he was greeted warmly and feted in a manner appropriate to his station. The following morning, after the Franks had had a good night's sleep, the Greeks placed Hugh and his men under arrest and escorted them under close supervision all the way to Constantinople.[15]

At about the same time as Hugh was preparing to cross the Adriatic, the two princes from northern France, Robert of Normandy and his cousin

Robert of Flanders, were still readying their followers for the long journey east. Sometime in mid-October 1096, probably at Chartres, their two armies rendezvoused with Robert of Normandy's cousin, Stephen of Blois, a wealthy and prominent count who had also decided to take the cross.

Stephen's army included a chaplain named Fulcher of Chartres, not a warrior or, in the conventional sense, a person of any significance, but in terms of history one of the most important of all crusaders. Fulcher, a somewhat officious man, had not only attended the Council of Clermont but had also jotted down notes about its more important decrees (though, curiously, he failed to mention Jerusalem in connection with Urban II's sermon). When he left with the French armies that October, he probably continued his record-keeping habits, or at least he made careful note in his own memory of the things he saw. At some later date, probably starting around 1102, he began to arrange these notes and memories more coherently in a book that he would revise often, entitled *The Jerusalem History*.

His description of the atmosphere around Chartres at the time of the Franks' departure was suitably vivid: "At that time a husband would tell his wife when he expected to return, and that if God permitted life to be a companion to him on the journey, he would come back to his homeland and to her. He commended her to the Lord, and he kissed her, and as they cried, he promised that he would return. But she feared that she would never see him again and was unable to hold herself up and fell to the ground lifeless, sobbing for her friend who left her, now alive but seemingly already dead." Crusaders may have expected a hundredfold return on their labors, but the immediate sacrifice and loss were no less daunting because of it.[16]

By October the French armies had crossed over into Italy. Along the way they stopped at Lucca, where Urban II himself received them. It was the first time most of the soldiers had laid eyes on the pope. It was also very likely the only opportunity Urban had to preach directly to an army of crusaders, though there is no evidence that he did so. Fulcher observed only that the pope spoke individually or in groups with several of the pilgrims (including Fulcher) and then gave the army as a whole his blessing.

From there the Franks marched down the coast to Rome, hoping to pray at St. Peter's. Unfortunately, the supporters of the antipope Clement III still controlled most of the basilica and were hostile to Urban's loyalists.

When the pilgrims entered the Vatican unarmed to pray, a few of Clement's men threatened them with swords and stole their offerings. When the Franks knelt before the altars, Clement's followers dropped rocks on their heads. The experience proved dispiriting enough for many of the crusaders that they decided to return home—victims of cowardice, according to Fulcher. More likely the grandeur of the papal vision, of which they would have at least had a taste at Lucca, clashed too sharply with the tawdry reality of Roman politics.[17]

Toward the end of November, the armies finally arrived at Bari. As they would have quickly learned, they were the third major crusading host to pass through this port, seeking transportation to Durazzo. Hugh the Great had sailed about six weeks before Stephen and the two Roberts, and Bohemond—having just delivered the rousing sermon that reached a crescendo with him cutting up his own cloak into crosses—had probably left about a month after Hugh. It was probably rumor of Hugh's army that inspired Bohemond to abandon his uncle at Amalfi and prepare to attack Jerusalem instead.

Once in Bari, the Franks would have gone at once to pray before the recently erected shrine of St. Nicholas, whose bones Italian adventurers claimed to have stolen from Asia Minor during the chaos that had followed upon the Seljuk Turks' expansion into that territory. They likely prayed for favorable winds and a quick crossing. If so, Nicholas did not listen. The winter seas had begun to turn ugly, and Robert of Normandy and Stephen both agreed that it would be wiser not to test them and instead to set camp in Italy until spring. Robert of Flanders, however, was impatient. He successfully led his army across the Adriatic to Durazzo. There is no record of how he fared upon arrival, but presumably he received the same strained welcome as Hugh the Great had before him.[18]

As for Bohemond, he was too familiar with Alexius's strategies to fall so easily into his hands. To avoid the emperor's traps, he arranged for his army to land at different points along the Adriatic coast and then to meet up on All Saints' Day, November 1, at the port city of Valona (Vlorë, in modern Albania). On his best behavior, Bohemond instructed his men not to plunder the country where they had arrived, since it belonged to

Christians, and not to claim more food than they needed. These rules were necessarily flexible. On Christmas Day, when the Byzantine town of Castoria refused to open its markets for the crusaders, Bohemond granted his men permission to plunder the countryside. And when, around New Year's, they stumbled upon what they took to be a castle full of heretics, they burned it to the ground and killed everyone inside.

This was all part of a drawn-out, slow, even leisurely four-month-long march to Constantinople. It was a kind of "purposeful procrastination," as a recent historian has phrased it, where Bohemond tried to make contact with other crusade leaders to propose to them an idea: that they begin their expedition with an attack on Constantinople. It was not as mad an idea as it now sounds. Bohemond was a veteran leader in the Norman wars against Alexius and had previously defeated the emperor in battle. Growing up, he had learned to think of himself as a potential Byzantine emperor. The crusade potentially gave him his chance. He only succeeded, however, in reaching Godfrey of Bouillon, who had arrived at Constantinople at about the same time Bohemond was looting around Castoria. The Lotharingian duke politely refused the invitation.[19]

GODFREY HIMSELF had left his homeland at the head of an army of "illustrious princes," according to Albert of Aachen—though most of these princes were related to Godfrey or else were members of his household. Most notable among them was Godfrey's younger brother Baldwin (his older brother Eustace, Count of Boulogne, as noted earlier, had departed with Robert of Flanders). They set forth around August 15, the semiofficial departure date and also at about the same time as Hugh the Great left France. Like the armies of Peter and Emicho, they followed the pilgrims' route through Hungary. But as they approached the German-Hungarian frontier, they met up with an alarming number of refugees from Emicho's and Gottschalk's armies, who told them how Coloman had betrayed their trust and how the Hungarians had closed all their markets and had refused them any hospitality. Godfrey wisely set camp on the Austrian side of the Leitha River and tried to discover the truth behind the stories.

Three weeks of tense negotiations followed. First Godfrey sent a small and undistinguished delegation to meet with Coloman. It included a knight named Godfrey of Esch, who had met Coloman in the past. Each side aired its complaints over the course of eight days, before Coloman allowed the envoys to return with an invitation to Godfrey that they meet together near one of his castles, called Sopron. Godfrey agreed, and at the advice of his men traveled there with three hundred soldiers. Leaving the main part of his army to mill about, he crossed a bridge with only two relatives to accompany him and walked into a marsh, where he found the king of Hungary awaiting. They sat together for hours and talked about friendship, peace, and love. Each man, king and duke, decided that he found the other to be sincere in his affections. But Godfrey still had more negotiating to do if he were to achieve a satisfactory accord. At no small risk, he walked back across the bridge and dismissed all but twelve of his three hundred followers and then, with this much smaller group, entered yet another of Coloman's castles. Negotiations and feasting continued for another eight days.

Finally, as the end of September neared, a deal was struck: Coloman would open his kingdom to the Lotharingians provided that they agreed to keep the peace and to respect Hungary's markets and properties and also provided that Godfrey offered Coloman hostages of sufficient importance. Godfrey agreed to these terms and turned over to the king as hostages his brother Baldwin, Baldwin's wife, and their household. Each side sent out heralds to proclaim the terms of the agreement. The penalty for even the slightest violation of the peace was death.[20]

Through this combination of diplomacy and fierce discipline, Godfrey steered his army through Hungary. Soldiers of the king shadowed his every step and effectively held his brother and his brother's family prisoner—very similar to the treatment Hugh the Great received at Durazzo from Alexius. After three weeks, around October 15, Godfrey's army reached Zemun, plundered just four months earlier by Peter the Hermit. They rested there for five days, in part because they heard that their diplomatic situation was unlikely to improve once they reached Byzantium.

The crossing of the Sava River to Belgrade thus became something of a preemptive military operation. Approximately one thousand soldiers managed to fit into only three ships and to establish a defensive line against any potential Greek attackers. The rest of the army, like many of

Peter's followers before them, used makeshift rafts constructed of timber and vines to cross safely. The operation proceeded without incident, and once all of the Lotharingians were across the Sava and outside of Hungarian lands, Coloman released Baldwin and his family from captivity and sent them to the other side of the Sava, too.

The next day, just as Godfrey's army was entering "the vast and mysterious woods of the kingdom of Bulgaria," envoys from Alexius met up with them and proposed yet another truce. Provided that, again, Godfrey respected the peace of the empire, Alexius would allow his army free passage and access to markets. At the city of Nish, where Peter the Hermit had lost nearly one-quarter of his army, the governor Nicetas now offered to the Lotharingians a generous gift of grain, wine, oil, and meat. The cities of Sophia and Philippopolis did much the same.

It was at Philippopolis, however, after an eight-day rest (where the soldiers might have occupied themselves visiting the first crusader shrine— the tomb of Walter of Poissy), that relations with Byzantium suddenly soured. A messenger arrived (it is unclear from whom) announcing that Alexius was holding as hostages and, rumor had it, in chains Hugh the Great, Drogo of Nesle, Clarembald of Vendeuil, and William the Carpenter. Perhaps this was honorable captivity, akin to what Baldwin had received from Coloman. There was also something like an expectation that Godfrey would join his fellow leaders in Constantinople. Instead, he stopped his advance and sent envoys to Alexius, demanding the captives' release. (Two other leaders in Godfrey's army rode ahead of the delegation, hoping to win a few last-minute presents from the emperor before the truce fell completely apart.) When Alexius refused this demand, Godfrey ordered his men to start plundering.

They did so for eight days. Alexius relented. Two new messengers reached Godfrey, promising that Alexius would release the prisoners provided the Lotharingians stopped ravaging the countryside. Godfrey ordered his men to cease their attacks and then moved camp up to the outskirts of Constantinople. Hugh, Drogo, Clarembald, and William were waiting to meet him, in the shadow of the city's great walls and its golden domes, intimidating in their splendor. The former prisoners and the duke rejoiced at their newfound fellowship, embracing and kissing one another.

Peace was, for a time, restored. But when messengers arrived from Bohemond a few days later and offered to make all-out war against Alexius, Godfrey must have been sorely tempted.[21]

THE FINAL ARMY TO LEAVE for the Holy Land was the first one that Urban II had recruited—the southern French. Though no one knows the exact numbers, it was the largest of the princely armies, a fact explained in part by the amount of time Urban II had spent recruiting in this area. Equally important was Raymond of Saint-Gilles's extraordinary wealth, which enabled him to finance a much larger army than any of the other princes could. Theoretically attached to the French crown, Raymond's Occitan— or as they are more often known, "Provençal"—followers would have formed a distinct cultural and linguistic group within the main army. One feature in particular would have immediately distinguished these Provençals from their fellow crusaders: the unusually large number of poor men and women who chose to follow in their wake. The care of these indigent pilgrims, as we shall see, Count Raymond took very seriously.

Before leaving Occitania, Count Raymond attended to his spiritual obligations, trying to resolve conflicts throughout his principality, including one of his own property disputes with the abbey of Saint-Gilles. As a final step toward putting his spiritual house in order, he arranged to have a candle left on the altar in the cathedral of le Puy, with a flame burning there before an image of the Blessed Virgin (likely the black statue of the Madonna, a replica of which sits in the cathedral today) as long as he should live. Perhaps because of the great care with which he approached these financial and spiritual obligations, his armies did not manage to leave until near the end of September, if not early October, well after Urban II's mid-August goal.[22]

In addition to a number of Provençal princes and castellans, Raymond's army included several distinguished churchmen—most notably, papal legate Bishop Adhémar of le Puy and Bishop William of Orange. In the long run, however, the most important and influential among them was an obscure cleric named Raymond of Aguilers, ordained a priest during the course of the march. This Raymond was a chaplain within the household of Count Raymond, and he had served some minor role in drawing up plans for the departure. By the time the armies had arrived in

Anatolia, as Constantinople neared, he certainly had a clear sense of what the crusade ought to be about, and he worried constantly that the army was losing its direction or else that deserters who had returned to the West were spreading lies about what was going on in the East. He wanted to make sure not only that the crusade succeeded, but also that his vision of the crusade prevailed. As often happened in the Middle Ages, he sought to control history by writing it. Probably realizing that his word alone would carry little weight, he recruited a knight named Pons of Balazun to help him with the project. And at some point during the march, certainly by the fall of 1098, like Fulcher of Chartres, they began writing a book, which is today simply called *The Book of Raymond of Aguilers*.[23]

It begins in the middle of things. Passing over the early stages of the march, where the Provençals skirted across northern Italy, Raymond opened his story with the army already in Dalmatia, or "Sclavonia," as he preferred to call it, a semiautonomous kingdom under the protection of the Byzantine Empire. Its land was, in Raymond's description, mountainous and devoid of all sustenance, and its natives were a barbarous and ignorant people. When the Slavs' harassment of the Provençals grew unbearable, Count Raymond ordered six of them captured and then had their eyes gouged out and their hands and feet cut off. Upon his command, they were left alive in public view, a warning of the consequences to be faced by those who would bedevil Christians. It was also a perfect example of the kind of rough justice characteristic of Christian lords in eleventh-century Europe—composed of small-scale acts of brutality intended to intimidate and subdue a potentially rebellious population. For Raymond the writer, the mutilations in Dalmatia were among Count Raymond's outstanding deeds, a shrewd tactic that made the final forty days in that wilderness pass in relative peace.[24]

By February 1, 1096, the Provençals entered into Byzantine territory at last, walking to the port city of Durazzo, where previously the northern Franks and southern Italians had arrived by sea. As soon as Raymond's men reached the city, Alexius began applying to them the same treatment he had given to the earlier armies. His envoys presented Raymond with letters of safe conduct but at the same time established armies to shadow them and—perhaps deliberately, perhaps owing to misunderstanding— engage them in small skirmishes. These encounters could be deadly. Early on Greek soldiers killed a knight named Pons Rainaud. Later in February Bishop Adhémar of le Puy himself was attacked. As the army entered "the valley of Pelagonia," Adhémar rode off alone on a mule, apparently looking for a congenial place to set camp. A group of Pecheneg soldiers or brigands (in the frontier regions of Macedonia, the distinction would have been a fine one) suddenly fell upon him, hit him sharply on the head, and knocked him off his mule. As much as the dazed Adhémar could later reconstruct things, most of the Pechenegs were ready to kill him, but one of them sensed that the bishop had access to more money than he was carrying. This brigand tried to stop his companions from killing Adhémar so that he might interrogate him, and in the process they all made enough noise to alert the rest of the army that the bishop was in danger. A group of Provençal soldiers quickly rode to his rescue.

This turn of events caused Count Raymond to take a more aggressive strategy against the emperor. Near a castle called Bucinat, he set an ambush for Pecheneg soldiers and routed them all. About a month later, around April 12, 1097, when the town of Roussa refused him supplies, he ordered an attack. His soldiers quickly broke down the walls, accepted the citizens' surrender, and then stole much of their wealth. As the crusaders marched away, they shouted Count Raymond's war cry: "Toulouse! Toulouse!" To all appearances, the Provençals were at war with the Greeks. Again, the crusade was turning into a war of Christians against Christians.

But at about this time more messengers from Constantinople arrived, along with envoys that Raymond himself had dispatched, carrying with them further promises of peace from Alexius. This time they carried news, too. The emperor was hosting at his palace Bohemond, Godfrey of Bouillon, and Robert of Flanders, among other princes. He was no longer keeping them prisoner; he was discussing with them whether to join the Latin army on the road to Jerusalem.

Important decisions were thus being made about the organization and financing of the crusade army. Raymond's presence was required if he did not wish losing, despite his wealth and his great number of followers, control of the crusade. Setting aside his grievances, he departed with a small escort, leaving the rest of his army to complete the journey to Constantinople without him. Up until this point, chaplain and writer Raymond observed, his tale had been pleasant to tell. But from the moment that Raymond left for Constantinople, the story became suffused with grief and anguish. The thought of Alexius made the chaplain regret ever having taken up his pen.[25]

IN THIS WAY THE CRUSADERS, little by little, reached Constantinople or else turned back, unable to maintain discipline and order while crossing Hungarian and Greek lands. The early armies—which historians have previously called "the popular crusade," "the people's crusade," or even "the peasants' crusade"—clearly had a less aristocratic character than did the later, "princely" armies, but as recent scholarship has demonstrated, a significant number of nobles did join their movement. What ultimately seems to have distinguished these early groups from the later ones is the character of their leaders. Among the commanders of the early armies were two priests, one lapsed monk, and a fanatical layman. They believed themselves divinely appointed, and one of them even had a letter from heaven to prove it. Many of their followers were also visionaries, men and women who claimed that God had branded them with the sign of the cross or else that He had inspired an animal to lead the way to the Holy Land. If we presume that these characteristics were more widely shared among their followers (and it seems a safe presumption), then we can observe that these armies were also more overtly apocalyptic than were the princes'. Their first acts were to massacre Jews because the pilgrims wanted to avenge Christ's death and to bring about the prophetic conditions necessary to enable the advent of the Last Days. Little surprise, then, that the leaders of these impatient armies had difficulty maintaining control over such large, disparate, and visionary gatherings during the one-thousand-mile march to Constantinople.

The princely armies were more successful because of better planning and finance and superior military discipline. Were these armies also less apocalyptic in outlook? Perhaps, but the leaders of the second wave of crusaders also struck a better balance between the ideals of holy war and the simple realities of war. In open battle it would be useful for soldiers to believe that they were carrying out God's will, bringing to fruition His designs for world history, but in the negotiating of truces and supply lines in unfriendly territories, such an overweening sense of divine mission could prove ruinous. Emicho of Flonheim's warriors discovered just that when they decided that Hungarians were false Christians and, like the Jews, deserved to be destroyed.[26]

The more explicitly apocalyptic vision of the crusade did not stay confined to the first wave of pilgrims. Peter the Hermit and a relatively small number of his followers, as we shall see, stuck with the expedition, and Peter continued to preach—not just to his original followers, but also to the rest of the crusading host. Emicho's chief lieutenants joined Hugh's armies and were waiting to greet Godfrey at Constantinople. Did Emicho's failures in Hungary dampen their own apocalyptic expectations? Probably not. They had seen the Danube run red with blood, and they had walked through fields littered with their friends' dismembered bodies. And all of the armies, as they closed in on the glittering city of Constantinople, had spent months trudging through unfamiliar landscapes, facing exotic and unfamiliar enemies, and living through what must have been previously unimaginable levels of privation and physical exertion. Now, with their homes far behind them and everything that had seemed familiar suddenly lost, the crusaders would have had every reason to believe that they were on a mission whose importance transcended the ways of men. All of them might justly believe that they were stepping into the Apocalypse.

MEANWHILE, almost forgotten because so long delayed, the armies of Robert of Normandy and Stephen of Blois finally began boarding ships in Italy on Easter Day to cross the Adriatic for Durazzo, on April 5, 1097. Some of the foot soldiers, unable to afford the long winter camp and fearing future deprivation, had sold their bows and returned home—proving themselves vile before God and man, Fulcher of Chartres assured his readers. The others gathered in Brindisi, ready for the short trip into Byzantine waters, the winds and the seas at last, presumably, in their favor. "But," Fulcher exclaimed, "deep and hidden are the judgments of God!" One of the first ships to leave port, for no apparent reason, broke apart and sank. All four hundred pilgrims on board drowned. It seemed that God had cursed the campaign, and indeed still more pilgrims grew faint-hearted at the thought of crossing the sea and returned home in shame. But then "there was joyful cry of praise raised up to God." For as the bloated and bluing bodies washed up on the shore or were picked out of the waves, many of them, like Walter of Poissy months before, were found to have crosses branded on their flesh, just above their shoulders, exactly like the ones that they had worn on their garments. The message was obvious, as Fulcher read it. It was a sign of victory given in return for the pilgrims' faith. God had called them home. They had justly attained the rest of eternal life.[27]

It is unlikely that any of the witnesses drew from this incident another lesson—that even within this most princely and patient of armies, lurking just below the surface, just below the fabric of their cloaks, the spirit of Peter the Hermit and the apocalyptic crusade was thriving.

5

Deals with Devils:
The Crusaders at Constantinople
(*August 1096–April 1097*)

Alexius Comnenus, the emperor who ruled the Eastern Roman world, did not anticipate the crusade. To hear his biographer and daughter Anna Comnena tell it, he had no idea that the Franks (or "Kelts," as she generally labeled all Europeans) were marching toward Byzantium at all until rumor of Peter the Hermit's approach reached him in the summer of 1096. The emperor "dreaded their arrival, knowing as he did their uncontrollable passion, their erratic character and their irresolution, not to mention the other peculiar traits of the Kelt, with their inevitable consequences: their greed for money, for example, which always led them, it seemed, to break their own agreements without scruple for any chance reason."

Anna's framing of these events is disingenuous. Because of the endless troubles that the crusaders would later cause the Greeks, she wished to protect her father's reputation from any direct association with them. But as we have seen, Alexius had been soliciting help from European leaders throughout the 1090s, and his request to Urban II before the Council of Piacenza may have helped to inspire the pope's own decision to preach the crusade at Clermont.

But Anna's characterization is correct in at least one important respect. Alexius had not wanted a religious war. He did not view conflicts in the

Middle East in purely confessional terms. He had struck alliances with the Turks in the past, and no matter what happened with the crusade, he and his successors would have to live with the Turks in the future. Instead of driving the Saracens out of the Christian world, he wanted only to restore a balance of power between his kingdom and the Turks. To do so, he was probably hoping only for a more substantial version of the military aid he had gotten five years earlier when Robert of Flanders had sent five hundred mercenaries to fight on his behalf. He certainly did not expect as many as 200,000 soldiers, preachers, and pilgrims—men, women, and children—to march toward Constantinople, intent on striking a blow for God by liberating Jerusalem and laying low "Persian perfidy."[1]

Nonetheless, the character of the army, especially its religious fanaticism, could not have come as a complete shock. After all, Alexius himself had framed his request for military help in religious terms—to save Eastern Christians from the unbelieving Turks—and he had requested that the pope act as one of his key military spokesmen. The decision to mix religion and war had thus been Alexius's own. Alexius had also known in advance the significance that relics and pilgrimage held in the hearts of Western Christians, and he must have suspected that a call to save the holy places of the East would kindle intense passions within the hearts of the great numbers of believers. If Alexius did not mention the Holy Sepulcher in his original plea, it was only because he didn't think to do so. If the Franks arrived at Constantinople with Jerusalem as their ultimate goal, Alexius could use them to inflict a few serious defeats against his Turkish adversaries and then send the crusaders on their way, no doubt to perish in the deserts between Antioch and Jerusalem. From a practical perspective, a great religious army might have been volatile and unpredictable, but it was not necessarily a bad thing. If five hundred seasoned mercenaries had proved helpful against the Turks in 1091, then a few thousand well-armed fanatics would be more useful still. Alexius himself did not want to fight a religious war, but he could have hoped to manipulate religious warriors to serve his own ends. A gathering of 100,000 zealots, however, was surely too much of a dangerous thing.

Anna Comnena's account does in general support this conclusion. In her eyes, "the Kelts" were easily manipulable. As a people, they were good at action but not so capable when it came to forethought or, for that matter, to any kind of thought at all. She saw them as "an exceptionally hotheaded race, and passionate." Once they had decided to invade a country, "neither reason nor force" could restrain them. In open warfare they were irresistible, almost unconquerable, but they were singularly inept at military strategy, for "if their foes chance to lay ambushes with soldier-like skill and if they meet them in a systematic manner, all their boldness vanishes." The Kelts' holy men were as belligerent as their warriors. Anna recalled one priest armed with a bow who nearly shot down a Greek naval commander called Marianus. When the priest ran out of arrows, he threw rocks at the Greeks, and when he ran out of rocks, he hurled bread cakes as if they were Eucharistic weapons. Christian though the Kelts might have been, they were also, in Anna's eyes, barbarians—not very bright and, again, easy to deceive and to control.

The Franks were also, as Anna Comnena styled them, a plague of locusts. Indeed, these insects preceded the arrival of each of the Frankish contingents, and "everyone, having observed the phenomenon several times, came to recognize locusts as the forerunners of Frankish battalions." These locusts avoided wheat but destroyed vines—a sign that the Kelts would not interfere in the affairs of Christians but would inflict severe injury on the Saracens, who were slaves to the pleasures of drunkenness.[2] [Plate 3]

Or at least that was Alexius's hope: to whip up a Frankish apocalypse and to inflict it on the Turks while ensuring that his own people suffered no ill consequences. When first Walter of Sansavoir and then Peter the Hermit arrived at Constantinople, Alexius must have realized that the last part of his plan would be more difficult than expected.

The Hermit and His Army

Peter arrived at Constantinople in August 1096, even as the first of the princely armies, led by Hugh the Great and Godfrey, respectively, were still preparing to depart from Europe. The day after his followers set camp, Peter was ushered into the emperor's residence in the Blachernae palace, where Alexius received him in full imperial majesty. The hermit apparently showed no disquiet in the face of Byzantine ceremony. Instead, he stood confidently before the emperor and explained his purpose and the ordeals that he and his followers had suffered. When Alexius asked what Peter wished to receive from him, the hermit replied, simply, food and money—requests to which Alexius, perhaps surprisingly, assented. He reportedly told Peter, along with Walter of Sansavoir, to remain outside Constantinople and to wait for the rest of the armies to arrive. By itself this group of pilgrims was too poorly trained to be of much use to Alexius's professional army, but in the context of a larger contingent of Latin zealots, they might prove their worth against the Saracens. Neither side probably expected that more than four months would pass before another group of Franks would reach Constantinople.[3]

But Peter and Walter's followers were incapable of waiting out the week, let alone the rest of the year. They grew bored in the suburbs and perhaps angry as well, since they were not allowed to enter Constantinople to pray in its rich churches and before its splendid relic collections. The latter included remains of several apostles and martyrs, the head of John the Baptist (on which some of the hair and beard still grew), and all of the relics of the Passion that the Empress Helena had collected during her pilgrimage to Jerusalem in 327. After all, the opportunity to pray before Christ's relics had attracted them to Jerusalem in the first place. Impatience and frustration soon turned to rage. "And so the Christians behaved abominably. They sacked and burned palaces of the city and stole the lead from church roofs so that they could sell it back to the Greeks." The emperor lost his patience in turn and ordered Peter and Walter and their followers to leave the suburbs and cross the straits of St. George into Asia Minor.[4]

At this point the two surviving armies numbered around 20,000 people, and perhaps more, including a few hundred knights, a few thousand foot soldiers, and an unknown number of unarmed women, children, clerics, and simple pilgrims. In a little over ten weeks, after they had left the relative safety of Constantinople, they would almost all be dead or enslaved.

The story of the destruction of Peter the Hermit's armies is well known, though much of what is known was no doubt invented by medieval historians who, lacking eyewitness testimony, were free to make embellishments. These historians also needed to resolve what ought to have been a difficult historical problem: Why did God allow an army of Christians, largely untainted by the worst excesses of Emicho's armies, to fail so miserably? It was largely a question, these writers concluded, of discipline. "They were a people without a king, without a duke, gathered from various locations, living without discipline, rapaciously attacking other people's property."[5]

True to this description, once these armies had reached Anatolia, they kept good order for barely a month. Peter and Walter first settled their troops in the port cities Civitot and Nicomedia, where, as promised, merchant ships regularly arrived laden with goods for sale at fair prices. But after a month, the army's resources were wearing thin, and Greek merchants were not interested in functioning as charitable institutions. Some of the Franks started looking inland for plunder, toward the city of Nicea, to fill out their supplies. Alexius had warned them not to do so—to stay close to the shoreline and to avoid engaging the Turks at all cost. "If you do otherwise," he had said, "the savage gentiles will fall on you and crush your ineffectual legions."

Peter the Hermit sensed the growing restlessness among his followers and around October 1 returned to Constantinople. He may have been attempting to negotiate an increased level of supplies at lower prices or perhaps just to ask for charity. But while he was gone, a few of the knights began striking off on their own, leading raids into the East and plundering the flocks of Greek Christians living under Turkish rule. The success of these first sorties inspired other warriors to more ambitious adventures, particularly the Germans and Italians, who were, anyway, finding the French pilgrims unbearable. Rather than wait for Peter to return or to share dwindling resources, they abandoned Civitot altogether and headed inland, against the emperor's advice, toward Nicea.[6]

Nicea was a capital of the Sultanate of Rûm, its name literally meaning "Rome" because the lands had been taken from the Roman Empire. It was ruled in 1096 by a still-seminomadic Seljuk leader called Kilij-Arslan. The Italians and Germans who entered Kilij-Arslan's territory in October 1096 found it largely unguarded. They marched for four days, coming within sight of Nicea itself, where, according to Anna Comnena, they engaged in behaviors that by both eleventh-century and modern standards were akin to war crimes: "They cut in pieces some of the babies, impaled others on wooden spits and roasted them over a fire; old people were subjected to every kind of torture."

The Niceans charged outside the city and attacked the German and Italian pilgrims but were quickly forced back behind its walls. The army next attacked a nearby castle called Xerigordos, which they quickly captured, sparing the Greek Christians but killing or expelling the entire Turkish garrison. Xerigordos was full of grain, meat, and wine, and flushed with victory, the pilgrims discussed how they might use the castle as a base to attack Nicea and, eventually, to drive the Turks out of Anatolia.[7]

But the ease of these raids had given the Italians and Germans a false sense of confidence. By entering into a major military engagement so close to Nicea, they had drawn too much attention to themselves. Kilij-Arslan quickly organized a counterattack. He marched on Xerigordos three days after the Germans and Italians had taken it. Overcoming an initial attempt by the Italians to set an ambush, he unleashed a fierce assault on the fortress. When the defenders did not immediately surrender, he established a formal siege around it (he also may have convinced one of the German leaders that the only way to survive was to surrender and betray the city—details are murky). According to one source, the siege lasted for eight days, with the defenders quickly running out of water. As the week dragged on, they drank blood from horses and pack animals, dipped cloths into sewers and squeezed out the liquid into their mouths, or else tried pathetically to suck moisture from damp earth until—with or without the collaboration of pilgrims' leaders—Kilij-Arslan's men set fire to Xerigordos's gates. The heat inside the castle became unbearable. Some of defenders, already dying of thirst, rushed out of the gates to surrender. Others hoped to escape by leaping through the flames, only to be burned alive. The survivors were used for target practice or, if pretty and young, were enslaved. "These men were the first ones happily to accept a martyr's fate," an anonymous historian, who likely saw the aftermath of the siege of Xerigordos, concluded.[8]

A few of the Germans, however, must have escaped the fires of battle, because they returned to Peter's camp with news of the army's destruction. The Franks—true to Comnena's caricature—wished for immediate revenge. The only leader present, Walter of Sansavoir, counseled patience, advising his fellow crusaders to wait until Peter had returned. Unfortunately, Peter's negotiations were taking longer than expected. And after a week, the pilgrims heard rumor that a Turkish scouting party had just captured and decapitated several more pilgrims.

The news set off a bitter debate as to whether to retaliate at once or to continue waiting for Peter. The knights, including Walter, by and large urged caution. The foot soldiers—or at least their leader, Godfrey Burel, who had led the attack on Zemun in Hungary—preferred immediate action. Pride entered into the equation, too, or so the story goes, with Godfrey Burel insulting the cautious, saying that "these distinguished knights were cowards and very little good in war." Unable to bear this mockery, the knights caved to Godfrey's demands, ordering their followers to set out in six divisions, each marching under a different banner, to attack Nicea. Only women, the unarmed, and the sick were left behind in the city.[9]

It seems a foolhardy maneuver, but the pilgrims may have had little choice. If Kilij-Arslan had sent out a scouting party, then he was likely preparing an attack. Time and again on crusade, the Franks would elect to take the battle to the Turks rather than become trapped in a prolonged siege. The danger was especially grave at Civitot, which apparently lacked adequate defenses to protect against a large army. And no help seemed to be forthcoming from Constantinople. The battle, fought on October 21, 1096, was therefore the first time the Franks attempted to take the fight directly to the enemy, rather than to hold a defensive position. It was not a hasty or disorganized operation, as modern historians have tended to paint it. But whatever their strategy, the Franks never had a chance to test it. They had scarcely marched three miles from Civitot when they ran directly into Kilij-Arslan's army, ordered and ready to attack. Kilij-Arslan had expected to ambush the Franks in their camps, but he was equally prepared for an open field engagement.

It was the first time that the Franks had seen the Turkish military in action, and it was unlike anything they had previously encountered. The Turks fought almost exclusively on horseback and with bow and arrow. Rather than arrange themselves in tight formations, advancing to attack at close quarters, they dispersed, scattering about as if they were hunters chasing prey, striking whenever opportunity arose and then retreating just as quickly, howling all the while in the most terrifying voices. Using their speed and maneuverability to their advantage, the Turks penetrated the crusaders' lines and began to encircle at least two of the six divisions. The fighting had barely begun before another line of Turkish cavalry had gotten behind the Frankish army and cut off its retreat. In a panic, some of the crusaders charged toward Nicea and into the heart of the Turkish forces. The Turks probably seemed to retreat in the face of this sudden onslaught, and the crusaders pressed what seemed to be their advantage. But they were in for a nasty surprise. Turkish soldiers were as skilled at firing arrows from behind while retreating as they were while attacking.

A few of the Christians managed to engage some of their enemies at close quarters and with great results. Albert of Aachen said that they cut down approximately two hundred Turks, though the number is necessarily a guess. At any rate, the Franks' success was short-lived. The Turks started aiming arrows at the crusaders' horses, turning the well-armed knights into common foot soldiers. A general massacre began, during which, among others, Walter of Sansavoir died. The sharp-tongued Godfrey Burel escaped, however, along with a few hundred other soldiers, heading back to Civitot.[10]

And the Turks were right behind them. They rode into Civitot and quickly dispatched the ill, the infirm, and the ugly. They took back to Anatolia attractive girls, nuns, and beardless boys. A few hundred of the pilgrims fled into an abandoned tower, but the rest were killed. Anna Comnena's description of the dead no doubt exaggerated their numbers, but it nonetheless provides a good sense of how the slaughter must have looked to survivors: "When they gathered the remains of the fallen, lying on every side, they heaped up, I will not say a mighty ridge or hill or peak, but a mountain of considerable height and depth and width, so huge was the mass of bones." A few years later, with the Turks pushed back into Anatolia and Civitot returned safely to Byzantine control, Frankish laborers working for Alexius would build walls around Civitot, using bones from crusader bodies to patch gaps between the rocks. "In this way the city became their tomb."

As for the survivors, the tower where they had enclosed themselves didn't have a gate to hold off the enemy, but they managed to create a makeshift barrier out of shields and rocks that at least would hold through the night. Rather than try to breach the barricade, the Turks fired arrows over the walls, intending to kill anyone unlucky enough to stand at the end of the arrows' trajectories. In the middle of the night, when the attacks slowed, a Greek man slipped out of the fortress and crossed the Bosphorus to Constantinople to plead one last time for Byzantine help.[11]

On this man's arrival, Peter the Hermit learned for the first time of the catastrophe that had befallen his men, and he went immediately to Alexius to beg him to do something. Anna Comnena wrote that news of the disaster distressed her father greatly. Another Western writer claimed that Alexius rejoiced to hear that the Franks had all perished. Whatever his emotions, he dispatched one of his generals, Constantine Euphorbenus Catacalon, at the head of an army of Turcopoles (ethnic Turks, believed by Christian writers to be the offspring of Christian mothers and Turkish fathers), to drive away Kilij-Arslan and to ferry the few remaining pilgrims back to the fields outside Constantinople.

Kilij-Arslan's men got word of the emperor's imminent arrival and withdrew. Perhaps they returned to Nicea. More likely they marched on to Nicomedia, where (as Peter the Hermit seemed to have forgotten) another army of Franks had encamped awaiting reinforcements before continuing to Jerusalem. These pilgrims were not expecting an attack. The Turks decapitated everyone they found and left bodies and heads unburied.[12]

The Emperor's New Son

Such was the situation that Godfrey of Bouillon discovered upon arriving at Constantinople. Hugh the Great, Robert of Flanders, and others had been held in honorable captivity or imprisoned, depending on one's perspective. All across Hungary Godfrey would have seen evidence of Catholics slaughtered by other Catholics. One of his fellow leaders on the crusade, Bohemond of Taranto, was aiming to turn the war for Jerusalem into an attack on Byzantium. The Greek emperor was harassing Godfrey's troops, and as he and his followers neared Constantinople, survivors from the armies of Peter the Hermit and Walter Sansavoir were no doubt pathetically recounting for him how, just two months earlier, the Turks of Nicea had slaughtered pilgrims by the thousands, as the emperor had sat idly by.

And now the same Alexius who so callously allowed the crusaders to be massacred was demanding that Godfrey leave his armies outside the city walls and enter his palace to discuss terms. It was December 23, 1096, just in time for the Christmas court—from Alexius's perspective, a fine moment to impress a gathering of German yokels with the full pageantry and spectacle of Greek imperial government.

Godfrey declined. He had apparently received warnings from certain unnamed Frenchmen (perhaps members of Hugh's entourage or an early legation sent from Bohemond) that he was not to trust Alexius, no matter what the emperor promised and regardless of the honeyed words he used. Alexius, for his part, took Godfrey's refusal as a snub and closed the markets to his armies. The Lotharingians responded predictably, plundering the land and stealing sustenance from the locals. Alexius in turn ordered his archers on the city walls to open fire on the pilgrims—but to shoot to frighten, not to kill, "without taking aim and mostly off target." But neither side had the stomach for this fight, and they quickly struck a new truce. Alexius agreed to open his markets temporarily for the Lotharingians, and Godfrey told his men not to destroy any more buildings or to kill anyone. It was, after all, Christmas.[13]

Alexius obviously was still trying to come up with a strategy for dealing with Godfrey and with the Latins more generally. It had been relatively easy to move Peter's armies along. They were, in Anna Comnena's words, "the simpler folk," who "were in very truth led on by a desire to worship at our Lord's tomb and visit the holy places." The strategy admittedly had ended in disaster for these credulous pilgrims, but things might not have gone so badly if they had not left so far in advance of Godfrey, or if the armies of Folkmar, Gottschalk, and Emicho had successfully passed through Hungary and had been able to reinforce them against the Turks. Hugh's and Robert of Flanders's armies, by contrast, had been small enough that Alexius bullied them around with ease. Thus, their time at Constantinople left barely a trace on the historical record. But Godfrey presented new problems. "A rich man, extremely proud of his noble birth, his own courage and the glory of his family," he was able to maintain a distance between his identity as a warrior of God and his identity as a more earthbound military leader. And his army was big enough to push back against Alexius—not big enough to take the city of Constantinople, but with Bohemond's army not far behind, big enough to seem a real danger to the Greeks. Alexius therefore dispatched groups of soldiers with instructions to break up any attempts at communication between Godfrey and Bohemond as they advanced toward his capital. In short, before the Franks could get their act together and turn their apocalyptic fury against a schismatic empire, Alexius needed to find a new way to exploit and appease the crusade.[14]

What he needed to do, fundamentally, was reassert his original vision of this venture: the recruitment of a few thousand religiously motivated Latin soldiers as allies against the Seljuk Turks. Success depended on Alexius's ability to bring Godfrey into his presence and, through a combination of charm and cajolery, to convince him that their interests were aligned. But Godfrey, having been warned against trusting Alexius, continued to resist his summonses. He did agree, on December 29, to move his troops to a less threatening position farther from the city and along the shores of the Bosphorus, where they might stay in abandoned buildings (perhaps storehouses, though Albert of Aachen understood them to be "palaces") rather than tents. But Godfrey still refused to meet with the emperor. Instead, he sent envoys to explain his reluctance: "The many evil things that have reached my ears about you, and which may have been invented out of jealousy or fear, frighten me." Alexius tried to assure Godfrey that whatever accusations he had heard were untrue, and he sent the envoys back laden with promises of all the benefits that would accrue from his friendship. But Godfrey continued to mistrust his words.

After two weeks of this back and forth, Alexius became aggressive. He once again began limiting the Lotharingians' access to markets, and lest they seek supplies elsewhere, he dispatched ships filled with Turcopoles to fire arrows into the Franks' camps, keeping them away from shore and away from alternative food sources. Godfrey's men in turn took up arms and began marching back toward Constantinople, ready to attack or besiege the city.

A full-fledged battle then began. Greek archers atop the walls opened fire on the pilgrims. Undeterred, Godfrey's brother Baldwin of Boulogne led five hundred soldiers to cross a bridge to attack the imperial residence at the Blachernae Palace and to attempt to set the city gate on fire. A division of Turcopoles exited the city and tried to drive the Franks off the bridge. They succeeded to a point, but Baldwin held his ground and continued the fight against the emperor's guards, starting "a grim, dour struggle on both sides." According to Anna, many of the Franks died, but few Greeks were injured. According to Albert, "On all sides the battle was fought violently; many fell on both sides; many of the Franks' horses died of arrow wounds." The Lotharingians ultimately surrendered their ground, or else the Turcopoles fled back into the city. More likely, night fell and the battle was called due to darkness. And for the next six days, Godfrey's men ruthlessly plundered the lands around Constantinople "so that at least the emperor's pride and his men's might be brought low."[15]

Finally, Alexius relented, sending a legation to Godfrey offering hostages as guarantees of peace, provided Godfrey would at last meet with him. In doing so, Alexius was either very lucky or else very well informed. It was on that very day (probably January 19, 1097) that agents from Bohemond, having eluded all of Alexius's traps, arrived at Godfrey's camp to propose an all-out war against Byzantium. After Godfrey learned that the emperor was going to send his own son John as hostage, and that the markets were already reopening, he rejected Bohemond's proposal. He "had not left his homeland and his kin for the sake of profit or the destruction of Christians, but had set out on the road to Jerusalem in the name of Christ." The next day, after receiving the imperial heir into his custody, Godfrey left with a small group of nobles to face the emperor. His brother Baldwin stayed behind, likely still mulling over Bohemond's proposition.[16]

Their meeting must have begun tensely. Alexius sat on his throne and did not rise for Godfrey. Rather, the emperor demanded that all Godfrey's entourage kneel before him and, in order of social prominence, kiss his hand. It may have been at this meeting that one of the crusaders attempted to sit before Alexius and was overheard later to mumble, "What a peasant! He sits alone while generals like these stand beside him!" Alexius, not understanding the words, called over an interpreter to explain what the man had been talking about. Rather than express impatience at the Latins and their primitive ways, he bore these indignities patiently.

He was, in fact, an impeccable host. He voiced wonder at the splendid appearance of the Latins, especially at their clothes, "lavishly fringed with both purple and gold, snow-white ermine, and gray and variegated marten fur, which the princes of Gaul use in particular." Godfrey had been warned to resist the emperor's flattery and promises, but he fell instantly under his spell. "I have heard about you," Alexius told him, "that you are a very powerful knight and prince in your land, and a very wise man and completely honest. Because of this I am taking you as my adopted son, and I am putting everything I possess in your power, so that my empire and land can be freed and saved through you from the present and future multitudes."[17]

As Greek courtiers stood in the shadows holding golden treasures destined for Godfrey, the duke delightedly accepted Alexius's offer. Perhaps he still doubted the emperor's promises, but he believed his treasure, and he grasped the imperial hands (which earlier he had been allowed only to kiss) and made himself a vassal of the Greek empire.

The exact terms of his oath remain unclear. He certainly promised (as Anna Comnena stressed and as events later in the crusade made clear) that he would return to Alexius whatever lands he had conquered that had recently belonged to the emperor. This included all of Anatolia as far as Antioch and perhaps the lands beyond. It certainly implied service obligations to Alexius on the part of the crusaders, though from their perspective it also required Alexius to protect and provision Godfrey's armies, as a good lord ought to do. Such was the Franks' custom, and their pledge was—again, according to Anna—"the customary Latin oath."[18]

The questions about vassalage and service obligations, however, might cause us to overlook the more interesting half of the story: namely, that Alexius made Godfrey his son, "as is the custom of that land." Whatever the emperor may have intended to accomplish by the ritual, according to Godfrey's interpretation, everything Alexius possessed was now "in his power, so that it could be freed and saved from the Turks and from other enemies." Albert surely exaggerated the importance of the ceremony, but some language of adoption probably did figure in to Alexius's new plan for mollifying the crusaders. When Stephen of Blois finally reached Constantinople in May and had his audience with Alexius, he would write excitedly to his wife, Adela, "Truly, my sweet, he often instructed me and instructs just as we might do for one of our sons!" No doubt cultural miscommuni-cations on both sides were thick in the air, but Godfrey left the palace with a belly full of fine food, his servants weighed down with gold, and a belief that he and the emperor were comrades in arms—perhaps even father and son. There is no evidence that before Godfrey met Alexius, he had dreamed of acquiring an empire for himself, as had the apocalyptically minded Emicho of Flonheim, but after dining within the Blachernae Palace, he very well may have begun to think on such prospects.[19]

Godfrey also began to see himself as Alexius's accomplice. He returned to camp and ordered his men to keep the peace. When Alexius asked Godfrey to lead them across the Bosphorus in late February, as Bohemond's armies neared, he did so without complaint, presumably taking the followers of Hugh the Great, Robert of Flanders, and Peter the Hermit with him. Alexius, for his part, supplied Godfrey's men with money and markets. The Franks made occasional accusations of price gouging against the Greeks, but Godfrey and Alexius were always able to reach an understanding and avoid a repetition of the grim and violent scenes of the previous January.

Yet not everyone was as impressed at Alexius's generosity as Godfrey. Some of the Lotharingians felt that the emperor was continuing to play them for fools. "Amazing to say! All of the emperor's gifts that the duke distributed to his soldiers went straight back to the royal treasury in exchange for food. And not just the emperor's money, but also the money that the army had brought together there from all over the world." From Alexius's perspective, the crusaders were a burden. They were primitive, they were violent, and they were fanatical, but with the right stage management and with quiet op-portunism, he might even turn a slight profit off of their service.[20]

Alexius and Bohemond: A Meeting of the Minds

The next crusading leader to reach Constantinople was Bohemond, who arrived with a few companions on April 20, 1097. The main part of his army had stayed behind at Roussa (the Byzantine city Raymond had at-tacked for refusing him supplies) under the command of Bohemond's nephew Tancred. In theory, Bohemond ought to have been the most dif-ficult crusade leader for Alexius to handle. Bohemond's father, Robert

Guiscard, had once set his eyes on toppling Alexius, and Bohemond himself, as we have already seen, had been testing the waters to see if Godfrey, and perhaps others, were willing to lay siege to the Byzantine capital before turning their attention to Jerusalem.

From Anna Comnena's perspective, among all the crusade leaders Bohemond's motives were the most suspect. Indeed, she found his obvious cynicism almost refreshing. "Apparently he left to worship at the Holy Sepulcher, but in reality to win power for himself—or rather, if possible, to seize the Roman Empire itself, as his father had suggested." His cunning and ambition were familiar to a Greek audience, but this made him no less terrifying: "The sight of him inspired admiration, the mention of his name terror. . . . There was a certain charm about him, but it was somewhat dimmed by the alarm his person as a whole inspired; there was a hard, savage quality in his whole aspect, due, I suppose, to his great stature and his eyes; even his laugh sounded like a threat to others." Even so, in comparison to earlier Western leaders, Alexius found Bohemond almost amiable. Perhaps this was because they spoke the same language: Bohemond knew Greek and was used to the customs, manners, and occasional acts of treachery characteristic of the East.[21]

Despite their many battles fifteen years earlier, Bohemond and Alexius were thus well suited to work together. Diplomacy, however, required them to perform certain rituals to overcome their mutual suspicions and establish something like understanding. At a ceremonial dinner, Alexius offered Bohemond two plates of food: one prepared in the Byzantine style and one left uncooked so that Bohemond's own chef could serve it as he wished. It was really an opportunity for the giant to show whether he trusted Alexius since the cooked plate could have been poisoned. Bohemond, cautious with his own life, turned the prepared dish over to his household, "for it was his habit to treat servants with utter indifference." Afterward (in a scene that is likely more emblematical than historical) Alexius had one of his servants take Bohemond into a room filled "with all kinds of wealth: clothes, gold and silver, coins, objects of lesser value filled the place so completely that it was impossible for anyone to walk in it." Bohemond mused that with such money he could long ago have conquered many countries, and the servant responded that he could indeed have it all as a gift of the emperor. Bohemond hesitated for a time, probably trying to decide whether such a gift would put him too much in Alexius's debt—typical Latin moodiness, according to Anna. In the end his practical instincts won out. He accepted the loot and got down to the serious business of negotiating with the emperor.[22]

What exactly Bohemond requested or what Alexius offered is unclear. Several near contemporary accounts survive, but none by anyone involved in the actual meetings. The two things they all seem to agree on is that the negotiations were secretive and that the two men struck some sort of deal about the future government of Anatolia. According to Anna Comnena, Bohemond asked that Alexius name him "Domestic of the East," or chief military commander for the empire's eastern lands. Alexius refused, apparently suspecting Bohemond's intentions, but nonetheless dangled hopes before him: "The time for that is not yet ripe, but with your energy and loyalty it will not be long before you have even that honor." An anonymous Norman historian differed, claiming that Alexius made a fairly specific proposal. In return for loyal service, Alexius would give him control of lands variously described as "in Romania" or "around Antioch" and fifteen days' journey in length and eight days' journey in width. The gist of the two stories is similar. Alexius offered Bohemond money and land and probably agreed to make him an officer in the Byzantine Empire, and Bohemond decided, for the foreseeable future, to be the most loyal servant possible to Alexius. It is doubtful that either man trusted the other. Even after the agreement, Bohemond probably still would have taken a plate of raw meat rather than cooked food had Alexius given him the same choice. But each man, for a time, was willing to pretend that all was well between them.[23]

Not everyone was happy at this unexpected détente. A member of Bohemond's army complained, "Maybe we are always to be deceived by our leaders from this point forward. For what did they do at the end? They will say that necessity compelled them to humiliate themselves in obedience to that wicked emperor, whether they wanted to or not."

Bohemond's nephew Tancred would likely have agreed with this assessment. Tancred arrived at Constantinople with the rest of the Italian-Norman army less than a week after Bohemond had sealed his pact with Alexius, but rather than risk having to take the oath, he marched straight past the imperial capital and immediately crossed the Bosphorus. According to his biographer, Tancred felt sad for Bohemond and fearful for himself. "What a crime! Where is faith? Where is prudence? Oh, the hearts of men! The duplicity of the one who would shamelessly harm the other! The foolishness of the other, who recklessly trusts the one!" On April 26 his men joined with those of Godfrey, Hugh, and Robert of Flanders, and together they marched toward Nicea, leaving the temptations of Constantinople behind.[24]

At about the same time, or a little before, Count Raymond of Saint-Gilles finally arrived at Constantinople, like Bohemond having parted from his army with only a few knights to accompany him. He was shocked to learn that all the other leaders had taken oaths of homage to Alexius and to find Bohemond acting as a sort of go-between for the emperor and the crusaders. Right away Alexius began demanding, presumably through Bohemond, that Raymond swear to become a loyal servant of the empire. But Raymond was having none of it. Imperial soldiers had been regularly harassing his army. Some of his men had died as a result. The bishop of le Puy had nearly been killed. Rather than take the oath, the count brought charges against the emperor, claiming that he was owed some sort of reparation for the treatment of his men (particularly because he had heard rumors that Greek troops at Roussa had again attacked his army soon after he left for Constantinople). Alexius, of course, denied the accusations, but he did offer to participate in some sort of trial. As part of the proceedings, Bohemond volunteered himself as hostage and guarantee of the emperor's innocence. An inquiry was held—unfortunately we know nothing of the procedure—and Raymond was unable to prove his case. By whatever law they were following, the count had to release his hostage, Bohemond, back to the emperor.

But Raymond was still not satisfied. Isolated in the palace, he continued to contemplate revenge against Alexius. The consensus of the other princes, however, was that "it would be stupid to attack Christians, when Turks threatened." Bohemond ratcheted up the pressure further by promising that he would stand as the emperor's ally if the count attempted anything against him or even if he merely continued to delay performing obeisance and homage to him. Under such duress from a Roman emperor and a mercenary giant, Raymond offered a compromise. He would take a limited oath of fidelity to Alexius, specifying that he would respect the emperor's life and property but nothing else. It was an oath between equals of a sort characteristic of the landholding nobility in the south of France.

All of this wrangling over law and honor took at least a week. Even when it was finished, Alexius delayed Count Raymond in Constantinople for several more days, using all his charisma and wisdom to try to win the count more completely to his side. "He explained in more detail the adventures that the Latins must expect to meet with on their march; he also laid bare his own suspicions of their plans. In the course of many conversations on this subject he unreservedly opened the doors of his soul, as it were, to the count; he warned him always to be on his guard against Bohemond's perfidy, so that if attempts were made to break the treaty he might frustrate them and in every way thwart Bohemond's schemes." How successful this charm offensive proved is unclear. Count Raymond still seemed to view any kind of dependence on the emperor as being less than honorable. His intransigence on this point, according to his chaplain, Raymond of Aguilers, had robbed the Provençals of the chance to acquire a lot of Greek money.[25]

Meanwhile, Bohemond left Constantinople a little ahead of Raymond, probably on May 7, now a firm friend of Alexius and expecting to be richly rewarded for it. If challenged about his motives, which seemed at the time and in retrospect transparently venal, he could have readily defended himself. Warm relations with Alexius brought many advantages to the Franks. For one thing, the emperor had sworn to provide logistical support to the army as it advanced to Jerusalem. These contributions would take many forms. First, he would provision them with food and weapons during the eight-hundred-mile march to Jerusalem. Second, he would provide military advice to help the Franks avoid a repetition of the disaster at Civitot—indeed, he had already begun dispensing such wisdom to the leaders and even to some of the regular soldiers at Constantinople (even to the angry and socially awkward Frank who had called the emperor a peasant and tried to sit down in front of him). Finally, Alexius indicated that he himself would join the crusade, though not right away. In the meantime, to accompany them, he dispatched a trusted general named Tetigus, an experienced leader who had once lost his nose in combat and wore in its place a golden prosthesis. Tetigus's counsel was no doubt invaluable, but the Franks grew to hate him. In the memorable phrase of Raymond of Aguilers, his "nose and virtue were completely truncated."

Each side depended on and resented the other. The crusaders needed Alexius's advice, his supplies, and his money if they were to reach Jerusalem. Alexius needed the crusaders' weapons if he was to regain Anatolia. It was also a marriage of convenience, a point that surely troubled most of the soldiers. For the pilgrims who desired only to walk in the sands where Jesus had lived and then to pray before His tomb, the crusade demanded, above all else, true passion.[26]

6

The Nicene Deal

(May 1097–June 1097)

T he last Frankish armies, led by Robert of Normandy and Stephen of Blois, arrived in Constantinople on May 14, 1097, blissfully ignorant of all the problems that had gone before. As far as they could see, Alexius was an ideal host and the crusade was moving forward as Pope Urban II had hoped—as a joint Latin-Greek project for the reconquest of Anatolia and perhaps even the eventual liberation of Jerusalem.

Having learned from past mistakes, Alexius allowed regular, small groups of Franks to enter his capital. They found it delightful. "My, what a noble and splendid city!" Fulcher of Chartres, in Stephen of Blois's army, said of Constantinople. "How many palaces, how many monasteries it has, and how wondrous is their construction! How many marvelous sites are there in the squares and roadways!" So vivid did the statues of men, women, horses, oxen, camels, and lions appear to Western eyes, accustomed to much more abstract and schematic artistic styles, that it was easy to believe rumors about times past, when these figures used to come to life through enchantment. All manner of exotic goods from around the world passed through Constantinople's ports, and there were, Fulcher concluded, at least 20,000 eunuchs living in the city. These are the observations of a happy tourist rather than the words of a pilgrim exposed to the travails of delicate and fraught diplomacy.

As far as negotiations went, Alexius asked Stephen and Robert to take the same oath as Bohemond, Godfrey, Hugh, and Robert of Flanders had, and they readily agreed. Fulcher was aware of the bad impression these oaths might create—from what he had heard, somewhat inaccurately, Count Raymond of Saint-Gilles had refused point-blank to take any oath at all. Nevertheless, from his perspective a pact of friendship with the emperor was the only sensible course to take: "Without his counsel and aid, we could not complete our journey, nor could those who might follow us on this road. And the emperor gave them all as much spending money and as many silken garments as they could want, as well as the horses and funds necessary to complete the journey." Gifts exchanged, soldiers rested, oaths of loyalty and mutual support offered—Alexius had finally perfected the system for welcoming and conscripting Latin armies. After two weeks Stephen and Robert and their followers were ready to march to the first major engagement of the crusade, the siege of Nicea.[1]

Nicea—the town of Iznik in modern Turkey—is one of the most storied locations in Christian history. It was the site of the first ecumenical council convened by the Emperor Constantine in 325 AD, where some of the most fundamental tenets of Christianity were worked out. Until recently, Nicea had been part of the Byzantine Empire. Now the Seljuk Turk Kilij-Arslan ruled it as the sultan of Rûm. Given Nicea's history and importance, it was the perfect testing ground for the new vision of the crusade promoted by Alexius and embraced, apparently, by most of the Frankish leaders. A recently held Greek capital with great spiritual significance, it gave the pilgrim armies a chance to strike a blow for Christianity while at the same time reversing Byzantium's territorial losses to the Turks. If all went well, Nicea would enable the development of a more controlled form of holy war: Frankish power mixed with Greek strategy and seasoned with just the right touch of militant piety.

But a holy war is difficult to control. Even though the armies of Peter and Emicho had been decimated, their influence survived. Emicho's lieutenants had signed on with Hugh the Great. A few hundred survivors from Peter's armies and Peter himself were continuing to Nicea, probably having joined either Godfrey or Bohemond. Untold numbers of crusaders still had crosses branded on their bodies as a sign that God had chosen them specially to carry out His work. The Frankish princes and Alexius may have settled on particular strategies and approaches to the crusade, but these other visions remained. The right combination of provocations and events might yet unleash them. At Nicea the apocalyptic crusade was largely kept in check, but the release of its energies may have begun there—if not at the city itself then during the march to it.

On May 30 Stephen and Robert's armies stopped at Nicomedia and found a grisly spectacle—the remains of dozens of Peter the Hermit's followers, massacred by the Turks and apparently brutalized after death: "Oh, how many severed heads and how many bodies of the slain we discovered lying in the fields near the sea around Nicomedia! In that year the Turks had annihilated our people who were ignorant of the arrow and new to its use. Moved by pity at this sight we shed many tears." The warriors further promised, "with God's help, to avenge their blood." [Plate 4]

The armies ahead of them on the way to Nicea would have necessarily seen these bodies, too. Godfrey, Tancred, Hugh, and Robert of Flanders had actually camped in Nicomedia for three days. The road beyond proved too narrow for all of the pilgrims, who at this point would have numbered close to 40,000. Godfrey therefore dispatched 3,000 men to cut a path with axes and swords, as the rest of the army waited, decomposed Frankish bodies scattered around their camp. Perhaps, like Fulcher, they wept over the dead, marveled at the cruelty of the Saracens, and vowed revenge. It is remarkable that no one seems to have thought to bury them, though it may have been a deliberate decision, intended to inflame the passions of the rank and file. As the armies marched along the mountain path cut by Godfrey's men and marked by crosses made of iron and wood, they would have ample time to ponder the black hearts of their enemies, who were filling heaven with new Christian martyrs and who were crucifying Christ anew every day in Jerusalem.[2]

The Siege

Nicea presented a formidable challenge. The city's fortifications had stood since the fourth century AD and had been regularly updated and strengthened by Byzantine emperors. The walls were probably a little over thirty feet high, and the towers (of which there were more than one hundred) were about twice that height. A ditch filled with water ran around the city, making the walls still more difficult to attack. If anyone did succeed in getting past the ditches to the walls, the towers were so cleverly positioned that one could barely avoid missiles fired from their heights. Finally, the city was impossible for a land army to encircle. The circuit of the walls was a little over three miles long, and for about half of that distance Nicea directly abutted the Ascanian Lake. As a result, the Turks were able to bring in by ship, almost at will, food, weapons, supplies, fresh soldiers, and even merchant vessels laden with goods. Barring a naval blockade, no army could cut off the city's supplies and starve it into submission. And even with naval support, Nicea seemed to the Franks "hardly conquerable by human powers."[3]

The soldiers who began to arrive on May 6 did not feel cowed by these great defenses. Confronted with the city's formidable walls and towers, according to Albert of Aachen, "they were incapable of feeling any fear. Instead, driven by every sort of heroism and knightly instinct they rushed to the city and attacked. Some of them provoked the city's defenders to battle, charging in on foot; others used bow and arrow. But many of those, who recklessly and blindly tried a sudden attack on the walls, were struck down under the heavy bombardment of spears hurled down from above." Seeing the uselessness of such assaults, the princes began organizing for a longer siege.

The defenders of Nicea, meanwhile, had dispatched messengers to Kilij-Arslan, who was occupied with affairs on the eastern frontiers of his sultanate (presumably having believed that he had successfully dispatched with the Frankish threat by wiping out Peter the Hermit's army). Hearing that his capital was in trouble, he returned quickly, arriving in the mountains around the city by Friday, May 14 (in 1097 that happened to be Ascension Day, the day that Christ rose into heaven), the day the siege proper began. According to Albert, immediately upon arrival Kilij-Arslan sent two spies, posing as Christians, to study the Latin armies and then to make their way into the city to prepare the citizens for a coordinated attack two days later on May 16. On that day Kilij-Arslan would lead a charge from the mountains on the south of the city, with all of the cavalry he had recruited (500,000 men, Albert recounted, with pardonable exaggeration), and the garrison should dispatch all of its men from the city gates. With surprise and numbers, they should be able to destroy this latest Frankish army just as they had done earlier with Peter the Hermit's.[4]

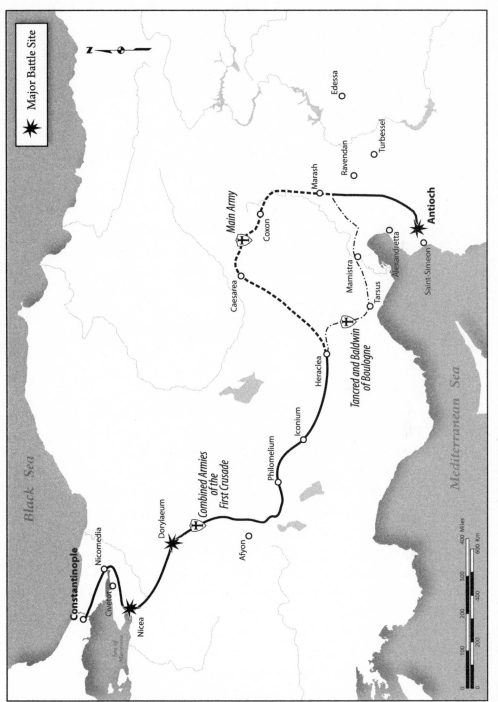

The roads taken from Constantinople to Antioch

Presumably, the two spies posed as Greek or Syrian Christians and tried to integrate themselves into the 2,000 or so men whom Alexius's advisor Tetigus had brought to the siege. The disguise didn't work. A few of the pilgrims stationed around the camp's perimeter spotted their approach, killed one of them, and captured the other. He was taken before Bohemond and Godfrey, and probably Tetigus, too, who barely had time to threaten the spy with torture before he was telling them all about Kilij-Arslan's plans. The spy also promised, Albert said, to embrace Christianity—a point that Albert found puzzling. Surely the Muslims would be as passionate about their religion as were the Franks.

It is likely that the spy's willingness to convert represented something other than fickleness on his part, something that Albert himself could not grasp. It was the story of Nicea writ small. The men whom Kilij-Arslan had sent out in advance likely spoke Greek and likely had, until recently, been subjects of Alexius Comnenus, just as Alexius himself had from time to time been allied with the Seljuk Turks. The Franks, now "in the land of Turks," saw the world with moral clarity—good and evil, Christian and Saracen. Not so for this spy. For him, as for most of the Niceans, it was a world of shifting alliances. The question was not whether Christianity or unbelief would prevail, but whether they would stay with the new Turkish regime or return to their former Byzantine administrators. Tetigus and Bohemond understood these distinctions. The other princes may have as well. It is unclear how well the rest of the army realized them. The Franks at Nicea, who imagined themselves "armed with the sign of the cross" or "offering their bodies to the fates, joyfully seeking the prizes of death," would have been displeased at the thought that their war was not about enacting God's plans on earth but rather about restoring balance to the complex network of Byzantine-Turkish alliances.[5]

Setting aside politics, the princes moved quickly to meet the danger presented by Kilij-Arslan's arrival. Immediately, they dispatched their own messengers back along the recently cleared pathway, decorated with crosses, to find Raymond of Saint-Gilles and his army and to urge them to hasten their march to the city. The messengers met up with the count, now traveling again with Bishop Adhémar of le Puy, who had been delayed at Thessalonica by illness for nearly four months. They were still about two days' march from the city. Nevertheless, Raymond and Adhémar responded with due haste. They ordered their men to march through the night, and they arrived at Nicea the next morning, May 16, 1097. They were still in the process of establishing their camps on the south side of the city when Kilij-Arslan rode down from the mountains and the battle began.

It seems to have been quick and decisive. Kilij-Arslan was expecting to face a much smaller army. Raymond's arrival, in fact, had probably doubled the size of the Frankish host. Kilij-Arslan had also been expecting to have a clear lane around the south side of the city. Instead, because of Raymond's camps, his army was caught up in a fairly confined space. The Provençals were doubtless exhausted from the overnight march and were still in the process of setting up tents, but they managed to hold off the initial attack and to keep the Turks from encircling them according to their custom. Adhémar urged the Provençals on, delivering the first of many battlefield orations designed to remind them of who they were and why they fought: "Oh race of people dedicated to God, you have given up all of your riches for God's love—your fields, your vineyards and your castles too! Now eternal life is at hand for you, indeed for anyone who might be crowned a martyr in battle! Go forth confidently against these enemies of the living God, and God will allow you today to achieve victory!" Godfrey's army, encamped nearby on the eastern side of the city and expecting just such an attack, joined the fight quickly enough for some of his men to hear the bishop's sermon. Within a short time, Kilij-Arslan's cavalry was put to flight. Even Anna Comnena acknowledged that it was "a glorious victory" for the Kelts.[6]

More remarkable than the battle was its aftermath. Albert of Aachen reported that, in celebration, "the Christians cut off the heads of the wounded and the dead and carried them back to their tents tied to the girths of the saddles and returned joyfully to their companions who had stayed behind in the camps around the city, to keep the besieged from escaping." If Albert's numbers are correct, the Franks must have made a grisly spectacle. They had gathered together over one thousand heads to send back to Alexius as proof of their victory. Other heads they threw into the city to frighten the defenders into surrender. Anna Comnena did not recall the Franks using Saracen skulls for saddle decorations, but she did remember the decapitations: "The heads of many Turks they stuck on the ends of spears and came back carrying these like standards, so that the barbarians, recognizing afar off what had happened and being frightened by this defeat at their first encounter, might not be so eager for battle in the future."[7]

In treating their enemies this way, were the Franks following the standard practices of eleventh-century warfare? This was, after all, a brutal time. Outside of the crusade, however, it is difficult to find evidence for Frankish warriors engaging in similar conduct. Questions of morality aside, desecration of the dead within Europe created bad publicity. William the Conqueror's conduct following the Battle of Hastings provides a nice comparison. In the aftermath of the Norman Conquest, according to William's biographer, it would have been fitting to leave the Anglo-Saxon dead unburied, "fodder for vultures and wolves. But to William such a punishment seemed cruel. He allowed anyone who wished freely to collect and bury the dead." William himself disposed of his enemy King Harold's body. He refused even to turn it over to Harold's mother, apparently out of respect for the other dead Englishmen. It did not seem just, William felt, to give a proper burial to the man who had been responsible for such carnage.

In even the most savage conflicts in the Middle Ages—and Hastings was one of the worst—there were expectations about how to treat the enemy dead. By collecting heads from both the wounded and the dead, hanging them from saddles, and giving them away as presents, the Franks were challenging their own standards of conduct. And they did this for a reason: to inspire genuine horror among the enemy, to break its will to resist, and, for the pilgrims as much as for the Turks, to show that the old rules of war did not apply to the crusade.[8]

A Troubling Victory

The remainder of the siege of Nicea went more or less as Alexius would have wanted. The rest of the army arrived on June 3 and was able to close all land access to the city. But as long as the lake remained open, the city couldn't be completely cut off from the outside world. There were only two options available for taking Nicea: to break down the walls or to establish a blockade on the lake.

Initially, the crusaders focused on the walls. The most direct approach was to charge the ramparts with siege ladders, with covering fire from catapults and archers, and to climb into the city. But with Nicea's cunningly arranged towers, no one could get close to the walls, no matter the ballistic support. If the armies were to have any success, they needed some kind of protection—specifically, hard armored shells designed to cover small groups of soldiers, allowing them to approach the walls and carry out siege operations. The first model, built by German soldiers, was called a "fox." Too heavy for its own good, the machine collapsed as it approached the walls, killing all twenty men beneath it. The second model, called, appropriately, the "tortoise," was built by the Provençal soldiers and had more success. It got close enough to the walls to allow pilgrims to start battering and picking at the rocks, digging their way into the city. The Turks, however, simply piled up more rocks to fill in the places where the crusaders had dug. No matter how much the Franks succeeded in weakening or clearing out the wall, the defenders just as quickly reinforced it.

Eventually, the Turks unleashed a forceful assault against the tortoise and managed to set it alight with "a mixture of grease, oil, and pitch with coarse flax and burning torches hurled from the walls." It was, in effect, a form of Greek Fire, perhaps the most feared and famous chemical weapon of the Middle Ages. Common as it was in the East—Alexius had vessels rigged up with terrifying animal heads that would spit Greek Fire at enemy ships—this was probably the crusaders' first direct experience of it. Its exact composition was a guarded secret (there certainly was more than one recipe), but its destructive effects were legendary. Not only was Greek Fire resistant to water; it could even burn on water. The tortoise never stood a chance. Those not killed by the fire were shot down with arrows or crushed by stones hurled from defenders on the city walls.[9]

Finally, a Lombard engineer boasted that for a price he could bring down one of the towers. In exchange for "fifteen pounds of the coins of Chartres," he designed and assembled a type of "tortoise," with walls that sloped at such an angle that none of the enemy's weapons could stick to it. Whatever the enemy threw against it, even Greek Fire, rolled off harmlessly. Directing operations from below the tortoise, the engineer had a group of sappers dig beneath the tower walls, putting wooden beams into place as others removed the earth, so that the structure would not collapse on top of them. "Now that a truly great cave had been dug, in width and length," the Lombard engineer directed the men to fill the spaces between the beams and the tower foundation with kindling and then to set it alight. The flames rapidly grew in strength, consuming all of the beams that the engineer had set in place and, with the foundation suddenly gone, the entire structure collapsed. Darkness fell before the army could take advantage of this good fortune, and anticipating the worst, Kilij-Arslan's wife slipped out of the city, hoping to escape danger via the Ascanian Lake. Inside Nicea, the defenders worked through the night, moving the rubble of the tower around in such a way that, by sunrise, the entry to the city was again blocked. Even so, at this point the Niceans must have begun to suspect that their city was lost.[10]

And the situation was worse still, as Kilij-Arslan's wife may have been the first to learn. Her attempt to escape via the lake was foiled when a Christian ship intercepted her boat and imprisoned her. While most of the Franks had been working so hard to bring down the walls of Nicea, the army's leaders had been exploring the other possible route to victory: shutting down the lake. They had sent word to Alexius, who was keeping an eye on the siege from the nearby city of Pelekanum, and explained that they needed boats if they were to complete their blockade. Alexius readily agreed and arranged to have several large ships sent to Civitot. From there a contingent of knights and foot soldiers collected the ships and, through the use of ropes, carts, oxen, and horses, carried the vessels seven miles overland and over mountains to put them on the Ascanian Lake. The Niceans thus awoke to find that one of their walls had been seriously compromised and the lake and all of their supplies had been cut off. Kilij-Arslan had left them to their own devices. Surrender was inevitable. The only question was how to handle it.[11]

Alexius made the decision easy. He sent Boutoumites, one of his generals, accompanied by a band of his Turcopoles, to make contact with Nicea's leaders. Boutoumites was armed with a chrysobull—an impressive imperial document usually sealed in gold and written in purple ink—that assured the Turks of merciful treatment and an abundance of gifts. Alexius promised his erstwhile enemies immunity from Byzantine justice, and, more importantly and immediately, protection from the Franks, who were, he seemed to indicate, the greater cause for worry. The Turks were likely beginning to realize that the emperor was right: The Franks were not Byzantine mercenaries. They were instruments of divine wrath who viewed Muslims as God's enemies. If they took the city, a general slaughter would surely follow. The Turks therefore did the only sensible thing and surrendered to the Greeks.

According to Anna Comnena, there was one final bit of stagecraft to be managed, mainly for the benefit of the Franks. Boutoumites, no doubt in collaboration with Tetigus, had told the Franks that there would be a final attack against the city on the morning of June 19. The Franks would strike from the ground and the Greeks from the sea. With the Turks, meanwhile, Boutoumites arranged to have the city's gates thrown open immediately so that his armies could enter safely and unopposed while his supposed allies were otherwise engaged. It was to be, she said, a "drama of betrayal carefully planned by Alexius" and deliberately concealed from the Kelts. The next day, trumpet blasts sounded and the Franks charged the ramparts. But they had barely begun to fight when imperial standards appeared on the ramparts. Nicea had fallen, and the Franks were still shut outside its walls. Alexius ordered the Turkish leaders shuttled out of the city after nightfall, lest the Franks capture them, and taken to Pelekanum in small groups, lest they have the opportunity to escape, reorganize, and cause him further grief. In Pelekanum he received the prisoners a few at a time and accepted terms of surrender from them. In sum, he treated them exactly as he had the Frankish leaders upon their arrivals at Constantinople.[12]

The quick victory was evidently a surprise for the Franks. Reactions were mixed. By and large the leaders were pleased. According to the knight Anselm of Ribemont, on June 19, 1097, the citizens of Nicea, making a circuit of the walls and carrying crosses and imperial banners, "reconciled the city to the Lord, as Greeks and Latins inside and outside walls shouted together, 'Glory to you, Lord!'" God had won a great victory, and the Frankish princes had won more treasure. Alexius invited them to an imperial residence on a nearby island and conferred with them about the next stages of their journey, rewarding them with still more treasure. To the knights he gave "gold, jewels, silver, cloaks, horses and such," and to the foot soldiers he distributed ample food or else a few bronze coins.

But not everyone was impressed by this generosity; a lot of potential wealth had been lost because the army hadn't plundered the city. As the Provençal priest Raymond of Aguilers observed caustically, "After Alexius had accepted the city he showed so much thanks to the army that for as long as he lives the people will always curse him and declare him a traitor." Some further grumbled about the wide disparity between the treasures being given to the rich and the alms being distributed to the poor. These complaints also led to what appears to be an outlandish conspiracy theory: The emperor had spared the citizens of Nicea so that he might one day arm them and use them to attack the Franks and bring their pilgrimage to an end. Beyond these grievances, many pilgrims would have been angry simply because there was not enough time for them to visit Nicea and pray in its churches. They would spend no more than ten days before its walls, and since Alexius would only allow them to enter the city in small groups, just a few hundred of the 100,000 pilgrims would have had a chance to view the magnificent old city. Simply put, something about this victory didn't smell right.[13]

On a more fundamental level, the Frankish warriors wanted blood. After seven weeks of often-brutal combat, they needed to take some measure of revenge. The Niceans had massacred the armies of Peter the Hermit and left their bodies at Nicomedia to rot. They had used a makeshift grapple that could reach down over the ramparts and pluck up Christian bodies from the ground by their chain mail armor. They hung one long-dead Norman from a noose in sight of the armies, as if executing him again. These sacrifices cried out for vengeance—never mind that the Franks had also made a habit of decapitating dead Turks and making sport with their severed heads. But vengeance would have to wait while Alexius fêted the crusade leaders and the Turkish generals in turns.[14]

Even Fulcher of Chartres, normally a sympathetic reporter of Greek affairs, felt that something had gone awry at Nicea. After the Franks had worn the city down with a long siege "and made the Turks frightened with our frequent attacks, talks were opened through envoys with the emperor, and they cunningly handed the city over to him, although it had almost been brought down through strength and cleverness. And then the Turks allowed entry into the city to Turcopoles sent by the emperor." Alexius, in sum, had gotten what he had wanted and the Turks had gotten to keep their lives. The Franks had gotten almost nothing. True, Alexius had enriched their princes, but he had given only a pittance to everyone else. He had also, true to his word, given the Latins further advice on how to fight the Saracens, urging them to begin negotiations with the enemy. Specifically, he advised them to send a legation to Egypt since these infidels, who were Shi'i, were the confirmed enemies of the Turks, who were Sunni. The Franks accepted his advice and sent at least three envoys to Egypt, hoping that the caliph would join them in their fight and would, perhaps, embrace Christianity. The story of their mission survives in the historical record in only the faintest of outlines, probably a sign of the ambivalence, or embarrassment, that the strategy inspired among the army in general.[15]

Alexius also took advantage of these gift exchanges to wring a few final concessions out of the Franks—namely, he forced Bohemond's nephew Tancred and a few other recalcitrant leaders to take an oath of homage to him and to swear to return all of the former Byzantine territories to his control. Tancred again resisted, believing that giving cities to the Greeks was no better than giving them to the Turks. Sounding like a Roman senator (or at least that is how his classically trained biographer wanted him to sound), he argued that he could not serve two masters, the Christian republic and the Greek king. He fumed and trembled and raged like a bull, but in the end, under compulsion, he took the emperor's hand and agreed to help Alexius provided that Alexius at some point fought alongside the Franks. "If you wish to dominate," he advised Alexius pedantically, "then you must strive to serve." Alexius tried to win Tancred over in the same way as he had done with his uncle Bohemond—with bribes. But Tancred refused the emperor's money, asking instead for his tent, a structure of magnificent workmanship that was the size of a city. Alexius refused the request, seething with anger. As they parted company, Tancred observed to Alexius, "I deem you worthy of being my enemy, and not a friend." He may have lost his battle of wills with the emperor, but he had at least preserved his dignity.[16]

Thus, despite a close alliance between Alexius and the princes, despite the oaths taken at Constantinople and afterward on an island several miles removed from Nicea, despite the significant military achievement that the victory of Nicea represented, there were significant rifts within the Frankish army, as well as uncertainty as to what the crusaders were doing and how they should be conducting their mission. For most observers looking back over the first six months of 1097, the time with the emperor was a shameful topic and the siege of Nicea a mixed and muted victory.

The ambivalence about these accomplishments is perhaps best expressed in an anecdote of Albert of Aachen's. After news of the surrender spread through the crusader camps, the Niceans unexpectedly began releasing prisoners from Peter the Hermit's armies, captured during the early battles of Civitot and Nicomedia. Among the freed captives was a nun from Trier, who, according to all reports, was a great beauty. Upon being captured, as she tearfully told the crusaders, she had been forced into "loathsome sexual acts" with a particular Turk and with others as well. Among the nobles she recognized a knight named Henry of Esch, most recently famous for having helped to finance the disastrous "fox" siege engine. The nun must have known Henry while in Europe since he had accompanied Godfrey's army, not Peter's, to Constantinople. (Esch, in modern Luxembourg, is relatively close to Trier, making it likely that Henry's family and the nun's moved in similar aristocratic circles.)

She called Henry by name and asked him "in a low and tearful voice" to speak on her behalf with whatever cleric should assign penance to her. Henry took her case to Duke Godfrey, who in turn spoke on the nun's behalf to Bishop Adhémar. He, conferring with a priest, decided that her penance for this "unlawful copulation" should be alleviated, though not eliminated altogether—an act of mercy for which there was ample spiritual precedent—because "she had unwillingly and under duress endured this foul rape from wicked and criminal men."

But the story was not as straightforward as it seemed. The Turk who had claimed possession of her body had been taken prisoner by the emperor. Only one night after his capture, and from his supposed Greek prison, he sent a message to the nun asking her to come back to him. "The same Turk burned because of her incomparable beauty, and he bore the loss of her quite badly; for he had promised her, who still occupied his thoughts, many rewards, so that she might return to that wicked marriage." He had even pledged, Albert said, to convert to Christianity if she would only come back. Of course, neither Albert nor his sources could have known any of these details for certain. They knew only that almost as soon as Christians had rescued her from her "wicked spouse and adulterous marriage," deceived by flattery or vain hope, moved by some unknown cunning or lechery, or perhaps just driven by lust, she returned to her Turkish husband.[17]

It is not difficult to fill the gaps in this story. Urban II had forbidden monks, and by inference, nuns, to travel to Jerusalem without the permission of their superiors. Monks, many of them confined to monasteries since childhood, likely saw in the crusade a great chance to escape the life that had been imposed on them. Nuns would have felt the same, only more so. In any case, it is likely that this nun—a young woman whose family mixed with nobility and who had broken her conventual vows to travel East—had never wanted to join a nunnery in the first place. Whatever the circumstances of her liaison with the Turkish man, she had found it a preferable life to what she had known in Europe. When she thought that her husband—for that is surely a better label for what he was than "rapist" or "kidnapper"—would be killed or imprisoned after the fall of Nicea, she returned to the Frankish army. The other prisoners who had been released with her likely knew that she had fared well in captivity and perhaps had not been a captive at all. For this reason she had asked Henry of Esch to intervene at the highest levels of the army on her behalf. But as soon as she knew that her husband was alive and that Alexius was not executing his prisoners but rather treating them with fairness and generosity, she returned, leaving the pilgrims confused and more than a little bitter, for they had earnestly believed that they had saved her life.[18]

Like Nicea as a whole, the Franks had fought hard to rescue this woman and to give her the opportunity to rid herself of the godless Turks, but neither the city nor the woman wanted their company or the brand of liberty they offered.

7

"Saracens," Through a Glass Darkly

With the victory at Nicea, the crusaders had had their first direct experience of fighting the Turks. But the conflict had been relatively limited, and the siege had ended through negotiations mediated by the Greeks rather than in an apocalyptic river of blood. The crusade was for a time just the proxy war that Alexius had imagined. After Nicea, however, the farther the Franks marched from Constantinople, the more the campaign became one of simple religious conflict—more akin to the holy war that Peter the Hermit and Emicho of Flonheim had preached. The crusade was entering a new, purely anti-Islamic phase, and the Franks would now have to confront an enemy they barely understood.

Ideas are often no less inspiring or powerful for being wrong, and the Franks on crusade had bought into fantastical misconceptions about their enemy. Not everyone in the army, of course, was equally ill informed about Islam. Bohemond and his followers, and some of the Provençals, too, had been fighting against Muslims in less spiritually charged locations, southern Italy and Spain, for years. But when faced with a choice between myth and reality, most medieval historians, presumably like many of the warriors, preferred to imagine the crusade not as a war fought against a rival faith but as one fought against figures of legend, villains of myth.

Eleventh- and twelfth-century fiction about Muslims offers the best portrait of what the crusaders actually believed about their opponents. Of particular use is *The Song of Roland*, an epic eleventh-century French poem about a war in Spain between Christians and Saracens. Composed by an unknown author, the story is loosely based on a historical event from the reign of Charlemagne in 778. After a brief and largely unsuccessful incursion across the Pyrénées and after a failed attempt to take the city of Zaragoza, Charlemagne decided to retreat to Francia. As his historical army (as opposed to the literary army in the *Song*) crossed the Pass of Roncesvalles, a band of Basque Christians ambushed the rearguard and killed everyone in it, including the famous warrior Roland.

As reimagined in 4,000 lines of poetry, Charlemagne agrees to accept the surrender of the Saracen King Marsilla after a seven-year campaign fought against Marsilla's Saracen armies. But as the Christians withdraw from Spain, because of the machinations of a traitor named Ganelon, Muslim armies attack their rearguard. Though they are outnumbered, Roland, his best friend Oliver, and the renowned Archbishop Turpin of Reims valiantly hold their ground. Roland, as leader, elects not to call to Charlemagne for help by sounding his horn Oliphant until almost all of his followers are dead. When Charlemagne later discovers their mangled, bloody bodies littering the field of Spain, he prepares for one last war against a vast army led by Baligant, the amir of Baghdad—the Saracen equivalent of an emperor. Charlemagne and Baligant, the two imperial figures, inevitably face each other in combat, each man determined to destroy the other and to prove that his religion is right. Charlemagne nearly fails. But with the help of God, and with the Archangel Gabriel coming down from heaven to inspire the weary old emperor to one last feat of valor, he manages to strike a deathblow against Baligant and secure a new triumph for Christ.

Such a story would obviously appeal to an audience of warriors. Skulls are split in two, brains ooze out of ears, and so much blood is shed that the green fields of Spain turn an eerie red. The poem's imagery would have been especially compelling for a Christian army going off to fight Islam. Did the First Crusaders know of the song? Probably. It was a well-known and often retold story. An English historian writing in the 1120s, for example, imagined that William the Conqueror's army together sang *Roland* before the 1066 Battle of Hastings. The poem would have likely inspired individual crusaders to see themselves as Roland or Charlemagne returned to life, and at least one contemporary historian, Ralph of Caen, said as much. Writing about Hugh the Great and Robert of Flanders plunging into the fray against the Saracens in a 1097 battle, he wrote, "You would have seen Roland and Oliver reborn, as you watched this count strike with his spear, and the other count with his sword."[1]

The enemies whom the crusaders imagined themselves facing, based on *The Song of Roland,* bore little connection to actual Muslims. Rather, as presented in the poem, they are distorted reflections of the Christian world. The similarities between the two worlds can be mathematical in their precision. Both sides in the poem, Christian and Muslim, have kings who hold meetings while seated beneath trees, and each king tugs pensively at his beard to indicate thoughtfulness. Surrounding and advising each king are twelve peers. Each side fights passionately for its religion, though it is never clear from the poem what either side believes. We learn mainly that the Saracen god is wrong and the Christian God is right, that the Saracens follow the path of heresy and error and the Christians cleave to truth. Christians worship Christ and the Holy Trinity; Muslims venerate three idols dedicated to Muhammad, Apollo, and Tervagant. When Christians die on the battlefield, angels descend from heaven and escort their souls back to paradise. When Muslims die, demons appear and gleefully drag their souls to hell. So finely balanced are the comparisons between the two worlds that of the 112 named characters in *The Song of Roland,* 56 are Muslim and 56 are Christian.[2]

This sort of imaginative structure, with its artistic and numerical rigor, is easy for modern readers to grasp. Like a photographic negative, Muslim characters perfectly reflect their Christian counterparts; in terms of shading, they are wicked and dark, whereas the Christians are virtuous and light. Medieval thinkers, however, did not have the luxury of a photographic allegory. Even "the concept of a distorted reflection" would not have come easily to them: Given the primitive state of mirror technology, all reflections were distorted, or "through a glass darkly," to quote the apostle Paul.

What medieval readers did have ready at hand were eschatological principles of death, judgment, damnation, and salvation. The two worlds of heaven and hell existed in perfect equilibrium to the extent that the structure of one world could be learned by meditating upon the shape of the other: "As the blessings of the saints, when they attain the vision of God, continue to grow in inestimable sweetness, so the souls of the wicked, united to their head the devil, in the most savage torment burn all the more vehemently with their desire to sin, and their will is in perfect concord with him who feeds on enticing others to sin (the devil). And just as the saints, once they have seen the glory of God, are ashamed that they did not expend more labor to acquire that glory, so do the impious grieve most bitterly, as they come into these tortures, that they were not more enslaved to their wicked wills during their lives." Heaven was like hell, but different; angels were like devils, but different; and Christians were like Muslims, but different. Indeed, they opposed and complemented each other with exactitude.[3]

Put another way: Whenever Christians wanted to understand or explain Islam, they thought about themselves and about the end of days. Christians and Muslims existed in perfect opposition to each other, just like angels and devils, and in the Last Days the former group would necessarily overcome the latter. This sort of worldview is not rooted in ignorance or superstition. To speculate about the Last Days is to look for the deep patterns and rhythms of history. From an apocalyptic perspective, historical actors do not just "make history." Nor do they, as with the modern proverb, "repeat history." Rather, they re-create and relive some of the key moments in history—the Exodus of the Israelites, the crowning of King David, the founding of Rome, and the Crucifixion, to take a few of the more popular historical road markers. These great moments from the past are precursors to current events, but they are also connected to current events. To enter apocalyptic time for the Frankish pilgrims meant that they needed, in some way, like their modern literary namesake Billy Pilgrim, to come unstuck in time.

The Muslims against whom the Crusaders fought existed in this timeless, nonhistorical world. Like the Jews, the Muslims were inseparable from events described in the Old Testament, forever re-creating the dramas in which siblings vie with one another for the status of favored son in hopes of earning for their offspring the title "Chosen People." This conflict surfaces in the Christians' preferred name for their enemies. As far as they knew, they were not fighting Muslims who practiced Islam. It is doubtful that most of the crusaders had even heard those words. The name they preferred instead was "Saracen"—a label born not of reality or experience but of apocalyptic time and Old Testament history. In a story most Christians would have known, Abraham and his wife Sarah had for years failed to produce a child. With Abraham in his eighties, Sarah suggested that he sleep with her maidservant Hagar so that he might at least have an heir. He did, and Hagar gave birth to a son named Ishmael. Later, when Abraham had passed his hundredth year, Sarah did finally, miraculously, give birth to a boy named Isaac, and at her prompting, Abraham disinherited Ishmael and drove the boy and his mother from their household.

According to prophecy, each of these children would found a great people—Isaac the Jews and Ishmael the Arabs. As the book of Genesis says, Ishmael "will be a savage man, his hand against all men and the hands of all men against him." In the fourth century, before the advent of Islam, St. Jerome was able to apply this passage to a nomadic ethnic group whom he labeled "Saracens": "These words signify that [Abraham's] seed will inhabit the desert—that is, they are the wandering Saracens with no fixed abodes, who attack all people who live beside the desert and whom all people there resist." By the twelfth century, Western scholars had linked Jerome's interpretation to Islam, making the connection between Ishmael and Muslims a historical and a theological commonplace.[4]

Western scholars did not invent this connection. The ancestry is an important point of Arabic culture and history, too. The application of the blanket term "Saracen," however, is a product of Western imagination. The Ishmaelites, Latin authors believed, desperately wished to conceal their base heritage. They wanted to pretend that they were not the illegitimate children of a slave. Hence, they called themselves the "Saracens," the descendants of Sarah, rather than, more properly, the "Hagarenes." One twelfth-century writer cautioned, "You should know and you ought never to doubt that these people, who take pride in their name, are not and never should be called Saracens. They are 'Agarenes,' and rightly named such." Despite this warning, European writers by and large rejected "Agarene." "Saracen" was simply too useful—by itself evidence of that faith's base ancestry (Muslims were born of a slave), its illegitimacy (they were bastards), and its mendaciousness (they used their name to lie about it).[5]

The origins of the Saracen faith, however, were almost a complete mystery to Europeans. Because none of the early Church Fathers had written a polemic against it or its founder—"Mathomus, if I'm spelling that correctly," one writer specified—they reasoned that the Saracen religion was "of no real antiquity." If it had been, surely some prominent thinker—Jerome or Augustine certainly—would have attacked it. The only reliable information about the faith's origins could be found, perhaps predictably, not in history books or in theological treatises but in prophecy—specifically in a series of popular prophetic manuals that were reaching something like the apogee of their popularity in the late eleventh century.[6]

Saracens, we learn from these books, first appeared in history around 4,000 years after the creation of the world (according to most respected chronologists, the crusade was occurring in the year of the world 6300). These Saracens were nomadic warriors who moved like locusts, traveled nude, ate raw meat stored in skins and drank the blood of oxen mixed with milk, desolated cities, and spread their destructive influence all around the Mediterranean. They had first attacked the Israelites in Old Testament times, but Gideon's armies defeated them. They disappeared for a while, but the prophecies warned that the Ishmaelites would return, fiercer than ever: "And their yoke will be double upon the necks of all people, and there will be no people or kingdom under heaven capable of defeating them."[7]

According to this prophet, the Ishmaelites would return from deserts in the East about 2,000 years after Gideon's victory and after the Romans had finally triumphed over Persia. Their arrival would be for the whole world "a punishment without pity." They would attain power not because God loved them, but because He wished to punish sinners. On account of sexual crimes committed by Christians, "God shall hand them over to the barbarians. Because of the barbarians they will fall into every sort of impurity and filth and pollution, and women will be contaminated by polluted barbarians, and the sons of Ishmael shall cast lots over their sons and daughters."

Ishmaelites would mock the poor and the infirm. They would stab pregnant women in their bellies, at a stroke killing both mother and child. They would murder priests in sanctuaries in order to defile the holy places. Not content with this crime, the Ishmaelites would burn the priests' bodies, along with the bodies of women, in the very holiest places where the sacred and "uncontaminated mystery" ought to be performed.

They would steal priestly vestments and use them to clothe their women and children. According to a later version of the prophecy, Jerusalem would find itself full of slaves driven there by Saracens. And as the final insult, they would bring beasts of burden into the tombs of the saints and there shelter them as if in a stable.[8]

The similarities between these images and the ones used in the sermons attributed to Urban II at Clermont are remarkable—enough to suggest that either Urban or the historians who composed sermons in his name drew upon prophetic histories in order to craft their stories of Saracen atrocities. Even the very last image of sheltering animals in the tombs of saints found its way into some of the propaganda circulating around the time of the First Crusade: "About churches that the pagans hold, having uprooted Christianity from them, there is a grievance because they have built in them stables for horses and mules and other animals." When preachers wanted to motivate soldiers, or when historians wanted to understand what the crusade was all about, the language they used was apocalyptic.[9]

These same apocalyptic instincts also shaped what Christians knew, or believed they knew, about "Saracen religion" and in particular about its founder, "Mathomos." Since Latin authors had no written evidence about his life, they relied on hearsay. The information was inaccurate, and they knew it, but there was no real harm in making mistakes. With a man as wicked as "Mathomos," the historian Guibert of Nogent wrote in 1108, "whoever sings evil things about him does so securely." Guibert may have chosen his words here with special precision. Two verse biographies of Muhammad survive from the crusade era. When writing about Muhammad, Guibert and other writers thus could have literally been basing their stories about Muhammad on a song. And as we might expect, the character of Mathomos in all of these biographies is a perfect parody, a negative image, of a Christian saint or of Christ. Latin writers thus did not seek the historical prophet Muhammad. Rather, they found Mathomos by looking at Christ through a glass darkly.[10]

The various biographies of Mathomos tell roughly the same story. They usually begin with a heretic: an embittered, failed Christian leader who, because of theological missteps, has been exiled to the land of the Agarenes. Angry and ambitious, eager to spread his doctrine and undermine true

Christianity, the heretical old man takes on a pupil, an impoverished youth named Mathomos. He trains the boy in the ways of his faith—essentially, a complete surrender to libidinous pleasure. According to twelfth-century writers, that was indeed the secret to Islam's rapid expansion and popularity: free love. Mathomos's followers called Christian moral strictures "cruel and bitter." They believed instead that God allowed only one thing: "liberty." It was forbidden to forbid. Or as a twelfth-century German summarized Mathomos's teaching, "Let food abound and let love be set free!"[11]

But giving free rein to the libido was not enough. The new religion needed miracles if it were to compete with Christianity. Thus, the cunning old heretic and his disciple grow practiced in the art of fakery. During one particularly important sermon, for example, a cow seems magically to appear, bearing on its head stone tablets that contain new divine revelations (not unlike the woman whose goose would lead her to Jerusalem). Unbeknown to a rapturous congregation, Mathomos had carefully trained the animal to respond to his voice and earlier attached the law code to its horns. The prophet also takes a wife, a wealthy widow in one version or the queen of the Agarenes in another, whose husband recently died at Babylon. The marriage nearly falls apart when Mathomos develops epilepsy, but his mentor, the old hermit, successfully convinces the woman that her new young husband is not suffering from a disease. Rather, angelic visitations are sending him into divine ecstasies. "I experience the conversation of the Archangel Gabriel," the prophet explains to his wife with precision, "and as a carnal being I am unable to bear his glorious visage. Hence, I fail; I fall!"[12]

According to most accounts, this same epilepsy kills Mathomos. While wandering alone, he suffers an acute seizure and falls to the ground. Wild pigs stumble onto his supine, trembling figure and consume his flesh, leaving behind only the feet, which, Guibert of Nogent said, Saracens still venerate. Because of the memory of this horrible death, Mathomos's followers abstain from eating pork. In another version of the story, Mathomos's body remains intact after his death, and his followers take his body to Mecca—Muhammad was laid to rest in Medina, but in the midst of such wildly inaccurate diatribes, this error is impressively close to the truth—and store his body inside a metal coffin. This coffin they then cunningly place inside a house constructed entirely of magnets so that the casket floats mysteriously in the air, one more faked miracle to deceive his regularly misled devotees. And as a poetic "Life" of the prophet reminds us, the name of the burial place, Mecca, is "not without hidden meaning" since Mathomos was a *mechus*, or "philanderer."[13]

However deliberately grotesque or inaccurate these stories might seem, they were not wholly products of ignorance. Their core elements (a law code given to a prophet through the Angel Gabriel, abstention from pork, an obligation to undertake the Hajj, or pilgrimage to Mecca) indicate some familiarity with the realities of Islam. But the method for constructing these tales has nothing to do with historical observation or analysis. It is instead another example of eschatological thought. Writers take a traditional element of Christianity, in this case a saint's biography, and invert it, applying this new negative characteristic to Muhammad.[14]

Crusade historians used the same technique. In their telling, Saracens were like Christians, but the opposite. They were "a people quite degenerate, despicable, and enslaved to demons." They worshipped idols. They hated Christianity, and they hated Christ. They venerated a man called Mathomos as if he were a god (rather than a man called Christ who *was* God). This Mathomos may have been an epileptic, or he may have been, one writer darkly hinted, a Canaanite god from the Old Testament. And what theologians knew about the Canaanites was similar to what historians believed they knew about Saracens. Among the Canaanites, "it was thought permissible to lust, to fornicate, and to commit all manner of debauchery." Just as Christians were members of the body of Christ, Saracens were parts of demons and servants of Antichrist, destined to battle against "Christ and all his limbs."[15]

Saracens were timeless villains, cut from an apocalyptic mold. They stood outside the normal rules of history. When the crusaders went to fight them in the Holy Land—a "real-world" landscape that existed also in heaven and eternity—they had to step outside of history and, to a degree, outside of reality as they had known it. Around Nicea the Emperor Alexius and the crusade princes managed to keep themselves and their armies in check, anchored very much in this world. The farther they marched from Nicea, however, and the more they engaged with this otherworldly enemy, the less bound by the old-fashioned rules of time and morality the Franks believed themselves to be.

As the crusade left Nicea behind, the campaign became what Peter the Hermit had long ago promised it would be. Still present in the army, Peter could now begin to remind everyone that he had been right. The Franks were not just battling for an earthly Jerusalem. They were not only struggling to save their souls. They also were fighting for heaven. They were waging an apocalypse.

8

Enemy Country

(*June 29, 1097–October 22, 1097*)

R obbed of plunder at Nicea and cheated of the satisfaction of their bloodlust by Alexius's diplomacy, the more fervent pilgrims were probably anxious to leave that city behind as quickly as possible. A few soldiers stayed with the emperor to tidy up negotiations about what help he might continue to provide. The rest of the Frankish army mustered at the nearby Göksu River, and on June 29 they began their march into Central Anatolia.

The immediate target was Antioch. Stephen of Blois mentioned the city in his letter to his wife, Adela, written on the eve of this departure: "I say to you, sweetheart, that from Nicea we will arrive at Jerusalem in five weeks, provided that Antioch does not slow us down." The siege of Antioch would wind up lasting nearly nine months, and the crusaders would not reach Jerusalem for another two years. In light of the enormity of the task the army would confront at Antioch, this passage brims with enough dramatic irony to call into question whether Stephen's letter is a genuine communication or else a witty forgery.

At the very least, if the letter is genuine, Stephen was badly misinformed about geography. The trek to Antioch was six hundred miles long at best, and the crusaders would follow a roundabout course to get there. The territory along the way would be complex and unpredictable, characterized by bewildering ethnic diversity and by shifting, kaleidoscopic patterns of religious and political alliances. The Franks' survival and the

success of the crusade depended on their ability to fend off Saracen attacks while at the same time striking up alliances with local Christian
groups, whose customs and languages they did not understand and who
were themselves justly suspicious of the Franks. However much the
armies might have wanted to fight and plunder, diplomacy would remain
the order of the day.[1]

But it all began with a grand battle.

Dorylaeum

Kilij-Arslan, the destroyer of Peter the Hermit's armies, had not ceded all
his territories to the Franks and the Greeks, nor had he been vanquished
by his own armies' defeat at Nicea on May 16. Instead, he had formed an
alliance with the Danishmend amir, one of his Turkish rivals. Together
they planned to ambush the Franks during the next phase of their march
near the ancient Roman trading post of Dorylaeum. Unlike the land
around Nicea, the relatively level ground by Dorylaeum would allow the
Turks to take advantage of their cavalry's speed and mobility.

The crusaders had unwittingly helped the Turks' cause. During the
first two days of the march, their armies divided into two groups. Why
they did so is a mystery. Some thought it a deliberate decision generated
by the difficulties in provisioning such a large army. Others thought it an
accident caused by darkness and disorganization. Whatever the case,
about one-third of the army, led by Bohemond, Robert of Normandy, and
Stephen of Blois, separated, broke off well ahead of the rest of the army,
and proceeded directly into Kilij-Arslan's ambush.[2]

On the night of June 30, only two days after the rendezvous at the
Göksu, rumor reached the Franks' vanguard that Kilij-Arslan had mustered another army against them and was preparing to spring a trap. Alexius had coached many of the princes about how to handle this situation.
Very likely Tetigus was with them as well and able to give advice. The next
morning, July 1, imagining themselves a grand Roman legion (as Fulcher
of Chartres described it), "weapons taken up, trumpets sounding,
arranged against the enemy in wings, centurions leading cohorts and centuries, standards raised, in an orderly fashion we began to set forth."

In about two hours, the Franks found the Turks waiting for them. Eye-witnesses estimated around 360,000 horsemen, a figure likely born of the crusaders' own bedazzlement at the speed and elegance of the enemy cavalry and terror at what they were about to experience. Bohemond and the other princes, however, kept their heads. They had already sent messengers to the rest of the army—the Lotharingians and the Provençals—to request help, telling them, "If they wish to fight today, they should come like men." The key to victory (or perhaps the only hope for survival) was to hold off the Turks until the others arrived. So rather than order an immediate attack, Bohemond directed the soldiers, in the face of imminent hostility, to set camp. They put their packs aside, pitched their tents near a marsh—or at least an area full of reeds—and prepared for combat.[3]

As the battle of Dorylaeum began, the Turks employed the same tactics Kilij-Arslan had tried at Nicea. His cavalry "encircled us on all sides, engaging at close quarters and throwing darts and spears and firing arrows wondrously far and wide." The Frankish soldiers had never experienced anything like this attack—full of clamor, speed, and savage beauty. "There was no pause, no respite before the army began slaughtering and fighting. As they rushed through the camps, some were struck with arrows, some beheaded by swords, with many others taken captive by so cruel an enemy. Everywhere a great shouting and shaking spread amongst the people, as women married and unmarried together with their husbands and children were beheaded."

The unarmed pilgrims hid inside the tents, trembling in fear as the Turks galloped about them with rapidity and precision. They "howled and shrieked and shouted, making a devilish noise in their high voices . . . crying and shouting like demons." Terrifying as the situation was, it wasn't surprising. These were, after all, harbingers of Antichrist, standing resolutely in the path of God's plan for salvation. Of course they looked and sounded like demons.[4]

The Franks withstood the devilish assault. The decision to pitch camp had enabled them to create a makeshift fortification. Their proximity to the marsh further ensured that the Turks could never completely encircle them. They could not defeat Kilij-Arslan from their camp, but they could keep him at bay—not forever, but with luck at least until help arrived.

And the battle dragged on. Clerics like Fulcher of Chartres prayed and cowered. The stouthearted women carried water skins to warriors clothed in full chain mail armor, fighting in the hot Anatolian sun. These women called out encouragement to the men, exhorting them to fight even more bravely. The warriors similarly passed reassuring words up and down the line: "Hold tight together in Christ's faith and in the victory of the Cross, since, God willing, at the end of the day you will all be rich!" Whether they would be rich with heavenly blessings or with the treasures, silks, and exotic foods that they hoped to claim as plunder is unclear. Probably they would be rich with both.[5]

After five hours, however, the crusaders were dying in ever-greater numbers. The Turks were closing in as their cavalry maneuvers took them closer and closer to the Franks' tents. The women, still taking water to the men, had a new duty: dragging corpses away from the field. Inside the tents among the poor pilgrims and the clerics, the mood grew darker. This catastrophe had happened, they decided, because of the army's sins. Luxury and avarice and other untold crimes—presumably connected to the payments from Alexius—had corrupted the Franks. Earnestly, the men and women in the tents confessed their misdeeds. Five clerics, all dressed in white, pleaded with God to show the army mercy one more time and lay low the enemies. "They sang and cried; they cried and sang. Then many more who were afraid to die rushed to confess their sins." Outside the tents, the Frankish warriors continued their attacks, not with the ferocity of lions but with the righteous anger of martyrs.[6]

About midday, after nearly six hours of fighting and with martyrdom seemingly inevitable, help finally arrived. First Hugh the Great, then Godfrey, and finally Raymond of Saint-Gilles and Adhémar of le Puy rode down from the hills to engage the Turks. Looking upon the fray, "our men marveled at where such a multitude of Turks and Arabs and Saracens could have come from, and I don't even know how to name the other peoples. For all the mountains and hills and valley and all the plains inside and out were filled with their excommunicate offspring." This second battle line began to encircle the enemy to cut off the opportunity for graceful and elegant horsemanship and to force the Turkish army to engage in close-range combat. In this style of fighting, the Franks had every advantage. Their heavier armor and weaponry made them almost invulnerable to their enemies' lighter weaponry.

The Turks, in genuine disarray, retreated to their camp. The Franks pursued them and continued killing them, plundering as they went—"gold, silver, horses and asses, camels, sheep, and bulls and many other things that I don't know about." In retrospect, the strategy looked deliberate: The crusaders had established a defensive camp, drawn the Turks in to close combat, and then suddenly ambushed them with the other half of the army. If it was an intentional strategy, however, the Franks had probably waited too long to seize their advantage. Approximately 3,000 Franks died during the fighting—a terrible loss that the army's leaders would later celebrate by proclaiming them as martyrs. "They perished in peace, and without any doubt they now glory in eternal life."[7]

God intervened in the battle as well. Some of the soldiers—in fact, Turks who deserted Kilij-Arslan and signed on to the crusade—swore that they had seen "two horsemen, with shimmering weapons and of wondrous appearance, riding ahead of our army, menacing the enemy such that they allowed them no opportunity for fighting." A later writer said that there were three knights of Christ at Dorylaeum, sitting atop white horses and carrying shimmering banners decorated with crosses. Their names were George, Demetrius, and Theodore, "Christian knights whom almighty God sent to help our people." All three were saints associated with the East, little venerated in the crusaders' homelands (though that would change after 1099, as crusaders returned to Europe with stories of the marvels they had witnessed), and all of them were soldiers. Theodore and George are frequently associated with killing dragons, Demetrius with spearing a gladiator. Thus, the crusaders were learning to work with the local power brokers in Anatolia on earth as in heaven.

Some observers may have been inclined to write off these ghostly apparitions as desert hallucinations or else as the inventions of Saracen prisoners anxious to curry favor with their captors, but the miracle would receive further confirmation. After the army broke camp at Dorylaeum on July 4 and during the three days that followed, the crusaders continually discovered Saracen corpses and their dead horses littering the roadways of Anatolia in places the Franks had not yet reached, far past the point where they had stopped pursuing the enemy. There could be only one explanation: The saints had kept up the chase and with their heavenly weapons had continued to cut down the enemy. The boundaries between this world and the next were blurring. Again, the farther from Constantinople the armies marched, and perhaps the more earnestly the soldiers prayed and confessed sins, the keener an interest God took in their affairs.[8]

Before these miraculous discoveries of Saracen corpses, the Christians rested. They mourned; they sang songs; they picked over their enemies' bodies, searching for jewels, coins, trinkets, and souvenirs; and they buried their own dead. The battle had left many of the Franks unidentifiable. Were it not for the crosses on their cloaks, the crusaders could not have even been sure which bodies belonged to Christians. They also told stories to one another, celebrating their victory and fictionalizing it at the same time. They imagined, for example, their vanquished foe, Kilij-Arslan, turning tail and fleeing to his masters in the East, warning every Saracen he encountered that the Franks were invincible, that surrender now was the wiser course. Some alternately imagined Kilij-Arslan pretending that he had won at Dorylaeum, proclaiming victory in front of every city that he approached, and then going inside and plundering it of all its goods lest the Franks find anything of value in Anatolian territory.

The pilgrims also took a moment to marvel at their own achievement. Clerics searched their memories of Scripture and prophecy (and perhaps through whatever portable libraries they had brought with them) to find words that encapsulated what had occurred. One theologically minded writer, looking back with hindsight from 1107, found the answer in Isaiah, the Old Testament prophet best known for forecasting the Virgin Birth. Perhaps Isaiah had also anticipated the crusade: *I will make you the pride of the ages, a joy lasting from generation unto generation. You will suck at the breast of many peoples and will drink milk from the breast of kings. And you will know that I am the Lord your God who saved you, the mighty redeemer of Jacob.* These words originally described God's promise to the Children of Israel. The Franks, however, were the new Israel—as many of them believed and would have proudly attested, they had wiped the old Jews from the face of the earth before leaving home. They would drain wealth and power from the kings of the East and establish themselves anew in the original city of God.

Dorylaeum had been their Red Sea, and with God's help, they had crossed it. Now they were set to enter the Promised Land.[9]

The Slow Road to Antioch

It took three days of rest and soul-searching, and three more days of joyfully discovering mutilated bodies on the desert sands, before the celebrations petered out. Despite Stephen of Blois's optimism, Antioch still lay fifteen weeks and several hundred miles in the future. The crusaders were venturing into an unknown and politically turbulent land with no sure allies and relatively few supplies. In these alien climes the wisdom and counsel of Alexius's man Tetigus doubtless proved essential—a point that would have galled many in the army. As far as some crusaders could tell, there was no real difference among Saracen, Jew, and heretic. They were "equally detestable," all "enemies of God." Now, to reach Jerusalem, the crusaders apparently were going to depend on one group of schismatic Christians to negotiate on their behalf with still other schismatic groups, particularly Armenians. The splendid and terrifying example of holy war at Dorylaeum notwithstanding, the crusade was again dependent on the search for allies, and not everyone would adapt well to this new reality.[10]

The first few days were especially difficult. The terrain was rocky, barren, practically waterless—apart from what the Franks were able to extract from cactuses—and difficult to traverse. The August sun was murderous. One Saturday, according to Albert of Aachen, five hundred men and women died of thirst, along with countless horses, mules, oxen, and other pack animals. This number sounds like an exaggeration, but Albert stressed that his information came not from hearsay but from the testimony of reliable witnesses, whose recollection caused "the human mind to tremble in horror." Besides the adult dead, several pregnant women went into labor on the march, many of them prematurely, but so desiccated were their bodies that "they simply abandoned their newborns in the middle of the road for all the world to see." The morning after this particular horrific Saturday, the army found a river. They charged its banks and fought one another like animals, as if its waters might suddenly go dry. Gratefully and voraciously, and excessively, not realizing the dangers posed by dehydration, they drank and drank, and several of them died on the spot, drowning in open air.[11]

The terrain became a bit more bearable after these harrowing experiences. Cities with large Armenian populations tended to welcome the Franks, seeing them either as Byzantine mercenaries out to restore Greek rule or else as simple allies willing to help them drive out Turkish occupiers. After forcing a large garrison of Turks to leave the city of Heraclea in early September, the Franks rested for four days and then decided, despite their bad experience at Dorylaeum, to divide the army in half once again. The larger group followed a long mountainous route to the north, through Cappadocia and eventually to Antioch, hoping to avoid the narrow passes and steep roads that characterized the more direct route through Cilicia. Two smaller groups, led by Bohemond's nephew Tancred and by Godfrey's brother Baldwin (who left his wife, an English noblewoman named Godevere, with the main army in his brother's care), took this latter, shorter route through Cilicia.

Relatively little is known about how the main army fared, apart from a few anecdotes. Godfrey, while hunting, saw an enormous bear attacking a poor pilgrim. It was "a cunning and wicked animal," and Godfrey, without hesitation, rushed to the unarmed man's defense. At first it seemed he might easily drive the bear away, but his cloak got caught up in its claws and he fell from his horse, landing awkwardly on top of his own sword. When Godfrey tried to unsheathe the weapon to stab the bear in the throat, he instead sliced his own leg open. The "poor peasant" he'd rescued was by now screaming wildly, and he managed to draw the attention of one of Godfrey's men, named Husechin, who in turn charged at the bear with sword drawn. He and Godfrey together killed the beast, but it had barely stopped breathing when the great duke turned pale and collapsed. Doctors were called in to treat him while the rest of his followers carved up the bear among themselves—they had never seen an animal with so much meat on its bones. The doctors did what they could for Godfrey, but it would be months before he fully recovered. For the next several weeks, and during the early stages of the siege of Antioch, he could only stray far from his tent if carried on a litter. By the time he was healthy enough to fight again, his men had deserted him by the hundreds.[12]

At about the same time, Raymond of Saint-Gilles fell ill and was confined to bed. His condition was grave enough that Bishop William of Orange stayed nearby, ready to deliver last rites if needed.

The rest of the army trudged on, "thirsting and burning for the blood of Turks" but finding only Armenians, striking treaties with them to recognize their control of particular castles, or else, on occasion, entrusting a fortification to a Frankish solider. The crusaders found a "hellish" mountain range—the Taurus Mountains, whose peaks rise as high as 12,000 feet—so steep and with paths so narrow that several horses tumbled over the side, as did beasts of burden. One ox would fall over the cliff and drag down the rest of the animals tethered to it. As knights lost their mounts and their servants, their weapons proved too great a burden. They tried to sell them, but the market became so glutted that their armor and swords proved almost worthless. As a result, many men threw away whatever was too heavy to carry and stood gloomily to one side, "wringing their hands in sadness and grief, not sure what to do with themselves." It was a badly depleted and much poorer army that in mid-October finally reached the foot of the Taurus Mountains and the city of Marash in southeastern Turkey, still about one hundred miles north of Antioch.[13]

As for the smaller armies that had ventured into Cilicia, their leaders rapidly abandoned the ethos of holy war in favor of more straightforward conquest and acquisitiveness, revealing in the process fundamental divisions that would later threaten to undermine the entire crusade. But this part of the journey started with a grand triumph for Tancred. He and his men reached the city of Tarsus, a former Roman capital and the birthplace of the apostle Paul. As Tancred assessed things, Tarsus was a place where Turks dominated, Greeks served, and Armenians fought for their liberty while hiding in the mountains. Impressed at the grandeur of the place and determined to make it his own, Tancred engaged in a bit of subterfuge. He dispatched a few Turcopoles—Alexius's Turkish mercenaries, presumably hired away from Tetigus—who pretended that they were bandits out to plunder the city's cattle, grazing in the nearby fields. As soon as the defenders charged from the city gates to attack, the Turcopoles retreated, and as the Turks followed, the rest of Tancred's army rose up from its hiding places. They chased the Turks back to the gates, killing as many as they could before archers atop the ramparts forced them back out of bowshot. During the night Tancred and his men set camp, planning their next attack. At the same time, the Turkish commanders evaluated their situation and thought the better of resisting. In darkness they withdrew from the city, leaving behind a small garrison but turning control of the place back over to the Greek and Armenian citizens. "Liberty had returned to the city because of its enemies—liberty which, because of its citizens, had once perished."[14]

It ought to have been a great crusader victory, but the next day, with Tancred's men still camped outside the city, another, much larger army marched into view, apparently ready for a fight. This was Baldwin of Boulogne and his men, who from a distance thought they were seeing a Turkish army camped in front of Tarsus. Baldwin and Tancred rejoiced upon recognizing one another, and they managed to celebrate one pleasant dinner together. The next morning, however, Baldwin demanded that Tancred share the spoils of Tarsus with him and his men equally or else turn the entire city over to him. Baldwin's apparently specious reasoning was that Tarsus had surrendered not out of fear of Tancred but in response to rumors of Baldwin's arrival. Were it not for his own army, Baldwin continued, without any real justification, the Turks would still be in charge of things. Difficult as it is to believe, the two crusaders were ready for all-out war against each other, but to avoid bloodshed, they agreed to allow the citizens of Tarsus to decide whom they wished to be their prince, Baldwin or Tancred. The leaders of Tarsus answered without hesitation: They preferred Tancred, not because of his innate virtue but because of his uncle Bohemond's fearsome reputation.

Baldwin flew into a rage. In the words of Albert of Aachen, "He cared not a wit for the pretension and rank of Tancred and Bohemond, likening them to mud and shit." For the Armenians' benefit, he used more measured and diplomatic terms: "You should not believe that Bohemond and this Tancred, whom you so respect and fear, are in any way the greatest and most powerful chiefs of the Christian army, nor that they bear comparison to my brother Godfrey, duke and leader of the soldiers from all Gaul, or any of his kin. For this same prince, my brother Godfrey, is duke of a realm of the great and earliest Roman emperor Augustus, by hereditary right of his noble ancestors; he is esteemed by the whole army, and great and small do not fail to comply with his words and advice on all matters because he has been elected and appointed chief and lord of everyone."[15]

Though not exactly true, Baldwin's arguments nonetheless carried the day. Bohemond and Tancred were *parvenus*. Godfrey's authority, and Baldwin's own, stretched back to Augustus. Baldwin may then have claimed as well that Godfrey's sword was the same one that the Emperor Vespasian had carried into battle in 70 AD when he had destroyed the city of Jerusalem and left its streets flowing with Jewish blood. Within a few years at least, the Armenians believed this to be the case. Tancred could not compete with such an imperial pedigree. Or, more prosaically, Tancred realized that he could not win in open combat against the Lotharingians. Whatever the case, he withdrew from St. Paul's birthplace, and the citizens raised Baldwin's standards over their walls. The city's gates were opened, and Baldwin's men were allowed to enter. Inside, they found a few Turks who had not left the city, and who were in no mood to fight. They had stayed in their towers along the wall, waiting to see what Baldwin and Tancred's intentions were. If it became apparent that the Franks were going to settle in Tarsus, then they would leave the tower peacefully.[16]

They got their answer the next day when about three hundred more Norman soldiers arrived at Tarsus's gates, presumably to reinforce Tancred's hold over the city. Baldwin, however, decided not to let them in. In his view, Tancred's followers were potential enemies, and he already had enough problems with the Greeks and Armenians. So he locked the gates, claiming that no more Christians would enter Tarsus until Godfrey arrived. The Normans, hungry and miserable, set up camp outside the walls. Only the Armenian Christians in Tarsus felt some pity for them; they lowered down live sheep and baskets full of bread, which the Normans received gratefully, happy at least to be able to go to sleep on a full stomach.

The Turks in Tarsus, on the other hand, probably knew nothing of the internal Christian conflicts. As far as they could tell, the city was lost, and it was time for them to escape and find new places to conquer. Taking all their valuables, all three hundred left Tarsus in the middle of the night, heading toward the mountains. On the way out, they passed through the sleeping Normans' camp and killed most of them before they had the chance to wake up—decapitating some, eviscerating others, shooting with arrows in the moonlight anyone who managed to get to his feet.

Such was the spectacle that greeted the citizens of Tarsus the next morning: the fields outside their city littered with Christian corpses. A riot broke out. Crusaders demanded revenge. They wanted blood—Turkish blood, preferably, but there was also talk of killing Baldwin, who barricaded himself in a tower until everyone's temper calmed. Fortunately for him, a couple hundred Turkish stragglers were left behind—poor workers whom the wealthier soldiers had not had time to bother over. The Lotharingians rounded them all up and cut their heads off. The Christian women of Tarsus also demanded justice for past crimes. The Turks had raped them, they said, and if a Christian woman had resisted, the Turks would cut off her nose or ears. Several women had the scars to prove it. The actual perpetrators had likely already fled, but the Franks were happy to inflict violence on whomever happened to be at hand. "The people of Jesus Christ were more greatly inflamed to hatred of the Turks by this scandal and horrendous accusation and they further increased their slaughter of them."[17]

By this point Tarsus was a bloody mess, inside and out, and Baldwin must have been anxious to move on. A near miraculous turn of events enabled him to do so. A few days after the slaughter of the Turks, a small fleet of ships approached the city's ports. Baldwin gathered his men together, expecting to find a contingent of Turks who had returned to challenge his rule. Boldly the crusaders approached the port and discovered the ships' crews instead to be—Belgian. One of them Baldwin had likely met before—a man named Winemer who had once served in the household of Baldwin's oldest brother, Eustace, now on crusade with Robert of Flanders. The newly arrived sailors said they were pilgrims who had departed from Flanders and Lotharingia eight years earlier, hoping to worship at the Holy Sepulcher. Along the way they had become distracted by the riches, and chaos, of the East and had decided to stay to make their fortunes, temporarily deferring the prospect of prayers at Christ's tomb. Baldwin straightaway administered the crusader's oath to all of them. They had probably been expecting to plunder Tarsus. Instead, they would govern it: Three hundred pirates would stay behind, along with two hundred of Baldwin's men. The rest would continue with him on the long road to Antioch and Jerusalem.[18]

Baldwin was at this point traveling in Tancred's shadows. Despite the setback in Tarsus, Tancred was moving from one success to another. Baldwin's men, of course, were not impressed. As they saw it (or as some of them would later repeat back in Germany), the Normans in Cilicia first conquered a castle of girls, then demolished a castle of children, and finally laid low a castle full of shepherds. In reality, Tancred had won control of the Armenian city Mamistra with the help of a local lord called Ursinus. As soon as the Turkish garrison in Mamistra had heard rumor of Tancred's approach, backed as he now was by Armenian allies, they had abandoned the place. After he arrived, Mamistra's Armenian citizens lined up to greet him and offer him an alliance. They also presented him with a great deal of the treasure left behind by the Turks, which Tancred distributed magnanimously to his followers. A few days later, Baldwin reached Mamistra and, apparently in a mood for compromise, asked for trading privileges. Tancred was inclined to agree—not to let him into the city but to allow him to barter with his new subjects. But not all of his men were as forgiving. "Ah Tancred!" one of them, Richard, Prince of Salerno, cried, "today you are the most worthless of men! You see Baldwin right there! By his treachery and jealousy you lost Tarsus. Ah! If you have an ounce of manhood left in you, you'll call up your men and bring down on him the same injury that he caused you!"[19]

What happened next is unclear. Whatever occurred, it reflected well on neither side. Either the two armies fought each other—prisoners were taken, and soldiers were killed—or else both sides lined up for battle, but neither was willing to engage the other. Whatever the case, prisoners were taken, and a few soldiers were killed. Barely a month after leaving the main army, Tancred's and Baldwin's crusade had become a war of Latin pilgrims against Latin pilgrims, meddling in Armenian and Turkish politics, with no very clear purpose or direction. The two groups may have been dispatched as part of an overarching "Armenian strategy" to secure local support necessary for the rest of the army to cross Anatolia, but they seem to have reverted quickly to stereotype—ill-tempered, small-minded European lords out to defend their pride and advance personal and familial reputations. Holy war was a fragile thing: Once outside the apocalyptic maelstrom of the main army, it was easy to lose sight of heavenly Jerusalem and its eternal rewards.

The day after the fighting in Mamistra, both Tancred and Baldwin reached this same conclusion, realizing "that they had both done wrong and had violated the devotion of the sacred road to Jerusalem." Prisoners were exchanged, plunder returned, and peace confirmed. Baldwin withdrew from Mamistra and left Tancred in control. "The whole thing could just be reduced to a nursery rhyme," Tancred's biographer Ralph of Caen observed: "*Finders keepers, losers weepers.*" Each side then at last made its own way toward the plain at the foot of the Taurus Mountains and toward the city of Marash, where the rest of the army awaited.[20]

Reassembling the Troops

Tancred and Baldwin, along with their followers, arrived at Marash around October 15, just after the main army had camped there upon crossing the Taurus Mountains. The numbers in both groups had diminished greatly. Some men had been lost to battle, others left behind in recently captured cities. The crusade had replenished its losses to a degree, having picked up a few Armenian recruits and advisors, as well as the two hundred Belgian pirates they had met outside Tarsus, but it was a much smaller army that prepared to march on Antioch.

The reunion of armies was not wholly joyous. At Marash Tancred learned that his uncle Bohemond had split from the army to investigate rumors of a roaming band of Turks, who were no doubt preparing some sort of trouble for the crusade. Baldwin likely was shocked to find his brother Godfrey bedridden, his massive, self-inflicted wound still not healed. They would have exchanged stories, Godfrey telling him about the illiterate peasant he'd saved from an enormous bear, Baldwin trying to put the best sheen on his falling out with Tancred and his subsequent abandonment of Tarsus. Baldwin also may have told Godfrey about the stories he had concocted during his diplomatic negotiations—how the Armenians now believed Godfrey not just a Lotharingian duke, but a Roman emperor armed with the sword of Vespasian. Godfrey, who recalled that Alexius had adopted him as a son and thus given him some claim to imperial title, must have appreciated that last detail. But Godfrey had sad news to pass on as well. In Baldwin's absence, his wife, Godevere, had contracted a disease that was still making the rounds among the soldiers, and she had recently died, buried outside Marash. It is impossible to guess what he felt upon hearing of his wife's death. She goes almost unmentioned in the medieval chronicles—unsurprising, considering how uninterested medieval military writers were in women. But that Baldwin had taken her on crusade at all suggests that he must have felt genuinely close to her, as does his leaving her with the main army rather than taking her on what promised to be a dangerous and undermanned expedition through Cilicia. The loss must have left him genuinely saddened and perhaps in doubt about whether his future lay in Jerusalem.[21]

As the army awaited Bohemond's return, Baldwin decided it was time to leave. He had accomplished great things in Cilicia and had shown a surprising knack for Eastern politics, successfully navigating the various ethnic, linguistic, and religious factions in southern Anatolia. Through the allies he had made in Cilicia, he learned that the Christians in northern Syria might be interested in recruiting him to resolve their own quarrels and to shore up their defenses against the Turks. Perhaps he could even establish his own lordship there and do some good for the pilgrimage at a distance.

One day's march beyond Marash and three days' march from Antioch, he broke away from the army. He took with him seven hundred knights, an unknown number of foot soldiers and servants, and at least one chaplain, Fulcher of Chartres, who had originally departed with Stephen of Blois but for unknown reasons decided to follow Baldwin in search of unknown goals in Syria. It might be that the experience of cowering inside a tent for hours at Dorylaeum waiting to die had proved too much for Fulcher. "Oh, battle!" Fulcher would write of a later conflict. "Hateful to the innocent, terrifying to those who see it. . . . I saw this battle. My mind trembled. I feared I would be wounded. Everyone rushed at one another's weapons as if they felt no terror at death. Such a cruel catastrophe, where there is no love." The siege of Antioch promised yet more dangerous encounters. The prospect of settling in a friendly Christian city must have appealed to him.[22]

At some point during all of these comings and goings (probably around the time of the army's arrival at Marash), Count Raymond of Saint-Gilles, long ailing, seemed finally ready to die. Bishop William of Orange performed last rites. And then something strange happened. Raymond of Aguilers knew his readers would be skeptical about this turn of events, but as a true miracle, he could not ignore it. "There was in our army," he wrote, "a count from Saxony. He went to Count Raymond and said that he was a legate of St. Gilles." St. Gilles, a seventh-century hermit venerated in Occitania and buried in the church of Saint-Gilles-du-Gard, was also, of course, Count Raymond's familial saint. St. Gilles had twice appeared to the Saxon count and told him to deliver a message to Raymond: "Be confident, for you shall not die from this disease. I have sought a truce for you with God, and I will always be with you."[23]

Nothing is known about this Saxon, including why he was with Raymond's army. Presumably, he had not originally departed with the count from southern France. He may have left with Godfrey and then abandoned the duke during his long illness (though it would be strange to leave one ailing leader for another). More likely he was a survivor of Peter the Hermit's fervent German followers or else a refugee from among Emicho's men. A true-believing apocalyptic or a cultist who looked to Jerusalem for the arrival of a Last Emperor, now he was receiving heavenly messages from the saints.

The appearance of such a man at Count Raymond's sickbed suggests two important points. First, the leadership may have been maintaining tight control over the army's more ecstatic members, but the spirit of Peter the Hermit was alive and well with some of the men. During the relatively peaceful days that followed Dorylaeum, characterized more by negotiation than conflict, they were still interacting with the powers of heaven, talking to saints and delivering their messages. Second, the pilgrims who had felt attracted to the ideals of Peter and Emicho were perhaps finding a new home among the Provençals. For as events would demonstrate, under the watch of Count Raymond and Bishop Adhémar, Urban II's handpicked leaders for the crusade, the most radical and visionary elements of the army were inventing their own doctrine of holy war and were aiming to seize control of the entire expedition.

9

Starvation and Nightmare: The Siege of Antioch Begins

(October 1097–January 1098)

During the siege of Antioch, the crusade became a full-fledged holy war. It is difficult to say exactly when this happened—the siege lasted eight months—but sometime during the army's sojourn at Antioch the rules of war completely changed.

When the Franks arrived, their leaders (and certainly Tetigus, their Greek advisor) were expecting to treat the city much as they had Nicea. As a recent Greek possession, it was subject to the terms of the oath that the Franks had sworn to Alexius at Constantinople. The crusaders also would have had some reason to expect Alexius eventually would meet them at Antioch or at least would send further military and logistic support, again as he had done at Nicea. Also just like Nicea, Antioch had a sizable Christian population, including Greek Christians, Armenians, and other local groups whom the Latins tended to lump into the general category of "Syrian." Considering all of the diplomacy in which the crusaders had engaged during the previous fourteen weeks, they were in theory well prepared to take advantage of these potential allies. If the crusade was able to implement another successful siege and force Antioch's defenders to capitulate, the crusaders could expect to march into the city, administer harsh justice to the Turks, and receive the adoring accolades of the Christians, schismatic though they might be. The Franks could then hand the city over to Alexius in exchange for new rewards and in doing so restore much of the territory that the empire had lost over the previous half-century. With the power of the Turks shattered and the Egyptians cowed by news of Frankish success, the crusaders might then undertake an easy, leisurely march to Jerusalem.

But Antioch was not Nicea. On a practical level, the city would be even more difficult to capture—perhaps outright impossible to take by force. It had enormous walls, "not able to be broken down by iron or stone, fashioned with an unheard of and unbreakable masonry and with a mass of great rocks." These walls, moreover, incorporated somewhere between 360 and 450 towers, according to the pilgrims' estimates. The actual figure was probably much lower, but the exaggeration gives us some sense of the city's imaginative impact, especially on Western observers accustomed to much smaller urban spaces.

Besides its towers, Antioch incorporated into its defenses four mountains and a massive citadel that reached hundreds of feet into the sky. Further complicating any potential attack was the Orontes River, which ran close along the city's west wall, dividing the territory around Antioch in half and thus complicating all ground movements. In Raymond of Aguilers's analysis (although this observation may belong to his collaborator, the knight Pons of Balazun), Antioch feared assaults from no army, no matter how well equipped, "even if every sort of man were to come out against it." Antioch could hold out as long as its inhabitants had bread to eat, and given the city's size and the character of its defenses, cutting off its food supply was nearly impossible. To warriors, however, there was something beautiful about these impenetrable defenses, even as they drove such admirers into starvation: "In every respect, the city is lovely."[1]

Antioch also exercised an imaginative appeal for the crusaders that far exceeded that of Nicea. Its importance was fundamental to the history of Christianity, being the first place where the word "Christian" had been used. It was the city where St. Peter had been bishop before leaving for Rome. It was a part of the Christian inheritance, more akin to Jerusalem than to Nicea. Indeed, that the army would want to claim the city for itself had always been a possibility. If the promised help from Alexius failed to arrive, anti-Greek voices and the ideas of the more radical and visionary pilgrims might start to carry the day.[2]

145

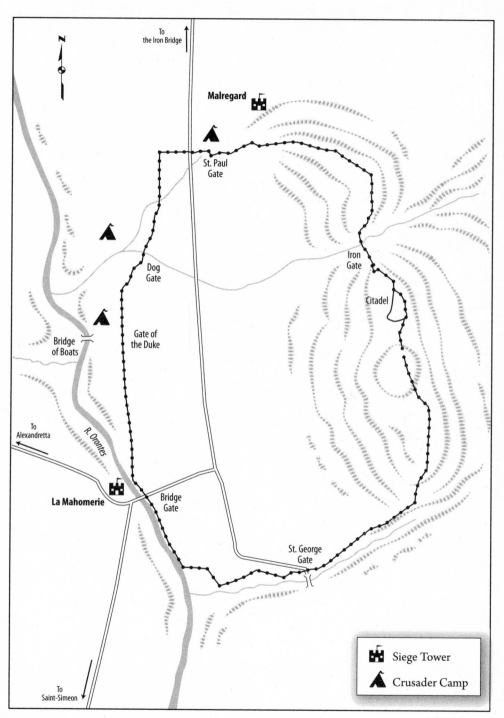

The city of Antioch

Cannibals and Severed Heads

Initially, the Franks had some hope of taking Antioch quickly, perhaps even without bloodshed. Before reaching the city, Raymond of Saint-Gilles, just recovered from his illness, heard rumor that the Turkish garrison had already abandoned Antioch. Holding a council of his own men, he decided to send five hundred soldiers in advance of the main army to see if the rumor was true and, if so, to take control of the city. This advance force discovered in the shadows of Antioch a castle held by the *Publicani*—likely an Armenian group whom the Franks could not otherwise identify except as heretics—who informed them that the Turks were still very much in charge of the city. The Turks, moreover, had learned of the Franks' approach and were currently preparing a vigorous defense. Raymond's men presumably sent the bad news back to their count. Most of them stayed near Antioch, trying to recruit to their cause Armenian Christians while also searching for some flaw in Antioch's forbidding defenses.[3]

As news of the city's defenses filtered back to the army, some leaders argued that they ought to postpone the siege until spring, when supplies might be more plentiful and when the much-anticipated aid from Alexius might finally arrive. But caution was not a virtue of God's army. Raymond of Saint-Gilles instead proposed an immediate attack. God had safely brought them this far. He had delivered the heavily fortified city of Nicea into their hands. "It would not be right for us to fear kings or the princes of kings, nor to tremble because of places and times, since the Lord has delivered us from so many dangers." Raymond's voice, and others, carried the argument, and the army marched on. Perhaps as soon as that same day, about twelve miles from Antioch, near a great stone bridge with iron gates—known as "the Iron Bridge"—that spanned the Orontes River, they encountered the first of Antioch's defenders.

According to French sources, it was a short battle. The Turkish garrison at the bridge was unprepared. The Turks saw the Franks, panicked, and ran. But Lotharingian soldiers had a very different memory of the engagement. It was a long and bloody fight, and the Franks won only after Bishop Adhémar thundered out in the voice of God, "Do not fear the blows of your adversary! Stand fast like men! Beat back these biting dogs! For today God fights for you!"[4]

The next day, October 21, 1097, the siege proper began. God's will or not, it was going to be a long, incremental affair. The crusaders could not begin to shut down the city as they had done at Nicea. The best they could do was to keep an eye on the walls that did not abut the mountains or the river. In line with this limited goal, they set camps around the northwest quadrant of the city, along the Orontes River, while also scouting out possible sources of food—which, at this early stage, proved surprisingly abundant. Meanwhile, Raymond of Saint-Gilles's men constructed a bridge of boats spanning the Orontes. It served both to control Turkish movement from one of the city gates—the "Bridge Gate"—and to enable the Franks to travel more easily to and from the nearby port of Saint-Simeon. The latter point was crucial since as the siege dragged on the crusaders would be dependent for survival upon goods shipped from Constantinople and Europe. (The first supply ships from Genoa arrived on November 17.)

The Franks seem to have carried out these projects in relative safety. For the first two weeks of the siege, the defenders of Antioch stayed behind their walls, waiting to see exactly what the Franks were up to while also anticipating the arrival of outside help from one of two sources. Before the Franks' appearance, the Turkish governor of Antioch, Yaghi-Siyan, had been able to preserve his independence by playing off against each other the more powerful cities of Aleppo and Damascus. Since 1096 two rival brothers, Ridwan of Aleppo and Duqaq of Damascus, had controlled the cities and had been at war with one another for control of Syria after their father's death. Now with Antioch under siege, Yaghi-Siyan began making diplomatic overtures to each brother, hoping one or the other might come to his aid. It would be over two months before one of them did.

As far as the crusaders could tell, this was simply a time of tranquility and abundance—perhaps too much of a good thing. In the eyes of the chaplain Raymond of Aguilers, such prosperity was a source of trouble. Discipline in camps grew so slack that the leaders weren't even bothering to post watches. The enemy could have inflicted a mortal blow on the army if they had but known to attack. This time of leisure, in Raymond's eyes, also exacerbated social divisions within the army. "Everyone wished only for his own private advantage. About the public good, they thought nothing."[5]

Once the Turks realized how carelessly the Franks were behaving, they began to make frequent raids on the camps, sometimes from the city but mainly from elsewhere. For a time the Franks couldn't figure out where the attacks were coming from. They knew only that large numbers of pilgrims were going missing, particularly the poor and unarmed who were wandering about foraging for food. News of these deaths grieved "the wealthier" members of the army, who realized that wicked men were boldly "unsheathing bloody swords" and using them to kill "saintly people."

At first, the Franks blamed the Antiochene Christians rather than the Turks. Many of these "Armenians and Syrians" claimed to have fled the city to seek shelter with the Franks. But the crusaders believed that the ostensible refugees were spies, relaying intelligence back to the city about the army's dispositions and its more vulnerable points of defense. Something had to be done about this "perfidious people."[6]

But the problem wasn't limited to Christian spies. Attacks were also coming from another location, toward the east. The task of finding these villains was assigned to Bohemond, who set out east on November 18, the day after supply ships had arrived from Genoa, accompanied by Robert of Flanders and 150 knights. In short order, Bohemond and his men discovered a garrison of Turks at the castle of Harim, about twenty miles from Antioch on the road to Aleppo. Once Bohemond had located the castle, he elected to employ against it a venerable tactic, used regularly by Turks and Normans alike. That is, he sent a small advance guard to harass the city and draw out its defenders. These men then pretended to retreat. It was no less dangerous a maneuver for being feigned. Two of the Franks were killed while falling back. The rest, however, led the Turks directly into an ambush by the greater part of the expedition. Bohemond, "Christ's most powerful athlete," led the charge, killing many Turks and taking the rest prisoner.[7]

It was a classic, even clichéd military tactic. Bohemond's follow-up to the victory, however, would prove more memorable, and controversial. Upon returning to the camp, he led all of the prisoners "to the city gate and decapitated them, in order to render sad those who were in the city." According to one later source, he then catapulted the heads into the city to make his message clearer still.[8]

Although the Franks had engaged in public, even theatrical beheadings at Nicea, they did not commonly desecrate the dead after victory in
battle. Under normal conditions, the Franks would not have employed
such tactics blithely. Decapitation was a violent act that the wicked inflicted upon saints, not a punishment that saints used against the wicked.
When the Franks thought about severed heads, they thought about the
martyrs whom the Romans had executed: for example, St. Denis, who,
after being decapitated outside medieval Paris atop Montmartre, carried
his head to a nearby town where a church would be founded in his honor.
The figure of a headless Denis was one of the most recognizable statues
throughout the Frankish heartland. In more recent history, even licit beheadings could have significant, and unintended, repercussions. In 1076
William the Conqueror ordered the decapitation of one of his political
adversaries, Earl Waltheof, who had repeatedly conspired and rebelled
against William's rule in England. Granted time to say the Lord's Prayer
before his death, Waltheof understandably stumbled over the last words.
He stuttered and stuttered and his executioners grew impatient, until one
of them drew a sword and chopped off the traitor's head. As the skull hit
the ground, its lips moved again and said, "But deliver us from evil. Amen."
So traumatic was the memory of Waltheof's execution that he gained a
wholly unearned reputation for sanctity. In the eleventh-century Latin
world, princes had occasion to cut off their subjects' heads, but it was not
a punishment that came easily. By 1097 it seemed a foreign practice.[9]

That is at least what Frankish writers liked to believe. The crusaders
wouldn't have cut off so many heads if the Saracens had not forced them
to do so. About a slightly later battle fought outside Antioch, the chronicler
Guibert of Nogent recounted that Bohemond ordered his followers to
hang up one hundred severed heads before the city walls to demoralize
the defenders. But then Guibert felt that some further explanation was
needed: "For this is the custom of the gentiles"—a biblical term for non-
Jews that Latin Christians regularly applied to Muslims—"they typically
set aside severed heads and display them as a sign of victory." By inference, the Franks would not have done such a thing if the Turks had not
taught them, or forced them, to do so (perhaps starting at Nicomedia,
where they had left unburied the headless bodies of Peter the Hermit's

St. Denis holds his own head in his hands, from the cathedral of Notre Dame in Paris. (Archive Timothy McCarthy/Art Resource)

followers). Other writers similarly stressed that this style of execution was fundamentally Turkish, lamenting that the enemy had decapitated local Christians and flung their heads into the Franks' camp or else that after one skirmish before the city gates the Turks had snuck out in the night to cut off the heads of dead Christians so that they could fling them back into the camp the next morning.[10]

How useful for the Franks were such practices? As with modern debates about torture, people disagreed. Baudry of Bourgueil, a worldly, urbane writer who never traveled to the East but who based his chronicle in part on eyewitness testimony, described the decapitations as pointless. They rendered the citizens "more savage," inspiring them to seek new heights from which to rain down arrows on the Franks. Specifically in response to this incident, they shot a Frankish woman dead, directly in front of Bohemond's tent.

Another writer working at the same time, Robert the Monk, saw the decapitations as legitimate. After Bohemond's savage gesture, it became easier for the soldiers and pilgrims to travel around the area—in part because of the discovery of the Turks' hiding place at Harim but also in part because of the fear that the executions had inspired.

Yet another European writer described the decapitations approvingly and mentioned elsewhere that Bishop Adhémar of le Puy, the Franks' spiritual leader, offered twelve *denarii* for each Saracen head brought to his tent so that he might stick it on a post. Like Bohemond, the bishop hoped that such a spectacle would frighten the city into surrender. Becoming "holy warriors" required that the crusaders on some level change their identities. And part of that change was that they learned to enjoy or appreciate the value of mass decapitations and desecrations of the enemy dead.[11]

At about the same time (according to a historian writing about seventy-five years later), Bohemond promised his fellow leaders that he would deal with their other major problem—the Antiochene spies in the crusader camp. After some careful thought, he ordered executioners to cut the throats of a handful of Turkish prisoners and then to have their bodies roasted on spits and prepared as if for a feast. Should anyone ask what was happening, Bohemond ordered his men to reply that henceforth anytime the army's leaders captured Turkish soldiers or spies, the cooks would roast them and serve them for dinner. All spies, naturally, fled the camp and spread word to Antioch and all over the region: "This people, for brutality, surpass not just all other nations, but even wild animals. It is not enough for them to rob their enemies of cities, castles, and all their wealth; it is not enough to cast them into chains, to torture them more cruelly than their enemies would do, and even kill them! No, they also fill their bellies with their enemies' flesh and grow fat off their lard!" The spy problem was thus solved, and the Turks had learned a terrifying lesson about who their enemies were and what it meant to be both a Christian and a warrior.[12]

Thanks to the giant Bohemond, then, the poor pilgrims were safer from Turkish attacks, but no less hungry. The springs of charity from the aristocracy must have begun to dry up fairly early into the siege as the warriors realized that they needed to conserve their own resources. Traveling too far beyond the camps to forage for food would have been a dangerous proposition. Resources had to be conserved, which meant that the poorest elements in the crusade host faced starvation.

Eventually—we do not know how early or late into the siege—the commoners may have begun to think on Bohemond's pantomimed feast and to see within it the easiest possible response to their situation. "There were some who nourished bodies with bodies, feeding on human flesh, but far away and in the mountains, lest others take offense at the smell of cooked meat." Cannibalism remained, at least at Antioch, a point of shame for the armies. Mass beheadings and desecration of the enemy dead, on the other hand, were becoming routine.[13]

The Crusade in Winter

Despite the ever-increasing levels of brutality, at the end of November the army remained optimistic. It had turned back challenges from the Antiochene defenders, and it had received its first major infusion of supplies from the Genoese ships. This included not just food but also building materials, thereby enabling the construction of further siege equipment to complement the bridge of boats over the Orontes.

The next major project, undertaken after Bohemond had roasted but did not eat—probably did not eat—Turkish prisoners, was the building of a wooden tower on a hill on the northern side of the city. The containment of Antioch was far from complete, but such a tower would at least enable the Franks to keep a closer watch on their enemy and even to look over Antioch's walls. They called the structure, appropriately, "Malregard"—roughly, "Evil Eye." Well supplied, thus far victorious, and continually extending and tightening their encirclement of Antioch's walls, the crusaders might well have imagined themselves on the verge of a relatively quick victory.[14]

But December was a long and uneventful month, with little further progress after the completion of Malregard. As Christmas approached, so, too, did fears of mass starvation. The countryside had been picked bare. The friendly Christian populations had run out of food or else were hoarding supplies to get through the winter. Supply expeditions grew evermore wide-ranging, with pilgrims traveling forty or fifty miles from camp in search of nourishment. How many Franks were surreptitiously slipping into the mountains with bodies and body parts of the recently deceased is anyone's guess.

Some of the crusaders, including princes, temporarily abandoned the siege. Robert of Normandy, for example, headed toward the Byzantine coastal city of Latakia late in December, apparently invited to stay there by Anglo-Saxon mercenaries who were serving on Alexius's behalf. Other pilgrims left the siege and never returned. Godfrey of Bouillon stayed but fell ill again, and camp conditions turned steadily unbearable: "Then the starving people devoured the stalks of beans still growing in the fields, many kinds of herbs unseasoned with salt and even thistles which, because of the lack of firewood were not well cooked and therefore scraped up the tongues of those eating them. They also ate horses, asses, camels, dogs, and even rats. The poorer people devoured the hides of animals and the seeds of grain found in dung heaps." On Christmas Day the crusaders as much as possible stayed in their tents for a furtive celebration. After a promising six weeks, the situation had become hopeless.[15]

The leaders, at least those who were still present and healthy, developed two responses—one rooted in this world and one aimed at the next. On a practical level, Bohemond and Robert of Flanders agreed to lead a major foraging expedition just after Christmas. On an idealistic level, probably at the instruction of Adhémar of le Puy, they decided that the army had to take responsibility for its own plight. Fulcher of Chartres, who had abandoned the main army with Baldwin of Boulogne a little over two months earlier, wrote with a certain comfortable priggishness, "We felt that misfortunes had befallen the Franks because of their sins and that for this reason they were not able to take the city for so long a time. Luxury and avarice and pride and plunder had indeed impeded them." This suffering served in effect both as punishment and purification. The crusaders were being burned like gold in a furnace, cleansed of sins through suffering and made all the mightier as warriors of God. The leaders further declared, in consultation with bishops and priests, that "all injustice and corruption" would be driven from the camp. Only fair prices would be charged, moneychangers would be strictly regulated, no theft would be tolerated, and anyone caught committing adultery, or just having sex, would be severely punished. "A man and a woman were found committing adultery there and were paraded nude before the army. With their hands tied behind their backs, men with lashes whipped them severely, and then the couple was forced to walk around the army so that everyone could see their severe wounds and be deterred from committing a similar wicked crime." Just in case deterrence did not work, all of the women were temporarily exiled. It was time, apparently, for holy warriors to earn the right to the title.[16]

The new moral code no doubt focused the crusaders' sense of purpose, but it did not feed them. Neither, unfortunately, did the foraging expedition. Accounts of what happened are vague, probably deliberately so. On Monday, December 28, Bohemond and Robert of Flanders set out with about two hundred knights and, probably, one thousand infantry, heading into Syria. Their goals were twofold—to gather as much plunder as possible and to clear the roads of Turkish armies so that the Frankish poor might be able to wander about and gather food in peace.

For three days the plan worked, and the armies seem to have captured enough food to supply the camp for weeks to come. But Bohemond and Robert did not realize that a Turkish relief force had finally answered Yaghi-Siyan's calls for help. Led from Damascus by the Seljuk amir Duqaq, these warriors were marching toward Antioch when, unexpectedly, they walked almost directly into the middle of Bohemond and Robert's expedition. According to one account, the Turks took flight almost immediately, realizing they could not hope to defeat Bohemond. According to another, the Turks caught the Frankish expedition completely unawares, as Bohemond was blissfully sleeping the night away. When he and the others awakened, they panicked. All of the knights, at least, escaped, but the foot soldiers, who were guarding the supplies, were massacred. Robert of Flanders eventually recovered a small portion of the plunder, but owing to the giant's carelessness and cowardice, the foraging expedition had come to naught.[17]

The situation was perhaps worse at the city. A significant number of the knights were away from the camps. Most of those who stayed didn't have horses and thus were reduced to the status of infantry. Godfrey of Bouillon was sick, and Robert of Normandy and his followers were away at Latakia. The crusader camp was badly undermanned, and the defenders of Antioch knew that a relief force was imminent. On December 29 they attacked. Count Raymond, according to his chaplain, crossed the bridge of boats and gave chase to the Turks, killing two of them. The sight of the count's courage inspired his foot soldiers to boldness, or perhaps foolishness. They abandoned their stations, threw down their standards, and followed the count to the Bridge Gate, throwing spears, rocks, and whatever else they could find at their enemies. The Turks then started to push back, both on the bridge and at a nearby ford in the Orontes.

It was close combat of the sort that should have favored the Franks, but something went wrong. According to the chaplain Raymond, a Provençal knight, who was trying to ride around the Frankish infantry and engage the Turks more directly, was thrown from his horse. The horse then wheeled around and sensibly tried to flee, causing several knights to pursue it lest the animal escape—warhorses were a precious commodity. The infantry, who had no banners and no real leaders, thought that the knights had surrendered and the day was lost, and began a panicked re-treat. It could have been worse. According to Count Raymond's chaplain, no more than fifteen knights and twenty foot soldiers were killed, among them Bishop Adhémar of le Puy's standard-bearer. But in the chaplain's eyes, they made a pathetic sight. The defeat was a "palpable shame" for the army, a punishment from God intended to call to true repentance the minds of the knights, whose thoughts were otherwise adulterous and bent on plunder.[18]

The armies at the gate were humiliated. Leadership was in disarray. Raymond of Saint-Gilles once more fell ill and withdrew to his tent. Ca-tastrophe and the end of the crusade seemed suddenly inevitable.

Then God spoke. The day after the retreat from the Bridge Gate, there was an earthquake—a great trembling of the land. The same night, shortly after sunset, "the heavens turned so red in the north that it seemed like dawn was ushering in the day." Fulcher saw it, too, from wherever Bald-win's army had camped in Syria: "At that time we saw a wondrous red color in the heavens; we also felt a great earthquake, which made us not a little frightened. Many then saw another sign, in the shape of a cross, white in color, cutting a path straight for the east." The visionaries in Fulcher's army could not have viewed these signs in a positive light. They had abandoned the road to Jerusalem in the name of some vaguely defined goals in Syria. The meaning of a heavenly cross flying quickly to the East (in brief: "You are going in the wrong way!") would have been obvious. As for the other signs, an educated cleric like Raymond or Fulcher would have likely turned to the Bible, perhaps to the book of the Apocalypse, where he would have read, or half-remembered, the description of the breaking of the sixth seal: "Lo! There was a great earthquake; and the sun became black as sackcloth, and the moon became as blood." The stars would soon fall from the heavens, and the kings, the great men, the rich men of the earth would retreat to the mountains and hide, begging for rocks to fall on them and kill them. Or they might have read the signs more simply, as did an observer in the Syrian city of Edessa: "It was an omen of bloodshed." The celestial activity was also visible in Europe. In Normandy people looked at the sky and shouted, "The East fights!" All agreed, as if with one voice, that signs in the heavens pointed toward war and blood on earth.

What the Lord's verdict about the siege of Antioch was, no one clearly understood. But everyone in the world had heard, or seen, Him speak.[19]

A Visionary's First Nightmare

That same night, a starving, barely literate pilgrim named Peter Bartholomew (not to be confused with the more famous crusade visionary Peter the Hermit) fell asleep and into a dream that would eventually re-make the crusade. After the initial earthquake, he ran into a little hut he had set up with some friends. Alone now and terrified, he just kept saying over and over again, "God help me. God help me." The aftershocks continued into the night, and Peter grew still more terrified until finally he fell asleep or else slipped into a trance. Two men stood before him. One was older, with red and white hair, a long bushy beard, and black eyes that seemed to suit his face. The other one was younger, taller, strikingly handsome.

The old man spoke first. "What are you doing?"

Peter, fearful and confused, answered with a question, "And who are you?"

"Get up," he said, "and don't be afraid. Listen to what I'm about to say: I am the apostle Andrew."[20]

What made Peter Bartholomew think of St. Andrew in this crisis is uncertain. Andrew was the brother of St. Peter, who had been bishop of Antioch before leaving for Rome. As the crusaders would later discover, some of Andrew's bones were kept inside the city. If Peter had been one of the ones lucky enough to be allowed into Constantinople, he could have prayed before some of Andrew's relics as well.

But there may have been a more immediate reason to associate this apostle with the siege of Antioch. Several apocryphal events from Andrew's later life had grown into a grand tale of adventure popular among medieval audiences. The settings and the characters were exotic enough to qualify it as a knightly romance. Andrew's most famous exploit involved his rescue of the apostle Matthew, who had been taken prisoner in the East in the land of the Mermedonians, a race of cannibals. It was in such a place, populated similarly by cannibals, in a campsite decorated by severed heads stuck on spears, that Peter Bartholomew found himself in February 1098 as the earth trembled and the skies turned blood-red. Perhaps in his dreams he fantasized that Andrew might be for him, like Matthew, a saintly liberator from a world inhabited by flesh-eating men.[21]

But St. Andrew had not come to rescue Peter Bartholomew. Rather, he wanted to charge him with a mission that, if carried out, could save the army. First, Peter was to call a meeting of the Provençal leaders, including Count Raymond and Bishop Adhémar, and he was to reprimand Adhémar for failing at his most crucial job. "Why does he not preach to the people and scold them and bless them daily with the cross he carries? It would benefit them greatly." But then Andrew changed tone altogether. "Come," he said, "I want to show you the lance of our father Jesus Christ, and you are going to give it to Count Raymond, as indeed God has intended to do since Raymond's birth."

The object to which Andrew referred was "the Holy Lance"—the weapon with which a Roman soldier, traditionally named Longinus, had pierced Christ's side during the Crucifixion. It was one of the most celebrated relics of the Passion—along with the True Cross, the Crown of Thorns, and the nails of the Crucifixion—and like those other relics, multiple churches (and both the Western and Eastern emperors) claimed to possess it. No tradition survived of Christians venerating the Holy Lance at Antioch, but, of course, Peter Bartholomew would be able to claim a source for his story higher than any mere book.

St. Andrew then guided Peter, wearing only a nightshirt (like so many dreamers, he was out in public in his pajamas), away from his hut and over the city walls. Together they approached a church—one Peter had obviously never seen while awake but with which he would grow familiar later on—and entered through its north door, passing through a "Mahomerie," or mosque, that the Saracens had built in the entryway. Inside the church two lamps were burning. Andrew guided Peter to a column near the high altar and said, "Wait here." He then ascended the steps and approached the altar from the south side. As he did, Peter noticed the apostle's younger companion standing silently by. Andrew reached toward the ground, his hands miraculously sinking beneath the earth, and then suddenly, magically, he pulled forth a long and exotic-looking spear. "Behold!" he said, "the lance that tore open Christ's side, from which salvation rained down on the earth." Andrew placed the Holy Lance in Peter's hands, and Peter wept copiously, promising to take it to Count Raymond.

But December was not the time, Andrew informed him. Peter would have to wait until the army had actually captured the city. Then he could guide Count Raymond, Bishop Adhémar, and twelve chosen men into the church. If they dug in the exact place that Andrew had indicated, they would find the Lance and be victorious against the Saracens. Andrew then reburied his treasure, guided Peter Bartholomew back into the city, over the walls, and to the camp, and left him in his little hut, bleary-eyed, wonderstruck, and more than a little frightened. Alone, Peter meditated on his dream. He looked at his own poor, ragged clothes and then thought about how magnificent Raymond and Adhémar always appeared as they paraded among the troops. And he feared to go to them. The story of the Lance would remain secret, at least for a few months longer.[22]

Two days later Bohemond's troops started to return, first with no food at all, then with the pitifully small collection of supplies that Robert of Flanders had been able to secure. An unknown number of soldiers had died. The army continued to starve. Armenian merchants, distastefully pleased at the crusaders' plight, began to engage in price gouging, unmoved as poor pilgrims fell dead in front of them from starvation. Bishop Adhémar, lacking guidance from St. Andrew, did not bless the troops with his cross. Rather, he declared a fast. For three days the starving soldiers would have to avoid food. And one starving pilgrim, Peter Bartholomew, kept his fearful secret to himself.[23]

An Apocalyptic Failure

Peter's caution was justified. It was a bad time to be a prophet in the army. God was angry, the poor were dying, and the leaders were little by little disappearing. Robert of Normandy had temporarily deserted the army, Raymond and Godfrey were ill, and now even the giant Bohemond had begun making noise that he might have to abandon the expedition since he could not bear to witness the suffering of his men. It was enough to make a person believe that God was not, in fact, on the Franks' side or, even worse, that the army's sins were so great that there was no point in seeking absolution. And thus the most visionary of all the pilgrims— the other, more famous Peter, called "the Hermit"—decided that he, too, had been wrong, and on the night of January 20 he snuck away from camp, taking with him as a companion that artist with the ax, William the Carpenter, who had joined the expedition because of the wild promises of Emicho of Flonheim that he would establish a new kingdom in Jerusalem, from which he would rule the world and do battle with Antichrist.

Rumor of their departure quickly reached Tancred. He had both the Hermit and the Carpenter hunted down and brought back to his tent. It was a high-level desertion and would require an appropriately severe and public response. Tancred therefore called in his oversized uncle Bohemond, who directed his rage, as far as we can tell, mainly against the Carpenter. A warrior's desertion probably seemed to Bohemond and Tancred a more serious matter than did that of a crackpot preacher. "Oh, you sad and disgraceful man, shame of all France," Bohemond thundered. "You Gallic outrage! The earth suffers no more wretched man than you! Why did you flee so outrageously?" William promised not to do it again, and after many of his friends begged for his life, Bohemond reluctantly agreed not to do William physical harm. Nevertheless, the giant branded him with the mark of Cain: "For the rest of the days of your life, you shall be held as a disgrace throughout the lands." William's promises were for naught as it turned out, for a few days later he deserted for good, this time without Peter. Furious, Bohemond ordered the Carpenter's tent turned into a latrine.[24]

Peter the Hermit stayed with the army, but at least a few of his critics must have taken delight at the stories of his near desertion. "As stars seemed to fall from the heaven in the book of the Apocalypse," one of them later wrote, "so that Peter, a most famous hermit, gave into foolishness and departed." Perhaps the apocalypse Peter had once hoped to ignite was beginning to fail as well.[25]

10

A Brief Account of Baldwin
of Boulogne's Adventures in Syria

(February 1098–March 1098)

While the rest of the army was starving, Baldwin of Boulogne, brother of the still-ailing Godfrey, was creating what would become known as the first of the "crusader states." His activity in Syria would eventually provide real, tangible benefits to the main army, bogged down as it was in the long siege of Antioch. But he was probably not moving with any real sense of urgency or purpose, apart from seeking opportunity for himself. That he would find in abundance in February and March when he miraculously transformed into a Syrian count.

About the early stages of this process, the historical record is hazy. Between his departure from the crusade in October 1097 and his reemergence in the historical record in February 1098, his chaplain, the much-admired historian Fulcher of Chartres, observed only that Baldwin captured several cities, some by guile and some by force. He did so with the help of an Armenian advisor named Bagrat, whom Baldwin eventually rewarded with the possession of a grand fortress called Rawandan. The two men subsequently had a falling out when other Armenian lords warned Baldwin that Bagrat was conspiring against him with the Turks. Baldwin had Bagrat thrown in irons and threatened to tear him limb from limb unless he willingly returned his possessions. Once Bagrat's son surrendered control of Rawandan, Baldwin released the father and continued his restless travels, "everywhere conquering the land and subjecting it to his power."

These brief bits of information allow us to see, if nothing else, that Baldwin was continuing to do in Syria what he had tried to do in Cilicia: play politics and, through intimidation more than actual force, assert his authority over as many people and places as possible. This time he was able to do so with no interference from Tancred, and he seems to have found several petty local lords willing and anxious to work with him as a way to advance their own careers. His activities were not exactly the glamorous stuff of holy war, but they were profitable, and Baldwin was proving himself astonishingly adept at working within the Armenian system.[1]

Around February 1 his fortunes took a turn that even he could scarcely have imagined. An embassy arrived from T'oros, the Armenian prince of the city of Edessa, asking Baldwin for military assistance. In return, T'oros offered immediate financial reward, indicating that he might even cede to Baldwin some more permanent authority. Possibly, the ambassadors added, given that T'oros had no children of his own, he might even name Baldwin his heir.

It was a proposal as attractive as it was unexpected. Edessa was a wealthy, well-fortified city, blessed with abundant vineyards, fruit trees, and olive groves, as well as established industries in cotton and silk cloth. Edessa's history stretched back into myth. Muslim tradition held that it was the birthplace of Abraham. Between Abraham's birth and 1097, all of the major Western and Eastern civilizations had conquered it—Greeks, Arabs, Romans, and Persians, to name a few. In the fifty years preceding the crusades, the Byzantines, the Turks, and the Armenians had held it at different times. T'oros, in fact, had only established himself as leader there in 1095, after driving out a Turkish governor who in turn had only recently wrested the city from Armenian rule. Surrounded by independent Armenian warlords and aggressively expanding Turkish princes, T'oros needed all the help he could get, and Baldwin of Boulogne had in a short time put together an impressive résumé.[2]

Taking with him only eighty knights, Baldwin crossed the Euphrates and traveled by night toward Edessa, hoping to avoid the Turkish camps scattered throughout the area. After a further four-day delay while his small force waited out a planned ambush from a much larger Turkish army, Baldwin and his men finally began something of a triumphal procession toward Edessa. Villagers lined the roads leading to the city and cheered them on. They carried crosses and battle standards, and as the Franks passed close by, they threw themselves to the ground and kissed their feet and the hems of the garments, hoping to be liberated, if not from the Turks, then at least from the political chaos that had engulfed the region. Similarly before the walls of Edessa, a crowd rushed out, exuberantly sounding trumpets and making a joyful noise unto the Lord.

T'oros, his wife, and his twelve closest advisors offered Baldwin formal greetings. So exotic were their dress and demeanor that they looked like something from ancient Rome, and Baldwin and his followers soon decided that these advisors must surely have been Edessa's senators. Feeling himself, no doubt, like a victorious Roman general, he led his Frankish legion through the gates and graciously accepted comfortable lodging.[3]

Later, T'oros summoned Baldwin and the twelve senators to a council. As it transpired, the prince of Edessa's terms were not as generous as they had originally sounded. He was willing to pay Baldwin handsomely in money, treasure, and silks provided that Baldwin fought on his behalf, but he was not willing to give Baldwin a position in the government, let alone any control over tax revenues. Baldwin refused the offer outright and instead asked for safe conduct so that he might rejoin his brother at Antioch. The senators and other leading men of the city erupted in anger on Baldwin's behalf, demanding that T'oros honor his original promises. Under pressure from all sides, he relented, not only accepting Baldwin into the government, but also agreeing to adopt him as his son and to name him as heir. So deftly did Baldwin handle this situation that one must presume that he had received good advice from local power brokers about how best to exploit T'oros's situation. One also suspects that there was something unsavory about the whole affair—deals had been struck behind the scenes that no one subsequently wished to acknowledge. Fulcher of Chartres, Baldwin's chaplain, seemed deliberately vague when describing these events, glossing over any difficulties in the negotiations with T'oros and saying only that the city and its prince fulfilled their promises without delay.[4]

The adoption ceremony was a public affair and, from the Franks' perspective, a strange one. Stripped down to the waist, Baldwin stood next to T'oros, himself wearing a long linen shirt. T'oros raised this garment up and over Baldwin's head so that the two men stood next to each other, bare chest to bare chest, and they exchanged promises, oaths, and mutual pledges of support, all sealed with a kiss. T'oros's wife gave Baldwin a kiss, too, and with that he was formally welcomed into the family of the prince of Edessa. He was therefore the second member of his family to be adopted by an Eastern lord, after Godfrey, who maintained that Alexius had made him his son during the exchange of oaths in Constantinople.[5]

Baldwin's adoption, however, yielded more immediate rewards than Godfrey's. He engaged in only one act of real service for T'oros, leading a brief campaign against the nearby fortress of Samosata and its Turkish leader, Balduk. Nothing much was accomplished there, and Baldwin quickly returned to Edessa, where a small group of dignitaries approached him in secret to express their displeasure with T'oros's leadership. They were confident that Baldwin could do a better job of protecting their interests. Succinctly put, just two weeks after the adoption, they planned to lynch Baldwin's new father and proclaim Baldwin prince in his place.

According to the Frankish version of the story, Baldwin reacted with horror: "It would be an irredeemable sin if I were to raise my hand against this man after just accepting him as my father and to whom I have pledged faith." The citizens then agreed to give Baldwin a little time to convince his foster father to resign for the benefit of the community. Baldwin ran to the tower and pleaded with T'oros. "All the citizens and leaders of this city are conspiring to kill you," he said, "and are coming here to this tower in a rage and impassioned, carrying every sort of weapon. I'm sorry to bring you such bad news." Even as he spoke, a crowd surrounded the tower, firing arrows, throwing rocks, and screaming death threats at the prince.

With Baldwin acting as intermediary, T'oros tried to buy the citizens off with promises of riches. But their bloodlust had become too intense. Baldwin, so the story goes, refused to give up and wanted to continue fighting for his father, driven on by "Frankish animosity." But T'oros, full of sadness and apparently full of love for his new child, miserably and tearfully told him to stop resisting; he preferred to die. T'oros lowered himself down from his window on a rope, into the hands of a waiting mob, who proceeded to beat him to death. They cut off his head and carried it around on a spear, allowing anyone who wished to spit in T'oros' face and insult it. And the next day they proclaimed a reluctant Baldwin to be their new "prince and duke of the city."[6]

A more likely interpretation, of course, is that Baldwin was complicit in the entire conspiracy. So argued a different version of the story that survives from an Armenian historian from Edessa. With Maundy Thursday fast approaching, forty citizens came together and plotted a Judas-like act of betrayal, assassinating the leader who had through "his ingenious sagacity, skillful inventiveness, and vigorous strength" delivered the city from the cruel dominion of the Turks barely three years earlier. During the night they went to Baldwin and "persuaded him to accede to their evil designs and promised to deliver Edessa into his hands; Baldwin approved of their vicious plot." And so on March 8, 1098, the forty traitors incited a crowd of citizens to attack the tower. T'oros commanded enough loyalty to put up a credible resistance, and he ultimately promised to surrender provided that the people gave him and his wife free passage out of Edessa. Perhaps at T'oros's request, Baldwin took an oath not to harm him, having a fragment of the True Cross brought forward so that he could swear not to do him injury. "Moreover, Baldwin vouched for his own sincerity in the presence of the angels, archangels, prophets, patriarchs, holy apostles, holy pontiffs, and all the host of martyrs—all of which was written down by the count in a letter to T'oros." Baldwin then moved his men into the tower.

The next day, March 9, a small gathering of the citizens of Edessa surrounded T'oros, probably while he was still in the tower and in theory under Baldwin's protection. A few of them threatened him with swords before someone with a club knocked him to the ground, allowing everyone to converge on him and kick him and beat him and then throw him over a rampart, still alive, into the midst of a mob. The people of Edessa beat and stabbed him to death, presumably with Baldwin watching from above. Still not satisfied, the crowd tied their dead prince's feet together and dragged his bloody body by a rope throughout the city, giving everyone the chance to desecrate and dishonor it as he wished.[7]

These two stories are broadly similar, differing mainly in how direct a role Baldwin played in T'oros's death. The man who knew Baldwin's heart best, his chaplain Fulcher, left his account deliberately vague. "The citizens criminally planned to kill their prince and to raise Baldwin in the palace so that he might rule the land. They certainly hated their prince. So it was said, so it was done. Baldwin was very sad about it, but had not been able to obtain any indulgence for him. When they had wickedly killed him, Baldwin accepted the principate as a gift from the citizens and immediately made war against the Turks who were then in that country, whom he again and again conquered and killed and overcame."

Baldwin's first act as prince of Edessa, in fact, was to return to Samosata and, upon the advice of his men, to offer the Turk Balduk a substantial bribe in gold, silver, purple cloth, and horses and mules if he turned over the fortress to him. "From that day forward, Balduk became a subject of Baldwin's, a member of his household, and a regular companion among Gallic men." Far from taking the war to the Turks, Baldwin allied himself with a former religious and political enemy and welcomed him into his household.[8]

Baldwin's activity in Edessa was not quite a conquest and certainly not a proper victory. Nevertheless, it brought the First Crusade immediate advantage. Baldwin opened up a supply line to the armies, alleviating much of the economic hardship they had endured throughout the long winter. Even so, we cannot conclude from this observation that Baldwin's adventures in Edessa were part of a grand plan designed to advance the goals of the crusade. Considering what Baldwin actually did do—abandon the pilgrimage to which he had vowed himself, leaving his two brothers potentially to starve at Antioch, venturing off with a small band of supporters and unbelievably establishing himself as prince of an ancient Near Eastern city—we can scarcely imagine how he would have understood his own goals during the winter months of 1098. What is clear is that Baldwin did not act as a conqueror. Rather, he recognized the complexities of Syrian politics, and he successfully inserted himself into that world. He learned to adapt to his new situation, which, given the utterly alien cultural landscape in which he found himself, was a remarkable achievement.

In December 1099 Baldwin would complete his pilgrimage to Jerusalem. A few months later, he would actually become king of Jerusalem. But after successfully scheming and manipulating his way into the leadership of Edessa in March 1098, he was, for all intents and purposes, an Armenian ruler. He was also effectively out of the crusade. It would fall to others, notably his brother Godfrey, to fulfill the apocalypse that Peter the Hermit had proclaimed in Europe.[9]

11

Reversal of Fortune and a River of Blood: The Battle for Antioch Continues

(*March 1098–April 1098*)

Around February 1, 1098, yet another prominent leader deserted the army. Unlike Peter the Hermit and William the Carpenter, he did so in the light of day and was successful. Tetigus, Alexius's representative, the man with the mangled nose and the crooked heart, announced that he was returning to Constantinople.

His excuse was airtight. He told the Franks that he wanted only to alleviate their supply problems, to contact Alexius, and to force him once and for all to meet his obligations to the pilgrimage. "Have no doubt," Tetigus told the army, "I will see that many ships come by sea from there loaded with all kinds of fruit, wine, grain, meat, flour, cheese, and the other goods that we are needing. I will have horses brought to be sold here, and there will be a market transported overland set up under the emperor's protection. Behold! All these things I faithfully promise to attend to." The same historian who recorded this speech observed that "he is a liar and always will be." Tetigus abandoned the army and never returned. Some of the Franks continued to hope for news from Constantinople, but they would not hear another word of support from the emperor.[1]

As much as the Franks mistrusted Tetigus, Tetigus feared and hated the Franks, and with reason. For as he would later tell the court at Constantinople, his closest friend in the army, Bohemond, the leader who spoke Greek with something like fluency, approached him in secret and informed him that a rumor had spread among the princes. The emperor was in contact with the Seljuk Turks, these anonymous princes were claiming, and he was plotting with the Turks to destroy the entire Frankish host. "The counts believe the story is true and they are plotting to kill you. Well, I have now done my part in forewarning you: the danger is imminent. The rest is up to you. You must consult your own interests and take thought for the lives of your men." The rumor was plausible since the Franks believed the emperor guilty of exactly this sort of treachery. In gratitude to Bohemond for his timely warning, Tetigus promised to hand over to him the same territory in Cilicia that Tancred and Baldwin had been fighting over the previous autumn. Then, assuring anyone who would listen that a relief force was in the works, that he would probably run into Alexius on the way to Constantinople, and that a legion of ferocious Turcopoles would arrive at any moment, Tetigus left the camp.[2]

As the Greeks departed, several unexpected guests arrived. The Franks' early experiment in Middle Eastern diplomacy, undertaken at the advice of Alexius, had borne fruit. The amir of Cairo—or, as the crusaders preferred to think of him, the king of Babylon—had taken an interest in the Franks' military efforts and had sent a delegation to discuss the possibility of pooling their resources to capture Jerusalem. Some in the army were understandably nervous about this foreign, infidel presence in their midst. And the Egyptians must have been equally baffled by what they had found at Antioch. They had expected a well-disciplined, well-supplied Byzantine army, supplemented by several thousand skilled mercenaries from the West. What they found instead was a ragtag band of starving soldiers (probably at about half of their original strength) whom the Greeks had abandoned and who, upon first glance, appeared incapable of reaching Jerusalem on a good day, let alone capturing it from a well-trained, formidable Turkish enemy. But the Egyptians stayed to talk terms, or perhaps they were just curious to see how the Frankish army would be destroyed.

Meanwhile, the princes were at odds over who ought to take command of the army—a point that thus far had remained unsettled—and, possibly, who ought to rule Antioch should it fall. The most likely candidates were the wealthy Raymond of Saint-Gilles and the charismatic Bohemond of

Taranto. But the issues at stake were more profound than who ought to be their leader. The princes were confronting the question of what the crusade was, at heart, all about—not just which person, but whose vision should give direction to the expedition.

The siege of Antioch would by no means settle the question, but it would bring back to the fore the army's prophetic, apocalyptic sensibilities. The prophets' fortunes, temporarily suppressed, would soon be revived as more and more pilgrims fixed their hopes not just on the end of their journey at Jerusalem but also on the end of time, which they intended to bring about.

Bohemond Becomes a Genius

Barely ten days after Tetigus's departure, on February 9, 1098, the Frankish armies received word of impending disaster. Ridwan, the ruler of Aleppo, had at last assented to the pleas for help from Yaghi-Siyan, governor of Antioch. His brother, and enemy, Duqaq had sent the relief force at the end of December that stumbled onto Bohemond's foraging expedition. Now it was Ridwan's turn to help. His goal was not so much to drive the Franks from Syria as it was to pull Antioch more firmly under his control in the ongoing conflict with Duqaq. But whatever his ultimate purpose, the immediate task was to destroy the crusade.

The Franks were, at best, dimly aware of these larger questions of Turkish politics. When they heard about the relief force, they developed a simpler explanation about its origin: A Christian deserter named Hilary had fled to Aleppo and there had embraced the Saracen faith. To win the trust of his new co-religionists, he had promised the amir, Ridwan of Aleppo, that if he attacked the Franks right away, he would find them defenseless. There would be only women and poor people to resist. Ridwan would also win for himself silver, gold, horses, mules, and various treasures brought from Gaul. Hearing this wondrous news, Ridwan rejoiced and summoned all of his followers, while Hilary spread news of the crusade's imminent collapse to other Turkish capitals—Damascus, Tripoli, and Caesarea.

The story of Hilary is, to say the least, highly improbable, and if true, the Franks could not possibly have known about it. As troubles multiplied, it was likely reassuring to blame an imaginary traitor rather than to ac-knowledge how overwhelming the odds were against capturing Antioch, not to mention how infinite was the number of enemies whom they faced. Already Ridwan and his army had reached Harim—the fortress that Bohemond had attacked in November.[3]

Upon learning of Ridwan's arrival, Bohemond tried to seize the initia-tive. He believed, as it rightly turned out, that he was the only one who could save the army. Even so, his options were not good. If the Franks set up defenses around their camps, they would be trapped between the city and the attackers, and they could not possibly survive a coordinated at-tack. The only other option, besides surrender and retreat, was to try to intercept the Aleppan army before it reached Antioch. Most obviously, they could return to the Iron Bridge, about ten miles from the city, and force a standoff at the Orontes. But that would potentially turn into a long, drawn-out battle. In the meantime the soldiers left at the camp would be vulnerable to attack from the city. A divided Frankish army fight-ing simultaneously against two enemies stood little chance of survival. It was an impossible situation and hence a good time for Bohemond to try to regain his reputation for military genius.

"Lords and oh so wise knights," he said before a meeting of the princes, "what are we going to do? We are now so few that we can't very well fight in two places. But do you know what we're going to do? We are going to divide into two parts! One part, the foot soldiers, are going to stay put and guard the tents and do what they can to check the city. The other part, the knights, are going to come with me and are going to meet our enemies, who are camped not far from here, in the castle Harim, just be-yond the Iron Bridge."

The rest of the princes accepted Bohemond's plan and seem to have placed him in charge of the battle arrangements as well. (According to one chronicler, writing somewhat obsequiously, Bohemond's followers on this occasion said to him, "You are wise and shrewd, you are great and magnificent, you are strong and victorious, you are a master of battles and a judge of conflict! Do this! All this is on you!") Owing to a dearth of men and horses, Bohemond could gather together only about seven hundred knights—and many of these were reduced to riding packhorses or mules. Undaunted, they left at night, to conceal their purpose from the citizens of Antioch. Perhaps still afraid of spies, Bohemond also hid his intentions from the soldiers, presumably letting them believe they were on some sort of foraging mission rather than about to confront an expeditionary force from one of the major Turkish capitals in the region.[4]

They stopped about six or seven miles from the city, choosing a site just behind a hill overlooking an open plain. It was also near the river and a lake. As with Dorylaeum, Bohemond aimed to prevent the Turks from employing their primary tactic of encirclement on the battlefield. He also hoped to surprise them. Very likely the Turks would have expected the Franks to try to cut them off at the bridge, but Bohemond had decided instead to attack them after the crossing, when they would be expecting a clear road to Antioch and a standoff at the city—and thus, perhaps, combat deferred for another day.

Bohemond also hoped to surprise them with the size of his army. Lacking sufficient numbers, he planned to create the illusion of a great host, and indeed one eyewitness said that when the Franks attacked, they appeared six times as numerous as they actually were. Specifically, Bohemond ordered the seven hundred knights to divide into six divisions. The first five groups would attack quickly, presumably in waves, one after another from behind the hill, trying to draw the enemy into close combat on the plain. The sixth group, under Bohemond's command, would wait in reserve. At the moment the battle seemed to turn against the Franks, Bohemond's warriors would enter the fray and, if all went according to plan, create chaos and force the Turks into a panicked retreat.

It was a risky scheme. Bohemond would not have known exactly how many enemies he was facing—only that his men were badly outnumbered. Latin historians estimated Ridwan's army at anywhere between 12,000 and 30,000 men. A number at the lower end of the scale seems likely, but that still leaves the few remaining Frankish knights outnumbered by more than ten to one. Rather than think about the odds, the soldiers passed the night singing songs, perhaps recalling the feats of Roland, "as if they took the imminent battle to be a game."[5]

The next morning Bohemond sent out scouts to locate the Turks' position. Within a short time—apparently shorter than expected—they found the enemy marching up from the river valley toward the plain. "Look! Look! They're coming!" the scouts shouted, riding back up to their

camp. "Come on and get ready, because they are already here!" Before
the Turks could order themselves, Bohemond sent the first wave of soldiers over the hill. "The clash sounded up to heaven. Everybody fought
against one another at once. A storm of spears darkened the sky." After
the initial clashes, in spite of Bohemond's careful plans, the Franks started
to give way. The Turks' numbers were simply too great. And when Bohemond, that "most learned man," saw his lines beginning to collapse—even
with his last division still in reserve—he started to weep. Turning to his
constable, summoning up the rhetoric of holy war (perhaps such language
came easily to him—battlefield descriptions make him sound more like a
preacher than a general), he cried, "Go as swiftly as you can! Be a strong
man and fierce to aid God and the Holy Sepulcher. For you truly know
that this war is not carnal but spiritual! Be Christ's strongest athlete. Go
in peace! The Lord is with you!"

Bohemond charged into the fray along with his final division, his giant
frame advancing so quickly that within moments his blood-red banner
was flying over the heads of the Saracens. Perhaps it was this last unexpected shock that frightened them. Perhaps it was the sight of this freak-
ishly large man careening down on top of them. Whatever it was, their
lines broke and the hoped-for panicked retreat began. The Franks—even
the ones riding mules and donkeys—sped down into the valley in pursuit.
Presumably there was a general massacre near the Iron Bridge as the
Turks tried to cross to safer ground. Some of the Frankish knights even
pursued them from there, riding all the way to Harim—which they found
abandoned and burned out.[6]

As for the fictitious Hilary, the Franks took some delight in imagining
his fate. According to legend, when word of the slaughter reached (presumably) Caesarea, where the traitor was staying, his hosts upbraided
him: "You son of a bitch! You would have led us right into the Franks'
hands! And if we had gone to their tents, what would have become of us?
If we had been found there, hardly any of us here would be alive! They
would have killed our brothers, our relatives, and our friends. You—you
don't get to live any longer!" And they cut off his head.[7]

In the real world, meanwhile, the Franks were cutting off a few heads
of their own. While much of the army stayed on the battlefield collecting
horses, weapons, and treasures, a few crusaders began, as they had done

at Nicea, sawing off the heads of the dead and wounded and tying them to their horses as saddle decorations. By some counts there were as few as one hundred heads and by others as many as one thousand. Many of these heads (two hundred, by one count) were put onto the ends of spears and paraded about the city walls before being planted into the ground. Others the Franks catapulted into the city "to worsen the Turks' grief." As had been true before, some of the warriors felt ambivalent about these tactics. But the clerics reassured them that their deeds were just. After all, in an earlier siege the Turks had captured a banner embroidered with an image of the Blessed Virgin and had turned it upside down and driven its point into the ground. "Thus it happened that the sight of these severed heads might cause them to think twice about making fun of us again."[8]

Diplomacy

Presumably, the Egyptians in the Franks' camp took a different attitude toward negotiation after the Franks had successfully dispatched the once-mighty army of Aleppo. A few of the Egyptian ambassadors had accompanied Bohemond to the battlefield. They were surely astonished, and strangely pleased, at what they saw. A few of them even joined in the festivities, finding dead or dying Turks, cutting off their heads, and tying them to their saddles. The crusaders offered several dozen other heads to the Egyptians as gifts. Some contemporaries imagined that they did so as another exercise in intimidation—wanting to frighten the Egyptians as surely as they hoped to terrify the Antiochenes—but there is no reason to think so. Offering a tribute of skulls was one of the customs of Eastern diplomacy that the Franks had learned during the course of the war. Nine months earlier during the siege of Nicea, they had sent a similar gift to Alexius, and the emperor was said to have rejoiced at the sight. The Fatimid caliph would presumably have had a similar reaction to the spectacle of his political and confessional enemies' skulls laid out before him.[9]

Everything else about these diplomatic overtures toward Egypt is hazy. The writers who described them usually did so with distaste, none more so than Robert the Monk. The legates arrived, he said, in March (though they had obviously been there since early February), identifying themselves as servants of the amir of Babylon, but then the chief ambassador added, "At the court of the King of Persia and of Our Lord a great council has been called because of you"—as if Persia and Egypt were the same thing. Whoever these legates were, they reprimanded the Franks for fighting while pretending to be pilgrims—a criticism not without merit. The Babylonians also wanted to make a deal. If the Franks laid down their weapons, then the Babylonians would allow them free passage to Jerusalem. They would even supply the knights with fresh horses and the poor with food. Once at Jerusalem the Franks could stay in peace for as long as a month. The crusaders responded belligerently, outlining their property rights in unequivocal terms. "Since God has given us Jerusalem, who can take it away?" The Egyptians left disappointed, and with the Franks' permission they entered the city of Antioch.[10]

Other writers give us a better sense of what transpired. The Egyptians probably offered to give the Franks control of certain neighborhoods in Jerusalem in return for their continued opposition to the hated Seljuk Turks. The vizier of Egypt, al-Afdal, may have suggested as well that he would give serious consideration to the tenets of Christianity, which some in the army took as a promise to convert or at least the first step toward conversion. In his initial overtures, then, al-Afdal proposed something like a truce, if not a full-fledged declaration of peace. At least that is what some in the army believed. The letter-writing knight Anselm of Ribemont boldly claimed that "the king of Babylon, through messengers sent to us, said that he will obey our will." As a result, he concluded, the doors of the Holy Land now stood open.

Not everyone was so bullish. About the same time, Stephen of Blois wrote to his wife, Adela, somewhat more cautiously, "The emperor of Babylon sent his Saracen messengers to our army with letters and through them confirmed an alliance with us as well as his affection." Stephen was likely heavily involved with the diplomatic outreach, for as he told his wife in the same letter, the princes had just elected him as "their lord and overseer and governor of all their actions." Stephen would have been especially qualified for the job. While in Constantinople, he had spent a great deal of time with Alexius, learning the intricacies of Middle Eastern politics. He was now one of the few sane, sober voices capable of carrying on negotiations with the adversarial faith. As leader of the army, he was also something of a compromise selection—someone who did not share the ambitions of Bohemond and Count Raymond and thus had less of a personal stake in the outcome of the siege of Antioch.[11]

To further impress the Egyptians (and probably to try to build up their own sense of self-confidence, as well as to keep their military skills sharp), the Franks began to host very public tournaments before the city walls. Eleventh-century knightly tournaments were not the orderly series of jousts characteristic of the later Middle Ages and the Renaissance. They were violent and loosely organized affairs in which warriors would divide into teams and have at one another, attempting to capture from the other side as many opponents as possible. The line between a tournament and real combat in Europe could be a fine one. Injuries were common, and deaths were not unheard of. It would have been a joyful, impressive exercise—made all the happier because it enabled the Franks to show off (and get to know) all of the horses they had captured after the battle with Ridwan. To further enhance the general feeling of bonhomie, the princes and clerics even loosened the moral regulations governing the camp, once again permitting the soldiers to play games of chance.

This public relations gesture worked. The Egyptians were surprised to find the knights so carefree when legends of their suffering were becoming proverbial. But the bravado was all based on sleight of hand. The situation at Antioch had improved but was just a little to one side of desperate. The city looked as impossible to capture as ever. For the rest of February, though, the crusaders could begin to believe that fate and God and prophecy were again all on their side.[12]

The River Battle

As the Egyptian ambassadors finally prepared to return to Cairo in March, the Franks had one other major stroke of good fortune, which would lend substance to whatever promises Stephen of Blois had been making to the Egyptians. On March 4 an English fleet laden with supplies arrived at Saint-Simeon. Not just food, the ships also carried timber and other building materials and carpenters and craftsmen as well. As a result, the Franks could at last extend their encirclement of Antioch, which they had been unable to do for lack of sufficient siege engines. As a first step, the leaders resolved to build a tower, called "the Mahomerie"—the Franks' preferred translation of "mosque"—overlooking the Bridge Gate. They also decided, or perhaps Stephen of Blois decided, to send the two most popular leaders and, before Stephen's election, the two fiercest rivals for control of the army, Raymond of Saint-Gilles and Bohemond, with about sixty knights and a few hundred infantry, to escort the English sailors and supplies back to Antioch. The Egyptian ambassadors probably accompanied them, too, at last ready to take a formal report back to al-Afdal, the vizier of Egypt.[13]

It took a full three days to reach Saint-Simeon and two more days to return. While Bohemond, Raymond, and the rest of the escort were absent, the garrison at Antioch made several minor sorties, harassing the main camp, but they were probably of a diversionary nature. The Antiochenes, too, had heard that about the supply ship at Saint-Simeon and probably realized that they needed to take immediate action before the crusaders had a chance to strengthen their siege works. All the time that Bohemond was gone, in the guise of making quick and violent strikes against the Franks' camp, the Antiochenes were in fact carefully dispatching warriors to hidden locations around the city, preparing an elaborate ambush for Bohemond and Raymond upon their return.

On March 7 the battle began. It would prove one of the most brutal, nigh apocalyptic, battles of the entire crusade. As Bohemond and Raymond returned from Saint-Simeon, laden with supplies and accompanied by the English sailors and carpenters, the Antiochenes attacked. Because they had left the city without being spotted, they achieved complete surprise. As far as the Franks could tell, the Saracens were like animals, wildly gnashing their teeth and howling in rage. Right away they killed, by one count, one thousand pilgrims. In retaliation for earlier humiliations, they decapitated at least five hundred of the dead. "We believe," one of the pilgrims wrote of the fallen, "that they went to heaven and there became white in the stole of martyrdom." Bohemond, riding at the rear of the army, panicked and fled—or else, according to his followers, he took a different route and didn't hear about the ambush until later.

Amid the bloodbath, some of the soldiers broke through the Turks' army and made it back to camp, telling the leaders—including a finally healthy Godfrey of Bouillon—that the expedition was being destroyed and that the precious military supplies were in danger. Criers were dispatched to spread the news throughout the camp. Pilgrims were enraged,

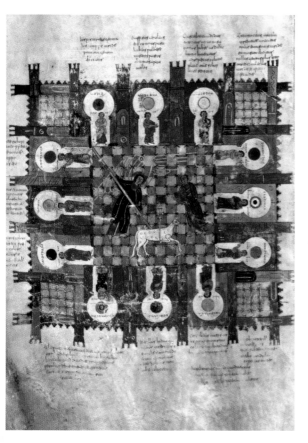

PLATE 1

Heavenly Jerusalem, as depicted in a tenth-century Apocalypse

The Granger Collection, New York

PLATE 2

Papal golden rose, a fourteenth-century golden rose commissioned by Pope John XXII, a no-doubt-more-splendid version of the gift that Urban II offered to Count Fulk of Anjou

Réunion des Musées Nationaux/Art Resource, NY

PLATE 7

Antichrist enthroned on a dragon, as depicted in a twelfth-century manuscript

Herzog August Bibliothek Wolfenbüttel, Cod. Guelf. 1 Gud. lat., 42r

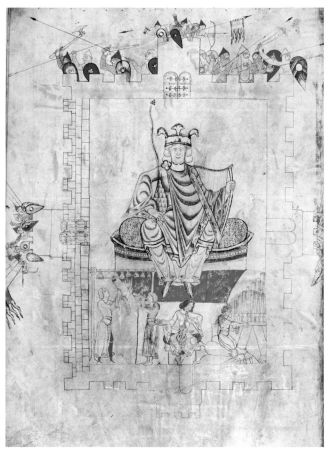

PLATE 10

The woman clad in the sun, as depicted in a twelfth-century manuscript

Herzog August Bibliothek Wolfenbüttel, Cod. Guelf. 1 Gud. lat., 14v

35

PLATE 12

The Children of Israel at war with the Amalekites and looking very much like the Franks

The Pierpont Morgan Library/Art Resource, NY

and they put their trust, notably, not in God, but in "the journey to the Holy Sepulcher." Calling on the name of Christ, with one heart and mind, they donned armor, crossed the bridge of boats, and set out to avenge their fallen brothers.[14]

On the other side of the bridge, they found a tearful Godfrey calling them to order. Messengers were also arriving from Bohemond, describing how many Turks there were and what paths they were taking. Then Bohemond himself appeared, along with all of the knights who had escaped with him. Quickly they reorganized themselves, aiming to confront the Turks who had ambushed them, when suddenly another contingent of Antiochene cavalry charged out of the Bridge Gate and attacked the Christians from behind. Yaghi-Siyan, the amir of Antioch, had decided that it was time to destroy the Frankish army by catching them unawares and trapping them between two cavalry divisions. After this second wave of horsemen had left the city, the gates were locked. There could be no escape route now for the Turks, except by killing Franks. Arrows fired on the crusaders from the city ramparts blackened the skies, and the battle that followed looked like Armageddon or else a scene from *The Song of Roland*.[15]

With Saracens attacking from two directions and Franks either retreating in terror or else charging in fury, the battle turned into a general, disorganized mêlée—the kind of mayhem that favored the Franks. For the first time, Godfrey of Bouillon distinguished himself against an opponent who was not a bear. According to many witnesses, he cut off several Turks' heads, in spite of helmets that protected their necks. More impressively, he sliced one mounted Saracen warrior in two through the waist. The horse galloped back toward the city with the rider's legs improbably stuck in the saddle. When word of this feat reached Edessa, his brother Baldwin likely reminded his subjects that Godfrey carried the sword of Vespasian, but for the Western knights it was just a particularly amusing example of a German warrior at the top of his game.[16]

At some point, alongside the individual swath of destruction that Godfrey had cut, the other leaders, notably Robert of Normandy and Raymond of Saint-Gilles, unleashed a coordinated charge against the Turks who had exited through the Bridge Gate. The crusaders then drove their enemies back over the river and against the city walls, forcing them into such a tight formation that if one of them died, he had nowhere to fall, his corpse standing upright on the bridge amid the press of his comrades. The river turned blood-red, almost as if the third angel of the Apocalypse had emptied a vase of God's wrath onto the earth. So many bodies now filled the Orontes that it ceased to flow.

Only nightfall brought the fight to an end, when the Turks cleared enough space in front of the Bridge Gate to open it up and slip back into the city. The Franks occupied themselves with prayer and the collection of plunder. "Thus our enemies were conquered by the power of God and the Holy Sepulcher, and from that day forward they were not able to muster strength as they had before, either in voice or in deed."[17]

On the following day in the early morning, a few Antioch citizens quietly exited the city gates to bury their dead, with no interference from the crusaders. This comes as a surprise. It shows the kind of restraint and empathy the Franks might typically show toward Christian enemies but certainly not toward Saracens, and it seems to indicate that even at this late stage of the siege, after nearly five months, some expectation of cooperation on both sides still existed. The Turks anticipated carrying out funerary rights in peace, and the Franks probably intended to let them do so.

But this interlude didn't last long. "When our men heard that the Turks had buried their dead, they prepared themselves and rushed out to that devil's courtyard and ordered all the tombs to be dug up and broken, the bodies to be dragged outside their graves. And then they threw all the corpses into a pit and carried away their severed heads to our tents so that we might be able to count their number." The total was somewhere between 1,500 and 7,000, not including the bodies lost in the Orontes River. Ecstatic at the level of slaughter, the Franks rigged up four horses to carry the skulls to the port of Saint-Simeon as a gift for the departing Egyptians—a final gesture of goodwill to take to Cairo.[18]

Again, the incident sparked some debate, and medieval chroniclers would continue to argue about the ethics of these acts for at least another decade. Some of the grave robbers, according to a historian writing in 1106, had hoped to demoralize the enemy, but others acted out of greed. They dreamed of finding valuables inside the tombs, perhaps because of rumors that Saracens, in pagan fashion, buried their dead with weapons and treasure, presumably to use in the afterlife. Another writer blamed the younger, more hotheaded soldiers for digging up the graves and added an uncharacteristic note of criticism: "What [the Turks] had buried with great honor, [the Christian youth] dug up with great shame." The events probably caused Guibert of Nogent some discomfort, too, since at this point in his chronicle he suggested the Franks learned such behavior from Saracens. With distance, these acts appeared increasingly more outlandish, but on the morning after the battle, the ground still damp with blood, they were cause for grim satisfaction, even amusement, as the sight of the heads caused the Turks "to weep and howl."[19]

Aftermath

Antioch's defenders may have been cowed by their defeat at the river. The sight of the Franks building yet another siege tower directly in front of the Bridge Gate probably intimidated them still further. But they were not ready to surrender. Instead, in answer to the pilgrims' desecration of the graves, they responded in kind with a new exercise in psychological warfare. They paraded one of the Franks captured during the Lake Battle, Reynald Porchet, along the ramparts of the city. He had promised his captors to shout down to the Christians and ask them how much they would pay for his ransom. Instead, he told them to save their money. "Be secure in your faith in Christ and the Holy Sepulcher, because God will always be with you. All the bravest and most important men of the city you have killed! That's 12 amirs and 1,500 nobles! No one remains who can fight against you, and no one can defend the city." Reynald then disappeared from the wall.

What happened? The Franks didn't know, but they were happy to invent a story. Yaghi-Siyan asked one of his men who spoke French what Reynald was talking about. His advisor replied, "He's saying nothing good about you." Flying into a rage, the amir ordered Reynald pulled off the wall and dragged back into the city.

"Reynald," the Turks said, "do you honestly wish to stay with us in happiness?"

"How?" he asked

"Deny your God, whom you worship, and we will give you anything you want. We will give you gold, silver, weapons, horses, many treasures, wives and plunder, and estates, all with great honor."

"Give me a little time," he said, "at least an hour to think it over by myself." They allowed this request. Then Reynald threw himself into prayer, hands joined, facing east, and humbly asked God to deem his soul worthy to be taken up into the bosom of Abraham.

Soon the amir called Reynald and asked the interpreter, "What does Reynald say?"

"He wishes in no way to deny his God," the interpreter said, "but he does refuse your treasure, gold, and silver."

Enraged, Yaghi-Siyan ordered Reynald's head cut off. Whereupon angels flew down to carry his soul into heaven. His anger still not sated, Yaghi-Siyan ordered that all the other prisoners in the city, "Christians, or knights of Christ," be burned alive, their voices echoing to the heavens and perhaps into the Franks' camps as well.[20]

Reynald was likely not the only Christian paraded along the walls at this time. When the Turks had first captured Antioch in 1084, they had forced Patriarch John IV out of the city's cathedral, along with five hundred monks and clerics, yet allowed them to remain in the city in a smaller church dedicated to the Virgin Mary. On the arrival of the Franks in 1097, the Turks had John put into chains. According to contemporary Christian historians, they did so mainly out of a childlike fear of Christianity and the magical power of its liturgy: "'This one,' they said, 'is a saint, and if he leaves the building, there is a chance that the Christians outside the walls might capture us through the power of his prayers.'"[21]

Now Yaghi-Siyan ordered the Greek patriarch to be dragged from the church where he had been imprisoned and had him dangled him from ropes over the walls, the shackles around his ankles further weighing him down. At this stage the Christians were too confident to let the Turks' jeering affect them. Instead, they retreated comfortably into fantasy. Even as they watched John IV hanging from the walls, they told stories to one another that transformed the jeering Turks into figures of fun and that demonstrated Christ's ongoing concern for the pilgrims—appearances to the contrary.[22]

The Turks, they told one another, had occupied Antioch's cathedral—
"or better yet, they had 'soiled' it," first converting it to their way of worship
and then dividing it into three temples dedicated to the devil. The gold
and silver mosaics that had adorned the walls and had glittered so splen-
didly they covered with limestone and gypsum, and over this material they
wrote words in "a demonic script." They left floors intact since the beautiful tile work had attracted them to the building in the first place.[23]

The details about how the Saracens were defacing the cathedral probably grew less out of knowledge of what was going on in Antioch and more
out of earlier experiences on the road. Unaware of Muslim distaste for
figural representations of religious subjects, the Franks had nonetheless
seen how Saracens had vandalized Christian churches before turning
them into mosques. In Syria the crusaders had passed through several religious buildings where the images on the walls had been scraped away,
where the eyes had been cut out, and where the pictures appeared to have
been shot with arrows. The Saracens, a later historian observed, often attacked paintings "as if they were living persons, digging out their eyes and
mutilating their noses."

From his prison, when Patriarch John heard rumor of such vandalism,
he sent a sternly worded message to Yaghi-Siyan and demanded that,
whatever else he might do, he must not touch one particular image of
Christ, a painted icon hanging high above the ground in the cathedral's
apse. It was a work beyond price, so carefully rendered that the Savior
Himself seemed to gaze down from it—so realistic that He appeared on
the verge of speech. Such icons were almost unknown in Europe, but the
Franks by this time would have grown accustomed to them. On the pay-
ment of five hundred *soldi*, Yaghi-Siyan agreed to John's demand.[24]

Later, probably after the river battle and as panic began to fall over
the city, the Turks held a war council. They could feel the Savior's cold,
angry stare burning into them from above. It caused them to lose their
self-control, and they began to shout at the rafters, "Hey, peasant! What
are you doing up there? Your men on the outside are besieging us, and
you want to watch us in here, too? Well, we don't want to have anything
to do with you or your men! Come down from there now! Either you come
down, or else we're going to shoot you down with arrows!" The picture
gazed impassively.

Archers opened fire. None of the arrows "dared approach the image of the Lord, and if one did get close, it immediately was broken by the Lord's power and fell at the Turks' feet." Still the Turks refused to accept the miraculous power of God. They believed instead that their bows did not have the range needed to hit Christ's face. Yaghi-Siyan therefore ordered one of his men to climb to the roof and with his own hands throw the picture to the floor. As the poor hapless Saracen approached the image, walking along the rafters, the structure gave way, and he crashed to the ground, his neck and limbs snapping in two. And the amir and his advisors gazed in wonder at the terrible face of the Lord. [25]

Nothing could rattle the Franks' confidence. They tightened their siege works, basked in the glory of successive victories against the Turks, and more and more felt themselves to be instruments of God, striding boldly through a world of myth and epic. They were prepared for almost any strategy the enemy might throw against them, except, perhaps, for what Yaghi-Siyan did next. He declared a truce. Unexpectedly, unimaginably, peace broke out.

12

Truce and Consequences:
The Fall of Antioch

(*April 1098–June 1098*)

Siege warfare had rules. They were written in the Bible, in Deuteronomy 20. Composed for a nomadic, tribal desert society, they did not always fit comfortably when applied to the more populous and prosperous eleventh-century world. According to Deuteronomy 20:10–15, if the Children of Israel intended to attack a city, they were obligated first to offer it peace. If the city accepted, its inhabitants would be spared but enslaved. By entering into negotiations, Yaghi-Siyan had raised the possibility of this sort of outcome for the siege of Antioch.

He would abandon the city to the Franks and recognize their lordship over it, and the citizens would become the crusaders' (or perhaps Alexius's) serfs. As Deuteronomy specified, if negotiations failed, the Israelites were to lay siege to the city, capture it, kill all of the men, and claim everything else therein—women, children, and livestock—as plunder. That was potentially the alternative for Antioch. But Deuteronomy describes a third possible outcome: "In the cities of the nations that the Lord God is giving you as an inheritance, do not leave alive anything that breathes. Completely destroy them." Antioch had once been the episcopal see of St. Peter. In the eyes of many crusaders, it would have fallen into the category of "special Christian inheritance." In that case negotiations would be altogether unacceptable. Only the destruction of the population and purification of the city would suffice. These were real choices faced by the theologians and moralists who might be advising the military leaders. For a time negotiation seemed likely to win out. If the truce failed, the more unforgiving laws of Deuteronomy might then be brought to bear.

The Truce

What exactly sparked the truce or when it began is unclear. In hindsight, no one wanted to talk much about it. Probably the truce started around May 1, 1098. By this time the Mahomerie tower was complete, effectively shutting down the Bridge Gate and the Turks' easiest access into the crusader camp. Tancred had established another stronghold near the Orontes River at the southern end of the city in a monastery's tower, keeping a close watch on the St. George Gate—a service he offered in exchange for four hundred marks of silver from the army's other princes. Almost immediately upon settling there, he captured a supply train of Syrian Christians who were trying to make their way into the city with grain, wine, barley, olive oil, and other such goods. The blockade was by no means perfect, but from April on it was good enough to make life uncomfortable for Yaghi-Siyan. He had to begin thinking about surrender. And after more than six months of siege warfare, many of the Franks were willing to listen.

But we know little about the talks that ensued. The only contemporary historian to describe this period in detail was Robert the Monk, who said that sometime in April Antioch's defenders had grown weary of the fight. They threw open the city gates, and the Franks and Saracens began to mingle together around the walls.

Predictably, the truce ended badly. According to Robert, a certain Walo of Chaumont-en-Vexin, constable to the king of France, happened to be wandering alone through a pleasant meadow, probably inside Antioch. He was "trusting too much in this faithless people." Suddenly, "armed dogs attacked him while he was defenseless and with wretched cruelty tore him limb from limb." Walo's wife, Humberge, now his widow, burst forth with a poetic lament addressed to Christ her king. Forgetful of "womanly shame," she threw herself to the ground, tore at her skin with her nails, ripped out handfuls of her golden hair, and decried her husband's dishonorable and senseless death—perhaps in the process attacking the rationale behind any attempts at negotiation: "Why did Walo deserve to die without battle? Oh ye, begotten of a virgin mother, cleanse the sins of Walo, whom you saved from death in so many other battles, and whom you have now permitted to be martyred." After this deliberate violation of the truce, "the gentiles" sealed themselves back inside their "walls and towers and caves" and the Christians resumed their siege operations, realizing that it was not a proper warrior's death to be murdered in peacetime.[1]

If Robert were our only source for the story, we might be inclined to reject the entire episode. But a letter from Anselm of Ribemont, written during the crusade, confirmed the existence of a brief cessation of hostilities when the leaders of Antioch and the Franks seriously discussed a peaceful handover of the city. In retrospect, Anselm believed the Turks never intended to surrender. Their real purpose was to lay traps for the Franks, resulting in the deaths of Walo and certain other unnamed soldiers. But during that time, "they so deceived us that they received many of our men in their city and many of them came to us."[2]

Although the truce failed, it did give Franks and Turks unusual opportunities to communicate with each other, helping to explain this somewhat surprising scene: "The people who were there tell how when this city was being besieged, and when the attackers and the citizens were mixing together in frequent encounters, the men on both sides would often cede ground, reason and council restraining the urge to fight. On those occasions, troops of boys would march forth, some from the city and some the sons of our men; and they would fight together in a worthy and admirable fashion."

These play armies included orphaned children who had attached themselves to particular princes and depended on their sponsor's charity for survival. The orphans also appointed leaders for themselves, whom they named after their patrons: One was a Bohemond, one a Hugh the Great, one a Robert of Flanders or a Robert of Normandy. "Such and so wondrous an army often attacked the city children, holding long reeds as spears, their shields woven from twigs, throwing darts and stones each according to his ability. And so these boys and the city's children would come together in the field, as their elders watched from either side, the citizens from the walls and ours from their tents. There you would have encountered the clash of battle, bloody blows without any danger of death." As the grown-ups saw children's bodies, all puny and helpless, bearing wounds for their cause, they would order the youngsters from the field, ready to renew their own more deadly combat. At heart, neither side seems to have wanted détente.[3]

And Yaghi-Siyan likely had a particular reason for ending the truce— a piece of news so good that it inspired him to order a hit on a prominent soldier like Walo. Word had reached him that a massive relief army was now only a few days' march from Antioch. It had originated in Mosul, along the Tigris River (in modern-day northern Iraq), but it encompassed many of the major factions in Syria. For about three weeks, this new army had camped outside of Edessa, then in the possession of Baldwin, collecting reinforcements from Damascus and elsewhere before beginning the long march to Antioch. Surely, this army would easily crush the Franks before the city walls and finally bring the crusade to an end.[4]

Consequences

The only way out of this dilemma was ugly. Our source for the truce, Robert the Monk, began preparing his readers for the measures that the crusaders would take in May 1098 when he first described Antioch. The city "could not be captured by strength, but only by strategy, through cunning and not through combat." To tell this story required finesse. Antioch was the central victory in the crusade. It was also morally suspect, a moment of conquest that potentially called into question the Franks' claim to be warriors of God. The situation was freighted with enough ambiguity that no writer who described it agreed with any other on exactly what happened, making it impossible to know when certain events occurred or why certain actors behaved as they did.[5]

A few days after Walo's death, probably around May 25, 1098, Armenian spies, likely dispatched by Baldwin from Edessa, reported to the Franks that this third and greatest Turkish relief force was fast approaching Antioch. Unsurprisingly, the leaders' initial reaction was to follow the strategy they had used in February, when under Bohemond's leadership they had ambushed Ridwan of Aleppo near the Iron Bridge. This time Godfrey and Robert of Flanders would lead half the army against the relief force, while the others would stay behind at Antioch to try to keep what remained of Yaghi-Siyan's garrison trapped behind city walls. Based on what the Armenian spies reported, however, this new relief force was much more formidable than the Aleppan one had been. If true, the Franks could only "put all their hope in Lord Jesus and pray in God's name that they would end their lives there as martyrs." To confirm these dreadful stories and, if possible, settle on a final strategy, the princes sent their own spies to gather and bring back reliable information. If the reports proved accurate, they agreed, they would need to keep the truth hidden from the majority of the warriors. Rumor of the new army's approach was already causing some common soldiers to desert, and at least one prince was thinking of doing so as well.[6]

Throughout these discussions Bohemond remained strangely calm, even chipper. His face was serene, his thoughts apparently untroubled. When he finally spoke, he did so lightly, almost jokingly. "Wise men, knights, see how terribly poor and miserable we all are! The greater and the lesser among us—there's no difference. And we don't have any idea how to make things better. Okay—if this seems to you like a good and honorable idea, let's elevate one of us above the others. And if, by any means or device he can acquire this city or engineer its capture, by himself or with others, let's all agree with one voice to give him the city as a gift."

No one liked the idea. The city, the princes responded, belonged to no one. They had all labored equally for its conquest, and they should share equally in its possession. One or two of them likely reminded Bohemond of the oaths they had sworn to Alexius—indeed, Bohemond had insisted that they do so at the time. The city ultimately should be returned to the emperor. Or at least that's how they felt while the size of the approaching army was unknown. As for Bohemond, he left the room, his smile now a little forced, though he perhaps tossed off a bon mot: "Woe to a city serving so many lords!"[7]

About three days later, right at the end of May, word came back from the scouts that the relief army from Mosul was indeed nearby and that it was as large, if not larger, than initial reports had suggested. By one estimate it numbered over 400,000 men. They would be at Antioch in less than a week. The desperate strategy Bohemond had used against Aleppo in February would not work a second time.

Some considered the possibility of retreat—not giving up the pilgrimage altogether, but leaving Antioch behind and continuing on to Jerusalem. Practical voices, however, shut down that avenue of escape. "If we abandon this city, it will not abandon us. It will follow us as a companion, as an adversary blocking our path, attacking from behind and from the front." Their only hope was that Bohemond had had a specific idea behind his earlier proposal—that they could enter the city before the new army arrived and use Antioch's impregnable defenses to their own advantage. Secure inside Antioch, they could worry about how to defeat the relief force later. They therefore agreed that if Bohemond might acquire Antioch in any way, they would all with one heart offer him complete authority over it. But there was a caveat: Should Alexius finally come to their rescue and fulfill the promises he had made at Constantinople, they would return the city to him according to those earlier agreements. Bohemond agreed to this provision, likely thinking that it would never be an issue. He knew the emperor's mind better than anyone else and knew that there was almost no chance Alexius would show up with his army to fight. And so, at last, having sat by patiently as a very real threat of complete annihilation had hung over the crusade, Bohemond revealed his plan. "Lords, my dearest brothers," he began, "I have a secret."[8]

For several weeks he had been cultivating an inside man in Antioch—a Turk or an Armenian (no one was quite sure) named Pirrus, or Firuz. Pirrus controlled three of the towers on the southern side of the city, near the St. George Gate (where Tancred had been keeping a close watch), and he was prepared to allow the Franks entry. Why he was willing to do so is unclear. Modern historians speculate that Pirrus was an Armenian who had converted to Islam after the Turks had captured the city thirteen years earlier and whose loyalty was suspect. According to twelfth-century rumor, Pirrus's motives were more personal. Bohemond had captured his son during an earlier battle and would free the boy only in return for the entire city of Antioch. Another story held that Pirrus had been an extremely wealthy and prominent citizen before the Turks conquered Antioch, but that as a result of predatory and punitive taxation, he had lost much of his status and was anxious to avenge himself upon Yaghi-Siyan.

The simplest, and perhaps most likely, story is that Bohemond bribed him: "He promised to give him Christianity and see that he became rich and much honored."[9]

An even simpler explanation: Pirrus and Bohemond just really liked each other. Indeed, in one version of this story Pirrus seems to have fallen in love with the charismatic giant. During the siege the two men had begun to exchange notes filled with the sort of emotion one would expect to find between lovers. To Bohemond, Pirrus became "my dearest." He pleaded with him for absolute trust, engaging in affectionate, ostentatious wordplay. "May you never disbelieve me, friend to friend, only one to one and only." Pirrus in turn promised to give Bohemond the city, saying, "I place my soul in the hands of my one and my only one, and I turn over this city, in faith, to my friend."[10]

For warriors fighting in God's name and with God's blessing, however, bribery, blackmail, and homoerotic romance were not satisfying explanations of why Antioch fell. A better explanation would involve God, making Pirrus into a sort of "saintly traitor." Robert the Monk provided it: Bohemond and Pirrus, he said, met during the truce (a likely observation). If it had not been for the truce, if Bohemond had not had the opportunity to exercise his outsized charms on a few of Antioch's disaffected defenders, then the Franks might have stayed stuck outside the city until the relief army arrived. But, Robert indicated, nothing would have come of these meetings had it not been for the wondrous judgments of God. For during one of their first encounters, Pirrus asked Bohemond where the Franks had stationed "the countless luminous soldiers" who had appeared to aid them in almost every military engagement. "By my guardian Mathomos, I swear that if they were all here present, the whole field would not be able to hold them. They all have wondrously fast white horses and vestments and shields and banners of the same color." Every time Pirrus saw them, he trembled as if caught in a whirlwind. Bohemond, inspired by God, explained that this army was a heavenly host composed of martyrs led by Saints George, Demetrius, and Maurice—the Eastern military saints who had first appeared in the campaign a year earlier at Dorylaeum. They were engaged in battles throughout the world against unbelievers. Their camps were not of this earth. Instead, they rested upon thrones in heaven.

Pirrus's next question was a perceptive one: Why then, if the saintly warriors were in heaven, did they need things like horses, shields, and banners? Bohemond admitted that he didn't know, and he called on his priest, a man familiar with the necessary technical jargon and thus better equipped to explain how God spoke heavenly truths through earthly signs. "They only appear to be armed," the priest explained, "so as to demonstrate that they are going to help those engaged in warfare." God transformed material appearances without actually affecting spiritual essences. Once the truce had broken down, and once Pirrus had had a chance to reflect further upon the priest's words, he agreed to give Bohemond the city.[11]

Now, perhaps with some distaste, the leaders assented to this treachery—an act possibly inspired by God but certainly made feasible through promises of money and power. Bohemond sent Pirrus the news: "Behold! The time is now! We can bring about whatever good deed we wish. Help me now, Pirrus, my friend!" The message pleased Pirrus, and the next day he sent his son to act as hostage and as a pledge of his integrity (assuming Bohemond had not already captured him in an earlier battle). After one or two more exchanges, they were ready to put their plan into effect. As Bohemond quietly informed a select few leaders—Godfrey, Robert of Flanders, Raymond of Saint-Gilles, and Bishop Adhémar—on June 2, 1098, "Grace of God willing, tonight Antioch will be handed over to us."

The tension, however, had proved all too much for the man so recently elected head of the entire crusade. Stephen of Blois was overcome with illness, or at least he claimed he was. He withdrew from the siege and traveled to the fortress of Alexandretta, about thirty miles northwest of Antioch, close to the shore and close to escape. He promised to return as soon as he could, but it was the last crusaders ever saw of him.[12]

That night Bohemond ordered a knight, nicknamed "Evil Crown," to summon a group of seven hundred warriors to accompany him on a march to nowhere. It was supposed to look like a foraging expedition or else to make Antioch's defenders believe that the Franks had left to confront the army from Mosul before it could reach the city, as they had originally proposed doing. Most of the Franks in this band didn't even know where they were going. Godfrey had told his men that they would be searching for a small group of Saracens camped somewhere in the mountains. The expedition's real purpose was simple misdirection: to convince Antioch that on this one night, out of all others, it had nothing to fear from the Franks. Because of the continuing problem of spies in camp, as few people as possible knew what the leaders were up to. So secret were the plans that Bohemond's own cousin Tancred later claimed to have known nothing of them.[13]

When the armies on the march returned to Antioch just before dawn, they approached one of Pirrus's towers, near the southeastern corner of the city. Bohemond sent forward an interpreter, fluent in Greek, to deliver some prearranged signal to Pirrus, who in turn passed down last-second instructions about when to approach the wall. In the meantime the princes and captains at the head of the expedition at last revealed to their men the real point of what they were doing, and they began choosing from the boldest among them the ones who should enter Antioch first. It must have been a terrifying prospect, climbing into the city whose defenses and defenders had so long mocked them and defied their every advance.

Godfrey tried to deliver encouraging words, but his tone, as his followers remembered it, was fairly gloomy. "Remember," he said, "in whose name you left your country and family, and how your renounced your earthly life, fearing to endure no danger of death on behalf of Christ." After exhorting them to be faithful knights of Christ, he concluded somberly, "We all must die in some way."

Silently they made their way to the city and hovered in the darkness. As their interpreter had learned from Pirrus, the night watch had yet to pass by. As soon as they saw the flame of a single torch flickering across the rampart, they approached the wall. A knotted rope fell down from the darkness, and some of Bohemond's men tied a ladder to it. Pirrus raised the ladder up and fixed it to the wall as Bohemond wished his men good luck. The giant stepped back into the shadows, waiting to see what would come of his plan.[14]

The Franks, somewhat gingerly, began climbing into the darkness. But not fast enough for Pirrus. Dawn was threatening, and as far as he could tell, hardly anyone had showed up for the invasion. As the first few pilgrims clambered over the ramparts, he panicked and called out, presumably for the benefit of his Greek interpreter, "*Micró Francos echomé!*" Or, "We have few Franks!" And then, "Where is that fierce Bohemond? Where is that unconquered man?" In the homoerotic version of their relationship, he added with fulsome despair, "You have lost not only us and the city, but also your friend, who laid bare in your lap all his hope and his very soul!"

The invaders ignored these histrionics. They focused only on seizing the three towers under his command, slipping inside and dispatching the still-sleeping guardians. One band of Franks stumbled onto a night watchman, but before he could call out for help, someone had cut off his head. Whoever crossed their path along the wall or in the towers died at once. Those killed included Pirrus's brother. Like Tancred, he had not been warned of the attack. "Such are the accidents, endless black night, that you bring to us," the monk Baudry lamented when pondering the unsuspecting brother's demise. "Such are the upheavals, O dark hours, that you cause!"[15]

On the ground no one else, Bohemond included, wanted to go into the city. Indeed, the first Franks on top of the wall had moved so stealthily and quietly that the rest of the army feared some sort of treachery. What if they'd all been strangled? Fifty or sixty men had disappeared into the dark, and no one wanted to join them—until an Italian man slid back down the ladder to report their progress and to see what everyone was waiting on. He called out to Bohemond in particular, "What are you doing standing there, O wise man? Why did you even bother to come here? Look! We've already got three towers!" Everyone rejoiced. They rushed to the ladder. In the darkness and from up above, they could hear screams of agony and shouts of "God wills it!" Saracens were dying, and all of the Franks wanted to be part of the killing. So many men got onto the ladder at once that it broke apart. Some of the other pilgrims on the ground approached the wall and began running their hands over the stonework, searching for a postern gate. They either found it, or one of the Franks atop the wall had made his way to street level and opened it for them. The conquest of the city now could begin in earnest.[16]

Everywhere there was confusion. The killing was complete and indiscriminate. The Franks who had broken through the gate were shouting, "God wills it! God wills it!"—the slogan that Urban II had taught them at Clermont now serving as the signal that the crusaders "were about to undertake some good work!"

"Everybody in the city was screaming at once." Like the guardians in the towers, many a Turk barely had time to wake up before a Christian had stabbed him. Some of the Turks were drunk, one contemporary noted with contempt. In the chaos only Bohemond kept his cool. "Impatient of delay," he ordered his blood-red banner to be raised above the city.[17]

When Christians in the camp heard the noise, they were momentarily confused. The men in Count Raymond's camp, awakened by the screams, initially concluded that the Muslim relief force had already arrived. Others disagreed: "That is not the sound of happy people." But when dawn broke and they saw their own flags flying over the city, they rushed to join the carnage. "They killed the Turks and Saracens whom they found there," though some managed to escape to Antioch's massive citadel. A few Turks stationed themselves on the walls and fired arrows, but they hit only the unarmed pilgrims, men and women, who had charged the city late, caught up in the general feeling of victory or else hoping to scavenge a little plunder for themselves while combat distracted the knights. Albert of Aachen estimated the number of Saracens dead at 10,000 and said that the Franks "spared none of the gentiles on the basis of age or gender, as the earth grew covered with the bodies and blood of the dead." As Raymond of Aguilers hurried to see the killing, he found it "an amusing spectacle," thinking on how the Turks, who had for so long resisted the Franks, now found themselves with no hope of escape—though he mentioned with sadness the deaths of three hundred horses. "All the public squares were filled with dead bodies," another eyewitness observed, "so that no one could stand to be there to endure the stench. In truth, no one could walk through the city streets without treading on corpses."[18]

Only two things detracted from the general celebration. First, a contingent of soldiers led by Godfrey and Robert had attempted to capture Antioch's massive citadel, perched on a mountain and dominating the city. The defenders of the citadel managed to drive away this first attack, and, as noted, it became a refuge for many survivors. During the next month, the presence of this garrison made the Franks continuously vulnerable to attack, even though they had established their control over the rest of Antioch.[19]

Second, on an ethical level there was some consternation about the killing of Syrian and Armenian Christians. Many of them had at first tried to join in the battle and fight for the Franks but then had gotten caught up in the massacre. For their deaths Albert of Aachen blamed accident and Saracen cunning. In the early stages of the fight, because of darkness, it was nearly impossible to tell Saracen and Eastern Christian apart. And the Saracens, moreover, faked being Christian, offering up counterfeit signs and words of faith. Or perhaps the supposed fakers really were Christian, for another historian observed that the local Christians—desperate not to be killed—took to singing the only shared words from the Latin and Greek mass, *Kyrie eleison*, in hopes that the Franks would recognize the words and spare them. He left unclear whether the tactic worked, but based on Albert's testimony, we may presume not. Incapable of telling friend from enemy, the Franks killed everyone.[20]

In the best of circumstances, it was difficult to distinguish Eastern Christians from Muslims. Their clothes and beards were almost identical. (Adhémar of le Puy had long before ordered the Franks to shave often in order to prevent such mix-ups.) But if any of the crusaders felt guilty or morally troubled over having struck down Antiochene Christians, they could always blame the victims and not just because of their appearance. Armenians and Syrians had aided the Turks periodically throughout the siege. Many of those killed had simply gotten what they deserved. At any rate these unfortunate deaths were soon forgotten. Fifty years later a Genoese writer would record that the crusaders sang *Kyrie eleison* on entering the city, turning the locals' cry for mercy into a song of triumph.[21]

To be sure, not all the Antiochenes were killed. Besides those who escaped to the citadel, several hundred others laid low during the battle and learned to live alongside the Franks afterward. We hear a hint of their survival in the complaints of the chaplain Raymond of Aguilers, who said that soon after the city fell, the crusaders succumbed to the charms of "pagan song girls," whom they presumably had spared. The unnamed sins committed with these women (along with other sins, like overeating) angered God enough that He elected to torment the Franks for another month, using the final Muslim army as His scourge.

Some of the Antiochenes also escaped the city and fled to the countryside, including the amir Yaghi-Siyan. He made for one of the nearby mountains, riding a mule and disguised as a commoner. But despite the lowly animal and humble garb, three Syrian men spotted a jeweled belt and scabbard around his waist. They approached him with pretended reverence but then threw him off his mule, unsheathed his own sword, and meted out the expected punishment, cutting off his head and sending it to Bohemond as a gift. It was, according to all reports, a big head, the ears large and hairy. The beard would have extended all the way to Yaghi-Siyan's navel, had it still been attached to a body. To Raymond, repulsed by all of the decapitations he had witnessed, this final beheading was an act of divine retribution. The same man who had made martyrs out of so many Christians had finally lost his own head at Christian hands.[22]

With this victory the Franks had applied the rules of siege warfare from Deuteronomy 20 almost to the letter. They had destroyed a population whom they had learned to demonize, but only after agreeing to at least one truce and only after each side had allowed its children occasionally to play rough with one another.

From a modern perspective, the massacre of an entire city population looks something like a war crime. But the Franks at Antioch, on June 3, 1098, did not do violence to their calling as holy warriors or as crusaders. Rather, the city's destruction was a way to embrace that identity, to align themselves as closely as possible with the Children of Israel (who had carried out similar massacres when they had marched to the Promised Land) and at the same time to displace those Jews forever from the title of "Chosen People." The corpse-ridden streets of Antioch set the pattern for the rest of the crusade. And it was difficult to deny the prophetic enthusiasms of the more radical elements of the army. All of the Franks had just lived through an apocalypse. Others were soon to follow.

13

Violent Men

The capture of Antioch signaled the advent of a new kind of war. The long siege, the desperate need to escape from a massive relief force, Pirrus's act of betrayal, and the street fighting in the dark all combined to create a singularly brutal event. But the slaughter was also a product of the crusade itself. It was, after all, the first "holy war."

Since the age of Constantine the Great, Christian knights, kings, and emperors had always fought with God in mind. The crusade, however, was a singular example of religious warfare because God and the warrior fought with a unity of purpose otherwise unimaginable outside of epic poetry. As contemporary historian Guibert of Nogent observed, "God has established in our times 'holy battles,' so that the erring crowd of knights—who after the fashion of the ancient pagan world busied themselves with mutual slaughter—could now find a new way to earn salvation." For these two reasons the crusade was new: It offered warriors a way to save their souls through combat, and it was a new type of war—complete with its own sets of rules and its own moral code.[1]

This last point might seem obvious enough, but it runs against what most historians have written of late about the First Crusade. The rules of war, so the argument goes, were the same in the East as in the West. Following the logic of Deuteronomy 20, the crusaders massacred all, or almost all, the inhabitants of a Muslim city, as they did in Antioch on the morning of June 3, because the city had refused to surrender. If the defenders did not negotiate and the city was taken by force, then the defenders' lives and property were forfeit. If, on the other hand, a city (Christian or Saracen) did surrender before or during a siege, the attackers (Saracen or Christian) would show mercy. Those were the eleventh-century rules of war, understood by both Turks and Franks. It was rough justice but justice nonetheless.[2]

Outside of the crusade, however, these rules were not very widely practiced. Great battles like Antioch were not part of an ordinary warrior's experience. Neither were great cities. Apart from Constantinople, many of the Franks would have never seen a city as impressive as Antioch, let alone have broken into such a place and killed most of the inhabitants. Compared to such a battle, war in eleventh-century Europe was commonplace and diffuse, less a disruption of the social fabric and more a seasonal event, like baseball. Grand battles such as Hastings in 1066 were the exception, not the rule. Most fighting was indirect, aimed at a rival lord's property, including his lands and his peasant laborers. No doubt such engagements were violent and terrifying for the unarmed victims, but they were a far cry from the great sieges of the First Crusade.

As for sieges in Europe, they typically targeted castles with small garrisons. The biblical rule of "surrender or die" might have applied, but the results would have looked very different from what happened at Antioch.

The eleventh-century siege of Échauffour is a typical example. The siege began when the knight Arnold, formerly lord of Échauffour, tried to reclaim his own lands after Duke William of Normandy had disinherited him: "One night [Arnold] came to Échauffour with four knights and entering the castle by strength made such an uproar that the sixty knights of the duke imagined he was bringing a great army with him and fled terrified, abandoning the castle which they ought to have guarded. He set fire to it, causing heavy loss to his enemies. He also set fire to the town of St. Évroul, and for many hours he and his minions stormed into every corner of the monastery, brandishing their naked swords and clamoring for Abbot Osbern's blood. But by the will of God he happened to be elsewhere." Property was lost in the fire, but most of the potential targets escaped before the fighting began.[3]

Sieges, on occasion, did end tragically, particularly if there were more than a normal garrison inside a castle's walls. To take one example, around the year 1020 an army of Normans invaded Burgundy and seemed to ex-

Siege warfare as depicted in the Bayeux Tapestry—violent but on a small scale (Scala/White Images/Art Resource, NY)

ercise something like "the rules of war" when they captured the fortress of Mimande. The Normans were enraged at the locals who had helped the Burgundian nobility resist the invasion, so they burned the tower to the ground, along with everyone inside it, "men, women, and children," who had earlier fled to the castle in hopes of escaping the Normans' fury.

Even in the worst cases, however, the small scale of the fortifications would have limited fatalities. Large castles, like William the Conqueror's White Tower in London, were unusual. In the eleventh century, most European fortresses were tall, narrow structures made of stone or wood. They were intended to provide shelter for aristocrats as they went about their business of plundering and terrorizing their own subjects. Such buildings were incapable of sheltering a large number of people, and they certainly would not have enabled casualties comparable to those of any of the great battles of the crusade.[4]

A possible exception to these rules is the siege of Beneciacum, a brutal massacre that, like the crusade, grew out of a spirit of peace. Around the year 1038, Aimo, Archbishop of Bourges, imposed an oath of peace upon everyone in his archdiocese over the age of fifteen. With all their hearts, they swore on the relics of St. Stephen, the first martyr, to fight against plunderers of church goods; against oppressors of monks, nuns, and clerics; and against anyone who would assail their mother church. "You would

have looked upon the army," the source for the story, a monk named Andrew, observed, "as if another Israelite people." Composed of ordinary folk
dedicated to peace, it proved itself an effective militia. "Fear and dread
of them so filled the hearts of the unbelievers that they trembled before
this unarmed multitude of commoners as if it were a division of trained
soldiers." But their achievements were fleeting. Archbishop Aimo over-
reached his authority and with no real cause accused a castellan named
Stephen of Beneciacum of breaking the peace. The church's army besieged his castle, where all of the locals—also mainly commoners—had
fled inside its walls. Archbishop Aimo, indifferent to the cost, ordered the
fortification set afire. According to Andrew (probably with some exaggeration), 1,400 people died, many pregnant women among them. Stephen
survived and was confined to the archbishop's prison.[5]

Later another castellan named Odo utterly destroyed the peace army.
In this battle at least seven hundred clergy died, and so many of their
corpses filled a river that they functioned as an effective bridge. Their
spears were left eerily stuck into the ground along the banks, like young
trees at the edge of a forest. Although exaggerations are likely in both
cases, these two battles were nonetheless remembered as massacres. They
resembled the crusade in at least two other respects as well: A bishop had
formally proclaimed the need for war, and the soldiers who formed the
army fought together in the name of God and of peace. Given the typically
small scale of European warfare in the eleventh century, these battles
were traumatic for eyewitnesses, though the numbers of dead were in no
way comparable to those of any of the major crusade battles.[6]

Aimo's story raises one other important point. When medieval observers were trying to contextualize battles that transcended normal levels
of violence, the likeliest place to appeal for precedents was the Old Testament. The peace army was, as noted, like "another Israelite people."
And in the aftermath of the battle, Andrew again turned to the Old Testament, comparing the fate of Aimo's army to what happened to the tribe
of Benjamin in the Book of Judges. Some of the Benjamites had committed a particularly brutal rape, but their leaders refused to allow the rapists
to undergo justice. The other Israelites agreed to make war against Benjamin. Their first two attacks failed, but on the third day they killed 25,000

of the tribe, and then afterward they destroyed their cities, their animals, their women, and their children.[7]

Had the crusaders ever followed this ethos in their European homeland, their actions would have been viewed as atrocities. But in the context of a holy war intended to re-create those same Old Testament battles fought in the same deserts where the Israelites had wandered, atrocities were standard practice. The result was a new level of violence, leading to battles that in scale and character were truly apocalyptic.

Even historians at the time recognized that to live through such battles would have been for the soldiers a transformative experience, and probably not a positive one. The levels of bloodshed and brutality were so far beyond ordinary warfare that the experience of it would have changed the warriors' sense of their own humanity. Around 1107 one writer, Baudry of Bourgueil, observed, "Of the fear of the dead customarily felt by the living there was none, since they had grown used to the dead being everywhere next to them just as the living. The stench hardly bothered them, for it had become normal to know and to see and even to sleep amongst the dead without revulsion." In describing the aftermath of a particularly brutal battle, Guibert of Nogent wrote, "The frequency of the sight and smell began to wear away the horror usually felt in all the senses, so that custom built courage and no one feared to step in the midst of those bodies scattered through the streets." Each of these writers apparently reached his conclusion independently of the other. Very likely the words were based on the experience of actual crusaders, men who had walked the new path to salvation, who had fought holy battles, and who in moments of unusual introspection recognized that the wars had wrought in their souls changes as profound as the ruptures created in history and in God's plans for salvation.[8]

Between the capture of Nicea and the fall of Antioch, the Franks had fought battles of an ever-increasing apocalyptic scale. The day after they took control of the city, when the relief army arrived from Mosul, they would encounter their fiercest opponent and their greatest challenge yet—a conflict in which they would need all the powers of heaven and its saints if they hoped to survive.

14

Kerbogah and the Lance

(*June 1098*)

B arely one day passed after the Franks took control of Antioch before a massive Turkish relief army reached the city. Its leader, the *atabeg*, or governor, of the city of Mosul, was named Kerbogah. More than any of the other enemies the crusaders had faced or would face, Kerbogah captured their imagination. The stories about him differ in detail, but his role is consistent. Unlike the Turkish leaders of Antioch, alternately shaking their fists and cowering in terror before the image of Christ, Kerbogah was a skeptic: a man who saw the crusade as a normal war governed by the ordinary rules of warfare. In this he was the inverse of a Christian warrior—yet another distorted reflection—not because he opposed his religion to theirs, not because he was superstitious or believed in pagan gods, but because he was rational.

Kerbogah's great mistake, almost a tragic flaw, was his inability to recognize the crusade as a new type of war—a series of holy battles rather than a conflict of men. To his misfortune, he placed his faith in rationality and in numbers at the very moment when, from the Franks' perspective, the wrath and wonder of God had been made everywhere visible.

A Worthy Villain: The Character of Kerbogah

Who was Kerbogah? As the *atabeg* of Mosul, he was one of the more prominent leaders in the Sunni Turkish world. His high status rested largely on a reputation for military genius and ferocity. When he decided to intervene at Antioch, he did so with the full knowledge and support of the Sunni Caliphate, but he was likely interested as well in advancing his own ambitions in the fractured political network of northern Syria. According to the twelfth-century Arab historian Ibn al-Athir, Kerbogah was an arrogant man whose abrasive character alienated many of his followers. But abrasive or not, he did manage to assemble a formidable coalition in advance of the battle, drawing support from many of the independent and semi-independent Turkish cities. His recruits included most notably Duqaq of Damascus, who had already attempted to relieve Antioch in December 1097. (Duqaq's estranged brother Ridwan sat out the rest of the siege.) How large Kerbogah's army was is a matter of guesswork. Estimates in the Middle Ages ran as high as one million. Modern writers tend toward a more realistic but still daunting figure of 40,000.[1]

Kerbogah, as the Latin writers understood him, was a "diabolical man" who felt horror at the word "Christian." But in this case such religious language seems more a matter of habit than conviction. Kerbogah, as they described him, kept his feet firmly grounded in this world, not the next. "These are men like us," Kerbogah said of the Franks. "We will be fighting against impure and uncircumcised men; we do not fight against God, nor God against us. An equal likelihood of death threatens us all." To borrow a modern phrase, from Kerbogah's perspective the crusade was a clash of civilizations, and he was prepared to take the fight all the way to Europe. "Let us pursue them tirelessly into their own countries. I would count it the greatest shame, my noble followers, to defend against them here and to conquer them in our own land if we did not inflict the same sort of injury on them in their land, too, and wipe out whatever they had there." In line with these grand plans for total war, he encouraged the sultan and the caliph in Khorasan (or Baghdad), through letters sent from Antioch, to promote sexual abandon at home. With more sex and more babies, the Saracens might put together an army large enough to conquer Europe.[2]

Part rationalist and part madman, Kerbogah was also a bully, a ruthless and selfish lord of a type that Frankish readers would have quickly recognized. His first thought when he reached Antioch had nothing to do with victory. Rather, he wanted to take possession of the great citadel of Antioch, where many of the Muslim survivors of the June 3 massacre had fled. This massive fortification was in the possession of Sensadolus (or Shams al-Daulah, "Sun of the Regime"), the son of Yaghi-Siyan, recently deposed as governor of Antioch.

Kerbogah opened negotiations with Sensadolus for possession of the tower right after he arrived. The vocabulary in the story is clearly Western, not Islamic, but there may have been some truth to the Latin reports. Upon meeting Kerbogah, so the story goes, Sensadolus observed to him, "I have waited a long time for your assistance, so that you might help me in this danger."

Kerbogah replied, "If you wish me to help you wholeheartedly and to be your faithful supporter in this danger, give this citadel into my hands, and then you will see how much benefit I can be. I will make my men guard it."

Sensadolus responded, "If you can kill all the Franks and bring me their heads, I will give you the citadel and gladly make homage to you, and I will guard the citadel in fealty to you."

To which Kerbogah said, "No, that won't work. Give me the citadel now." And willingly or not, Sensadolus gave him the citadel.[3]

Warriors in eleventh-century France would have found this a familiar story. A great lord had forced someone in a precarious situation to surrender his liberty. Not satisfied with loyalty and service, the lord wanted property, too, effectively extorting a castle from its rightful owner. Kerbogah, again like a thuggish, Frankish strongman, turned the property over to one of his close followers—a "new man" in the area, upon whose loyalty he could more safely depend.[4]

This new man was Ahmad ibn-Marwan, known in Frankish chronicles as "the amir." He was "a gentle and peaceable man"—curious qualities in a warlord but appropriate for a cringing sidekick. "The amir," however, was uncomfortable with Kerbogah's actions. He accepted command of the citadel, but only on the condition that if the Franks defeated Kerbogah, he would surrender the fortification to them peacefully. Kerbogah agreed because he knew Ahmad ibn-Marwan to be an honest and prudent fellow. According to a barely remembered tradition, however, immediately upon giving the citadel to this faithful friend, Kerbogah returned and demanded right of entry. Another series of negotiations ensued, with the amir offering his lord whatever gold Yaghi-Siyan had left in the tower, as well as the service of the men there, provided Kerbogah used the soldiers to kill Franks. "But I will not," he concluded, "pay tribute to you for the castle." Again, using medieval legal language, Ahmad ibn-Marwan wished to hold the castle as an *allod*, given in gift from his lord, and not to obligate himself to permanent, recurring payments. Kerbogah, however, was both acquisitive and erratic—on the one hand enriching his followers while on the other hand reminding them that the largesse he had showed remained in his possession, regardless of earlier promises.[5]

Yet in the world of Frankish gossip and historical legend, Kerbogah's coalition was already collapsing. Ahmad ibn-Marwan immediately entered into negotiations with Bohemond's nephew Tancred, who spoke a little Syriac. The amir promised that he would hand over the citadel to Bohemond should the Franks prevail against Kerbogah.

As unlikely as it sounds, this story is not merely the product of crusader legend. Kerbogah's great army at Antioch almost immediately began to fracture. Its great size was at once its biggest strength and its greatest weakness. For Kerbogah had cobbled together his army from numerous, semiautonomous warlords, and it was, inevitably, riven with mistrust. Could the Franks have learned of these divisions and exploited them? It is not impossible. Bohemond had already used similar diplomatic tactics to capture Antioch. It was within the abilities of his kinsman Tancred (armed with a little Syriac) to exploit similar diplomatic openings during this final stage of the siege.[6]

Oblivious to the difficulties he was creating among his own men, Kerbogah continued to prepare for what he saw as an easy victory. The Franks, after all, had starved Antioch of most of its supplies. The Turkish garrison inside the citadel was constantly harassing them. And, above all, Kerbogah had numbers on his side. "I have more amirs with me here than there are Christians, both greater and lesser ones," he is said to have boasted. Victory was for him an article of faith. The Franks were mad to have invaded Syria. They did not have the necessary manpower, riches, or weapons to prevail. When some of his followers presented him with a few broken and rusted Frankish weapons, he burst into laughter. "Are these the fierce and shiny armaments the Christians have brought against us into Asia?" he asked. "With these do they think and believe that they can drive us back beyond Khorasan?"

So confident was he in victory that he had brought with him "a countless and infinite number of every kind of chain and fetter" with which he planned to enslave the enemy. A herd of dumb animals, he believed, presented a greater threat than the Christians did. "He was so proud and stubborn that he did not believe any of the Franks would dare to come against him in the field."[7]

Only one person in Kerbogah's army had the courage to tell him otherwise: his mother. For unknown reasons, again, according to Frankish rumor, she was staying nearby in the city of Aleppo. As soon as she had heard news of the impending battle—and this story, told by the Franks, is almost surely wholly fictional—she rushed to her son's army and begged him not to fight. "Oh, dearest son, the Christians cannot make war against you. I know that they could never bring the fight to you, but their God fights for them every day!" To support her argument, she marshaled a series of Old Testament citations to demonstrate that a small army supported by the Christian God could easily triumph over a numerically superior foe. If Kerbogah fought, she concluded, he would lose, and he would die within the year.

Kerbogah was incredulous. What possible reason was there to spout such nonsense? The prophecies, she answered, appeared "in our scripture and in the books of gentiles"—the former, presumably, the Qur'an, and the latter, perhaps, any of the popular apocalyptic prophecies that circulated in eleventh-century Europe. Kerbogah's mother had also consulted the signs of the zodiac, all of which showed the same result: The Christians would win. It was uncertain, she concluded, whether this victory would be the final Christian triumph over Islam or just a preliminary battle. Like a lot of Christian prophets in the 1090s, she did not know if the crusade had ignited Armageddon itself, but she was relatively sure that the Last Days were beginning.[8]

Kerbogah refused to listen, even to his mother. The Franks were vastly outnumbered, they were trapped in a city with no supplies and no horses, they were starving, and they were, after all, only men. "Hugh their standard bearer, and Bohemond of Puglia, and Godfrey the gladiator—are they gods? Surely they eat the same ordinary food as we do? Can their skin not be cut with iron, just like ours?" The battle would occur on earth, not in heaven.[9]

That is, at least, what the Franks like to believe about Kerbogah. These were the stories they told one another by torchlight. And from the Franks' perspective, these stories had an obvious moral: If they were going to win this battle and reach Jerusalem, they could not afford to treat it as an earthly conflict. They had to look to the angels for help.

In the Real World: The Crusade Forsaken

For the actual crusader army, trapped in Antioch and far removed from heaven, the siege of Kerbogah against them began disastrously. On June 4, the day his advance party arrived, about thirty Turkish warriors rode close to the walls, inspiring a prominent crusader named Roger de Barneville to ride out of a city gate and challenge them. Unfortunately for Roger, there were another three hundred Turks hidden and waiting. He and his companions tried to retreat back to the city. A crowd of Franks stood on the city walls and cheered him, but before he could reach the gates, a Saracen shot him in the back with an arrow, knocking him off his horse and to the ground. A few of the Turks quickly fell on his body and cut off his head, which they carried around the perimeter of Antioch out of bowshot. What Roger had intended as a bold gesture to inspire his friends had demoralized the entire Frankish host. "They averted their eyes, unable to bear to watch as his body was torn limb from limb."[10]

The Franks tried to maintain some tactical advantage by preserving the Mahomerie tower outside the Bridge Gate. Its construction had been crucial in closing the siege around Antioch, and they hoped it would be equally useful in keeping Kerbogah at bay and leaving open the road to Saint-Simeon. For two days Robert of Flanders and a small band of Franks, fighting with lances and crossbows, maintained possession of the Mahomerie. After three days, however, the fighting became particularly brutal. Several of the defenders died or suffered serious injury. Kerbogah's army suffered losses as well, and that evening his troops retreated to seek reinforcements. Count Robert, meanwhile, realized that retaining the tower was a lost cause. He allowed his weary and bloodied men to retreat back into Antioch in the middle of the night, setting the Mahomerie on fire as they left lest the Saracens turn it against them. The next morning, June 8, about 4,000 Turks turned up for the fight but instead picked through the wreckage left behind.

With the siege tower out of the way, Kerbogah began to relocate his army to the southeast corner of the city, near the citadel. From outside the walls, he could run his army through the massive keep and directly into Antioch. The Franks recognized the danger and tried to cut the Turks off, attacking them near the St. George Gate. That fight raged all day, and those involved experienced a whole new level of exhaustion and delirium. Some of them reported something like combat fatigue—an out-of-body experience or, perhaps, a hellish visitation. "Something happened to our men there both horrible to mention and unheard of. Amidst the hail of arrows and the continuous blows from stones and spears and among so, so many dead, our men were asleep."

It was perhaps at this moment that one of the poor pilgrims, fighting courageously alongside the knights, became crushed between two horses. What happened next he could never say. As if waking from the dead, he found himself lying on a rock outside the city at twilight. The battle was winding down, and so with the rest of the survivors, he scurried back into Antioch. The poor pilgrim was Peter Bartholomew, the man whom St. Andrew had visited months earlier to tell of the Holy Lance. By this point Peter had come completely unstuck in time and disconnected from reality, moving easily between this world and the next. Once awake outside the walls of Antioch, he was ready to tell his tale, but over the next five days hardly anyone would hear of it.[11]

For the rest of the army, trapped in the hell that was Antioch, the most intense fighting of the siege began the next morning around the citadel as Kerbogah, securely in control of the land outside the walls, began trying to funnel his men directly into the city. At the end of the first day, a Frankish warrior called Hugh the Insane became trapped at the top of a tower, fighting alone against several Turks. Realizing that he could not escape, he struggled valiantly for as long as he could stand. "Finally, his body burned with a thousand arrows, as he saw that he could not avoid death, he hastened the moment for himself by leaping with shield and weapons into a thick crowd he had seen, and made himself into a missile against his killers"—one of the first instances in history of suicide, martyrdom, and murder combined in a single gesture.[12]

At about the same time and near the same place, Bohemond was hit in the leg by an arrow. "Blood flowed copiously from the wound, and the noble prince's heart began to decline from its former courage." Besides the physical effects, the injury seems to have made him skittish. At the very least, he was losing his touch. A day or two later, when his men were reluctant to leave the houses they'd commandeered and risk their lives outside the citadel, Bohemond attempted to force them into action by setting fire to the city. It was an act born of frustration. Simply put, Bohemond had not anticipated this fight—he had not expected there to be a battle against Kerbogah at all. When he had agreed to the other leaders' terms about his possession of the city, he did so thinking that Alexius had, at best, only a few days to reach Antioch before the fighting would end and the agreement about surrendering the city to the emperor would expire. The city, including the citadel, would fall into Bohemond's hands. Kerbogah would arrive with his army, but he would find Antioch as daunting a challenge as the Franks had done. The relief force would then disperse in short order. But when the citadel did not fall, giving Kerbogah nearly direct access into the city, Bohemond must have realized that his genius had failed him. The flames born of his anger spread rapidly, destroying about 2,000 houses and, reportedly, devouring temples that would have made a Greek painter or an Arab goldsmith or an Irish metalworker weep.[13]

As bad as the fighting was, the hunger was worse. Over the previous eight months, the Turks had exhausted almost all of the city's useful supplies. Soon the army would be experiencing levels of starvation beyond anything that had happened the previous winter. Already the pilgrims were picking through soil with trembling fingers, chewing on branches and roots, hoping to find a little nourishment. They cooked the skin of long-dead horses and oxen or else just chewed leather shoes vainly trying to suck out some protein. A mother held a baby to her breast, but her milk had run dry, and she knew that her child would die.

Food was available, but only at unattainable prices. Some survivors kept a list: "A hen cost 15 shillings; an egg, 2 shillings; a walnut, a penny;

3 or 4 beans, a penny; a small buck, 16 shillings; the buck's stomach, 2 shillings; a ram's tail, 3 shillings and 8 pennies. A camel's tongue, which is small, cost 4 shillings." A similar but shorter list appears in the Old Testament in a description of the siege of Samaria. It "lasted for so long that a donkey's head sold for 8 shekels of silver, and a quarter of a cab of seed pods for 5 shekels." This biblical famine had been so bad that one mother had eaten her own child. Similarly in Antioch, the hunger grew so fierce that the Franks could barely restrain themselves from "human banquets." Perhaps not all of them did.[14]

The starvation, hopelessness, and constant danger were all more than most of the crusaders could bear. After one day of fighting around the citadel, a large group of warriors, including many prominent men (Bohemond's brother-in-law among them) met in secret and agreed that they could never prevail. And so in the dead of night, they hung ropes from the ramparts and quietly slid down the walls—earning for themselves at home the nickname "Secret Ropedancers." Outside the walls, they picked a stealthy path around the periphery of Kerbogah's camp and made their way to the port of Saint-Simeon. There they found several European ships and informed their crews that "Antioch had been captured by the Turks and the pagans had annihilated the Christians." Some of the ships immediately cut anchor and started home. One of them stopped at Alexandretta along the way, where the same deserters told a convalescing Stephen of Blois that he had been right to flee. Sadly, Stephen joined them, and together they sailed to Constantinople.[15]

The Heavens Open

But even as the Secret Ropedancers fled and while most of the army was starving, the crusaders' fortunes began to turn. The heavens were opening up, and Christ once more smiled on His warriors, sending them clear signs of His affection and consolation.

Near the citadel of Antioch, a group of soldiers wearied by the fight were wondering, for obvious reasons, what had been the point of it all. Why had they traveled so far in the name of Christ, now to die while defending a city captured through treachery? In answer, a priest from Lombardy told a remarkable story. "Don't think that you are suffering in this way for nothing," he said, "but hear and think about the reward that Lord Jesus will give to all those who are going to die on this road for his love and grace." He had it on good authority that two years earlier another Italian priest had met a strange pilgrim who eventually identified himself as St. Ambrose of Milan. Ambrose had died seven hundred years earlier, but even so, there he was. He told the priest that God had approved of the crusade and that anyone who kept faith and died on the journey would immediately receive a crown of martyrdom. Lest anyone doubt the vision, Ambrose added, "When three years have passed from this day, know that the surviving Christians, after many struggles will reach the holy city of Jerusalem and there gain victory over all the barbarian nations." With that, the saint vanished. Two years after the vision, the men at the makeshift ramparts around Antioch's citadel took heart. Burning with hope and longing for eternal life, they set aside fear of death and resumed the struggle.[16]

AT THE SAME TIME, a priest named Stephen of Valence ran away from the citadel, believing himself about to die, and entered the church of the Virgin Mary. There he found several clerics gathered together, praying and preparing for death. Stephen confessed his sins, as did the others, and then they sang psalms late into the night. After everyone else had fallen asleep, Stephen maintained a vigil.

The next morning he breathlessly hurried back. Many of the leaders, including Adhémar, Raymond, and Bohemond, had gathered there, shaking their heads at the impossible battle before them. "Gentlemen!" Stephen said. "If it please you, listen to this thing that I just saw in a vision!"

That night, after his friends had fallen asleep, an extraordinarily handsome man approached him. "Do you know me?" the man asked.

"I don't know you at all," Stephen answered, "except that I can see a cross on your head like our Savior."

He said, "That is who I am."

Christ was angry. The Franks had forgotten all of the help He had already given them and had begun to satisfy their lusts "with Christian women and pagan tramps." Their sin was creating a veritable stench unto heaven. The Lord's rage, boiling over, could be mollified only through the intervention of His mother, Mary, and St. Peter, who threw themselves at

His feet and pleaded that He spare the Christians. Peter was particularly eloquent: "Lord, through so many years the pagan people have held my house and have performed there many inexpressible evils. If they are driven out, the angels in heaven will rejoice!"

Christ turned to Stephen. "Who is leader of the army?"

The priest answered, "Lord, there has never been one leader"—at this stage everyone wanted to forget Stephen of Blois—"but for the most part they trust the bishop."

Christ therefore ordered Stephen to carry His message of repentance directly to Bishop Adhémar. If the crusaders followed His directions, they would receive unexpected help within five days. Stephen tried to wake his friends. He wanted to introduce them to Christ, Mary, and Peter, but the heavenly visitors disappeared before he could.

Stephen finished his story in the shadow of the citadel, but Adhémar did not entirely believe him. He asked the priest to swear to the truth of his words on a Bible. Stephen offered instead to walk through fire or to throw himself from a tower. So electrifying was this answer that all of the leaders on the spot used the proffered Bible to swear that they would never dance down ropes to escape Antioch. They would see the siege through to the end. And Tancred went a step further. As long as he had forty knights, he would not quit the pilgrimage until he had seen Jerusalem.[17]

THE MOST REMARKABLE VISIONARY of them all was Peter Bartholomew. When he had spoken with Andrew outside the walls of Antioch during the ferocious struggle with Kerbogah, when so many of the Franks had entered into a trance, he learned that the apostle was losing his patience. He threatened serious consequences to Peter if he did not finally tell Adhémar and Count Raymond the secret of the Holy Lance. And finally Peter worked up his courage to do so—perhaps convinced by his miraculous delivery on the field of battle.

By then this was the fifth time that Andrew had appeared to Peter. On the first occasion, of course, the earth had trembled and the skies had turned blood-red. The second, third, and fourth visions all happened while Peter was on the road. Once, on February 10, Peter was near Edessa begging for food (before Baldwin arrived there). The other two times he was at the ports of Saint-Simeon and Mamistra, on March 20 and May 4, respectively, looking for ships on which to stow away and thus escape the nightmare that Antioch had become. At Mamistra when St. Andrew stopped Peter and ordered him to return to the army with news of the Lance, he "burst into the bitterest tears," thinking of the impossibility of survival. And he disobeyed Andrew, boarding a ship for Cyprus. It sailed on calm seas and with favorable winds. But at night the weather turned ugly, and the crew returned to Mamistra. Two more times the ship set out and turned back, the third time going to Saint-Simeon, where Peter fell deathly ill. He had recovered and gone back to Antioch just before the city was captured.[18]

Born of disasters where it seemed the very earth around him was coming apart, the dreams of Andrew returned at times of intense hunger, disorientation, and despair. Peter probably found comfort in them. Not only did his ghostly, apostolic friend promise eventual relief, but he also hinted that Peter might yet prove to be the hero of the crusade. Peter hesitated to tell others about the visions, however, not because he doubted their truth or feared they were "the mere distraction of dreams, which affects us almost constantly." Rather, he stayed quiet because he believed people would not take a poor man seriously. He again and again imagined his own "impoverished garb" set alongside the ecclesiastical and secular "magnificence" of Bishop Adhémar and Count Raymond and feared to approach his lords.[19]

But for eleventh-century Christians, poverty could also be a source of authority, so much so that Peter pretended to be illiterate even though he did have some learning. In a later vision, Saints Andrew and Peter would make the point explicitly. While asleep in the chapel of Count Raymond, Peter saw the apostles before him, "clad in poorly cut and filthy clothes, standing near the coffers where the relics were kept, and he thought them poor men who were intending to steal something from the tent. St. Andrew indeed was wearing an old cloak torn at the shoulders, with a patch sewn over the opening on the left shoulder, and nothing on the right, and he wore the meanest of shoes. St. Peter was wearing a long and baggy shirt that went down to his ankles. Then Peter Bartholomew said to them, 'Who are you, lords, or what do you want?' And blessed Peter answered, 'We are legates of God. I am Peter, and this is Andrew. But we want you to see us in this dress so that you might know how useful it is for devoted servants of God. In this condition and dress, as you see us, we went to God, and so we are now.' And at these words they changed so that nothing was brighter, nothing more beautiful." The message that the apostles—and Peter Bartholomew—wished to convey was clear: The poor were closer to God. It was because of Peter's frayed clothing, not in spite of it, that his message ought to seem credible.[20]

And so as the fighting raged around the citadel, the poor Provençal visionary finally told his prince and his bishop about the Holy Lance and where they might find it. Adhémar, as expected, did not believe him. Count Raymond, however, was hopeful, and he handed the ragged visionary over to his chaplain, Raymond of Aguilers, for safekeeping and perhaps also to make a formal record of his testimony.[21]

This vision needs to be set in context with the other two—the priest who had told how St. Ambrose had endorsed their cause and Stephen of Valence, who brought reassuring words from Christ. At this point in the never-ending siege, the army's leaders had decided to cast their lot with the miraculous. Claiming total confidence in Stephen's words, they took a public oath intended to inspire and motivate the ordinary soldiers. They also made a conscious decision, whatever their doubts about Peter Bartholomew, to connect his vision to Stephen of Valence's.

Stephen had promised, through the voice of Christ, that heavenly aid would arrive in five days. Count Raymond decided that the excavation for the Lance should occur on June 14, the fifth day after Stephen's vision. A cynical observer might think that this delay gave someone time to hide a lance in the church. It likely did. But it also gave Raymond, and other leaders, the opportunity to circulate Peter Bartholomew's story among the soldiers. It was five days to build up hope, to create excitement about the possible discovery of a major relic, and to instill confidence among the common soldiers that the words of the Lombard priest and St. Ambrose were true: Their final victory at Jerusalem had been preordained.

The princes also received an unexpected assist from heaven. The night before the dig, a meteor streaked across the skies of Antioch. It came from the West, like the crusaders themselves, and it seemed to crash into the middle of the Turks' camps. As signs from heaven go, this one wasn't subtle: God was hurling fire at the Turks. The chaplain Raymond, who had volunteered to dig for the Lance the next morning, described it thus: "A great star stood above the city during the night and then, after a little while, it split into three parts and fell into three parts. Our men drew comfort from it, and awaited the day that the priest [Stephen of Valence] had predicted."[22]

On that fifth day, Raymond and eleven other men—including Count Raymond, the bishop of Orange, and Pons of Balazun, the knight who was working as Raymond of Aguilers's coauthor—began to dig behind the altar of the Church of St. Peter in search of the Holy Lance. Adhémar, notably, was not present. If he hesitated, it was not because he doubted the Lance's authenticity. A pious fraud was clearly in the works. Adhémar knew it was a fake and was complicit in the deception. He was more likely absent because he had doubts about the messenger, Peter Bartholomew. It was dangerous, even foolhardy to invest such an unknown and possibly unstable figure with so much prestige.

After a full day of digging, the blue ribbon panel of archaeologists found nothing. Peter ordered a stop to the work, stripped down to just a shirt, stepped into what must have been by this time a sizable hole, and prayed to God to show them mercy. Everyone present followed his example. And at last, with only a little more digging, the exotic, ornamental head of a clearly foreign, Eastern lance poked above the earth. The chaplain Raymond was one of the first to see it. "I, who wrote these things, when only the point had appeared above the ground—I kissed it." Peter Bartholomew and Raymond carried it out to the city, where it inspired joy and fear at the awesome power of God.[23]

Probably in the midst of all these signs and miracles, the army's leaders unveiled one final visionary, who on the night of June 10 had tried to escape down the walls with the other Secret Ropedancers. Halfway to the ground, he unexpectedly ran into his brother, a crusader, and, more to the point, a dead crusader. "Where are you running off to?" the dead brother asked. "Stay! Don't be afraid. The Lord will be with you in your battle, as will your friends, who have gone before you in death during this journey. They will fight with you against the Turks!" The dead crusaders would return for the fight against Kerbogah. Peter Bartholomew, at the apostle Andrew's instruction, similarly proclaimed, "Truly God will aid you. All your brothers who have died, starting from the beginning of the journey, will be here with you in this fight, and you shall fight only a tenth of the enemy, since your brothers will destroy the other nine tenths, through the power and command of God."[24]

The heavens were opening. The Christian God, like Zeus, was hurling firebolts against an unbelieving enemy. The dead were readying their ghostly mounts to ride out in force alongside the living, an army of spirits brought back to life to eviscerate the slaves of Antichrist. At about the same time, Kerbogah was withdrawing his men from the citadel, settling in for a longer siege. Apparently, the brutal combat had worn them down as well, or perhaps the meteor had rattled them as much as the Franks liked to think that it had. Ever the empiricist, still trusting in numerical advantage, Kerbogah continued to expect to wear the Franks down. They were starving. They would surrender. Kerbogah, in short, had no idea what he had unleashed.

The Prophets' Crusade

The crusaders still needed a plan, and their resident military and diplomatic genius, Bohemond, may have at last found one. Predictably, he decided to forego caution. Waiting out the siege was pointless. The army couldn't survive the summer. They might just possibly make it until the end of the July, but no further. The only hope for victory lay in a frontal assault. But apart from a general plan to "ride out the gates in groups and attack," he never revealed exactly what he had in mind or why he expected it to work. Keeping his counsel on this point may have been a wise decision. More than ever, the army had staked its identity and its mission on miracles. It was not a time for strategy and cunning. It was a time to unleash God's wrath.

Divine intervention aside, Bohemond's plan remained a long shot. The princes therefore (presumably with Bohemond's approval) decided to investigate one other way to resolve the siege, one that did not potentially involve destruction of the entire army. They sent two men to negotiate with Kerbogah. One of them, named Herluin, spoke enough Arabic to act as an interpreter. The other person, the true legate for the princes, was the original apocalyptic crusade preacher, Peter the Hermit. If ever a sign was needed that Bohemond had learned to appreciate the power and importance of prophecy to the crusaders' mission, this was it: Peter the Hermit was to be his *porte-parole*. To borrow a phrase from the French historian Jean Flori, the apocalyptic-minded members of the army were at this stage "leading the dance."[25]

In what must have been a terrifying experience, the two men left the relative safety of the city and walked into the heart of the Muslim camp under a flag of truce. Kerbogah received them inside his tent, a fabulous structure. It was, according to later tradition, embroidered with golden thread and held together with cords of silk and stakes of ivory, decorated with the ancient laws (presumably Arabic lettering) going back to the time of Adam. If Kerbogah had hoped to overwhelm his guests with showy displays of wealth and power, however, he had miscalculated. The Franks' chief negotiator was an inflexible hermit who dressed like a barefoot peasant.

Kerbogah must also have been surprised at the terms offered. Through his interpreter Peter gave Kerbogah the chance to surrender, to leave Antioch at once, since the city belonged "to St. Peter and to the Christians, according to law." For "the blessed apostle Peter had converted it by his preaching to the worship of Christ." The Franks were willing to take the matter to court: "If you wish to contend for this land according to legal judgment, surely it pertains to the Christians?" The Turks were usurpers who could hold the city only through "proud tyranny." It was a stark argument, made from strength rather than weakness, and Kerbogah no doubt greeted it with equal parts amusement and derision.[26]

Peter also suggested a middle option between surrender and war: a judicial ordeal, trial by combat. In doing so, he was again suggesting that at the heart of the battle was a property dispute. Each side, Peter proposed, could choose anywhere from five to one hundred men. Hostages would be exchanged and oaths taken before the Christian God and the Saracen god respectively, and then the two teams would fight to the death, the winning side to receive Antioch.

Like many other elements in the crusade story, this proposal sounds outrageous, but it was not without precedent. A few years before in 1066, William of Normandy had made a similar offer to King Harold of England.

William would prove his right to rule England in a trial, either according to English or Norman law, as Harold preferred. And if Harold did not wish to risk a legal decision, they might settle everything through an ordeal, thus preventing an eventual massacre on the battlefield. The story could have served as the model for Peter the Hermit's legation—perhaps Robert of Normandy, who had been at Hastings, suggested it. But like King Harold of England, Kerbogah rejected the idea. According to one report, he offered instead to spare the Franks only if they renounced Christianity. Converts would receive lands, cities, and castles. Indeed, all of the Frankish foot soldiers could become mounted warriors. According to another version, Kerbogah promised nothing except to enslave the Franks' beardless boys and virgin women and to kill everyone else—postpubescent men and married women alike. He then showed Peter the vast collection of chains he had brought with him to shackle prisoners. There was, it seemed, no possible settlement outside of battle.[27]

The Arab historian Ibn al-Athir offers a slightly different version of events. Peter went to Kerbogah hoping only to surrender. The only thing the crusaders requested was safe conduct back to Europe. Kerbogah laughingly refused. The Franks would have to fight their way out, he told Peter.

Given the contradiction between the two accounts, which should we believe? Recent historians have tended to accept Ibn al-Athir's story on the grounds that the evidence behind it is "less partisan." We should probably be more circumspect. Ibn al-Athir was a remarkably lucid historian, but no less partisan than the Latin writers. (In this case he might have wanted to show how unreasonable Kerbogah was being, how he had the chance to turn the Franks away, but in his arrogance rejected the opportunity.) Ibn al-Athir also knew much less about the mindset and intentions of the Franks than did contemporary Christian writers. Peter certainly might have floated some sort of handover of the city, probably asking for a guarantee of safe passage to Jerusalem—terms that Kerbogah did not accept. But the fact that Peter offered a possible compromise does not invalidate the impression created in chronicles that diplomatic bluster formed the better part of his presentation. Whatever the case, the two sides could not come to agreement, and Peter and Herluin returned to the city.[28]

Back inside Antioch Peter announced that Kerbogah would have only war. Drawing a crowd, as he was wont to do, he started to go into detail about the things he had seen, but Godfrey ordered him to be silent, "lest the people, already suffering from fear and deprivation withdraw from the battle." Godfrey may have had still another reason for telling Peter to be quiet. Peter, or Herluin, may have been sent to gather other intelligence about the Turks, information that the princes did not want the rest of their armies to know. Or they may have feared that there were still spies in the city in communication with Kerbogah, and they did not want these spies relaying back to Kerbogah everything that Peter had learned.[29]

Over the next three days, in preparation for battle, the princes declared a fast. It was likely unnecessary. The army was already starving. The clergy also arranged liturgical processions in and around Antioch's churches, along with ceremonies of mass confession. Every available cleric preached, including the Provençal visionary Peter Bartholomew. Andrew was still talking to him, and the apostle's young spiritual companion had by now revealed himself to be Jesus Christ. (He made His identity known somewhat grotesquely—ordering Peter to kiss His foot. When Peter knelt down, he recoiled in horror at the sight of the bloody open wound. Whether he then pressed his lips to the gory mess, as requested, is unknown.)

Speaking to the crowd, Peter Bartholomew delivered three important messages. First, everyone who was able should perform five acts of charity in commemoration of the five wounds of Christ. Even in these tense circumstances, Peter was thinking of how best to alleviate the suffering of the poor. Second, the Lord wanted the crusaders to change their battle cry. It should be "God help us!" rather than "God wills it!" It is doubtful whether anyone followed him on this point, even among the Provençals. Adhémar of le Puy, who distrusted Peter anyway, would not have tolerated going against Urban II's instructions. Finally, he proclaimed, "know this well: the days have come that the Lord promised to Blessed Mary and to his apostles, that He would raise up the kingdom of Christians while casting down and trampling the kingdom of pagans." In other words, based on what Andrew had told Peter, the Apocalypse was at hand.[30]

Few in the army would have contradicted this opinion. More than ever, the crusade belonged to the prophets.

The Battle with Kerbogah

The fasting over, on June 28, 1098, the Franks did what Kerbogah had least expected: They attacked. Their forces were badly outnumbered. Many of the knights were riding packhorses and mules. Nevertheless, most of the Franks left the city in waves, directly engaging Kerbogah's army at close range. Another group, under the leadership of Raymond of Saint-Gilles, stayed behind to guard the citadel lest Kerbogah's lieutenant Ahmad ibn-Marwan suddenly decided to fight aggressively on behalf of his lord. Outside the walls, according to Frankish lore, Kerbogah sat idly by, playing chess with one of his followers. When news of the battle reached him, he refused to believe that it was actually happening. His surprise at the news led him to berate one of his noble followers, a Turk named Mirdalin, who had assured him that the Franks were trapped in the city and would never dare challenge him. "What's going on? Didn't you tell me that there were very few Franks and that they'd never fight with me?"

"I never said that they wouldn't attack," Mirdalin responded. "But come! I'll have a look and tell you if they can be easily beaten." At that moment a third wave of Franks, led by Bishop Adhémar, exited the city, and Mirdalin observed, "They can be killed, but you can't make them retreat." (Some Latin writers maintained that Mirdalin was an apostate Christian from Aquitaine. In their version of the story, Kerbogah turned to him and shouted, "You clod! You wretched criminal! What nonsense you told me about these men—that they were eating their horses, in the death throes of hunger, planning to flee! By Mathomos, this lie will come back on your head, and it will cost you the price of your head!" Kerbogah then summoned his "gladiator" and ordered him to unsheathe his sword and cut off the man's head in a way worthy of his prattling apostasy.)[31]

It was time for a new plan, but Kerbogah continued to hesitate. Rather than attack, he pathetically sought another parlay, ready now to accept the Franks' offer of a judicial duel. As a result, his army entered the fray too late and too little prepared. (Or did Kerbogah order his army to delay its counterattack in order to crush the Franks all at once, as one Latin writer and one Arab writer argued? Nearly a decade later, the circumstances of the battle remained controversial.)[32]

As Kerbogah would soon realize, the time for negotiation had passed. And despite all the Franks' previous talk of their cause being based on property rights secured by St. Peter, and despite their willingness to settle it according to legal procedure and to consider surrender, they had now crossed over into heaven. Or heaven had crossed into their world. The true holy war had begun. Lines of priests and monks clad in vestments marched in front of the armies, chanting and summoning heavenly aid for the battle.

Help from above arrived. First, God sent a light rain to refresh the wearied Franks and their mounts. Then, a cross that some of the Normans were carrying began to shine brightly, striking fear into the Saracens. Adhémar of le Puy's chaplain, none other than the chronicler Raymond of Aguilers, held aloft the Holy Lance of Antioch and wielded it as a talismanic weapon. The very winds struggled to determine the outcome, and when for a time things seemed to go poorly for the Franks, Eurus, the east wind, appeared to prevail over Zephyrus, the west.[33]

As some of the veterans remembered the battle, what really turned the fighting was the appearance of ghost riders. Their number included the fallen crusaders, just as Peter Bartholomew and the former ropedancing priest had promised. Many saints were there as well. God loved the Franks so much, the apostle Andrew had earlier told Peter, "that the saints, who are now at rest and who know in advance the gift God has planned, were willing to be in the flesh and to fight with us." Their number included George, Theodore, Demetrius—"You have to believe these words," an eyewitness wrote, "since many of our men saw it"—and all the other white-clad riders whom Pirrus had often seen riding down from a mysterious camp in the hills. Saints Peter and Paul, meanwhile, vigorously offered prayers of intercession for the soldiers, without actually becoming directly involved in the fighting.

The ghost army marched in five divisions, exiting the city along with the crusaders, their numbers freely mingling with the living Franks. "For truly as they said, our princes had established only eight divisions, and once outside the city we were in thirteen orders." With this army in the fray, with priests chanting psalms of victory, with the Holy Lance keeping the Saracens and their arrows miraculously at bay, Christ was at last conferring the victory at Antioch of which "the pilgrim church of Franks" had so long dreamed.[34]

Shortly after Adhémar and the chaplain Raymond took to the field, a grass fire broke out. Was it a Saracen battle tactic—a deliberate attempt to blind the Franks and their horses and thus more easily kill them—or an agreed-upon signal for the Saracens to retreat? Yet another point of controversy. Regardless, a panicked, disorganized withdrawal began, the Turks blinded with their own smoke and terror—or else with dread instilled in them from the Holy Lance of Christ. Bohemond emerged from the city at the head of his reserve force only to find the battle, to all appearances, ended. Kerbogah's massive army was fleeing, with the ragtag band of the crusaders in pursuit on their mules or oxen or half-dead horses. Most of the Turkish cavalry escaped, their horses in far better condition than the Franks'. Their foot soldiers were captured. As for the Turkish women, the historian Fulcher of Chartres bragged that the Franks did not rape them but only pierced their bellies with lances. "They left behind their tents, their gold and silver and many treasures, their sheep and oxen, their horses and mules, their camels and asses, their grains and wine, their flour and many other things that we needed to live." The battle for Antioch was over, and the Franks, unbelievably, had won.[35]

Surely some of the crusaders, like modern historians, wondered just how they had survived. Their success in battle had always depended on two things: the opportunity to engage the Turks at close quarters and the strength of their knights. But as Kerbogah would have readily agreed, the numbers didn't add up. By June 28 the Franks had fewer than two hundred horses left. A few thousand infantry and two hundred poorly equipped knights seemed a poor match for an army so large that contemporaries numbered it in the hundreds of thousands. Kerbogah's decision to delay his attack until the Franks were in the open field seemed a wise decision— to wait until the enemy was most vulnerable to encirclement and false retreats, basic tactics of Turkish cavalry. With any kind of discipline, Kerbogah could not have lost and a commander like Bohemond could not have believed that his pathetic, starving warriors would ever win.[36]

So how did they? The Arab historian Ibn al-Athir (the same historian who I have suggested was not trustworthy on matters of crusader psychology) offered a straightforward solution: Kerbogah's armies betrayed him. They had only joined his cause with reluctance. Kerbogah, he wrote, "thinking that the present crisis would force the Muslims to remain loyal to him, alienated them by his pride and ill-treatment of them. They plotted in secret anger to betray him and desert him in the heat of battle." That appears to be exactly what happened. Remarkably, Ibn al-Athir's portrayal of Kerbogah was perfectly in line with what the Franks said about him. He was an arrogant man, someone so anxious to impose his own will on Antioch that he first disinherited Yaghi-Siyan's son in favor of his own man, Ahmad ibn-Marwan, and then promptly began to bully Ahmad ibn-Marwan.

The Franks, particularly Tancred, seem to have been aware of this situation. They also could have readily understood how the Turks drafted into Kerbogah's service would have viewed their general. Kerbogah was a representative of Baghdad, a ruthlessly ambitious man anxious to impose his own vision of a unified culture on what was essentially a frontier society. Many of the men in Kerbogah's army would have been no more enthusiastic about his presence than, for example, Raymond of Saint-Gilles would have been if King Philip I had marched to Occitania to impose order on Raymond's principality or if representatives of Henry IV had showed up in southern Italy trying to coerce Bohemond's clan into more predictable and subservient behavior.[37]

Yet there is even more to the story. It may be that Kerbogah's followers not only deserted him in the battle but also that Bohemond, and perhaps the other crusader princes, knew—or at least suspected—that this would happen. Perhaps Ahmad ibn-Marwan raised the possibility in his discussions with Tancred. He may well have identified other dissatisfied leaders in the Turkish army whom the Christians could try to contact. And on the eve of the battle, the Christians had had the opportunity to pursue such leads in the form of the legation led by Peter the Hermit and at least one fluent Arabic speaker. In this scenario the sudden grass fire in the Turkish camp may indeed have been a signal to retreat, as the author of *Deeds of the Franks* suggested, a signal about which the Franks had been warned in advance.

In any case Ahmad ibn-Marwan knew that the fix was in. As soon as the battle started to turn, he sent word down from the citadel that he wanted to surrender. Raymond of Saint-Gilles, who had been left behind to block the citadel, immediately sent up his banner, and Ahmad ibn-Marwan had it displayed from a tower. Some of the Normans, however, informed the Turks in the citadel that the banner was not Bohemond's. Ahmad ibn-Marwan returned it at once and only formalized his surrender when he received the banner of the man whom Tancred had helped to establish as his ally.[38]

If this were the case—if Christians had conspired with Turks to gain victory at Antioch—then neither side would later want to make the fact known. The Turks had betrayed their leader and allowed the Franks to establish a second capital, along with Edessa, in Syria. It would not have been a proud moment in Muslim history.

As for the Christians, they preferred the illusion of a great—no, rather, a miraculous—victory. Adhémar of le Puy, who by now had embraced the Holy Lance of Antioch, was a man who knew something about faking a miracle. He, Bohemond, and the other princes would have been content in this case to let appearances speak for themselves. Through the miracles of God, the crusaders had achieved the impossible. Why let on that it had been another negotiated betrayal, instead of a heroic last stand gone unbelievably right?

And to a degree we ought to accept this explanation. The Franks believed that their enemies were idol worshippers. They were adherents of a cult whose founder, Mathomos, was a heretic and a libertine. The Franks saw in this same Mathomos a cruel parody of Christ and indeed a precursor to Antichrist. They believed that as warriors the Turks were very much like themselves, and if only they would renounce their misguided and misbegotten religion, they might stand alongside Christians as brothers. But because they would not, the Turks and Saracens were limbs of Satan and legates of Antichrist. Kerbogah may have believed that he was fighting a traditional war in which numbers, strategy, and, perhaps, law would play a role. But the Franks knew their battle fit into a much grander apocalyptic drama, one whose ending had long been written.

15

Feasting on the Fallen:
Antioch to Ma'arra

(June 1097–January 1099)

After the defeat of Kerbogah, the army went into something like early hibernation. Jerusalem, by some reports, was a mere ten days' march away if the crusaders committed to going. Instead, the princes decided to rest until at least November. Fulcher of Chartres, who was in Edessa, indicated that the leaders did not want to advance until the beginning of the harvest season when supplies would be more plentiful, but no one else supported this explanation. The Franks instead seemed to have lost their direction.

In the meantime the armies dispersed into different parts of Syria, each group foraging for food and looking for adventure on its own. The leaders, meanwhile, fought among themselves. Their struggles were in part political and personal, with Bohemond and Raymond vying for control of Antioch and seeking out allies among the other lords. But these leaders were at the same time engaged in an ideological battle over the meaning of the crusade. In question was not only whether their campaign was, at heart, an apocalyptic enterprise. They also faced a subtler problem: What kind of apocalypse would it be?[1]

Aftermath

The political problems (as distinct from the ideological ones) had begun before the battle with Kerbogah ended. As we have seen, the Turks in the citadel preferred to surrender to Bohemond, not Raymond. And Bohemond had already secured a promise from all the other Frankish leaders that should he play an instrumental role in Antioch's capture, he would gain possession of it. He had now played that sort of role twice, first by securing Pirrus's cooperation in betraying the city and then by simultaneously defeating Kerbogah and securing Ahmad ibn-Marwan's agreement to hand over the citadel. To secure his claim to the keep, Bohemond expelled from it all but his own men. Raymond, his chief rival and critic, forced his way inside a tower near the Bridge Gate, the area of the most intense fighting during the siege, and established a stronghold there. The princes were unsure how to settle these claims, particularly if Alexius or Tetigus turned up with their long-expected army, asserting imperial rights to the city.

This last problem was especially pressing. Alexius had it in his power to wreck the whole crusade if in the name of Antioch he decided to set his armies against the Franks. The princes, with the exception of Bohemond, therefore decided to take the question directly to him. They dispatched Hugh the Great to Constantinople, charging him either with inviting Alexius to come to Antioch to claim his prize or else with denouncing him to his face as a traitor and informing him that the Franks had broken all ties with him. As is sometimes the case, equally reliable sources give diametrically opposed reports. Whatever the tenor of Hugh's mission, it didn't matter. Alexius never rejoined the Franks, and Hugh never returned to the crusade.[2]

Bohemond continued about the business of establishing himself as prince of Antioch. He set the clergy to work restoring the cathedral of St. Peter to its former glory, as the fearsome icon of Christ no doubt gazed down approvingly. He allowed Patriarch John IV—who had become somewhat of a folk hero after the Turks had hung him from the wall during the siege—to return to his office. Not everyone, on earth or in heaven, was happy with that decision. Barely a month later, in a vision the apostle Andrew told Peter Bartholomew that the Franks needed to appoint a new patriarch, one who followed Latin law. But the decision to retain John IV was probably politic if Bohemond wished to pacify his new subjects, the survivors of the long siege and the sacking of the city. He also granted a church dedicated to St. John to the people of Genoa, whose fleet had provided crucial supplies over the previous nine months. As part of this deal, the Genoese obtained possession of thirty houses near the church and the rights to run a market on the square. The giant's guiding philosophy was that if he acted as if he owned the place, everyone, Raymond included, would eventually go along with him. And for the most part, they did. Perhaps grudgingly, at some point Bohemond received the title of "lord and advocate of the city."[3]

A spirit of melancholy, however, was settling over Antioch's new ruler. Comfortably ensconced in his citadel, he invited Robert of Flanders and Godfrey of Bouillon to dine with him. At the end of their meal, he began to play sullenly with a knife. Robert chided him, telling him to lighten up, given all that he had accomplished. Bohemond attempted to brighten and rise to the occasion. In a show of bravado, he pointed at a large candle and boasted that he could slice it in two with a single stroke. Robert bet him that he couldn't, and each man agreed to wager a cloak on it. Bohemond swung the knife and cut the candle into two unequal sections, in itself an astonishing feat, but "wondrous to say, one candle became two." That is, the smaller half fell to one side and suddenly caught fire. It glowed for a short while and then burned itself out.

Word of the sign spread throughout the city, and according to a later Italian writer, it left Bohemond badly shaken. He not only refused to accept Robert's cloak but, bothered by the candle's behavior, also handed over his own cloak and other gifts. In hindsight, the story seemed to portend the death of Bohemond's son, killed in 1130 while campaigning around Antioch. But the younger Bohemond had not been born in 1098. A more likely interpretation at the time would have been that Bohemond's own rule of Antioch would burn out as swiftly as had that candle. His glory was already fading.[4]

The army had still other causes for melancholy. On August 1, 1098, Bishop Adhémar of le Puy fell ill and died. Albert of Aachen said that he was the first victim of a plague that ravaged the crusader camps for months, killing more than 100,000 men and women, although none of the other writers, including the ones who would have lived through the crisis, mentioned any such epidemic. According to their telling, Adhémar simply passed away.

It may have been an ordinary death, but its effects were tremendous. If the Franks were the Chosen People wandering through the desert, Adhémar had been their Moses—a cleric as comfortable, if not more so, leading a battlefield charge as he was delivering a sermon. But his first eulogist, the author of *Deeds of the Franks*, chose not to emphasize his military achievements or even his role in the crusade. Rather, he described Adhémar as "sustainer of the poor, counselor to the rich," and reported a sermon that the bishop had once delivered on the theme of charity: "None of you can be saved unless he honors and refreshes the poor, and you cannot be saved without them and they cannot live without you." He had died on the feast day of St. Peter in Chains—a coincidence that seemed appropriate since Peter held the keys to heaven. "Upon his death, he found someone to absolve his sins; he deservingly met one who welcomed him into heaven."[5]

Or maybe not. Shortly after Adhémar's death, St. Andrew again approached the discoverer of the Lance, Peter Bartholomew, accompanied now by Adhémar's shade. The dead bishop confessed to Peter that he had, for a time, gone to hell because of his initial doubts about the Holy Lance. "I was led into hell, and there punished most bitterly, and my head and face were burned, as you can see. My soul was there from the hour that it left my body, until my corpse was handed over to the dust." God provided some protection from the flames, covering him with a special cloak that Adhémar had once given to a poor man, but it left his head unprotected. Whoever doubted the truth of the vision, Adhémar added, need simply look inside his tomb, for the hellfire had consumed a large part of his physical head, too. He had escaped only because his friends offered a candle for him and because before his death, in penance for his doubts, he had donated three *denarii* to the Holy Lance. Among all the soldiers, Adhémar singled out Bohemond as playing a key part in releasing him from hell. Think on the fires of the afterlife, Adhémar concluded. They are both heavy and horrifying. Yet no one should grieve at his death. Adhémar continued to live with the army, as did everyone who had died on crusade. "And I will appear to them and I will give them better counsel than ever I did before."[6]

Andrew spoke in the same vision and urged Count Raymond and Bohemond to settle their differences. Addressing Raymond directly, the apostle said, "Let there be concord, Count Raymond, between you and Bohemond, and let there be the love of God and of your neighbor. And if you two make peace, nothing can separate you." Andrew did not want Raymond to hold Antioch at all. Rather, Raymond should consider all of the potential claimants to the city and give possession of it to the person with the truest faith, which could be judged by how generously he distributed charity to the poor. Given Bohemond's crucial role in helping to save Adhémar's soul, the giant was probably a strong candidate. And for a time, the chaplain Raymond concluded, everyone believed what Peter Bartholomew had said. But then they forgot his words, and some began to say that they should give the city to Alexius—an outcome that, in Raymond's eyes apparently, the very heavens would oppose.[7]

The crusade was thus on the verge of disintegrating over the questions of what to do with Antioch and whether to revive the alliance with Byzantium. Perhaps a living Adhémar could have crafted a compromise. In his absence, on September 11, 1098, the leaders wrote a letter about their difficulties to Pope Urban II. It is a remarkable document because it demonstrates both the army's turmoil and its optimism. "We have already subdued the Turks and the pagans," the princes claimed. "But the heretics—Greek and Armenian, Syrian and Jacobite—we have not been able to conquer. We therefore entreat and enjoin you, our dearest father, that, as head and father, you come to this, the place of your father, Peter. For since you are St. Peter's vicar and sit in his cathedral and hold us as your obedient servants in all things needing rightly to be done, then by your authority and by our might you shall uproot and destroy every sort of heresy here."

It is an ecstatic, almost apocalyptic vision—the entire world united under papal guidance and Latin Christianity. And the apocalypticism became more explicit in the conclusion: "Then you shall open for us the doors of each Jerusalem, and you will free the Lord's Sepulcher and make exalted the name of Christ above every name. If you come to us and complete with us the pilgrimage begun through you, the whole world will be obedient to you." A thoroughly Christianized world with the doors of "each

Jerusalem" (two Jerusalems, the earthly one and the heavenly one) opening simultaneously—so closely in sync had the Franks' wars and the designs of God now become.[8]

Frustrated Desire: The Crusaders Scatter

By the time the princes sent this letter, their armies had largely dispersed.
Leaders at all levels—princes and petty lords—were busily pursuing their
own interests. One of the first to depart in search of fortune was a
Provençal knight named Raymond Pilet, who led an expedition into the
Jabal as-Summaq region in northern Syria. He briefly besieged a castle
called Tel-Mannas before its occupants, Syrian Christians, welcomed him
inside and accepted his lordship.

A week later Raymond Pilet, his men, and a few of his new Syrian followers attacked an unnamed "castle full of Saracens." They seized the
peasants who lived around it and forced them to accept baptism—a rare
example of forced conversion on the crusade, or of any interest at all in
conversion. The peasants who did not accept Christ, Raymond executed.
From there he attempted an ambitious strike against the city of Ma'arra,
but that venture proved a little too ambitious.

Ma'arra, modern-day Ma'arrat al-Numan, was a compact, well-fortified,
and densely populated city beyond the reach of a small-time warlord like
Raymond Pilet. The Turks engaged his men before the city gates, and the
fight quickly turned into a rout. By the end of the day, Raymond and his
Syrian and Provençal followers were fleeing back to the castle, once full
of Saracens, that they had recently conquered. By the time they reached
it, the few survivors in his army were almost dying of thirst. There undoubtedly were dozens of other minor lords like Raymond engaged in similar small-scale adventures at the same time with similarly mixed results,
but their stories have been lost.[9]

As for the princes, Bohemond spent much of August in Cilicia (the
territory promised to him by Tetigus in February, though presumably with
different circumstances in mind). Godfrey went to Edessa and became
embroiled in its regional politics. For what seems to have been the first
time in the crusade, he and his men fought on behalf of one Turkish amir,
Omar of Azaz, against another, Ridwan of Aleppo. Raymond of Saint-

Gilles, who had been plundering the Syrian countryside to relieve the poor pilgrims, joined Godfrey in the campaign. To convince a few of the increasingly radical Provençal soldiers to follow him into this battle, Raymond apparently put out the word that a few Turks in Azaz had been spotted making the sign of the cross while fighting against the Turks of Aleppo—secret Christians perhaps? Together, Raymond and Godfrey succeeded in driving Ridwan from Azaz. Godfrey also established a treaty of friendship with Omar, gained some small amount of treasure, and even got a lesson in carrier pigeon technology. Like the truce at Antioch, this was a surprising interlude, suggesting, as it did, that given a slightly different vision, the business of holy war might have gone in a radically different direction.[10]

Many other soldiers would have accompanied Godfrey to Edessa, either fighting alongside him for the sake of Omar's independence or living in Edessa and working as mercenaries for Baldwin. Indeed, so many Franks came to Edessa that Baldwin's subjects feared he was turning their city into a European outpost, and some of them began plotting a coup d'état. It was probably inevitable. They would overthrow Baldwin just as he had replaced T'oros. One of the conspirators, however, lost his nerve and revealed the plans to Baldwin, who showed no hesitation. He learned the names of all the potential traitors, called together his most trusted bodyguards, and ordered them to arrest everyone involved. The more prominent among the prisoners, he ransomed. As for the others, he cut off their noses, hands, feet, tongues, lips, and testicles in various combinations. "From that day on Duke Baldwin became feared in the city of Edessa, and his name spread to the farthest reaches of his land."[11]

Clearly, the crusade had become aimless. Not everyone was happy following Baldwin and Godfrey's lead, playing Middle Eastern politics. They had an obvious goal, but none of the leaders wished to pursue it. St. Andrew, for one, was furious. The next time he spoke to Peter Bartholomew, around October 10, accompanied this time by Christ and an unnamed bearded man, he rebuked the visionary on many counts. First, there was the shoddy treatment his relics had received at Antioch. Peter had apparently discovered a few of Andrew's bone fragments (where and when we don't know) and set them aside in "an unworthy place." What were these bones? "When unbelievers threw me off of a mountain top," Andrew explained, "two of my fingers were broken. After my death, this man"—apparently the bearded stranger—"kept them and took them to Antioch. But then you, when you found them, allowed one of them to be stolen, the other to be treated poorly." Andrew waved a spectral hand in Peter's face. Two fingers were missing.

But the apostle was mainly angry at Raymond of Saint-Gilles. The count had received a special gift from God—the Holy Lance—yet he continued to sin grievously. To lend power to the warning, Peter reminded the count how he had five days earlier left in his chapel a large candle that should have shone for three days but had burned out almost immediately. The night before, by contrast, Raymond had donated a much smaller candle, but it continued to burn. What did this mean? Andrew didn't explain, but as when Bohemond chopped the candle in two, it betokened nothing good.

When told of the vision, Count Raymond denied any wrongdoing, but Peter whispered into his ear a secret sin (apparently related to him by Andrew) for which the count had not done penance. And at last he confessed his guilt, and Peter directed him both to perform penance and to expel his wicked advisors—presumably the men who were encouraging him to postpone the march to Jerusalem. "The Lord commands you not to delay any longer, since if Jerusalem is not captured, you will receive no help."[12]

It was an awkward position for Raymond. His hopes to seize control of the crusade had begun to depend more and more on his possession of the Holy Lance and his relationship to its eccentric prophet. But now the prophet was turning against him and trying to take control of military decisionmaking. Raymond couldn't take Jerusalem by himself. He would have to wait for at least three more weeks, until November 1, when the other princes were ready to depart. And he still had not given up hope of wresting control of Antioch from Bohemond. So under pressure from Peter Bartholomew and St. Andrew, Raymond settled on a middle course. He would lead his army in a generally southerly direction, following in the footsteps of Raymond Pilet, toward the Jabal as-Summaq plateau. Such a course might generously be seen as a first step toward Jerusalem. It could also be, as Count Raymond claimed, an attempt to find yet more supplies for the poor. And from Count Raymond's perspective, it was a way to continue exerting pressure on Bohemond by seizing control of territory that might otherwise pertain to Antioch.[13]

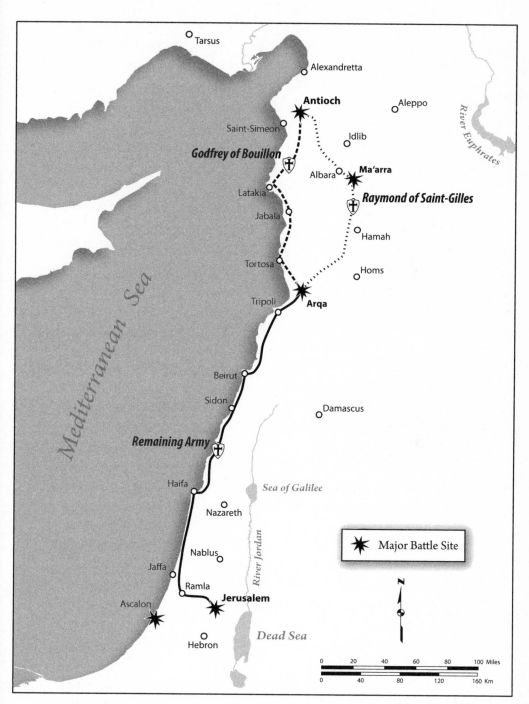

The roads taken from Antioch to Jerusalem

His first target was Albara, a once-prosperous trading city that had steadily decayed until by the eleventh century it was a small town inhabited by Turks and dwarfed by Roman ruins. Raymond's goal for Albara was, quite literally, colonial. He wanted to eradicate the Saracens and, according toone writer, fill the city with new landholders, or *colonis*.

The population of Albara was small, but Raymond seems to have treated it brutally. "He killed all the Saracen men and women, great and small, whom he found." The chaplain Raymond said that his count enslaved several thousand citizens, though he added somewhat disdainfully that Raymond freed any cowardly citizens who had surrendered before Albara fell. Careful to preserve the sacred character of his actions, the count also ordered that his followers elect a bishop, and they solemnly chose a Provençal cleric, Peter of Narbonne. Shortly thereafter Peter traveled to Antioch to receive consecration from John IV. Raymond also entrusted to Peter half of the city and the territories that pertained to Albara and established his rule in a newly consecrated church (recently a mosque, or "devil's house").[14]

Raymond then left most of his followers behind—for a time they were sated with blood and war—and returned to Antioch for the proposed November 1 departure. The other princes were already there, with Godfrey accompanied by an impressive number of Saracen slaves, pathetically carrying the heads of their dead friends. As it turned out, no one wanted to leave. The chief troublemaker was Count Raymond, who announced that he would never give Antioch to Bohemond. He was, he explained, reluctant to violate the oath he had made to the emperor. More to the point, his men were still in possession of the Bridge Gate and of Yaghi-Siyan's former palace, and he had just established a foothold in Albara. Bohemond was furious, and the other princes seemed to agree. Raymond had, after all, made a show at Constantinople of preserving his honor and not giving in to Greek pressure. His sudden conversion to Alexius's cause—a road to Damascus moment—must have struck everyone as disingenuous.

In the end Bohemond and Raymond could only agree to follow the will of the other princes—Godfrey, Robert of Flanders, and Robert of Normandy—and not to delay the road to Jerusalem. The rank and file seemed to believe that the leader had agreed on a new date to begin the final march, but in reality they had decided to do nothing except wait for a month and talk about it again in December. Effectively, Bohemond and Raymond were scuttling the crusade.[15]

Ma'arra: Those Belonging to Jeroboam

Raymond returned to Albara, accompanied this time by Robert of Flanders. Rather than recuperate for the month, the two princes set a new target: the city of Ma'arra, whose defenders had earlier humiliated Raymond Pilet and his Latin and Syrian bandits. The people of Ma'arra, according to the chaplain Raymond, had grown arrogant because of their easy victory over Raymond Pilet. When the Franks arrived on November 28, the citizens stood on the walls mocking them, ridiculing their leaders, and desecrating crosses. Raymond and Robert, likely prodded by the anger of their followers, decided to attack at once but failed for lack of ladders. Bohemond arrived shortly afterward, no doubt suggesting that things might have gone differently if only they had waited for him. But in reality the city was too well fortified to fall easily, Bohemond's presence or not. Once again, as at Antioch, the Franks settled in for what promised to be a long siege.[16]

And again, as at Antioch, the common soldiers started to feel intense hunger pangs. Perhaps to reassure them, Peter Bartholomew announced that St. Andrew had spoken to him once more, now accompanied by his brother St. Peter. The apostles had wished to scold the army and to reassure them. They explained that the soldiers deserved their suffering. They had forgotten their previous blessings and had not fully appreciated the miracle of the Holy Lance. They had also sinned greatly—theft, adultery, and violence to the poor. If they repented of these practices, established true justice, married their harlots, and offered tithes regularly to the poor, they would again know God's mercy. But in fact God was prepared to give them Ma'arra anyway. "Whenever you want, attack the city," St. Peter told him, "since without doubt it shall be yours." The chaplain Raymond was delighted at these instructions. Some, however, were beginning to weary of the little Provençal rustic. The Normans in particular had started to ridicule him and his relic—probably at Bohemond's suggestion. Undermining belief in the Holy Lance was an easy, albeit indirect, way to dislodge Count Raymond from Antioch.[17]

In any case no one was willing to attack Ma'arra just yet. The siege would continue for two more weeks—a time spent in part building a massive, wheeled siege tower and several more siege ladders. It was not an inordinately long time compared to the epic ordeal at Antioch, but even so this waiting period had shocking repercussions. The hunger grew intense more quickly, and the radical elements in the army were not willing to bear their suffering. For Jerusalem they might have endured it, but not for Ma'arra.

Spurred by the combination of severe hunger and prophetic rage, some members of the army turned to a now familiar, if horrifying, solution: cannibalism. This time they did so proudly, having learned how to use psychological warfare to their advantage. In the words of Fulcher of Chartres, reporting what he had heard from Edessa, "I tremble to say it, but many of our men, seized by the madness of hunger, cut pieces from the buttocks of the Saracens, who were dead at the time, which they cooked and ate, and even if they were barely warmed over they savagely filled their mouths and devoured them." Another writer said that he learned these details from some of the actual cannibals, apparently proud of what they had done: "Adults were put in the stewpot, and boys were skewered on spits. Both were cooked and eaten."

If, as described earlier, Bohemond publicly faked cannibalism at Antioch as a way to flush out Turkish spies, the crusaders at Ma'arra genuinely indulged in it, hoping to terrify the enemy—a step beyond desecrating Saracen graves or using Saracen heads as saddle ornaments. In the goal of inspiring horror, they were successful: "Indeed the Saracens and the Turks said amongst themselves, 'Who is able to stand against this people, who are so resolute and cruel that—after a whole year of not being driven away from the siege of Antioch, either by hunger or sword or by any other danger—they now eat human flesh?'" But not all of the Franks were pleased at the result. Some were so shocked that they abandoned the expedition altogether, close to Jerusalem though they were.[18]

Crusade chroniclers agonized over this story. One of them, Guibert of Nogent, blamed the cannibalism on a band of poor soldiers he called the "Tafurs." Not really warriors, they were mainly helpful peasants or poor pilgrims, carrying out useful tasks for the Frankish aristocracy. The Tafurs' own leader, whom they called a "king," was reportedly a Norman knight who had lost his horse. In the epic poetry of the twelfth century, the Tafur king and his earnest peasant band would be transformed into savage warriors, hardened by the deprivations of poverty—an imaginative leap made possible by Guibert's decision to blame them for the cannibalism at Ma'arra. Modern writers have either followed Guibert's lead and accused the Tafurs for what went wrong, or they have preferred the testimony of Raymond of Aguilers and the author of *Deeds of the Franks*, who both placed the cannibalism after the siege had ended and blamed it only on sharp, unexpected hunger. They also were eyewitnesses, and modern historians, like medieval ones, tend to put greater weight on eyewitness testimony.

As eyewitnesses, however, they were also potentially implicated in the cannibalism. It was in their interest to explain it away. Writers like Fulcher, Ralph of Caen, Guibert of Nogent, and Albert of Aachen, who were well informed about the crusade and who had talked to other participants at the siege of Ma'arra, had heard too many reports of deliberate, aggressive cannibalism to dismiss it out of hand, including from some men who claimed to have cut their enemies up and put them on spits in full view of the city's defenders. They weren't ashamed. For them it would have all been a part of the process of holy war.

The cannibals, or their confessors, might have even appealed to the Bible to justify their actions since the God of the Old Testament often threatened cannibalism against His enemies, and sometimes against His followers, too. The consumption of human flesh was but one weapon in the divine arsenal. "I will feed your enemies with their own flesh, and like new wine, they shall be drunk with their own blood," says the prophet Isaiah. "They will eat the flesh of my people," the prophet Micah says; "they will flay their skin and break their bones and chop them into pieces for the pot, with flesh as if in the midst of the cauldron." In the book of the Apocalypse, God through an angel commands birds to feed upon the kings of the earth, their servants, and their horses. [Plate 5] And in the Old Testament, He promises a similar fate to the wicked Israelite king Jeroboam: "Dogs will eat those who die in the city belonging to Jeroboam, and the birds of the air will feed on those who die in the country." Perhaps Albert of Aachen had this passage in mind when he wrote of Ma'arra, "Christians did not shrink from eating not only killed Turks or Saracens, but even dogs, whom they snatched and cooked with fire."[19]

Peter Bartholomew's Crusade

Finally, on December 11, with some soldiers starving, others cannibalizing the dead, and the leaders all but at war with one another, the Franks attacked Ma'arra from two sides. Priests prayed to God to "raise up Christendom and cast down Pagandom." Raymond's men pushed and wheeled their siege tower as close to the city as possible, somehow preserving the structure against Saracen attempts to bring it down with catapults and fire. Atop the tower a knight named Evrard "the Hunter" sounded repeated trumpet blasts and probably tried intermittently to earn his nickname by laying low human prey with his bow. Other knights crowded into the tower's upper stories and threw rocks onto the wall's defenders. More effective than arrows, the rocks crashed into their shields and knocked them over into the city.

Finally, by the end of the day, the sun just beginning to set, the Provençals had cleared out enough of a space on the ramparts to raise a ladder. Protected by their siege tower, as its occupants fired arrows and debris down on the wall's defenders, a knight named Gouffier of Lastours (later famous for having a pet lion) ascended the ladder, followed en masse by a swarm of warriors anxious to bring this battle to an end. So many crowded onto the ladder's rungs that it started to split apart, several Franks in full chain mail armor crashing hard to the ground. Gouffier and a few other warriors managed to stake out a place on the ramparts, with Gouffier fighting back Saracens "like a bear beating back a pack of yipping dogs." The Frankish youth on the ground "forgot about themselves but remembered their friends" and set up another ladder. Soon a few dozen warriors had scrambled up beside Gouffier and were widening their hold on the city's ramparts. It remained a desperate fight—too much for some men, who jumped off the wall rather than face the continual onslaught of arrows, stones, swords, and fire—until sunset. But by nightfall the Franks had claimed a large portion of the wall and likely a tower or two. They had also broken through one of the city's gates. In the morning they could expect to capture Ma'arra easily.[20]

A few of the Turkish citizens recognized the impossibility of their situation. Trying to exploit a loophole in the laws of war, they offered to surrender. Their city was all but conquered. Bohemond, as Raymond had at

Albara, agreed to their terms. But Bohemond was not as merciful as Raymond had been. The next day he would kill many of the Turks who had surrendered and would enslave the rest. In the meantime, in the dead of night, as Bohemond engaged in stealth diplomacy, or stealth duplicity, several of the poorer knights, maybe the Tafurs among them, scrambled through the breach in the walls and roamed the dark streets, looking for Saracens to kill and wealth to claim. They'd learned from experience; this time they would not risk the aristocrats scooping up all the Saracen valuables. The rest of the army waited till morning, when it could sack the city with impunity.

The scene that followed would have readily recalled the carnage of Antioch. "No corner was clear of Saracen corpses; you could hardly go anywhere in the city without stepping on Saracen corpses." According to Arab historians, it was the worst massacre of the crusades. More were killed there than at Antioch or later at Jerusalem. At times the Saracens unwittingly imitated the Jews of the Rhineland, preferring suicide to captivity. They would, for example, offer to lead Franks to hidden storerooms where they might grow rich, but then on the way hurl themselves into wells, "preferring to pay the price of death rather than to show where their supplies were, or anything else." Because of their stubbornness, Raymond concluded, all of the defenders died. It was the second time that the crusaders had inflicted upon their enemy the rules of war set down in Deuteronomy 20.[21]

Politically, Ma'arra threatened to turn into a repeat version of Antioch. Bohemond stationed his men in several towers around the city—more than Raymond managed to take—as if to claim Raymond's prize for his own. Raymond took the high ground, at least formally so, arguing that the city belonged by right to Peter of Narbonne, recently anointed bishop of Albara. Predictably, Bohemond would not give up anything in Ma'arra until Raymond had first abandoned Antioch.

With the princes' squabble on display for the whole army to see, many soldiers were on the verge of open rebellion. The march to the Holy Land had begun years ago, they argued, and yet each day it seemed to start anew, so irksome were the princes' delays. But Bohemond was not intimidated. In light of current circumstances, he announced, he did not expect to leave for Jerusalem until Easter, and on December 29 he withdrew to

Antioch. Let Raymond clean up the mess they had made at Ma'arra. And all the while, more and more pilgrims continued to desert.[22]

The people still put their hope in Count Raymond and recruited Bishop Peter of Albara (whose interests Raymond was claiming to defend against Bohemond) as spokesperson. Peter, surrounded by an entourage of commoners and knights, approached Raymond to express their frustrated longing for Jerusalem. The laypeople all knelt around the bishop as he spoke. Count Raymond, Peter said, should depart immediately. God had chosen him as His special instrument by giving him the Holy Lance. He had no need of the other princes. If, however, he preferred to stay at Ma'arra, he should at once hand the Lance over to the people, who, leaderless, would march on to Jerusalem without him.

Bishop Adhémar's worst fears had been realized. The eccentric vision of Peter Bartholomew had taken hold of the Provençal contingent. Count Raymond had put too much trust in him. Despite all his military achievements and money, he was about to lose his army to a peasant. He had one last chance to stem the tide of deserters and to regain control of his followers: a council to be held at nearby Rugia, midway between Antioch and Ma'arra, on January 4, called to try yet again to settle his dispute with Bohemond. The people were willing to give him that much time, but again, at Rugia, neither side was willing to budge. Bohemond returned to Antioch, planning to forcibly expel the Provençals from the city. Raymond hired more knights and headed back to Ma'arra. With the help of his new subjects, or mercenaries, he would begin to fortify the city as the new capital of his own Syrian principality—a rival and enemy to Bohemond's capital at Antioch.[23]

But even before Raymond's return, the army's poor took control of the situation. They had either heard how badly the council at Rugia was going or they simply didn't care. They said among themselves, "Huh. Quarrels because of Antioch and quarrels because of Ma'arra, and in every other place that God would give us, our princes fight and the army grows smaller. Certainly there will no more be a fight about this city." And they began to dismantle the walls. As the demolition progressed, it seemed yet another miracle. The weak and the infirm pushed away rocks so large that three or four pairs of oxen could not have moved them. The bishop of Albara, recoiling at the forces he had let loose, ran among the people trying to convince them to stop. The vandals hid when they saw him approach with his guards, but as soon as he had departed, they left their hiding places and returned to methodically destroying the city.

Once Raymond arrived, he flew into a new rage at what was happening. When he had heard how the bishops and the nobles had been unable to deter the people from their purpose, however, "he understood that there was something godly there," and he ordered the men who had come with him, originally to fortify the place, instead to destroy the walls completely. He had given up, temporarily, dreams of a Syrian principality and was now embracing anew his mission to guide and protect the poor. In preparation for leaving, he announced that he would lead one more foraging expedition through Syrian territory for the benefit of his starving people—food other than the rotten bodies of the dead, upon which the Franks had continued to dine, with varying degrees of secrecy.[24]

During this series of raids around Ma'arra, the Provençals killed many Saracens, though on their return a Turkish raiding party dispatched six or seven of the poor. Remarkably, the chaplain Raymond observed, each of these poor men was found to have a cross branded onto his right shoulder. Word of this sign spread back to the garrison in the city, but not everyone believed it. Another faked miracle? To prove the story true, the count sent to the city "one of the dead who was still breathing." His body was so battered and torn that "he had barely enough of it left to cover his soul." But he survived for several days and convinced the doubters of the miracle: Christ alone had burned this sign onto his body.

The crusade was still on track. Raymond had maintained the goodwill of his followers, though he had now tied his prestige even more closely to the poor and to the dreams of Peter Bartholomew. At last, on January 13, 1098, the Provençal army processed solemnly out of Ma'arra, believing that Jerusalem was only a few days ahead. Count Raymond was a barefoot penitent. It was still his army, but it was Peter Bartholomew's crusade. And the crusaders' sense of purpose had, if anything, grown stronger from having slaughtered and feasted on the enemy.[25]

16

Trial by Fire

(January 1099 – April 1099)

Raymond had no intention of going to Jerusalem without the other princes. Indeed, the next three months of the crusade would look very much like the previous three. The armies stayed divided, and the princes continued to pursue their own ends, sometimes in competition with each other. The armies did move more deliberately to the south, keeping close to the coast, but the focus of the leaders remained on acquiring cities and territories in Syria rather than making a quick advance on Jerusalem.

This seemingly aimless period grew out of an ongoing crisis in leadership. Without Adhémar of le Puy, no one could effectively unite the different regional and linguistic divisions within the army. But another struggle was occurring at the same time. It grew out of the princes' personalities and the increasingly conspicuous rifts between the Provençals and the northern Europeans, but it also transcended politics and regional identity. At heart it was a debate about what the crusade meant. This conflict had dogged the expedition from its beginnings, with Pope Urban II and Peter the Hermit offering competing visions about Jerusalem and why Christians needed to go there. The more radical ideas of Peter the Hermit and Emicho of Flonheim had survived the disasters that befell the first wave of crusaders and perhaps had helped inspire the increasingly frenetic followers of Raymond of Saint-Gilles. In the months between the cannibalism of Ma'arra and the final march on Jerusalem, the number of visionaries would increase, and the content of their visions would grow ever more radical until—finally—the leaders would force Peter Bartholomew, the most extreme of these visionaries, to undergo, quite literally, a trial by fire, where the Franks would turn directly to God and ask for an immediate verdict as to the truth of the apocalyptic crusade.

Rendezvous at Arqa

The day after Raymond left Ma'arra, his followers crossed paths with a contingent of Normans led by Duke Robert and Tancred. For a brief moment, it must have seemed to everyone that all parts of the crusading host were finally reassembling after the long winter of 1098, ready for Jerusalem. And, indeed, Raymond, Robert, and Tancred did make quick progress. Supplies had suddenly become, if not abundant, sufficient, and even the perpetually dour Raymond of Aguilers noted with approval how the nobles actually were sharing their wealth with the poor. The health of everyone in the army improved markedly. Rumor of the brutalities at Ma'arra had spread throughout northern Syria, and most cities were now willing to offer terms rather than risk a siege and the attendant consequences. The roads to Jerusalem were opening.

But a minor disagreement arose as the armies marched near the coastal town of Jabala. Raymond's inclination was to change course and lay siege to it. The rest of the army wanted to press on, and the ordinary soldiers found a surprising spokesperson in Tancred. "God has bestowed his presence on the poor people and us. Should we now stray from the path?" It was impossible, Tancred argued, for so few soldiers to conquer all of the Saracen towns between Antioch and Jerusalem. There were, apparently, only 5,000 men left from the original—as he estimated it—200,000 warriors who had departed Europe. They needed reinforcements. "Do we really expect people to come from our homeland when they hear that we have conquered Antioch and Jabala and the rest of the Saracen cities? But let us go to Jerusalem, our reason for setting out, and surely God will give it to us." Once Jerusalem fell, the other places would surrender out of fear and awe at what the Franks had done, and then tens of thousands of reinforcements would surely follow, to see the Holy Sepulcher, if nothing else. Tancred's argument carried the day for a time. The armies continued south.[1]

About seventy-five miles farther down the coast, Raymond again became distracted. It began with an offer of friendship from the amir of Tripoli, which lay near the end of the Seljuk sphere of authority. An alliance with this amir could open up the road for immediate access to Jerusalem. Raymond therefore sent a delegation to finalize the agreement. The amir not only accepted his proposal but also agreed to let Raymond fly his banner above the city walls, just as the count had managed to do for only a moment at Antioch. But for some reason—probably for many reasons—Raymond decided to renege on the deal. His formal excuse was that he would not negotiate with "the king of Tripoli" unless the king first accepted baptism. The chaplain Raymond was more suspicious of his count's intentions, and rightly so. After all, the army had now been making pacts of friendship with amirs all along the Mediterranean. There must have been another reason for the sudden change of heart, and the chaplain Raymond settled on the obvious explanation: money. The negotiators who had gone to Tripoli had been astonished by the city's extraordinary wealth, and they impressed upon their count the great treasure he might win if he captured it. A slightly later historian echoed the charge: "The count of Saint-Gilles desired that land and its government very much, because it was rich and because it was more celebrated than the others."[2]

Strategic factors likely played into Raymond's decision, too. As Tancred had pointed out, the crusade's numbers had grown thin, and Raymond and Robert must have recognized, even if Tancred did not, that by themselves they lacked the manpower to take Jerusalem. Raymond's legates in Tripoli may also have delivered to him some remarkable news: Jerusalem had already fallen.

About six months earlier, in August 1098, the Egyptians had driven out the Seljuk Turks and regained control of the city. The Franks, as we have seen, had opened diplomatic channels to Cairo as early as the summer of 1097. Once allies against the Seljuk armies, they were now set to become enemies. In venturing past Tripoli, then, the crusade was entering into a new sort of hostile country—out of frontier regions dominated by the Turks and into frontier regions under the Fatimids' influence. At the very least, this turn in Cairo's fortunes required careful consideration. And Raymond was happy to bide his time with a potentially profitable war against Tripoli—provided he could hold his army together. Even then, he did not attack Tripoli itself but rather the fortified town of Arqa, just a little to the north, beginning on February 14, 1098, barely a month after he had left Ma'arra.[3]

News of Raymond's rapid progress did yield results from the other princes. Around the beginning of February, Godfrey, Robert of Flanders, and Bohemond met together at Antioch. They were hearing complaints similar to the ones Raymond's men had raised at Ma'arra: "They were being held up in the city of Antioch only for the sake of delay and were not making any progress to Jerusalem, out of desire for which they had abandoned their homes and suffered so many things." Desertions were growing so common that the princes had to forbid their followers from boarding ships lest they try to return home. To restore a sense of order and purpose, Godfrey, Robert, and Bohemond held a public meeting on March 1 and announced that all of the soldiers who were not already with Raymond would rendezvous at the Byzantine port city of Latakia, about fifty miles to the south of Antioch. And from there, "thinking nothing of the dangers to their own lives," they would delay no longer the road to Jerusalem.[4]

The armies met at Latakia as planned, but the resolve to cease procrastinating lasted barely a day. Setting camp just a few miles to the south of Latakia, they laid siege to Jabala, the same city that had tempted Raymond but that Tancred had convinced him to pass by. Bohemond wasn't interested. According to Albert of Aachen, he was worried that there was a plot afoot to steal Antioch from him. Upon arriving at Jabala, he may also have realized that the army would not be leaving for Jerusalem anytime soon and that his time and money were better spent preserving the city he had already won. There would be other opportunities to pray at the Holy Sepulcher.

Whatever his true motives, Bohemond left the crusade and this time did not return. Why? Perhaps (contemporaries would have said if they had had the phrase) because biology is destiny: "From Bohemond's father, who was a Frank, he had the best of beginnings, but of his mother, who was Southern Italian, there were still traces."[5]

At any rate the siege of Jabala was to be short-lived. About ten days after it began, a panicked message arrived from Raymond of Saint-Gilles, borne by Bishop Peter of Albara. Word had reached the Provençals that "the pope of the Turks" had organized "the numberless Turkish people" for war and that they were about to attack the pilgrims en masse to drive them away from Arqa. The Saracen armies had gathered at Damascus and were now just a few days away. If the other barons did not come soon, half of the crusading army might be destroyed and Jerusalem never attained, and the army at Jabala could expect to suffer a similar, swift martyrdom.

Godfrey and Robert of Flanders thus had no choice. They pulled up their tents and marched down the coast to Arqa. "Meanwhile," the chaplain Raymond wrote, "the story turned out to be false, the Saracens having composed it to put us off for a little bit so that they might gain some relief from the siege."

Godfrey and Robert were furious. The whole story about Damascus, they believed, had been a fraud. More to the point, Raymond had invented it as a favor to the amir of Jabala, in exchange for a hefty bribe, to draw the Franks away from that siege. So angry were Godfrey and Robert that they set camp two miles from Arqa and for the next several days refused to cooperate with Raymond at all. Tancred, by this time, had begun to weary of Raymond, too, though for a different reason. Specifically, he hadn't been paid enough. As quickly as he was able, he broke with the Provençal count, symbolically returning to him a staff of lordship, and then joined Godfrey's army.[6]

Save Bohemond, the armies had now all reassembled, and they were all tired of or unimpressed with Arqa. The siege dragged on interminably, with no progress and with no apparent purpose beyond enriching Raymond or whoever else might happen to enter the city first. The voices of the doubters grew sharper as heroic and popular knights began to die. The learned Anselm of Ribemont, who had written at least two letters home to discuss progress on the crusade, was hit in the head with a stone flung by a catapult and died instantly. The warrior Pons of Balazun, who had been Raymond of Aguilers's collaborator for the first half of his chronicle, died in the same way. By April 1 even the chaplain Raymond was turning against his count. "God did not wish this siege to succeed," he wrote, "since we obviously undertook it for reasons that ran against justice and God, and He disposed that all things ran against us there."[7]

Whatever practical motives might have driven the princes to continue the siege, soldiers and clerics like Raymond did not believe their explanations. Arqa was about greed and about the corruption of the crusaders' mission. A new vision was needed to galvanize the army, to enable it to reclaim the initiative from the princes. That vision came from Peter Bartholomew. But Peter had to speak with care and in measured tones when announcing his latest apostolic mandates. Already at Ma'arra, Bohemond's followers had begun to mock Peter and his Lance and his sponsor, Raymond of Saint-Gilles. If Peter phrased his message at all indelicately, he might undermine his own visionary authority and his patron's credibility with it. But instead of words of clemency and unity, framed around the image of the Holy Lance and the memory of Antioch, Peter this time advocated social revolution and an all-out civil war.

A Dangerous Vision

It happened on April 5, 1099. That night Peter Bartholomew was alone in a makeshift chapel set up by Count Raymond. He was thinking, as he rested there, about the original vision of Stephen of Valence at Antioch, who had been allowed not only to speak with Christ but also to see his cross, and Peter wondered, a bit petulantly, why he had never known a similar blessing. Almost instantly four men stood next to him. Three were familiar: Christ, Andrew, and Peter. The fourth was heavyset and partly bald—probably St. Paul, though he was never explicitly identified.[8]

"Christ said to me, 'What are you doing?'

"I answered, 'Lord, I'm standing.'

"And the Lord said, 'You almost drowned with the others [what Christ refers to is unclear, but Peter apparently had suffered another near-death experience, as often happened before his visions], so now what do you think?'

"And I answered, 'Lord Father, I was thinking about that priest you appeared to with the Cross.'

"And the Lord said, 'I know that. And henceforth believe that I am the Lord on Whose behalf you have all come here, and Who for the sake of sinners suffered at Jerusalem on the Cross, as you will now see.'"[9]

There appeared before Peter two planks of black wood, rounded but not carved or worked over in any way, except that the midsections had been cut so that they might fit easily together. Christ called out, "Behold the cross, which you desired!" Then suddenly the Cross was before Him and He was stretched out upon it, with Peter and Andrew holding either arm as Paul supported the Cross from behind. And the Lord ordered Peter (in a way typical of later medieval mystics like St. Francis, but still unusual in the eleventh century) to gaze upon His wounds and meditate on them and then preach to the whole army about what he saw.

"You see these five wounds of mine," Christ said, "just as all of you stand in five orders." The mystical vision of the wounds was turning into a metaphor for the entire Frankish army. The first order of pilgrims, Christ told Peter, consisted of those who feared neither spear nor sword nor any weapon. They were like Christ, who entered Jerusalem without hesitation, despite the lances, clubs, and even the Cross that threatened Him. Did Christ intend to say that these people were the bravest members in the army, the men who were most ready to fight and least likely to flee? Or was He saying that the first order was composed of people who followed his example and entered Jerusalem peacefully, humbly, and unarmed? In other words, was the first order composed of soldiers or of the army's poor, unarmed pilgrims? The answer became clear only when He described the second order. They were the ones who supported the first group, guarding their backs and providing shelter for them—perhaps the "knights of the people" and the "poor foot soldiers" described in another section of Raymond's chronicle. If they were the men who defended and sheltered the first group, then the members of that group, by implication, did not fight; they were the poor pilgrims, who would enter Jerusalem as Christ had done on Palm Sunday more than one millennium before the crusade.[10]

Each of the other ranks, by turns, was further removed from the action of holy war. The ones in the third order provided logistical support to the second group, giving them stones and spears to use in combat. Christ compared them to the people who witnessed the Crucifixion and grieved

254 | Armies of Heaven

the injury done to Him. The fourth group comprised "those who see battle and hide themselves in their homes." They were like the witnesses to the Crucifixion who just barely believed it. The fifth order included those who heard the roar of battle, looked into the reasons for it, and then hid, offering examples of cowardice, not prowess. "They refuse to undergo dangers not only for me, but also for their brothers." They hid, and they encouraged others to run away, to watch the battle from a distance. "They are similar to the traitor Judas and to Pontius Pilate."[11]

Interpreting this vision is not easy. The five orders that Peter described do not represent cultural groups since they are neither linguistic nor geographic. The second and third orders (fighters and servants) serve military functions, but the first, fourth, and fifth (the fearless, the deserters, and the cowards) do not. They certainly do not correspond to the usual military divisions within the crusade army: horsemen, foot soldiers, and noncombatants. They seem to be based on something else altogether—the unknowable content of the crusaders' character. How to make this analogy conform to the wounds of Christ defies any coherent program of allegory since it implies that some wounds are better than others, or perhaps that some wounds are more efficacious than others.

How to make these secret divisions reveal themselves, however, was easy. When Peter Bartholomew protested, as he often did, that people would not believe him, Christ ordered him to tell Count Raymond to call together all the princes and the people and attack Arqa. Let the army's best-known criers shout three times "God help us!" and then the divisions described by Christ would visibly form. The group who charged forward would be the army's true pilgrims—a category that overlapped with the people who believed Peter Bartholomew's visions and trusted in the Holy Lance. When Peter asked Christ what to do about the unbelievers in the last two ranks, the Lord answered, "Do not spare them. Kill them. For they are my traitors, brothers of Judas Iscariot." Their property would be redistributed to the people in the first order. "If you do these things," Christ concluded, "you will have found the right path, around which you have so far only drifted."[12]

What Christ was proposing was a bloody purge—a massacre of the cowardly. The survivors would constitute the Frankish elect, divided into three parts: true pilgrims, their warrior guardians, and the squires

and servants who could attend to practical needs. If the crusaders followed Peter's instructions, they would march straight to Jerusalem, the
last several miles barefoot, and quickly capture the city, regardless of
how many or few siege ladders, catapults, and battering rams they possessed. For it was characteristic of the traitors in the fourth order to
think like Kerbogah—to see victory as something attainable only through
the cunning of man and not through the power of God.[13]

If Peter's vision had stopped here, most of the army would have turned
against him. But Christ added one other set of instructions that demonstrated just how radical a transformation He was advocating. The problem
that had so often hobbled the crusade's progress, in the eyes of Peter, was
a lack of concord among the leaders. After the purges, therefore, judges
would be appointed to represent households and larger families. If anyone
suffered any sort of injury, the accuser was to approach the offending party
and inform him that he was bringing the case to trial. If the malefactor
did not make things right, a judge would intervene with the proper authorities to confiscate all of the accused person's property. Half the goods
would go to the plaintiff, with the other half going to the "sovereign." If
the judge refused to act at all in the case, or delayed unnecessarily, then
it would be at his own spiritual peril. Someone (the princes? the other
judges? Peter Bartholomew?) would inform the accused of the dangers
he faced at Judgment Day. Any act of injustice, Christ explained, was like
Adam's original sin. But as always the Lord's thoughts and Peter's were
with the poor, since He concluded, "About giving tithes, some are doing
quite well, because they offered as I commanded. I shall magnify them
and make them known amongst the others."[14]

This program of reform was both sweeping and dangerous. Peter
Bartholomew was proposing to remake the army, violently, in order to create something church doctrine had long recognized as impossible: a pure
City of God on earth. The ranks and distinctions within this army would
be determined not by social status or family position but by a willing embrace of poverty, by the quality of a person's character, and by practical
considerations such as who was best equipped to fight and who best
equipped to serve. At the head of the army would be the true pilgrims,
those who, if they should die, "will be raised up on the right hand of God,
when, at the resurrection, ascending into heaven, I have taken my seat."

Peter's reform brings to mind another vision—Chapter 20 of the book of the Apocalypse: "And I saw thrones, and they sat upon them, and the power of judgment was given to them. And I saw the souls of those who had been decapitated because of their witness for Jesus and the word of God. . . . The rest of the dead did not live until 1000 years had passed. This is the first resurrection." After the victory of the heavenly army in the Apocalypse, a government of saintly judges—the souls eligible for resurrection before Christ takes His final seat of judgment—shall rule alongside God for a millennium. What Peter Bartholomew and Raymond of Aguilers were now advocating was unadulterated millenarianism, created through a purge of nonbelievers, through purity of heart, and through military victory. [Plate 6]

Whether Count Raymond embraced this ideology, too, or, as seems more likely, found himself uncomfortably associated with it because of his enthusiasm for the Holy Lance, we cannot say. But such was the situation in April 1099 when the other leaders finally began to speak against Raymond, his prophet, and his relic.[15]

Burning the Messenger

Such a vision was sure to divide the army, and indeed after reports of Peter Bartholomew's latest proposals began to spread, his critics finally spoke out loudly and forcefully against him. All of the aristocratic warriors would have had a stake in quashing his ideas, but the ones who took the lead in doing so were Norman. Duke Robert of Normandy must have played a major role in discrediting Peter, as did his chaplain, a man named Arnulf of Choques. Our best evidence for the antimillenarian case, however, comes from the biography of Bohemond's nephew Tancred, the Norman leader from southern Italy, written by the cleric Ralph of Caen some twenty years after the fact.

Ralph, as a Norman partisan, was hardly an objective observer. The case he made against Peter Bartholomew was composed less of historical analysis and more of raw invective. As such it probably provided an accurate portrayal of what the Normans were saying about the Provençals and their eccentric visionary in the spring of 1099.

The Holy Lance was, Ralph said, not a relic at all. It was instead an exotic-looking Arab weapon whose strange appearance struck European observers as fabulous. Peter Bartholomew had managed to hide it in a dark church and then faked its discovery amid the crowds summoned to dig for it. But belief in the Lance was strong, especially after the victory over Kerbogah. Its fiercest support came, naturally, from the Provençals, whose leader Count Raymond was using the Lance to promote his own status. In Ralph's version of the history, Bohemond, "a man not lacking in wisdom," conducted a formal investigation into the character of Peter Bartholomew and then presented a lawyerly case against him to the army. In reality, Bohemond had withdrawn from the crusade a month earlier. The likely prosecutor was Arnulf, Robert of Normandy's chaplain. Why Ralph did not credit the speech to him is a mystery, but we can hazard a guess—that belief in the Lance years later was still strong enough in Jerusalem, where Arnulf would eventually settle, and that he preferred not to be associated with its debunking.[16]

In any case Bohemond's presentation, as Ralph imagined it, was a mixture of character assassination and logical argumentation. First, Bohemond wondered, why would the apostle Andrew appear to a man like Peter, a frequenter of brothels, a keeper of loose company, and a generally unreliable fellow? Surely the saint would have chosen a more honorable man if he wished to reveal the secrets of heaven? Next, on a historical level, why was the Lance buried at all? If a Christian man had brought it to Antioch, then surely he would have placed it inside the altar. If a pagan or a Jew had done so, then obviously he would have never brought it into a church in the first place. More damningly, how did the Lance ever travel to Antioch? It was supposed to have belonged to one of Pilate's soldiers, and no historian told of Pilate visiting Antioch after the Crucifixion. (Another crusade writer tried indirectly to answer this charge by saying that Saints Andrew and Peter had themselves sent the Holy Lance to Antioch.) Bohemond finally noted that it was Peter Bartholomew who had found the Lance after everyone else had failed (he was apparently unaware of Raymond of Aguilers's initial sexually charged encounter with the relic's tip). If Peter were a true messenger from God, then someone else should have made that discovery.[17]

Ultimately, Peter's claim about the Lance foundered on two basic points, one cultural and the other economic. Culturally, the Lance had become too much a Provençal relic and too obviously a political tool of Count Raymond. The Provençals, Bohemond said, wanted to usurp for themselves the victory at Antioch, instead of allowing all the army to share in it. In this respect Bohemond's argument resembles many modern interpretations of this story: that by April 1099 the Lance was a Provençal symbol and thus no longer had the widespread support that it had once enjoyed.[18]

But that argument is only half true. Whatever local pride Peter may have felt, he had no hesitation about attacking Raymond for delaying his march to Jerusalem or, as noted, reminding the count about his secret, unconfessed sin. But this argument also ignores the other half of Bohemond's argument as Ralph presented it: "Oh, the rustic stupidity! Oh, the gullible rusticity!" It was poverty that stigmatized Peter Bartholomew, just as he had always feared it would.[19]

The attack against Peter and the Lance set off something of a firestorm among visionaries. A priest named Peter Desiderius stepped forward, saying that he, like Peter Bartholomew, had spoken with Adhémar of le Puy after his death and could confirm that the bishop had spent time in hell for his doubts about the Holy Lance's authenticity, which, the dead Adhémar admitted, "I ought to have accepted enthusiastically." Fortunately, by the time Peter Desiderius saw him, Adhémar was standing with St. Nicholas, singing in a heavenly choir. Much of his hair had burned off his head and face because of the hellfire. "Although I am not in pain," Adhémar explained, "I nevertheless can't see God clearly until my hair and beard grow back as they used to be."

The bishop of Apt next described how a man visited him in his sleep and asked him three times whether he believed in the Lance. The bishop admitted he had doubted it in the past, but in part because of being browbeaten in his dreams, he now accepted its authenticity.

A priest named Evrard described how before the final battle of Antioch he had met a Syrian Christian who told him about meeting the evangelist Mark. Mark had informed the priest that, just as Peter Bartholomew had described, God was ordering all saints to converge on Antioch to support the pilgrims. The Syrian man added that he had read in an apocryphal gospel of Peter that one day Christian men and women would become trapped in Antioch and would not be able to escape until they had first discovered the Holy Lance hidden there.

Stephen of Valence recalled his own vision of Christ and the Virgin and how five days later the army had discovered the Holy Lance, as predicted. And, finally, Bertrand of le Puy described how Adhémar and his dead standard-bearer both appeared in a vision to reprove him about doubts in general, though apparently not for doubting the Lance.[20]

These visions were not all relevant to Peter's case, but the speed and the passion with which the visionaries stepped forward, along with the outrage they created, must have given the Norman priest Arnulf, chief of the doubters, pause about pressing his case. He agreed to withdraw his accusations and do penance for doubt. But at the appointed time, Arnulf did not confess. He asked for a postponement. Peter Bartholomew sensed trickery, and rather than wait for the Norman's next move, he demanded that he be allowed to prove his own innocence, as well as the authenticity of the Holy Lance, by undergoing an ordeal by fire.[21]

The notion of a "trial by fire" sounds terribly dramatic, but in the eleventh century it was a relatively common procedure. As the historian Robert Bartlett has summarized it, "A man accused of a crime, or a man seeking to claim or defend his rights, would, after a solemn three-day fast, pick up a hot iron, walk three paces, and put the iron down. His hand would be bandaged and sealed, then, after three days, inspected. If it was 'clean'—that is, healing without suppuration or discoloration—he was innocent or vindicated; if the wound was unclean, he was guilty." This procedure would have required both a waiting period and heads calm enough to judge the condition of Peter's burns, but the stakes were too high to wait three days or to allow anyone other than God to determine the outcome. Not only the authenticity of the Holy Lance but also the leadership of the army were in doubt. We don't know what Count Raymond thought about the proceedings, but he must have recognized that he would walk away from the affair either badly humiliated or unchallenged as the leader of crusade. The ordeal also had the potential to reshape the meaning of the crusade, to transform it into the millenarian venture that Peter Bartholomew and perhaps Peter the Hermit before him had imagined. And, of course, there was always the possibility that Peter, in victory, could ignite the bloodletting that Christ had ordered, the nonbelievers having revealed themselves through their opposition to the Lance. A special ordeal was therefore created: a massive bonfire, built on two mounds of dried olive branches, separated from one another by only one foot, each pile four feet high and thirteen feet in length.[22]

It happened just three days later, on April 8, 1099—by coincidence, Good Friday. Raymond estimated that a crowd of 60,000 men gathered for the spectacle. He exaggerated, but probably not by much. The drama would have engulfed all the Franks at Arqa (and perhaps intrigued the city's Muslim defenders, too).

The ceremony began with Peter of Narbonne, the bishop of Albara, leading the priests of the army, barefoot but clad in their finest vestments, three times around the woodpile, singing psalms and carrying crosses in their hands. After the third time around, the bishop and the priests set fire to the branches, and then they all circled it three more times, sprinkling holy water around it and praying loudly to Christ over the roar of the flames. Raymond of Aguilers was one of them: "When the fire was raging, I myself, Raymond, said to all the multitude, 'If omnipotent God spoke to this man, face to face, and if blessed Andrew showed him the Holy Lance while he kept vigil, let him walk through the fire unhurt. If it was a lie, let him burn, along with the Lance he shall carry in his hand.'" Another chronicler attributed a similar speech to Peter the Hermit. Probably both men—and several others—delivered nearly identical sermons to educate and incite onlookers. In the absence of public address systems, several preachers all offering the same message would have been necessary to reach such a large audience.[23]

In the meantime Peter Bartholomew had shed his clothing and put on a simple black tunic. He fell to his knees before the bishop of Albara and accepted charge of the Lance, now wrapped in a white cloth. He made the sign of the cross, rose to his feet, and, Raymond the chaplain said, "walked boldly toward the fire," which had now risen to unbelievable heights—about fifty feet. No one could bear to stand near the pyre, let alone to step into it. Arrows could not have passed quickly enough through the flames to escape incineration.

According to two accounts, Peter ran quickly through the fiery corridor. Raymond, however, remembered him pausing halfway through before continuing to the other side. When later asked why, Peter explained that Christ had stopped him and said, "Since you hesitated about the discovery of the Lance when blessed Andrew showed it to you, you will not cross unhurt; but you will not see hell."[24]

A knight, delightfully named William Badboy, supported Peter's story. William spotted another man in priestly raiment, he said, entering the flames just ahead of the prophet. When only one man emerged at the other side, Badboy burst into tears, thinking Peter dead. At least two other people—a priest named Evrard and another knight named, more sedately, William Goodson—saw a bird swoop into the flames, perhaps another sign of divine protection. However it happened and whatever supernatural forces intervened, Peter did emerge at the other end of the corridor of fire, alive, though injured and understandably exhausted.[25]

Twelve days later he was dead. When Raymond of Aguilers thought on the circumstances, he broke dramatically into the present tense, "But now I am so caught up in care and anxiety that I cannot write further on these things." His explanation for what happened is almost pitiable. Peter would have survived the ordeal, he argued, if only the riotous crowd had not closed so tightly about him and injured him in its raucous celebration. They sought relics from his clothes and even tore at his flesh.

Peter nearly died on the spot, but the knight Raymond Pilet gathered him up and took him to Raymond of Aguilers's residence. In his chronicle Raymond then slips into the third person, when speaking of himself, saying that Peter called to "the count's chaplain, by the name of Raymond" and demanded to know why he had wanted Peter to go through this ordeal. "I know well enough," Peter continued, "that you have thought this and this, too." Raymond denied those thoughts—whatever they were—and Peter snapped at him that the Blessed Virgin and Bishop Adhémar had told the truth. "Raymond recognized himself as guilty before God and burst into bitter tears. Peter replied, 'Do not despair, for the pious Virgin Mary and St. Andrew have obtained indulgence for you from God.'"

Later, worn out by illness, Peter called Count Raymond and the other Provençal leaders to his bedside, swore once more to the truth of everything he had said, and charged them in good faith to preserve his words. And then he died in peace, being buried at the place where he had undergone the ordeal, either as a sign of victory over the fire or as a reminder of his failure.

The millenarian crusade had come to an end. All its hopes for a recast social and economic order, with Christ the King and His saintly judges ruling in Jerusalem, were burned and beaten to death during the pointless siege of Arqa.[26]

17

Seeking a New Apocalypse

(*April 1099–May 1099*)

Peter Bartholomew's spectacular failure and death outside of Arqa left a void in both the leadership of the crusade and the meaning of the expedition. Without him, Count Raymond of Saint-Gilles had lost significant prestige. With Peter alive, he had successfully manipulated all of the leaders into joining his siege of Arqa. Through the Holy Lance of Antioch, he had won symbolic prestige and miraculous assistance, punctuated by occasional spectral visits from St. Andrew, Adhémar of le Puy, and even Christ. But the overreaching of Peter Bartholomew had undermined all of Raymond's careful planning. Fortunately, he still had enough followers and money to credibly reclaim control of the expedition. Indeed, in the weeks following Peter Bartholomew's ordeal, he managed, with judicious bribes, to win back the friendship of all the important leaders except Tancred.

Yet barring the sudden conquest of Arqa, military and financial prestige alone would not suffice to assert control of the expedition—the crusade lacked meaning. Peter Bartholomew's apocalyptic vision had provided much of the army with a sense of unity and purpose. After his death the Franks needed not just a new commander to fill the void left by Bohemond's desertion and Raymond's failures. They also needed a new vision—or perhaps a new apocalypse altogether.

A New Vision

An apocalyptic mind-set, as we have seen, had shaped much of the action of the First Crusade. Preachers had proclaimed it. The first waves of soldiers had tried to eradicate the Jews in fulfillment of its prophecies. A vision of the enemy as servants of Antichrist had shaped crusader understanding of the Saracens. And the scale and brutality of warfare would have called to mind stories from the Old Testament and prophecies from Revelation. When Peter Bartholomew revealed the location of the Holy Lance, he was perfectly poised to seize this furor and channel it in whatever direction his passion and his meager knowledge of Scripture suggested.

But with his emphasis on poverty and his desire to remake the social order, Peter subscribed to a very particular type of apocalypticism known as "millenarianism." It is a very old idea that grows out of Revelation 20, where John describes events following the first defeat of Satan. At that time the beast and his prophet will be cast into a lake of fire, and an angel will consign the dragon, who is the devil, to hell, the doors to be locked for one thousand years. Then there will be a time of peace on earth and government by saints. After the dragon's release at the end of the millennium—John does not say why it must be released, observing only that "it is proper"—the enemy will call together the peoples of Gog and Magog and make one last stand against heaven. It will be short and violent. Fire will consume the devil's armies, and God at last will cast the dragon forever into the lake of fire. Peter Bartholomew perhaps believed or hoped that the crusade was the first of these battles and that the judges he would help to appoint to rule the army and then Jerusalem would inaugurate the era of peace that the Bible had proclaimed.[1]

Most educated readers in the Middle Ages did not accept this literal interpretation of Revelation 20. At least since the time of St. Augustine in the early fifth century, churchmen had learned to read it allegorically. The age in which they were living, after the Crucifixion, was itself the time of the saints, a symbolic millennium in which the church would gradually expand to fill the entire earth before the advent of Antichrist. Christ would then appear to strike down Satan and to judge the quick and the dead. In other words, according to Augustine, the millennium was now. Christians were living in the age of peace, the age of the church, awaiting final judgment. Yet the force and popularity of Peter Bartholomew's message showed that a literal interpretation of Revelation 20 remained possible. As Peter himself discovered, however, its vision of peace and perfect justice was dangerous, particularly when applied to a society dominated by a military aristocracy.[2]

Augustine condemned millenarianism, in part because it encouraged Christians to speculate about the precise date of the Last Judgment, which violated Christ's declaration that "no one knows the hour or the day, not even the angels of heaven." On the other hand, in the same passage Christ warns his apostles that they can recognize the end times when certain signs appear—false prophets, wars, rumor of war, earthquakes, famines, wonders in the sky, and an abomination occupying the holy place in Jerusalem. Within the first year of the crusade, if not on the eve of its departure, all of these signs were readily apparent. And to speculate as to whether these events presaged the Last Days did not violate Christ's words. Rather, it obeyed them, since He compares these signs of the end times to the changing of the seasons. When fig trees "sprout leaves, you can see for yourselves and know that summer is near. In just this way, when you see these things happening, you know that the kingdom of God is near." It probably was not lost on the army's clerics that at that very moment in May 1099 the crusaders were surrounded by the very fig trees that had inspired Christ's parable and their leaves had begun to sprout.[3]

By the eleventh century, apocalyptic speculation about the end of the world had developed some fairly specific contours. Out of a potent cocktail of Scripture—chiefly, the books of Daniel, II Thessalonians, and Revelation—medieval prophets had produced a detailed description of the Last Days. They would begin after the Roman Empire had ended—a time of "rebellion" or "falling away" foretold in Thessalonians, or the collapse of the giant statue with clay and iron feet dreamed of by Nebuchadnezzar in Daniel. According to medieval interpretations (and contrary to modern understanding), Rome had not fallen; though much decayed, it still lived through the imperial rulers of Germany or else through the kings of the Franks, depending upon one's national prejudices. But the empire itself was in disrepair. The theoretical Western Roman emperor, Henry IV, was at war with the Roman pope—a sign of rebellion and falling away if ever there was one. Hence Daniel's description of the statue's feet as "iron mixed with clay"—put colloquially, Rome wasn't what it used to be. But nonetheless a pitiful, doddering Roman Empire existed, and as long as it did, the Last Days could not commence. (Latin writers do not seem to have considered Byzantium a legitimate successor to Rome, at least not after Charlemagne was crowned emperor in 800 AD.)

The Last Days would begin, however, not with the gradual failure of Rome but with the appearance of a new emperor, a king of the Greeks and Romans who would reunite the empire and make it more powerful than it had ever been. And when his power was at its apogee, he would travel to Jerusalem, there to wear a crown and thus signal the triumph of Christian government. This vision had inspired Henry IV to dream of conquering first Rome, before marching on Constantinople, and then eventually arriving at Jerusalem. The same vision, as noted much earlier, seems to have inspired Emicho of Flonheim, who encouraged his followers to believe—for reasons now unfathomable—that he was the Last Emperor. And though Emicho had long ago abandoned the expedition, after his disastrous failure to cross Hungary, some of his followers remained, from time to time likely retelling the Last Emperor legend and speculating if either Bohemond or Raymond might be more likely to fulfill the role.

But the Last Emperor had a problem. According to prophetic understanding—enshrined in Western Europe in the 950s when a book called *The Life of Antichrist* was written—the most dramatic act of that emperor would not be to rule in Jerusalem but to abdicate. For upon his arrival in the holy city, he would lay down his scepter and crown on the Mount of Olives. After nearly a millennium and a half, Roman government would draw to a close, "the end and the completion of the rule of the Romans and the Christians." The way would be open for the terrifying armies of Antichrist, whose servants the Saracens so closely resembled. [Plate 7] As visions of one thousand years of unbroken peace started to fade, these dreams of a final world empire striking one last blow against the dragon would have haunted the thoughts of the crusaders. This happy fantasy just needed a prophet to give it substance.[4]

New Visionaries

There were several plausible candidates to assume this visionary role. One of them, Peter the Hermit, had never really left. As we have seen, he served as the princes' emissary to Kerbogah before the final battle of Antioch, and he also seems to have delivered sermons and helped to preside at the trial of Peter Bartholomew. Just before the trial by fire, probably before Godfrey and Robert of Flanders arrived at Arqa, Peter the Hermit had taken responsibility for the distribution of charity within the army. According to a system established by Raymond of Saint-Gilles and Robert of Normandy, all of the pilgrims were to contribute tithes. From this sum, one-quarter would go to bishops, another quarter to priests, and half to Peter the Hermit, who would give the money to impoverished clerics and laymen. For a man who had begun the crusade brandishing a letter sent from heaven and inspiring his followers to massacre Jews, it was a surprisingly responsible position. Peter had obviously managed to regain the trust of many important people after his near desertion and disgrace at Antioch. But he also had become the princes' prophet and as such might not have been the most effective person to capture and direct the energies of Peter Bartholomew's supporters.[5]

The person who most immediately sought to fill that role was Stephen of Valence, who at the siege of Antioch had spoken with Christ, Mary, and Peter and who had defended Peter Bartholomew during his trial. After the great ordeal but before Peter had died, Stephen informed Count Raymond that instructions continued to arrive from heaven. Most recently, as Stephen had been walking through the camp, the dead Bishop Adhémar had come out of nowhere and hit him with a stick. Stephen fell to the ground, understandably surprised, but Adhémar had already approached him twice before. "Why have you failed once and now twice," Adhémar asked Stephen, "to do what I told you about the Cross of the Lord and of the Virgin Mary our Mother? I told you about that cross that I used to have carried before me in the army. What better sign is there than the Cross?" Adhémar's personal cross had been left behind, just to the north, in the Greek city of Latakia. It was time to bring it back. Indeed, the Virgin Mary had decreed that until the cross was returned, the army would receive no useful counsel.

"Oh, most beloved lord, where is Blessed Mary?" Stephen cried, no doubt remembering his previous encounter with her in Antioch and wanting to see her again.

Adhémar pointed to a woman standing about thirty feet in the distance, alongside two other virgins. One of them Stephen did not recognize. The other he knew to be St. Agatha, likely because of her distinctive appearance. A third-century martyr, she was most famous for having had her breasts cut off. Mary declined to talk directly to Stephen, so Adhémar carried his request to her. She refused to grant it. Instead, she ordered Stephen to give his ring to Count Raymond and tell him, "Whenever you seem to fail in anything, remember the Lady who sent this to you. If you call on her, the Lord will help you."

Stephen also asked Adhémar if he had really been burned in hell, a rumor that must have left some in the army incredulous. "Look!" Adhémar said. "See my face? Doesn't it look burned?" Adhémar, through Stephen, thus tried again to strengthen belief in the stories of Peter Bartholomew, even as Peter lay dying. In line with this goal, Adhémar ordered that the Provençals continue to carry the Holy Lance in public, but that it should be wrapped in sacred vestments, held by a priest, and carried behind Adhémar's cross (still at Latakia) hanging from the tip of a spear. To illustrate his instructions, Adhémar dangled his cross from a spear, as a priest marched behind him with the Lance. The bishop then sang, "Rejoice, Virgin Mary! You alone crush all heresies!" It became a heavenly roar, as 100,000 voices joined in.

Then the chorus vanished. Silence followed. Waking from the dream, Stephen ran to the count in part to discover if the Holy Lance still existed. As far as he knew, the fire had consumed it. When Raymond revealed the relic to him, Stephen burst into tears, and the count was so moved by Stephen's story that he sent William Hugh of Monteil, Adhémar's own brother, to recover the cross at Latakia. Peter may have died, but something of his message and of Raymond's reputation might yet survive him.[6]

By the time of this vision, political events were moving faster than Raymond or any of the visionaries could predict or control. For even as Adhémar was beating Stephen of Valence with a stick, a delegation had arrived from Alexius demanding that Bohemond return Antioch to the emperor. They were probably surprised not to find Bohemond at Arqa. Alexius also strongly recommended that the crusaders wait until July 25 before going to Jerusalem. At that time he would finally join them and march to the Holy Sepulcher. Some in the army were sympathetic to these requests. Raymond in particular still had hopes both of conquering Arqa and bringing Tripoli to heel. Most of the soldiers, however, had grown tired of this endless wrangling over Antioch. And many of them believed as well, based on rumors out of Tripoli, that Alexius was actively negotiating with the Egyptians, trying to find a mutually acceptable course that would allow Greek and Saracen together to drive the Franks out of the East. If anything, July 25 seemed like a deadline—a date by which the army needed to have conquered Jerusalem, before Alexius could arrive and interfere with its plans.[7]

About the same time, the Franks received still more ambassadors into their camp. These men were from Cairo, and it seems to have been the first direct contact that the crusaders had had with "the Babylonian king" since they had sent his ambassadors, loaded down with severed heads, away from Saint-Simeon. At the time the Franks had been willing to strike an agreement with Cairo along the lines of what they had proposed to Alexius—they would restore Fatimid cities that the Seljuk Turks had recently captured in exchange for uncontested possession of Jerusalem. Al-Afdal, the vizier of Egypt, however, was no longer interested in power sharing. Jerusalem was his. He would allow the Franks to visit it unimpeded, in groups of two hundred or three hundred pilgrims, but he was no longer willing to concede possession of any part of the city. The Franks probably kept talking and kept making proposals, but they no longer believed anything the Egyptians told them. From Tripoli they had learned that al-Afdal was making diplomatic overtures not only to the Greeks but also to the Turks. The chaplain Raymond of Aguilers had even heard that the Turks were offering to convert to Shi'i Islam and become tributaries of Egypt if only Cairo would join them against the crusaders.[8]

Before any of these diplomatic maneuvers had a chance to succeed, or before the Egyptians had a chance to consolidate their hold on Jerusalem, the Franks needed to move. They had two problems: extricating themselves from Arqa and convincing Count Raymond to leave with

them. The former problem was relatively easy. The amir of Tripoli had always wanted a negotiated settlement with the Franks (and probably would
not have minded seeing the crusade inflict real damage on Egypt). In
order to reopen negotiations from a position of strength, the princes made
a threatening advance on Tripoli itself. The amir decided to engage them,
resulting in a brief, violent battle outside the city that ended with Tripoli's
Roman aqueduct filling up with Turkish corpses. It was, Raymond of
Aguilers observed, a delightful sight. The amir then offered terms, promising to pay the Franks a handsome tribute and release all of the prisoners
he had taken during the previous three months of the siege. And if the
Franks took Jerusalem, he would consider conversion to Christianity.[9]

But Raymond was reluctant to give up his prize. Supernatural pressure
was needed to change the count's mind, and it came from all directions.
Arnulf the Norman priest motivated his people into action by sculpting a
golden cross, strangely reminiscent of the golden calf Aaron cast for the
Children of Israel in the Book of Exodus while Moses was receiving the
law on Mount Sinai. Arnulf then delivered a simple sermon to the people
that moved them to feel shame at their indolence. Closer to Raymond,
the priest Peter Desiderius, who had spoken at Peter Bartholomew's trial
and confirmed that he had seen Bishop Adhémar in hell, approached the
count of Saint-Gilles and told him that he now had just seen St. Andrew,
who had asked Peter Desiderius to talk to the count. Raymond was, Andrew commanded, to give up his designs on Tripoli and Arqa. Neither of
these cities would fall unless the Franks first captured Jerusalem. But if
they did conquer Jerusalem, then both of these prizes, and others still,
could be his.

At the same time, William Hugh of Monteil returned with Adhémar's
cross. "And when they had seen this cross, even the count's closest friends
became so keyed up about the pilgrimage that they set their tents on fire,
over the objections of the count and the other princes." Like the destruction of the walls of Ma'arra, it was a powerful symbolic statement. The
Provençal nobles and commoners alike wanted to go. When Raymond realized what was happening, he grew "disturbed to the point of tears, and
he hated himself and his followers." He still made some abortive efforts
to divert the army to Tripoli, pleading with the princes and offering them

substantial bribes, but the crusade was moving on with or without him, prodded into action by the army's new visionary, Peter Desiderius, and by the disaffected followers of Peter Bartholomew.[10]

It was no longer Raymond's crusade. Nor was it Peter Bartholomew's. The millennial apocalypse had ended. The apocalypse of the Last Emperor was about to begin.

18

Jerusalem

(May 1099 – July 1099)

nriched by 15,000 gold pieces from the amir of Tripoli, not to mention a fresh supply of horses, pack animals, and food, the crusaders were ready to abandon both Arqa and Tripoli for Jerusalem. The amir was happy to see them go. He even provided a guide, "an elderly man, since the paths through the mountains by the shore were convoluted and unmarked." The army also decided, against custom but with the guide's help, to march at night.

They moved quickly. In the two days after leaving Tripoli, they covered over fifty miles to reach Beirut on May 19. Their goal was to reach Jerusalem before anyone in Egypt even knew that they had left Arqa. They also likely wanted to arrive in advance of any Greek expeditionary force, whose leaders might complain that Jerusalem had long ago belonged to the Greeks, having last been conquered by Heraclius in 629 AD, and that to the Greeks it should return.[1]

The other Muslim cities that the Franks encountered along the way largely followed Tripoli's example, rushing the crusaders along before they could do any real damage, rather than trying to prevent them from reaching their destination. The citizens of Beirut offered them supplies on May 19, requesting only that the Franks respect the locals' property for as long as they camped nearby. The princes happily agreed.

The next day near Sidon, after another exhausting twenty-five-mile march, the Frankish camp became infested with poisonous snakes. Many people were bitten; their limbs swelled up tremendously, their wounds bursting. Some died. The inhabitants of Sidon, after some brief resistance, decided not to fight but to give advice. The Franks should set men around the camp to beat on their shields throughout the night. This noise would keep the snakes at bay. As for the people who were sick, the locals recommended having the leaders place their right hands on the wounds. The touch of a crusading prince—like the miraculous touch of French kings who were at that time curing their subjects of scrofula—would stop the flow of venom. If that didn't work, the ailing people should try having sex. Albert of Aachen, our source for this story, did not say how successful either of these remedies was.[2]

After a three-day rest, the Franks began another, two-day, fifty-mile march, this time camping outside the walls of Acre. Once again the local amir, fearful of a siege, offered the Franks terms, going so far as to promise Acre would become a tributary state of Jerusalem should the Franks capture the city. In the meantime he pledged them his friendship. It was a lie, as the Franks learned in miraculous fashion. While they were camping before Acre and scavenging for food, the bishop of Apt appreciatively watched a hawk in the sky pursue and kill a pigeon. The bishop ran to where the pigeon fell, somehow getting there before the hawk, and found attached to its body a note, written in Arabic letters—that the hawk, or rather God through the hawk, had delivered to the crusaders a carrier pigeon of the type Godfrey of Bouillon had seen a few months earlier during his negotiations with Omar of Azaz. The letter, as best the Franks could translate it, read, "The King of Acre to the Duke of Caesarea. A generation of dogs has passed me by—a stupid and violent people, without government, whom you and others should want to kill, as much as you love the law. And you can easily do it." On another day the Franks might have made Acre pay for its amir's treachery and insults. For now they pretended to be friends. The pilgrims' beloved city awaited them. On June 3 she was within reach.

The Franks camped at Ramla, a mere thirty miles from Jerusalem. They took two more days to consider their strategy (a few independent voices at this stage, either from fear or simple pig-headedness, urged a last-second change of course and an attack on Egypt; they were ignored).

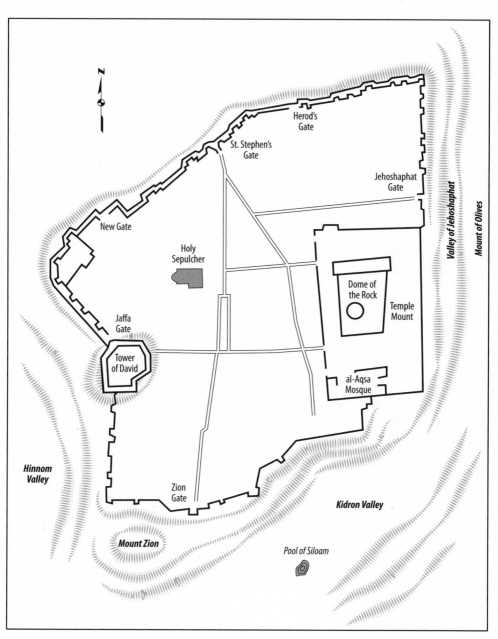

N

Mount of Olives

Valley of Jehoshaphat

Herod's Gate

St. Stephen's Gate

Jehoshaphat Gate

New Gate

Holy Sepulcher

Dome of the Rock

Temple Mount

Jaffa Gate

Tower of David

al-Aqsa Mosque

Hinnom Valley

Zion Gate

Kidron Valley

Mount Zion

Pool of Siloam

The city of Jerusalem

Then finally on June 6, the army set forth toward the destination which the soldiers had so long desired and of which they had so long dreamed.

Jerusalem Syndrome

Tancred couldn't wait. Throughout the crusade he had showed all of the ruthlessness, ambition, and independence of his uncle Bohemond, but by the time he was approaching Jerusalem, he had learned to combine these qualities with theological instincts that had always eluded his larger and more famous kinsman. As the rest of the army marched toward the village of Imwas, associated with the biblical town of Emmaus, where Christ had appeared to two of his disciples after death, Tancred, along with one hundred other knights, broke off and hurried instead toward Bethlehem.

The people at Bethlehem, hearing the sounds of charging horses in the early dawn, feared a Saracen attack. At the sight of Tancred, they rejoiced, picking up crosses and banners and starting a makeshift liturgical procession. Joyfully, they proclaimed, "You, our Christian brothers, are here to cast off our yoke of slavery, and to restore the holy places of Jerusalem, and to eliminate the rituals and impurities of the gentiles from that holy place." Tancred accepted their gratitude and offered them his lordship.

Presumably, he and his knights then entered the Church of the Nativity to pray. Just to the side of the main altar, the Christians of Bethlehem would have shown him the entrance to a cave, allowing the Franks to descend into the earth to the stable where Christ was born, there to see and touch the grotto where he had lain and the spot where the ox and the ass had stood nearby. Arising from the sacred earth, Tancred turned to his men and ordered them to plant his banner atop the Church of the Nativity, "as if over the town hall." It was an unseemly claim to own a church—and what a church!—and the gesture would draw increasing criticism in the weeks to follow. But in that one action, Tancred managed to encompass all the piety, fervor, and raw greed that together defined the crusade princes.[3]

From Bethlehem Tancred and his men rode quickly to the Holy City itself, arriving just a little ahead of the main army. With the walls and tow-

The tombs of the Kidron Valley—one of the sites Tancred would have passed as he approached the Mount of Olives (Erich Lessing/Art Resource, NY)

ers of Jerusalem in sight, still under the spell of Bethlehem's sacred history, Tancred dismounted, dropped to his knees, and sent kisses to the place for which he had so longed, his heart carried off to heaven. He ordered his men to set up camp near the gate at the Tower of David, but he rode alone toward the other side of Jerusalem, wanting to see for himself the places where Christ had lived and died.

The best views were to be found on the Mount of Olives. This was, perhaps coincidentally, the place prophecy indicated that the Last Emperor would make his presence known. The ride there would have been dangerous, the landscapes and monuments a little eerie, leading Tancred through the barren Hinnom Valley (known as *Gehnna*, the earthly incarnation of hell), past the ancient tombs in the Kidron Valley, past the garden of Gethsemane where Christ had prayed in agony as his apostles slept, and finally up the mountain to the site "where, Tancred had learned, the divine Christ had ascended to the Father."

Tancred's description of what he saw, related years later to his biographer, retained a note of genuine wonder. "He was watching the people hurrying about, the armed towers, the soldiers making a din, men rushing to arms, young women bursting into tears, priests intent on prayers, calling them out with a shout, a scream, a noise, a shriek. He marveled at the temples, the ethereal dome of the Temple of the Lord, and the marvelous length of the Temple of Solomon, with the undulations of its grand portico: the whole place was like another city within the city."[4]

Whether Tancred went to the Mount of Olives primarily because of Scriptural association or because of a desire to gather tactical information, his visit soon took on a prophetic air. For as he surveyed the land and the city, and as his eyes drifted longingly from the Temple Mount to the dome over the Holy Sepulcher, a mysterious hermit stepped beside him. In the manner of a friend or a tour guide, he indicated to him, one by one, all of the important Christian sites in Jerusalem. The hermit also expressed surprise to see Tancred, a Christian, alone in such dangerous territory, but when he learned who Tancred was, descended from Robert Guiscard, Bohemond's father, "at whose threats all Greece trembled," the situation became clear. "I will no longer marvel if you do marvelous things. Rather, I would wonder if you did not do marvelous things. Born from that family, it is not your lot to cleave to the path of ordinary men."

As if to prove the accolade, five Saracen knights charged out of Jerusalem, through the Valley of Jehoshaphat, to attack Tancred, "believing him a spy"—which, presumably, he was. Tancred rode against them and killed three, forcing the other two into a shameful retreat. He then returned to camp at last, knowing himself to be the lord of Bethlehem and a figure of prophecy.[5]

For the rest of the army, the final hours of the march were less eventful but almost unbearable. "Other nights had brought them bitter cold, or great fear, or battles; but this night was the hardest of all, because it kindled in their minds a desire long deferred." At sunrise, at the mere mention of the city's name, "everyone poured forth floods of happy tears, because they were so close to the holy site of the city they longed for, on whose behalf they had suffered such hardship, such danger, and so many forms of death and hunger." And when they actually saw the walls in the morning light, these few thousand pilgrims—probably about 20,000, just under one-fifth of the soldiers who had originally left Europe—"stood stock still, fell to their knees, and kissed the holy earth." Some of them burst into song, loudly singing "hymns of praise, still weeping for joy." Or as a poetic scribe entered into the margins of Robert the Monk's history, "Oh good King Christ, your people did weep how many a tear, when they saw that Jerusalem was near?"[6]

The language of one contemporary historian, Guibert of Nogent, shifted here from battle narrative to something like spiritual adoration mixed with romantic desire. The whole army felt "a burning love of martyrdom." Jerusalem was "their most intensely pleasurable destination, an enticement toward death and a lure toward wounds, to that place desired, I say, by so many thousands upon thousands." All warfare involves an effort to correct a perceived wrong and in doing so to achieve a desire. But because of the intensity and complexity of the emotional associations with Jerusalem, these "affections" proved uniquely powerful. No group of aristocratic warriors had ever risked and suffered so much for the sake of spiritual gain alone. "This is my conclusion, and it is unprecedented."[7]

These thought processes sound similar to the modern, controversial psychological concept of "Jerusalem syndrome": an overidentification with biblical characters experienced by visitors to Jerusalem that leaves them unable to distinguish between their world and Scripture. A similar sort of hallucinatory feeling captured the Franks as they finally achieved their goal. As one writer described it, the pilgrims wept the sweetest tears over Jesus, "and with the deepest affection they embraced Him, the cause of their daily labors and sufferings, as if He still hung there on the cross, as if He still lay shrouded in the tomb, through all space of remembered time."

This derangement would prove dangerous during battle. According to Tancred's biographer, Ralph of Caen, at a later point in the siege some pilgrims lost control of their faculties altogether. As if with one mind, they charged the city's walls and embraced the stones like spouses, apparently thinking, "I will kiss my beloved Jerusalem before I die." The city's defenders dropped rocks on the amorous pilgrims, killing them all, lost in their mad desires.[8]

In this atmosphere of excitement, the army decided on an immediate attack, in part because the hermit whom Tancred had met on the Mount of Olives encouraged them to do so. The Franks' victory was, he assured them, preordained if they followed his instructions. The leaders were at first skeptical, pointing to their lack of siege equipment. The hermit responded, "Almighty God, if he wishes, will conquer the wall with a single ladder. The Lord is ever present for those who struggle on behalf of truth." He further recommended June 11 as the day God had chosen for victory, but the army waited another two days as it searched for wood to build additional ladders. The region, however, had been exhausted of supplies, owing in part to the battles over the city between Turks and Egyptians. On the day of the attack, the Franks still had only one ladder, "without a companion."[9]

On June 13 the crusaders did storm the city, and somehow, with no siege equipment to speak of, managed to raise their lonely ladder up against the walls. The first Frank to climb to the top, a young man named Raimbold Croton, had his hand instantly sliced off but escaped with his life. Several other knights fell beneath stones thrown from the walls or else had their eyes shot out with arrows.

In sum the attack failed; "the result did not meet their desire." Perhaps it was because the Franks had doubted the hermit's words and waited two extra days. Or maybe it was because they had failed to show Jerusalem due respect in their initial approach. Raymond of Aguilers quietly complained that, according to the late Peter Bartholomew, they should have walked the final two miles barefoot—an injunction that only a few of the pilgrims had followed. The soldiers who left their shoes on defended the choice. The approach, they said, was risky. They could not afford to get caught shoeless. For Raymond, however, the army had grown lazy. With a barefoot procession, the city would have fallen as predicted.[10]

Preparations for the Final Battle

A more protracted siege would be necessary, but the army could not afford an engagement as lengthy as the one at Antioch. The danger from Egypt was imminent, but even without Egypt, the scarcity of drinking water threatened to destroy the army. Jerusalem lies near no major body of fresh water and has almost no natural sources of potable water beyond what is collected in underground cisterns. What few wells there were the Egyptians had either blocked or poisoned. The nearest source, the Pool of Siloam, flowed only every three days. Even there, when water appeared, men and women would fight with one another to be the first to drink it while it was still clear. Sometimes in the struggle the Franks would drown one another. In the meantime the poor and infirm would lie helplessly nearby, pointing at their mouths, unable to use words to beg because their tongues had gone so dry. The only other option for drinkable water was to risk a five- or six-mile journey to the nearest springs. Those who managed to bring any liquid back sold it at exorbitant prices. Survival for the army depended on getting quickly inside the city and out of the summer desert sun.[11]

Barring a new traitor like Pirrus, the Franks would have to break into Jerusalem on their own, which would require procuring enough supplies for massive new siege engines. In the days that followed the initial, failed attack, the leaders began a renewed and more intensive search of the region. They met with some greater success this time through "a type of miracle," albeit an unusual one.

All of the princes were involved in the search. Tancred participated reluctantly since he was suffering from dysentery. When the pain in his bowels became too much to bear, he looked for a cave to hide in—an easy enough task in the valleys around Jerusalem. Finding one that looked suitable for his needs, whose entry was somewhat concealed, he darted inside to relieve himself and perhaps to nap. In the indirect light of the cave, as he squatted down to employ his "excretory virtue," he noticed, against the opposite wall, a neat pile of lumber, apparently left behind by either the Egyptians or the Turks in one of the recent battles. Construction at last could begin.

More important (if not as miraculous) was the unexpected arrival on June 17 at the nearby port of Jaffa (in modern-day Tel Aviv) of six ships from Europe. The ships provided both supplies and engineers to help with the siege works. A quick, brutal attack to finish the crusade was now feasible.[12]

In terms of an overall strategy, the leaders organized their camps in a way intended to stretch the Saracen defenses, forcing the Egyptian garrison to defend two separate points at opposite ends of the city. Most of the Franks set camp around Jerusalem's northwest corner (protected by a double wall: an exterior curtain wall and a more formidable interior wall), while the Provençals at first concentrated around the Tower of David and the Jaffa Gate.

A little later Count Raymond relocated farther south, onto Mount Zion, seemingly against the wishes of the other leaders and against those of his own followers. The new setting offered Raymond several advantages—notably, higher terrain and more level ground for an attack. But with Jerusalem no decision was ever purely strategic. Mount Zion was the burial place of King David and King Solomon and of the first Christian martyr, Stephen. It was the traditional site of the Last Supper, the place where Christ had appeared to his apostles after death, and the location of the Dormition of the Virgin Mary, where she fell into a final deep sleep. After Count Raymond had seen these places, many of them in ruins, largely destroyed by an earthquake in 1033, he turned to his companions and asked, "If we pass by the holy things that God has shown to us here, and if the Saracens take them over, what will become of us? What if their hatred leads them to pollute and destroy them? Who can say whether God has given us this moment as a test, in order to discover just how much we love Him? I can tell you one thing for sure: If we do not faithfully guard these holy sites, He is not going to give us the other things inside the city."[13]

Even so, many of Raymond's followers did not want to move from their camps at the Jaffa Gate—put off either by the dangers of the new location or simply by the inconvenience of pulling up stakes. To make them accept his vision, Raymond offered fresh stipends. Holy war did not preclude making a profit after all. The count would later pay his followers—soldiers and commoners, men and women alike—to carry rocks to fill in the ditch between Mount Zion and the city walls (one penny for every three stones) in order to level out the ground and to pave the way for the final attack.[14]

By early July all was ready for the Franks to storm the city, except for one vital piece of business: a procession of penance and humility around Jerusalem's walls. From a military perspective, it was an exercise in morale building. The struggles between Raymond and Bohemond over Antioch, as well as the endless delays along the road to Jerusalem at places like Ma'arra and Arqa, had created serious divisions. A liturgical procession in which everyone participated would have been a useful corrective.

The ceremony would serve one other fundamental purpose: It was a last-ditch attempt to appease a wrathful God on the eve of this most important battle. The military probably consulted with all the available and respected visionaries, including the hermit from the Mount of Olives, and concluded that July 8 would be the best time for the ceremony. The hermit recommended another regimen of prayer and fasting, too, and assured them that God would finally enable them to surmount Jerusalem's walls.[15]

Raymond of Aguilers tells a more exotic version of this story, and in doing so makes a case for his own man, Peter Desiderius, to act as the army's new prophet. Bishop Adhémar of le Puy, Raymond said, now dead for almost a year, appeared again to Peter Desiderius and through him ordered the army to undertake the procession. The Franks needed to be "sanctified from impurities" before entering Jerusalem. If they marched around the city, barefoot like angels or apostles, invoking God and fasting, then they would "fight manfully for the city, such that it will be captured on the ninth day."

Peter took the orders first to William Hugh of Monteil, Adhémar's brother, and to his own count Isoard of Die, before the proposal went before a council of all the princes and the people on July 6. Everyone agreed to the procession—to reconcile themselves brother to brother, to embrace humility, and to seek the mercy of God through His saints so that "He might grant judgment against His enemies and ours, the ones who hold the place of the Passion and burial and who contaminate it, and who try to keep us from our own redemption and from such a blessing of divine humility."[16]

Two days later the armies gathered for the march. It started near Count Raymond's camp on Mount Zion, in front of the Church of St. Mary, and moved on toward the Church of St. Stephen. From there they traveled through the Valley of Jehoshaphat, ending up on the Mount of Olives, the place of Christ's final ascension into heaven—thus roughly following Tancred's itinerary when he had broken off from his followers on June 7 to explore Jerusalem alone. The armies then walked back down the mountain to the tomb of the Virgin before once again returning to the place of the Ascension.

This procession was in part a reenactment of Joshua leading the Children of Israel in a six-day march around the walls of Jericho. As such, it was an outright act of aggression. For in Joshua's case, on the seventh day the trumpets sounded, the Israelites let out a shout, and the walls crumbled to the ground.[17]

The Egyptian garrison, however, found the whole thing amusing. Along the ramparts they set up crosses and held mock crucifixions, spitting on the images of Christ or urinating over them. A cleric named Peter Tudebode remembered a group of Saracens breaking apart a crucifix and shouting, "*Frangi agip salip?*' In our language that means, 'Franks, is this a good cross?'" Such ridicule probably encouraged rumors that Muslims were physically attacking the Holy Sepulcher, hurling spears and stones at it—much like the pathetic leaders of Antioch who had tried to dislodge the icon of Christ in the cathedral. As the pilgrims' march drew to a close, one cleric who wandered too close to the walls was shot through the eye with an arrow. He fell dead immediately in front of Peter Tudebode, who never forgot the mocking words that the Saracens shouted at this humble procession.[18]

The enemy's jeering provided immediate fodder for the preachers in their sermons at the place of the Ascension. One of the men who spoke was the chaplain Raymond of Aguilers, who urged brothers to reconcile with one another so that God might grant them the city. Albert attributed the same message to Peter the Hermit and to Arnulf of Choques, Robert of Normandy's chaplain, and says that their words helped soothe the rancor that had grown between Tancred and Raymond. Probably, as was the case with the trial of Peter Bartholomew, several preachers spoke at once to different groups, all of them delivering roughly the same message.[19]

The most dynamic of these sermons, however, appears in the history of Baudry of Bourgueil, a chronicler who wrote in 1107, having never left Europe. He didn't accredit it to any particular preacher. It was most likely the message that he wished he had delivered if he had been able to participate in the crusade. In any case it nicely summed up what would become conventional historical thought in the twelfth century about what the crusade had meant and what the stakes of the expedition had been.[20]

"You know with what gall they are polluting God's sanctuary," he said of the Saracens, "how they have subjected the holy city to so many poisons!" Just as Jerusalem pointed toward higher and more beautiful truths—toward heaven—so did these Saracens cover a darker reality. They were not just Egyptians; they were demons. Not metaphorical demons, but real, physical, hellish servants of the devil. "In this little city the ones who are snarling at us are the limbs of others, and they are lesser and weaker than their masters." The stakes of this battle were therefore greater than the control of an earthly Jerusalem. Heaven itself was in the balance: "For if these enemies, who are nothing, are able to triumph and to take away from us the city we now see, what do you think their lords will do, when servants dare such things?" If the Franks should prove unworthy of this earthly Jerusalem, then the heavenly one, too, might be forever closed. Physical danger, moral danger, and otherworldly danger all were converging in this single apocalyptic moment where Christians met pagans and saints fought demons.[21]

In order to win, the crusaders needed to become like Joseph of Arimathea, who took Christ down from the cross and gave Him a tomb where He might rest. Then they could claim victory over all enemies, external and internal. But, above all, their war was for heaven, both the crusaders' right to enter heaven and, perhaps, the very survival of heaven itself. These are esoteric concepts, but Baudry framed them in simple language any warrior could appreciate. "I am speaking now to fathers and sons and brothers and nephews: If some foreigner struck down someone in your family, would you not avenge their blood? How much more ought you to avenge your God, your Father, your Brother Whom you now see mocked and punished and crucified, Whom you hear crying out alone, begging for help?"

At heart this was a blood feud, an extended war between families typical of early medieval culture. Christ's blood had been shed. The divine Christ, who was both Father and Son, continued to suffer, to cry out for vengeance. Historically speaking, Christ's killers were not Muslims but pagan Romans and (especially according to medieval interpreters) Jews. Were the Franks really, then, avenging Christ, or were they attacking the wrong enemy? Baudry had resolved this difficulty dozens of pages earlier when he observed that Jews, heretics, and Saracens were, in the pilgrims' eyes, all enemies of God and all equally detestable.[22]

Whatever else the crusade might have been, it was an exercise in vengeance for the crusaders' suffering and for the Crucifixion of Christ and destined to happen on a Friday, the day when "the Jewish race, desiring to put to death their master Jesus, instead put themselves to death." A slightly later poet, writing about the crusade in the vernacular, asked his audience to imagine Christ on the cross at Calvary, facing death but attempting to comfort the good thief Dimas, crucified beside Him. "Friend," Christ said, "there is a people, not yet born, who will come here to avenge me with sharpened spears. They will kill these devils' pagans, who have never kept my commandments. Then all of Christendom will be cleansed, my land will be conquered and my country freed! After 1000 years it will be baptized and raised up high! And then the Holy Sepulcher shall be visited and venerated anew."[23]

These were the stakes at the end of the First Crusade.

Apocalypse 14:20

Their heads may have been in heaven, but the Franks had to keep their feet on earth. In particular, they needed to finish building siege towers—mobile wooden castles whose height exceeded a city's ramparts. In a typical assault, armies would maneuver these towers as close to the walls as possible, using them to rain down arrows on the city's defenders. The towers themselves were not intended to provide access to the ramparts but to create sufficient cover for the soldiers on the ground so that they could raise ladders against the walls, clamber to the top, and engage the enemy in hand-to-hand combat. The Franks were building two great towers, one under the command of Godfrey and the other under the command of Raymond, and apparently two smaller towers as well. They would be used in a two-pronged assault: from Raymond's camp at Mount Zion to the south and from the other princes' camp at the city's northwestern corner.

The first attack, from Mount Zion, would be relatively straightforward. The second involved some trickery, perhaps necessarily so. A double wall surrounded North Jerusalem. The Franks would need to break through the first barrier before they could attempt to surmount the second. Rather than hit the wall at the point where they were building their tower (and hence where the Egyptians would expect them to strike), they instead planned to shift their equipment at the last moment to a more favorable location near Herod's Gate. That was the trickery. They had built the tower so that it could be easily disassembled and moved. If the plan succeeded, the Saracens would not have adequate time to reallocate their manpower and defensive equipment and thus would be less able to repel the assault. The night before the attack began, July 13, 1099, they carried out this plan. It worked brilliantly, though it seemed to Raymond of Aguilers more miraculous than strategic. "For it was at that point manifestly obvious to the all the faithful that the Lord's hand was with us."[24]

The battle began the next day, as at Jericho, with a blast of trumpets. To the north around Godfrey's tower and under cover of rocks flung from catapults, the Franks maneuvered a massive battering ram into position against the wall. The Saracens did everything they could to destroy the weapon, including trying to set it on fire, but without success.

By the end of the day, Godfrey's men had smashed through Jerusalem's exterior wall. They then set the battering ram on fire to clear an opening for their siege tower to pass through the next morning. The Egyptian defenders, having passed the day trying to burn up the battering ram, now fought to extinguish the flames, but this effort, too, was unsuccessful.[25]

At Mount Zion the city did not have a double wall. Raymond's army needed only to move a siege tower into position and attack with ladders, but these warriors faced heavier resistance than Godfrey's men did. Jerusalem's defenders had concentrated most of their resources—nine of their fourteen catapults—against the Provençals, perhaps because the walls there seemed more vulnerable. And the defenders' effort did prove more effective against Raymond. By nightfall the Provençals had suffered heavy losses, and their tower had taken serious damage from catapults. After an exhausting day of combat and with these mixed results, the Franks passed a sleepless night, keeping watch so that no further harm came to their siege engines.[26]

Fighting resumed the next morning. "Everyone girded himself with weapons and sought the city together. Each man was preaching to himself; each one was his own priest, his own bishop."

The northern Franks had only to move Godfrey's tower closer to the wall. It probably stood about forty feet high and had at least three different levels, with Godfrey at the top, directly under a golden cross—probably the one Arnulf had crafted in the deserts near Arqa. Godfrey was now "no longer a knight, but an archer, the Lord directing his hand to battle, his fingers to war." Two other towers under the command of Tancred and

Robert of Normandy were proving impossible to move. Only when priests surrounded one of them and chanted "*Kyrie eleison*" did the massive building come unstuck. Each side, Christian and Muslim, the chaplain Raymond observed, was fighting for its religion, one army wishing to capture Jerusalem for God, the other resisting with all its might, compelled by the laws of Muhammad and tapping into the powers of the occult as well. "Two women were trying to hex one of our catapults, but a stone powerfully flung from this same machine struck the women as they sang, along with three little girls. Their souls cut down, the incantations ceased."[27]

This victory over the occult notwithstanding, the Provençal cause was failing. Most of the siege equipment had broken apart, and the great tower was starting to crumble. Raymond and his closest advisors convened an emergency council, trying to devise a strategy on the fly when—suddenly—someone spotted a mysterious warrior on the Mount of Olives, brandishing a sword and signaling that the city was open to attack. "Who that knight was," Raymond reported, "I was never able to discover." Another writer, possibly an eyewitness, suggested an answer: The soldiers "saw a beautiful person sitting atop a white horse." Perhaps it was a saintly warrior or the soul of a fallen comrade or maybe even the first rider of the Apocalypse, who rode a white horse and who, according to exegetical tradition, was Christ. If the identification is correct, the rider's anonymity was no accident, for according to prophecy he would have "a name written on him that no one but he himself knows."[28]

What had actually happened (in historical, rather than apocalyptic, time) was that Godfrey's army had breached the northern defenses and had thus created a panic in the city. No one could agree who was the first over the walls. It may have been a knight named Lethold or his brother Englebert or Bernard of Saint-Valéry or Godfrey and Tancred together. Or was it, as some claimed, a spectral Adhémar of le Puy?

This breach occurred after one of the most dramatic moments in the battle. The Saracens atop the wall had brought forth an enormous tree trunk, attached to an equally enormous chain, and they had set the trunk ablaze with Greek Fire. This primitive chemical weapon they hurled into Godfrey's tower. But the Franks had anticipated this attack; local Christians—perhaps Tancred's friends at Bethlehem—instructed them to counteract the fire with vinegar. Thus, before the battle they had cov-

Christ as the apocalyptic rider on a white horse, a ceiling fresco from
the crypt of the cathedral of Saint-Etienne in Auxerre, France
(Bridgeman-Giraudon/Art Resource, NY)

ered Godfrey's tower in ox and camel hides soaked in vinegar, and the
flames never caught. At the same time, soldiers on the ground managed
to latch hooks onto the chain and to drag both it and the flaming tree to
earth. In the general confusion, some of the Franks inside the tower may
have torn lumber from their own walls and dropped them onto the ramparts, effectively improvising walkways into Jerusalem, or else Godfrey

himself broke apart a section of the wall at the top of the tower and turned it into a makeshift bridge. Whatever the case, Lethold, Engelbert, Bernard, or Godfrey and Tancred staked a place on Jerusalem's ramparts. Other crusaders approached the walls with ladders, and a celebratory massacre began.[29]

One writer described it as "more a slaughter than a fight." Another said that the pilgrims pursued and killed the Muslims from behind, their backs still turned. Neither cruel nor cowardly, the killings were "deserved retribution inflicted upon the worst of men."

Those who saw the massacre, and those who just imagined it, delighted in the simplest details. Of the Muslims, "one was laid low, struck through the head, one through the belly, another through the guts, one through the neck, another through the back." The Franks sliced open human bodies, eviscerating them from the head to the kidneys and cutting them lengthwise from left to right. Duke Godfrey "had showed such a capacity for killing in no previous battle," even at Antioch, when he had cut the giant Muslim in two. The deaths were, in Raymond of Aguilers's mind, "miracles." "Some had their heads cut from their bodies (which was fairly merciful) or were hit with arrows and forced to jump from towers. Others suffered for a long, long time, and were consumed and burned up in flames. Horses and men on public roads were walking over bodies. But these things I say are trifling. Let us go to the Temple of Solomon."[30]

About the killing on the Temple Mount (or Noble Sanctuary), historians reached for new literary heights. "Our pilgrims entered the city, pursuing and killing Saracens up to the Temple of Solomon. They gathered there and fought our men hard all day, so that their blood flowed through the whole temple." This picture—of Christians tramping through rivulets of enemy blood—haunted twelfth-century writers. And still they tried to improve upon it. Guibert said that blood rose so high that it seeped through the tops of the Franks' boots. Baudry wrote that the Franks splashed around in Saracen blood up to their calves. Robert the Monk outpaced all of them. Rivers of Saracen blood flowed fast and deep and carried severed limbs and heads down the streets, torsos and extremities mixed and intermingled so that no one could have put them back together again, if anyone had been inclined to try.[31]

But no writer raised the level of violence, and blood, higher than Raymond of Aguilers. "And what happened there? If I tell you the truth, it will be beyond belief. Let it suffice to say that in the temple and around the portico of Solomon they were riding in blood to their knees, and up to the reins of the horses." Raymond drew upon a specific source here: Revelation 14:20. [Plate 8] There, an angel of the Lord gathers the harvest of the earth and runs it through the wine press of God's wrath. "And the wine press was trodden outside the city, and blood flowed from the wine press, as high as a horse's bridle, for a distance of about 200 miles." The fact that Raymond used a biblical allusion here does not mean that he did not at the same time remember seeing exactly what he described. As the chaplain witnessed and recollected the battle, in his mind he saw the Apocalypse.[32]

At least one other warrior felt the same way. Tancred, upon entering Jerusalem, attacked the most impressive structure in the city, the Dome of the Rock (where he had heard the greatest wealth in Jerusalem was to be found), and began immediately stripping it of its gold. While plundering the temple, he noticed a mysterious silver object. It seemed to him a statue. And as he liked to tell for years afterward, he stood before it and began to speak, or else he burst into song.

> *Perhaps you are a likeness of Mars? Or Apollo?*
> *Surely you are not Christ? No, this does not look like Christ!*
> *There's no cross, no wreath, no nails, no pierced side.*
> *Therefore, this is not Christ, but rather the first Antichrist,*
> *Wicked Mahummet, cunning Mahummet.*
> *Oh, if only his friend were here, too, the next one!*
> *Then I would stomp on you both, one foot for each Antichrist!*

His men carried out the statue with difficulty. At the end of the day, they spared only one vessel in the entire building: a vase hanging from the ceiling, rumored to contain some of Christ's blood, or else manna gathered in the desert by the Children of Israel.[33]

It was a time to plunder, to kill, to bluster, but it was also a time to worship. As the fighting raged on, Godfrey of Bouillon, a descendant of

Charlemagne who, according to his brother Baldwin, carried with him the sword of the Emperor Vespasian and who had been adopted by the Emperor Alexius as his heir—in sum, an ideal candidate for the title of Last Emperor—withdrew from combat, shed his armor, and left the city with three companions. Outside the walls they took off their shoes in a way that Peter Bartholomew might have appreciated and processed around the perimeter of the city barefoot. They then entered Jerusalem at the foot of the Mount of Olives, near where the Lions' Gate is today, and marched humbly to the Church of the Holy Sepulcher. The route they traced would be roughly equivalent to that later invention and pious fraud, the Stations of the Cross, or Via Dolorosa, which pilgrims of Jerusalem still follow.

At the Holy Sepulcher, Godfrey shed tears, prayed, and gave thanks to God. Perhaps he also paused to consider the Prophet Isaiah, whose words were being fulfilled around him: "And his Sepulcher will be made glorious."

Others soon followed his example. They cleaned the gore from their hands but walked barefoot through the still bloody streets, making their way to Christ's tomb, tracking in red footprints and offering sacrifices of peace in the church they believed to mark the center of the world. It was, Raymond of Aguilers believed, a day that would be celebrated annually forevermore with similar processions throughout the world, the day when Christendom was raised up, the pagan world brought low, and the true faith everywhere strengthened. Raymond, perennially disillusioned and unhappy though he may have been, surely must have looked joyfully and expectantly toward the skies in the direction of the Mount of Olives. Prophecy had been fulfilled. The Apocalypse had begun, or perhaps it had ended. How much longer, he and others asked themselves, would Christ's triumphant return be deferred?[34]

19

The Last Emperor

(July 1099)

J erusalem had fallen. What to do now?

The question seems not to have come up before the crusaders' victory in July 1099. The chances that they would actually succeed had probably looked so remote that no one bothered to think beyond the next battle.

Should Jerusalem become a European outpost? A city with a king? A fiefdom of the pope? Some had the impulse to look to Urban II for an answer, but that turned out to be impossible. Back in Europe, he was on his deathbed even as the last battle occurred. He would never hear the news of the grotesque glories wrought because of his pronouncements at Clermont.

In leading a barefoot procession to the Sepulcher of Christ, treading through gore-filled streets, Godfrey may have been trying to give an answer. After "shedding more blood on that day than can be believed," he struck the pose of a penitent pilgrim and encouraged others to follow his example, to forget plunder, to forget about taking hostages or prisoners, and to meditate for a time on their singular achievement. Godfrey was offering himself as the conscience of the crusade, revealed in the last days of the campaign—if not in the last days of time—as God's own instrument for the advancement of history.

Few other leaders were willing to take control of the apocalypse they had started. Of the original princes, three were gone—Bohemond,

Stephen of Blois, and Hugh the Great. Neither of the two Roberts—Flanders and Normandy—seems to have wanted to stay in the East. They might be kingmakers at Jerusalem, but they would not themselves be kings. Raymond of Saint-Gilles, despite all his missteps and the many failures at Arqa, was one of a very small group who still remained viable as a ruler. The only other contender, in the absence of Bohemond, was Tancred, whose several important military contributions to the crusade (not to mention a few sly political maneuvers) made him an unlikely but credible candidate to govern Jerusalem.

A final struggle for Jerusalem would follow. Of the three men—Godfrey, Raymond, and Tancred—the one to prevail would need to balance the humility of a true Christian with the ferocity necessary to repel Antichrist. For the simple act of accepting the crown of Jerusalem was to invite the onset of the Last Days. Up to this point, Godfrey had not been particularly adept at manipulating prophecy. His public procession around Jerusalem, however, was a brilliant first step in that direction.[1]

The Merciful and the Greedy

Godfrey's rivals had not performed nearly so well. While Godfrey was weeping at the heart of Jerusalem and the heart of the world, Raymond and Tancred were doing what they would have done in an ordinary war: collecting hostages. They were not alone. Despite the massacre, several hundred Saracens had survived, taken into custody by princes and petty warlords. To do so was an act of both mercy and greed—mercy because the knight had somehow curbed his instinct for killing, greed because hostages would pay ransoms to save their lives and escape the city. Seen from that perspective, to spare an enemy was little different from a practice common among the poor pilgrims—disemboweling Saracen corpses in the hopes of finding gold hidden in their guts. The honorable slaughtered. The avaricious spared.[2]

Raymond and Tancred were the worst offenders on this front. In the early stages of the battle on July 15, Raymond concentrated his followers at the citadel on the western side of the city, known as the Tower of David. Many high-value hostages had taken shelter inside, including Iftikhar-ad-Daulah, the Fatimid governor of Jerusalem. These men sought a pledge of security from Raymond, and in return they offered him possession of the citadel, along with a huge sum of money. Raymond, "corrupted by greed," accepted. He not only let these Saracens leave safely; he even arranged for an escort to accompany them all the way to the Egyptian city of Ascalon. He also began to stock the tower with all of the food and weapons and money he had managed to plunder, as if in preparation for another war—this time against either Tancred or Godfrey for control of the city.[3]

Tancred, too, took prisoners. Along with another knight named Gaston of Béarn, he spotted a crowd of Saracens atop al-Aqsa mosque (or as the Franks called it, the Temple of Solomon). There were about three hundred men, women, and children, who had made their way to the roof, all now begging for their lives. Benevolently (or avariciously), Tancred and Gaston gave them assurances and Tancred's standard as a sign of protection.

The prisoners stayed there throughout the night, but the next morning a few pilgrims, enraged at the sight of Muslims on what seemed to them a sacred Christian building, "attacked the Saracens, both men and women, cutting off their heads with drawn swords. Some of the Saracens threw themselves headlong from the Temple." All of them died. Tancred had lost his prizes and was furious, both at his hostages' deaths and at Raymond's success in the same enterprise. Tancred demanded justice, presumably in the form of monetary compensation, and if not justice, revenge.[4]

The dissensions created by this second, smaller massacre threatened to open new, unbridgeable rifts within the army. That is, until some of the "greater and wiser men" shared their counsel: Rather than allow the Franks to fail through "avarice or sloth or mercy," they should kill all of the prisoners, regardless of whether they were being held for ransom or even if the ransom had already been paid.[5]

And so on the third day of the conquest, the final stage of the Jerusalem massacre began. Albert of Aachen was the only writer to describe it. As with his account of the pogroms along the Rhine, he showed a startling degree of empathy for the victims: The Franks "were beheading or striking down with stones girls, women, noble ladies, even pregnant women, and very young children, paying attention to no one's age. By contrast, girls, women, ladies, tormented by fear of imminent death, and horror-struck by the violent slaughter, were embracing the Christians in their midst even as they were raving and venting their rage on the throats of both sexes, in the hope of saving their lives. Some were wound about the Christians' feet, begging them with piteous weeping and wailing for their lives and safety. When children five or three years old saw the cruel fate of their mothers and fathers, of one accord they intensified the weeping and wretched clamor. But they were making these signals for pity and mercy in vain. The Christians gave over their whole hearts to the slaughter, so that not a suckling little male child or female, not even an infant of one year would escape alive the hand of the murderer. The streets of the whole city of Jerusalem are reported to have been so strewn and covered with the dead bodies of men and women and the mangled limbs of infants, not only in the streets, houses, and palaces, but even in places of desert solitude numbers of slain were to be found."[6]

Just enough Saracens were spared so that the Franks might have slaves charged with removing the bodies. Rather than giving a formal burial, these few survivors piled their friends and family in heaps outside the gates. "They made mountains from the bodies. They were as big as houses." Six months later at Christmas, the bodies were still there. Fulcher of Chartres, the historian who had settled at Edessa, traveled to Jerusalem as a pilgrim for the holiday, and he wrote, "Oh, how great was the stench at that time, both inside and outside the city walls, because of the Saracen corpses, still rotting there, killed when our comrades captured the city! It was so bad that we had to stop up our noses and mouths."[7]

The Election of a King

During the same meeting when the princes decided to execute all of their prisoners, they also treated another vexed question: Who would rule Jerusalem? And how? On July 17, the day of the third massacre, they did little more than offer prayers and charity, hoping that God would show them the right answer. For the next five days, they argued among themselves, as the various pretenders to the throne made their cases, each trying to present himself as best suited for the job while maintaining due humility.

The topic had been broached only once before, around July 1, when some of the army's clerics had discussed the possibility of making a king. It would be no light undertaking. Kings were semidivine incarnations of secular authority, enforcers of God's will in earthly affairs. The trappings of office dated back to the Old Testament, and all European kings to a degree would have seen themselves as partaking in a form of government created by David in Jerusalem. The Israelite kings were effectively the founding fathers of medieval Europe, their images celebrated in, among other places, the western façade of Notre-Dame, the royal cathedral in Paris. A king of Jerusalem—like a king of France, England, or Germany— would be David's heir, too, only doubly so since he would actually sit in David's city in a direct line of succession to his rule. [Plate 9] To restore a king in Jerusalem, like the crusade itself, was to tinker with the funda- mental patterns of history, and not everyone was ready for that.

The chaplain Raymond of Aguilers was especially opposed. His mil- lennial program had failed, and without Peter Bartholomew or an equally visionary prophet—Peter Desiderius does not seem to have captured the army's imagination—he was not sure how to proceed. In fact, given the prophetic implications of crowning someone in Jerusalem, he earnestly believed that there shouldn't be a king there at all. When the topic was first broached during the siege, he said, the bishops and clerics argued that "they ought not elect a king where the Lord had suffered and was crowned, that if the king were to say in his heart, 'I sit on the throne of David and I hold his kingdom,' his faith and virtue might decline from David's. Perhaps the Lord would bring him to ruin and grow angry at the place and the people." These clergymen preferred instead to have some- one who "would be an 'advocate,' to guard the city and distribute the trib- utes and rents collected from the area to the city's guardians." Others simply wanted a king, and there could be no compromise between these groups, except to delay a decision.[8]

When the topic came up again after Jerusalem fell, no one heeded Raymond's arguments. There was a strong movement to create a king, though his duties were essentially the same as what the chaplain had en- visioned for an advocate: "The princes came together to elect someone as king, who might take care for all, who might collect the tributes in the area, someone to whom the people might run and someone who would take care lest anyone's land suffer destruction." Some of the clergy spoke up against the procedure and demanded that the army follow the natural order of things—that is, elect a "spiritual vicar," a patriarch, first, and then a king who might look after secular affairs. But most everyone rejected this idea, including many priests, and they pushed for an immediate royal election. How greatly had clerical authority diminished, the chaplain Raymond mused, since the death of Adhémar, that second Moses.

Without dwelling on voting procedures, the leaders first offered the crown to Raymond of Saint-Gilles. It was a surprising choice. Even more surprising, Raymond refused. Perhaps he had found his chaplain's arguments about the need for an advocate convincing. Maybe at this juncture his authority was so bound up with the Holy Lance and Peter Bartholomew's millenarianism that he could not accept a crown—the new Jerusalem should be ruled by Christ and saintly judges, not by a man wearing a crown.

More likely, Raymond was trying to emulate Godfrey's July 15 public display of humility. By refusing a crown, he would show that he was, in fact, the only man worthy to wear one. Raymond of Aguilers said only that the count "felt horror at the name of kings in that city." Another writer suggested that Raymond refused because he "was truly worn down with age and had only one eye." Whatever his rationale, the barons and priests next turned to Godfrey, who on July 22, 1099, accepted.[9]

What office he accepted on that day is somewhat unclear. According to historical tradition, he matched Raymond's humility by refusing the title of king, preferring instead to call himself "Advocate of the Holy Sepulcher." So venerable is this tale, still related earnestly by the Franciscans who today maintain Godfrey's sword and spurs in Jerusalem, that it seems rude to question it. But the tradition is wrong.

Raymond of Aguilers had originally proposed that Jerusalem should not have a king but an advocate. If Godfrey had accepted this title, surely Raymond would have trumpeted the decision? It would have been, for him, a rare victory. Instead, Raymond left the impression that Godfrey, unlike Count Raymond, felt no horror at the name of king and took upon himself all the burdens and privileges of monarchy. Even the writers who did not call Godfrey king, like Fulcher of Chartres or the author of *Deeds of the Franks*, called him "prince" or, in Fulcher's case, "prince of the kingdom." Chroniclers writing in Europe in the early twelfth century, by and large, just called Godfrey "king."[10]

The best way to resolve these contradictory reports is to conclude that Godfrey compromised: He accepted the office of king but refused to wear a crown. "Never in the city of Jerusalem did he bear the crown of kings, out of reverence for Jesus Christ, the author of our salvation, who because of human mockery there wore a thorny crown." "Though elected a king," an epitaph from Godfrey's tomb read, "he preferred not to be so titled, nor to be crowned, but rather to serve Christ." He preferred not to wear a crown, and the evidence on this point suggests that he did not. He preferred not to be called king, but the evidence on this point is at best ambiguous. The one thing he absolutely did not call himself was "Advocate of the Holy Sepulcher."[11]

Despite the absence of a crown and the ambiguous title, Godfrey's office seemed no less splendid or royal. If anything, it was imperial. As a descendant of Charlemagne, he could make a plausible case to have fulfilled the rumors that had circulated through Lotharingia in 1096 that the first Holy Roman Emperor had returned from the grave and would liberate Jerusalem. More importantly, he could also make a case that he was fulfilling the predictions about the Last World Emperor, the "King of the Greeks and Romans." As Charlemagne's descendant, he could be king of the Romans. As Alexius's adopted son, he could be king of the Greeks. It might seem a dubious claim, but Godfrey's brother Baldwin had used a similar adoption ceremony to make himself prince of Edessa. In this light, Alexius's words to Godfrey at the time of the supposed ceremony would have seemed portentous: "I am accepting you as my adopted son, and everything that I possess I place in your power, so that through you my empire and my land shall be safe and free from the forces here now and from those still to come."[12]

It was a title confirmed by visions, many of them related around the time of Godfrey's election. The first one had occurred ten years before the march to Jerusalem when a knight named Hecelo, after spending a day hunting with Godfrey, dreamed that he saw the duke standing atop Mount Sinai, a new Moses to the Christian people. Mount Sinai was the place where God had handed down the law to Moses and with it the authority to govern, as the Children of Israel wandered through the deserts,

searching, like the Franks, for the Promised Land. In the dream two unnamed men in ecclesiastical garb rushed forward, hailing Godfrey as the
"duke and guide for his Christian people," praying that he might find
blessing and grace in the eyes of God, just as Moses had done. Of all the
princes to liberate Jerusalem, Albert of Aachen explained, Godfrey was
the only one to do so in the spirit of Moses, "preordained by God as spiritual leader of Israel." Albert did not point out the obvious difference between Godfrey and Moses: that the duke actually did complete his
journey and took his people to the Promised Land.[13]

In another precrusade vision, one of Godfrey's servants, Stabelo,
dreamed of a golden ladder stretching from earth to heaven. Godfrey attempted to climb the ladder with another servant named Rothard, who
carried a lamp in his hand. Halfway up the ladder, Rothard's lamp went
dark. At the same moment, the rung under his foot broke, causing him to
retreat down the ladder in fear—unable to arrive safely with the duke at
"the heavenly gate" and thus reach "the throne of heaven." Stabelo then
climbed the ladder himself, and he and Godfrey together entered "the
court of heaven." Rothard was a deserter, as Albert of Aachen explained,
but Stabelo completed the pilgrimage (and remained a political player in
Jerusalem for many years). The ladder was made of gold to signify free
will and a pure heart. It reached heaven to demonstrate that Godfrey's
entire mind was focused on the city of Jerusalem, "which is the gate to
the heavenly homeland." Earthly and heavenly Jerusalems once more
melded together, and our dream interpreter, Albert, did not even mention
the obvious royal symbolism here: a heavenly court and a heavenly throne
welcoming Godfrey, the new king.[14]

Finally, seven months after the Lotharingians had departed for the
East, a cleric named Giselbert, from Aachen, learned in a vision that Godfrey would be "head of all and prince of Jerusalem, foreknown and established by God." Giselbert saw the duke seated upon the sun, surrounded
by innumerable birds. Many of the birds suddenly took flight, for a time
obscuring both Godfrey and the light of day. The sun, Albert explained,
symbolized Jerusalem, which "surpasses all the cities in the world because
of its name and sanctity, just as the sun by its brightness surpasses all the
stars of heaven." To sit upon the sun was to sit "on the throne of the kingdom of Jerusalem." The birds symbolized the army, some of whom stayed

in the Holy Land out of love for their leader, many of whom returned home upon his death. The choreography of the scene seems deliberately reminiscent of Revelation 19, where an angel standing upon the sun commands the birds of the air to feast upon the kings of the earth.[15] [Plate 5]

We might add to this list of stories a series of miracles associated with Ida of Boulogne, Godfrey's mother. She developed a reputation during her life for sanctity, based in large part on the achievements of her sons in the Holy Land. In one of her biographies we read that she, too, had a dream of the sun. It appeared to descend from heaven to settle in her lap: a sign of the auspicious lives prepared for her children, including Godfrey, "predestined to be the first King of Jerusalem by a new dispensation." Revelation 12:5 speaks of a woman clothed in the sun and about to give birth to a child who is to rule the nations of God. [Plate 10] In an imaginative variation on this story, Ida, while pregnant with Godfrey, saw herself standing inside the Holy Sepulcher. She noticed a crucifix suspended from the ceiling, and she wished to abase herself before it. Instead of receiving her worship, however, the image of Christ came to life and lowered itself to pay homage to her womb since the child therein would liberate the city where He had died.[16]

Godfrey may not have a worn a crown, but he was still a figure of royal and imperial dignity—just what Jerusalem needed as it prepared for the next confrontation with the minions of Antichrist and perhaps with Antichrist himself.

The Millenarian Strikes Back

Soon after the election, Godfrey demanded that Raymond turn over the Tower of David. Raymond, naturally, refused. He explained that he and his men intended to stay in the region until Easter 1100 and needed a suitable place to live. His feud with Bohemond over Antioch seemed destined to replay itself in Jerusalem. This time, however, he was to be even less successful in staking out a position in the city.

Godfrey was a more formidable adversary than Bohemond. He was also more popular. The two Roberts sided with him, and several of Raymond's own men, who wished to return to Occitania as soon as possible, secretly opposed the count. Under pressure, Raymond agreed to give over the tower to his new right-hand man, Bishop Peter of Albara, in anticipation of a trial. Peter, however, handed it directly to Godfrey, claiming later that he had been threatened with violence if he did not do so and hinting as well that Raymond's own men had been the ones who had threatened him. His honor lost, Raymond and his entourage left the city. As the chaplain Raymond bleakly summed up the affair, "And so the feuds multiplied."[17]

Once a likely candidate for kingship, now unwelcome in Jerusalem, Raymond had only one stratagem left. He and his few remaining men one last time paid homage to their fallen prophet. For Peter Bartholomew had given the count one set of instructions he had yet to fulfill. When Peter had first approached him and Bishop Adhémar with news of the Holy Lance, he had described how they ought to behave at the end of the crusade. From Jerusalem Raymond was to go to Jericho. There he would cross the Jordan, but he must do so in a boat and not on foot. On the other side, he would clothe himself in a shirt and a pair of linen breeches and allow himself to be sprinkled with water from the river. Once his clothes had dried, he would set them aside, thenceforth to be preserved with the Holy Lance.[18]

When Raymond arrived at Jericho, his retinue could not find a boat. He therefore ordered them to build one from tree branches so that he might cross the river while staying dry. The chaplain Raymond exhorted everyone to pray for the lives of the count and of the other princes. Raymond of Saint-Gilles then stepped forward, wearing only a shirt and a new pair of breeches as ordered, and Raymond of Aguilers baptized him at the same place and in the same fashion as John the Baptist had baptized Christ. But the chaplain's patience was wearing thin: "Why the man of God would have ordered these things, I still don't know." When they returned to Jerusalem in early August, they would learn that Arnulf of Choques, chaplain to Robert of Normandy, Peter Bartholomew's prosecutor, and chief of the doubters of the Holy Lance, had been elected patriarch of Jerusalem.[19]

Two months later, perhaps still puzzling over the judgments of God and wondering just what that last bit of pantomime at the Jordan had meant, the two Raymonds, count and chaplain, were staying in Latakia, a Syrian port city under the control of Byzantium. There they had met a man named Daimbert, Archbishop of Pisa, now acting as papal legate, sent from Rome to fill the void left by Adhémar's death. Daimbert was delighted to encounter veterans of the crusade. They could help him compose a letter to send to the new pope, Paschal II, to update him on the situation in Jerusalem. Based on the letter's style and content, Raymond of Aguilers appears to have written the entire document in Daimbert's name, and with a few strokes of the pen, he managed to reshape the history of the end of the crusade. He did it not so much with the letter's content but with its salutation, signed on behalf of Archbishop Daimbert, Count Raymond of Saint-Gilles, and Godfrey, now styled "Advocate of the Holy Sepulcher."

The letter circulated widely. Over time it became one of the most frequently read descriptions of the crusade in medieval Europe. Godfrey had had no input into its content—he had long since parted company with Raymond—which explains why in this one instance he bore the title "Advocate," the office that the chaplain Raymond and his party had tried to force upon him at Jerusalem but that Godfrey had refused. And thanks to the wide circulation of this letter, the title stuck. Historians, clerics, and tourists to Jerusalem embraced the idea of Godfrey the Advocate, too humble to be a king. For the first time perhaps since the discovery of the Lance, Raymond had won an argument. He had never liked the idea of a king in Jerusalem, and in history, if not in life, the millenarian had his revenge.[20]

20

Ascalon, the Sixth Battle

(*August 1099*)

The crusade was not yet ended. Near the beginning of August, at about the same time Raymond was bathing in the River Jordan, Tancred and Godfrey's older brother Eustace learned that a massive Egyptian army—Turks, Persians, Syrians, Agarenes, Arabs, and "the rest of the infidel people from Eastern nations"—was coming together to attack the Franks. Unbelievably, the exhausted soldiers—their numbers greatly reduced by battle, starvation, famine, and desertion—having just secured an astonishing, near unimaginable triumph at Jerusalem, still had one more battle to fight.

Tancred and Eustace sent warnings back to Godfrey. The Franks, under the king's leadership, decided to ride out to face the enemy rather than risk being caught in an intractable siege. It was by this point a venerable strategy: Catch a numerically superior foe by surprise while it is still on the march and while its leaders were anticipating a later battle at a fixed location. The Franks would meet the Egyptians at Ascalon, the port city where less than a month earlier Raymond had escorted his ransomed prisoners from the Tower of David. Devising a strategy at this point was relatively easy. The more difficult task would be to re-create the apocalyptic fervor that had driven the crusade to those earlier victories. The pilgrim-warriors had captured their prize. They were ready to go home.[1]

For this problem Godfrey, or perhaps his patriarch, Arnulf, employed another well-worn strategy: the discovery of a miraculous relic. Sources in the local Christian community maintained that they had recently possessed a small fragment of the True Cross but that it had been lost. Such a prize would do nicely.

This time there was no Peter Bartholomew to reveal its whereabouts. Godfrey and Arnulf had to rely on more conventional methods: putting out inquiries among the locals and asking if anyone knew where the relic might be. After several denials a Syrian gentleman reluctantly admitted where to find the True Cross. "It is clear that God has chosen you and delivered you from every tribulation, and that He has bestowed upon you this city and many others, not because of your virtue or strength, but because of His own fury. Your Lord and Leader has opened for you extraordinarily well-fortified cities and through Him you have won fearsome battles. Since we see that God is on your side, by what stubbornness should we hide from you His treasures?" He then led Arnulf to an abandoned house and showed him a darkened corner where the Syrian had a year earlier buried away the sacred treasure out of fear that the Egyptians would destroy it.[2]

What they unearthed was a cross-shaped reliquary made of wood and decorated in gold and silver. Inside was a smaller piece of wood—a particle of the True Cross, a *particula*—also shaped like a cross. There were similar fragments scattered throughout the world—not enough to build a battleship, as conventional wisdom held, but probably enough to build one very big cross. Compared with more significant portions at Rome and Constantinople, this particle must have seemed unremarkable. Because of its location, however, and because of its nearly miraculous delivery from the Saracens, the Franks believed it especially valuable. Quickly, instinctively, they organized a procession to carry it to Mount Calvary and the Holy Sepulcher and then to the Temple Mount, under the leadership of Arnulf and Peter the Hermit, who was now working closely with the new regime.[3]

The timing of the battle was advantageous, if not providential. Godfrey's election as king two weeks earlier had been a divisive process. Not everyone had wished to accept him as leader or obey his commands. A new enemy might at least unite the various factions temporarily and for one last time.

But not right away. Even the rumor of an imminent Egyptian attack could not move some of the leaders to follow Godfrey into battle—particularly Raymond of Saint-Gilles. He had by now returned to Jerusalem from Jericho and announced that he did not wish to follow Godfrey anywhere. More surprisingly, Robert of Normandy indicated that he, too, would not leave the city until he had proof that the threat was real. Godfrey did not intend to wait. Accompanied by Robert of Flanders and the Patriarch Arnulf of Choques, he led the march toward Ascalon while the others held back. Peter the Hermit stayed behind, too, but he was tending to heavenly problems—organizing processions; encouraging all of the Christians in the city, Greek, Latin, and Syrian, to join together in prayer; collecting alms; tending to the poor; and as best as possible propitiating the wrath of a still-angry God.[4]

Outside Jerusalem Godfrey dispatched a party of scouts to gather more information about what the Egyptians were planning. Within a day the scouts had completed the ninety-mile round-trip journey to Ascalon and confirmed that a massive Egyptian army was indeed gathering before the city. With visual confirmation Godfrey sent Bishop Arnulf of Martirano (not to be confused with the Patriarch Arnulf) back to Jerusalem to rouse Robert and Raymond and all of their followers from a self-induced torpor. Arnulf must have arrived on the morning of August 10, exhausted from twenty-four hours of constant travel. Fortunately for him and for Godfrey, Raymond and Robert now believed his story and agreed to leave later that day. Rather than wait for them, the bishop rushed back alone to Godfrey and was never seen again.[5]

The Normans and the Provençals finally set out later that day. They caught up to Godfrey the next afternoon, presumably after traveling through the night. Godfrey at this point was riding alongside an Egyptian spy, the prefect of the city of Ramla, located on the road between Jerusalem and the port of Jaffa. The spy was, according to Albert of Aachen, "a faithful man in his intentions, although a gentile," and was able to warn the Franks about Egyptian tactics. Very likely, he told Godfrey, the Egyptians would attempt to distract the army from thoughts of battle. And perhaps they did. At about the time of day when Raymond and Robert joined the other princes, they came upon a small band of

Egyptian soldiers (or perhaps they were just shepherds) and captured from them large herds of sheep, cattle, and camels. Based on what the spy had told them, Godfrey assumed that the vizier of Egypt, al-Afdal, had placed this tempting target before them deliberately. The Egyptian leaders wanted them to focus on plunder and forget about fighting. If that was the case, the ploy failed. The crusaders left the animals alone and continued toward Ascalon. Strangely, the animals followed. They even seemed to arrange themselves in something like military formation, arrayed in wings along the left and right flanks of the army, marching as if of their own accord. It was a miracle—or else the animals found the shiny armor and weapons attractive. Opinions varied.[6]

The animals may have been unified, but the people were not. The Provençals were still carrying the Holy Lance of Antioch. Arnulf, riding near Godfrey, was brandishing the True Cross. That night Raymond of Aguilers would deliver a sermon to his people while holding the Lance, just as the Patriarch Arnulf would preach to the rest of the army with his relic. Their message, delivered in different languages and with different emblems of divine authority, stressed the need to set aside, one last time, selfishness. Whoever started to gather plunder before the battle ended would be excommunicated, but if everyone stayed dedicated to the cause, then he could later claim whatever treasure he liked. The soldiers were also encouraged to confess their sins, even the slight ones, and each probably received a blessing as well, touching the Cross or the Holy Lance, as preferred. The ritual complete, they passed an uneventful and unpleasant night, with no tents, little bread, no wine, but, at least, more meat than they could possibly eat.[7]

At daybreak they marched on the Egyptian camps in front of Ascalon. As they did, Albert of Aachen said, they sang together happily, perhaps performing a new song about the battle for Jerusalem, playing flutes, stringed instruments, and bagpipes.

The prefect of Ramla was amazed at the soldiers' demeanor. How could they be so cheerful with such a terrible battle looming? Godfrey explained to the prefect that the Franks rejoiced at the thought of dying. They would go to a better place to join their Lord. Pointing to the True Cross, he concluded, "This sign of the Holy Cross, which fortifies us and sanctifies us, will no doubt serve as a spiritual shield against all our enemies' spears. Because of our hope in the sign, we dare to stand more firmly against any danger." The cross—and not the lance, Provençals be damned—was now protecting Jerusalem, a spiritual talisman against pagans who would blaspheme the Lord. So impressed was the prefect that he decided to convert to Christianity on the spot, as soon as they could find someone to baptize him.[8]

It was this noisy, happy, divided army that marched against "the camps of Mahummeth." Their enemy was not ready for the fight. The battle began while many of the warriors were still tying flasks of water around their necks, wanting something to drink after pursuing their enemies all day—or so the Franks speculated. In the half-light of dawn, the crusading army seemed numberless, surrounded as it was by hundreds of pack animals marching in a miraculous and orderly fashion. Shocked at the size of the army before them, the Egyptians panicked. Apparently, God struck them blind. "If indeed we are to believe the gentiles, they often said afterwards that they found themselves stupefied. Their eyes were open, but they could barely see the Christians and could not hurt them at all."[9]

The battle-hardened contingent of Franks thus overwhelmed their enemy—unprepared, confused, and possibly blind. After a fight of uncertain duration, they drove the Egyptians back into their own tents and to Ascalon's gates. Some Egyptians were caught between the army of Raymond of Saint-Gilles and the sea. A few vainly hid in trees. The hero of the day was Robert of Normandy, "a fearless warrior," who spotted the standard of al-Afdal by the golden apple at its tip. The duke charged at the vizier, drove away his men, and thus broke the entire enemy's will to resist. Robert later presented the standard before the Holy Sepulcher.[10]

The defeat for the Egyptians was total. In one writer's words, "The fields were bedewed—nay, flooded—with blood, and gradually covered in gentile carrion." Another chronicler mixed the language of history with that of the Apocalypse, saying, "And in a moment the field was covered with prone bodies, and none of ours could step anywhere except on a corpse. The land everywhere was wet with blood, as if a bloody rain had fallen from the clouds." "In this battle," a German writer observed, "the strength of the pagans and of the devil was broken, and the kingdom of Christ and of the church spread from sea to sea."

The Christians liked to imagine the Egyptian vizier al-Afdal tearing his hair in frustration, realizing the scope of the disaster: "Whatever may happen, one thing is certain: I will never again rise up against them. Better for me to return to my own country, there to dwell in shame as long as I live." Another writer, Robert the Monk, imagined that al-Afdal—whom Robert bizarrely named "Clement," presumably because in Latin it rhymes with "demented": *Clemens demens*—screamed vain threats at the Christians: "O Jerusalem, debauched city! Whorish city! If at any time by any chance you should fall into my hands, I will raze you to the ground and destroy entirely the Sepulcher of your corpse!"[11]

One contemporary historian, Fulcher of Chartres, took a slightly different tack in describing the outcome. Rather than focus on the amir, he talked about the Egyptians' wealth. It was vast, including not just gold, silver, and valuable cloth, but also twelve types of precious stone: jasper, sapphire, chalcedony, emerald, onyx, sardius, chrysolite, beryl, topaz, chrysoprase, jacinth, and amethyst. It is a curious and exotic list, until one realizes that it comes from Revelation, where the prophet John lists all of the gems that adorn Heaven's foundations. The crusaders plundered from Babylon the spoils of heaven, and perhaps with this treasure, their earthly Jerusalem could become a bit more like the heavenly one.[12]

Yet climactic as it was, this battle would not be the last. Raymond of Aguilers, in his letter written under the name of Daimbert of Pisa, described Ascalon, in a rather odd system of numbering, as the "sixth battle." Apocalyptic events tend to happen in sevens. Raymond's implication was that the final battle, the seventh battle, was still to occur. For Fulcher of Chartres, too, despite the heavenly treasure gained at Ascalon, the war for Jerusalem had not yet ended. But there would come a time six years later when he would believe that the end had arrived—that he had seen Armageddon. The new king of Jerusalem, Baldwin I, Godfrey's brother, would defeat a combined army of Egyptian and Damascene soldiers. In that battle's aftermath, a storm struck the Egyptian fleet, destroying Babylon's seapower as well. It was a fittingly victorious note on which to conclude Fulcher's book: "This battle occurred, the last of the battles. And this is the end." The next chapter followed with a brief list of apocalyptic phenomena—a terrifying earthquake, a comet that lit up the skies for seven straight weeks, and, finally, in February 1106, just six months after the defeat of Babylon, two new suns appearing in the heavens, one to either side of the real sun, arced by a four-colored rainbow and creating a splendid and dazzling burst of lights the size of the city. A New Jerusalem, perhaps, descending from the sky to inhabit and revivify the Old—had the final act of Revelation 21 begun? [Plate 11]

What it all signified, Fulcher said, "we entrust entirely to the Lord."[13]

Conclusion

The Never-Ending Apocalypse

On September 7, 1101, a battle occurred between the Frankish Kingdom of Jerusalem and the armies of Fatimid Egypt near the city of Ramla—the city whose prefect had been so helpful before the battle at Ascalon. In typical fashion the Franks were badly outnumbered, but once they managed to engage the Egyptians at close quarters, they butchered them. The Franks were helped in no small part by the True Cross, which deflected all spears and arrows thrown at it—a heavenly shield covering a small corner of the Franks' army.

Many esteemed knights from Jerusalem died that day. Among their number was the standard-bearer Galdemar Carpenel, a First Crusader who had elected to stay in the East after Jerusalem's conquest. He had done so not to build a principality for himself but rather, as the Knights Templar would later do, to protect pilgrims—to be "the guardian and champion of Christians coming and going, especially to that sacred river [Jordan], as much as he could." King Baldwin I of Jerusalem later took revenge against Galdemar's killers and managed to recover the body. His friends and followers carefully cut out Galdemar's intestines and allowed his corpse to dry in the sun before carrying him back to Jerusalem. There, at the command of Archbishop Hugh of Lyon, who had arrived in the Holy Land as a pilgrim that year, he was placed before the Holy Sepulcher, an unusual honor for an ordinary knight and against the practices of the Frankish church. He was later given a solemn burial in that same building, songs and litanies sung before his tomb in Latin, Greek, and Armenian.[1]

The night after the funeral, Archbishop Hugh saw in his sleep someone dressed as a deacon who ordered him to step outside. There, beyond the door, Hugh saw the recently buried Galdemar, seated atop a white horse, with one hand shaking a spear, the other holding a blood-red banner. Hugh caught his attention, and they began a simple conversation.

The archbishop said, "Are you Galdemar?"
He answered, "I am—honestly."
ARCHBISHOP: "How are you?"
GALDEMAR: "Okay."
ARCHBISHOP: "Tell me everything! Where are you? How are you?"
GALDEMAR: "I'm not allowed to say what I want."
ARCHBISHOP: "Why are you turned away and not looking at me?"
Galdemar said, "I'm threatening Babylon."

The apocalyptic crusade continued. Galdemar, entitled to a heavenly reward, was not yet ready to abandon his comrades in their never-ending struggle against Babylon.[2]

FROM OUR VANTAGE POINT, with nine centuries of hindsight, it is tempting to look smugly or dismissively at the dreams and nightmares born of the First Crusade. The expected Apocalypse, after all, didn't happen. It is a diverting, if at times disturbing, story, but at the end of the day, so what? In the twenty-first century, we expect our history not to have morals but to at least have some sort of connection to the modern world. Important events change the course of history. They lead to discoveries, to inventions, to new ideas. They concern heroic events that can be celebrated, or they tell cautionary tales of what might be if we are so foolish as to repeat past mistakes.

I have told the story of an idea that ultimately went nowhere. It concluded with what seemed to be the Apocalypse but, inevitably, wasn't. And even that false apocalypse was eventually forgotten. The whole affair is today remembered as a military and religious victory without the trappings of Armageddon. The war's greatest heroes, like their apocalyptic dreams, faded into quiet obscurity, their fates serving more as a warning about the world's dimming glory than providing fodder for further celebration of apocalyptic glory.

None fell harder than Robert of Normandy, the hero of the battle of Ascalon. He returned home to great fanfare and nearly to a great stroke of fortune as well. In August 1100 his younger brother King William of England, to whom he had mortgaged his duchy in order to pay for his crusade, died in a hunting accident on the eve of Robert's return from the East. Before Robert could lay claim to both kingdom and duchy, however, his youngest brother, Henry, established himself in William's place as king of England. Five years later Henry would defeat Robert at the battle of Tinchebrai and would hold his brother, the crusade hero, a prisoner for the remaining twenty-eight years of his life, a man largely forgotten by the time of his death.

Siding with Henry in this conflict was none other than Robert of Flanders. In 1103, in a treaty negotiated between the two rulers, he pledged to provide one thousand warriors to the English king should he choose to invade Normandy. So fleeting and fragile did the ties formed on the road to Jerusalem prove to be. It was just one of many shrewd decisions made by Count Robert upon his return to his increasingly prosperous and urbanized homeland. Until his death in 1111, he proved himself a capable and effective ruler. He also drew upon the mystique of the crusade, occasionally styling himself "the Jerusalemite" on legal proclamations. From time to time, though, during the last five years of his life, as he thought about his pilgrim comrade imprisoned in an English castle, he must have questioned the decisions he had made after 1101 in the name of political expediency.[3]

Unlike Robert, Stephen of Blois and Hugh the Great were never able to settle comfortably back into Europe. These two men, who at varying times had harbored pretensions of leading the crusade, both returned home in disgrace, having abandoned the armies during and just after the siege of Antioch, respectively. Both men faced intense public pressure to return to the Holy Land and make right their cowardice. Stephen in particular became a popular figure of ridicule. A later poet writing an epic poem of the crusade chose to present Stephen as a pitiable weakling, trembling visibly before every battle and constantly trying to desert. A Norman monk named Orderic Vitalis, writing around 1120, liked to imagine Stephen's wife, Adela of Blois, calling him a coward in the midst of their conjugal embraces. In 1101 both Hugh and Stephen joined a new crusade intended to shore up the gains of the first expedition. Hugh died of battle wounds in October 1101 in the city of Tarsus. Stephen at least made it to Jerusalem, but he died a few weeks later fighting alongside Baldwin I at Ramla. Despite their good endings, most knights in Europe never forgave them their character failures or the abandonment of their friends at Antioch.[4]

Some of the princes never returned to Europe, Count Raymond of Saint-Gilles among them. His reputation had obviously suffered toward the end of the crusade, owing to his connection with Peter Bartholomew, his constant wrangling with Bohemond over Antioch, and his inability to match the political and spiritual savvy of Godfrey of Bouillon at the fall of Jerusalem. Still, he might have gone home to Toulouse a hero had not the allure of a Middle Eastern principality maintained a hold on his imagination. After his encounter with Daimbert of Pisa at Latakia in 1099, where his chaplain wrote a letter proclaiming Godfrey "Advocate of the Holy Sepulcher," Raymond sailed to Constantinople and stayed for a time with the Emperor Alexius. When word reached him in 1101 that a new crusade was coming from Europe, he decided to join it and spent the next two years sometimes fighting against Turks, sometimes fighting against Tancred, now based in Antioch. In 1102 Raymond's attentions returned to Tripoli, the city whose wealth and prestige had first drawn his attention in 1099 in the final stages of the original crusade. In 1103, after capturing a couple of nearby coastal cities, he built a castle on a hill outside Tripoli and dug in for a long siege. It lasted six years before the city finally fell. Raymond himself died in 1105, his dreams of a new principality still unrealized.

Most puzzling of all is the case of Bohemond. The great hero of the crusade, the military genius who had led the Franks to a series of improbable or impossible victories over the Seljuk Turks, he withdrew from the campaign before its final chapter in the name of establishing a Frankish state around Antioch. It was to be an enduring political creation, lasting for 170 years. But Bohemond himself played little part in securing its survival. In August 1100, just two years after the defeat of Kerbogah, he made an ill-advised expedition to the north and was captured by a Turkish amir. He would spend the next three years in prison and would escape only by paying a massive ransom and promising military support to his captors against their Muslim rivals. A year later he would sail for Europe and with the blessing of the pope would begin organizing a new crusade, this one to be fought against his traditional enemy, the Emperor Alexius. As part of this new campaign, Bohemond traveled all over France and Flanders delivering sermons that condemned the Greeks, that celebrated the crusade, and that placed himself squarely at the center of things—securing his reputation to this day as the greatest hero of the First Crusade. The new expedition, however, fizzled. After a months-long siege of the Byzantine port city of Durazzo, through which so many of the Frankish armies had passed in 1096 and 1097, Bohemond surrendered to Alexius almost unconditionally, returning in quiet disgrace to his homeland in southern Italy. His remains lie today in the Italian town of Canosa di Puglia, just outside the cathedral. The mausoleum, which Bohemond surely designed for himself, was built in the style of a Greek imperial tomb. From the grave he thus continues to threaten the empire, long after it had finally, decisively, defeated him.

Of all the major crusade leaders, only Godfrey left this world with his reputation intact—perhaps because he died in 1100, less than a year after the victory at Ascalon. Like a medieval JFK, his followers were free to imagine the long reign that he might have had and to paint him as whatever sort of hero they wished him to be.

The lesser lords, Godfrey's brother Baldwin and Bohemond's nephew Tancred, were the only ones who put together truly lengthy and impressive careers as crusading princes. Baldwin, of course, established the first crusader state around the city of Edessa. Two years later, in 1100, he claimed the throne of Jerusalem immediately after his brother's death. Within a year he also overcame whatever scruples his brother had felt about wearing a crown in the Holy City, proclaiming himself defiantly king of Jerusalem and governing from the Aqsa Mosque, or as he preferred to call it, the Temple of Solomon.

Tancred, meanwhile, beginning in 1100, ruled Antioch as regent after Bohemond's imprisonment. His effective administration probably helps to explain why his uncle abandoned the Levant for Europe shortly after his release from captivity in 1103. The giant was a fine battlefield commander and an inspirational figure, but when it came to managing the day-to-day affairs of a principality, his nephew seems to have been better suited for the job. Tancred continued to rule Antioch, albeit as regent in the name of Bohemond's infant son, until his death from ill health in 1111.

It is remarkable, and probably no coincidence, that the two men who first broke from the main armies in 1097 in order to explore political opportunities in Armenia were also the most successful rulers in the Latin East. Working in the shadows of more famous relatives, they learned the ruthlessness and cunning needed to survive in the frontier societies of eleventh-century Syria and Palestine. When the apocalypse finally calmed in 1100, Baldwin and Tancred were the men best prepared to impose a new order onto the madness they had helped create.

BALDWIN AND TANCRED's careers also serve as a fitting symbol for the First Crusade's historical legacy: a two-hundred-year saga of continual warfare, increasingly disastrous for Europe, a dark chapter in Western history that most would rather forget but that recent events in what we call the "war on terror" suggest we ought to remember. Given what we know of the eventual scope of the crusades, of their political importance, of the poisonous effect that their memory continues to exert on relations between adherents of Christianity and Islam, why should we concern ourselves with the failed and eventually forgotten prophetic dreams of those first unfortunate souls who set their culture onto this nightmarish path?

Apocalypses and history are, from any perspective, uncomfortable bedfellows. History is the study of what happened, and the Apocalypse, by definition, hasn't happened. At least not yet. When it does, there will be no more history. People still believe in apocalypses. They still think one to be imminent. They have done so interminably, and they will probably always do so. Historians are only now learning to appreciate the importance of this recurring phenomenon. Thanks to the work of my colleague Richard Landes, for example, most historians now admit that some, and perhaps many, European men and women looked expectantly, either hopefully or fearfully, toward the year 1000 and then 1033 as likely times for the Apocalypse. We have seen in this book how thousands of German pilgrims felt similarly about the year 1064. In all three cases, the years passed, Christ did not return, and memory of those expectations largely, but not completely, faded from historical memory.

The First Crusade is different. It was an apocalypse that for a time worked. The grandest predictions were fulfilled. Christian armies marched east, they witnessed miracles, they bathed in rivers of blood, and they remade history. The crusade then became part of an ongoing Apocalypse. As late as 1120, many highly educated people still believed that they were witnessing the Last Days. Theirs was a shared Apocalypse, a lived Apocalypse, an Apocalypse without end.

History had been transformed, these educated observers would have sworn. And they would have been correct. Their world was in the process of being remade, although perhaps not because of what had happened in Jerusalem.

Every facet of life around the year 1100 was in the midst of some sort of transformation. Medieval historians have long written about the years 1050–1200 in these terms. It was the time of the twelfth-century renaissance, the age of medieval humanism, the era of the discovery of the individual. As tempting as it is to say otherwise, the First Crusade did not cause all of these changes associated with "the Long Twelfth Century." In many respects it was a product of the early phases of this movement—a product of the economic, political, and intellectual revivals just gaining traction in the later eleventh century. But the First Crusade was a catalyst for all of the social, intellectual, and economic changes that followed. Western European Christians in the twelfth century believed themselves not just to be witnessing history but also to be remaking history, working in concert with the divine plan, serving as instruments of God's will rather than suffering through life as objects of His wrath. And they believed this, I am suggesting, because for a time—in fact, for decades—they were living with an ongoing Apocalypse. They were God's agents remaking the world in preparation not for history's end but for its culmination. Let us consider for a few moments what some of the effects of this continuing Apocalypse were.[5]

One of the most famous, if troubling, formulations of what happened in the twelfth century is that of Colin Morris, who defined it as the time of "the discovery of the individual." It is an esoteric idea, but one not without bases in the sources. As even a cursory reading of twelfth-century history will indicate, it was an era that developed a new fascination with questions of psychology, motivation, and internal spiritual life.

For these widespread concerns we ought to consider the First Crusade a primary cause. The application of the crusade indulgence as proclaimed by Urban II required confessors all across Europe to sort through the intentions and personalities of warriors who had accomplished great things in the East but who were, on the face of it, wholly irredeemable. To understand the erratic violence of a man like Raimbold Croton (who lost a hand while trying to scale the walls of Jerusalem and who would later castrate a monk at home), the inexplicable cowardice of Stephen of Blois, or the myriad contradictions that together created Bohemond of Antioch required speculation and investigations of intention and psychology on a grand scale. If anything necessitated a discovery of the individual, interpreting the First Crusade did.[6]

The apocalyptic First Crusade could also be seen as playing a part in the establishment of national identities, particularly in France. The argument grows in part out of a habit of thought that by now is easily recognizable: the tendency to conflate the Israelites of the Old Testament with the Franks. This association was one of the "revealed truths" contained in Revelation. The new Judah, the true Chosen People, would step out of the allegorical shadows of the Jews and claim their rightful inheritance. The Franks, in this case, were the new Jews, but they also saw themselves as better than the Jews. It was a theological point that even Saracen characters—specifically, Kerbogah's mother—understood: "What had been with the Jews was transferred to these nations by the gift of adoption." And this idea could help to justify some of the crusaders' most questionable actions, such as the massacres at Jerusalem, which according to one observer did not grow from tactical necessity but from a desire not to repeat the mistakes of King Saul: "They spared neither women nor children, remembering, I think, King Saul, who spared Agag and thus incurred the wrath of God and perished." For God had ordered Saul, the first king of Israel, to destroy the Amalekites completely, "man and woman, child and infant, ox and sheep, camel and donkey." Saul, however, spared their king, Agag, and preserved some of their most valuable possessions. As a result, God rejected Saul as king and promoted David in his place. Godfrey's army avoided that error.[7]

This obsession with "Chosen People" is one of the most powerful catalysts toward the creation of national communities. It is strikingly apparent in the sermon of Urban II as imagined by Robert the Monk, where the pope addressed his audience as the "race of Franks . . . chosen and beloved by God." The language was a deliberate gloss on Deuteronomy 7:6–8: "Since you are holy, the Lord your God has chosen you that you might be to him a particular people out of all those who are on the earth. The Lord is not joined to you and has not chosen you because you will conquer all peoples through numbers, for you are fewer than all other peoples. Rather, the Lord has loved you and He kept the oath sworn to your fathers and has led you with a mighty hand from the slavery and the domination of King Pharaoh of Egypt."

The biblical passage recalls several scenes from the crusade. In particular, while fighting in the same deserts as the Children of Israel, the Franks were lifted by God in victory over numerically superior enemies, who were also by coincidence lineal political descendants of the pharaohs. Both the Israelites and the Franks had entered the Promised Land, taking as their leaders Joshua and Jesus, respectively—two names that, according to the rules of medieval biblical commentary, were allegorically the same.[8] [Plate 12]

The Franks were not the first to claim this sort of affinity with the Jews, and they would not be the last. The books of the Old Testament, particularly the story of the Exodus and the return to the Promised Land, have proved enduring sources of national passions, continually appealing to religious groups who believed that they, like the Franks in 1099, were taking a lead part in God's plans for history. The citizens of the Dutch Republic, the Parliamentarians of Cromwell's England, and the Puritans who settled in America (to take three seventeenth-century examples) all conceived of themselves as an elect—a Chosen People like Israel—in order to strengthen their sense of community and purpose. The same ideology would inform the American experience, with its sense of Manifest Destiny and of the United States as "a shining city upon a hill."

Similar rhetoric had played an important part in the history and politics of the early Middle Ages. Most notably, Charlemagne liked to style himself as a new David and his people the Franks, a new Israel. As a recent study by Matthew Gabriele demonstrates, the memory of Charlemagne in France and Europe more broadly may have played a part in the calling of the Crusade. But Charlemagne's use of this Old Testament language in 800 would have looked very different from the Franks' use of it three centuries later. Whereas Charlemagne's "New Israel" centered on his personality as a new David, the crusaders did not get their David, Godfrey, until after they had arrived in the Promised Land. Their achievement belonged to the people as a whole, and they were encouraged to celebrate that fact, to see themselves as the bountiful and brilliant race whose accomplishment dozens of crusade chroniclers would extol.[9]

This shared Frankish identity went beyond France. It was an achievement that all Latin Christians could celebrate, and in doing so, they helped to forge a broader category of "Christendom." The idea of Christendom, the subject of a recent book by Brett Edward Whalen, entered into common parlance in twelfth-century Europe. Expressed in the Latin word *Christianitas*, it can refer to the belief system of Christianity, to the people who subscribe to those beliefs, or, sometimes, to a geographic entity.

The crusade chronicle of Baudry of Bourgueil used *Christianitas* in every one of these senses. As a belief system: "[The Turks] claim that they are descended of Frankish stock, but that their ancestors broke away from Christianity." As a people: "In our times God called up almost all of His Christendom, from lands everywhere, to snatch Jerusalem, where He especially suffered, from the hands of the filthy Turks." As a geographic entity: "There was [after the victory of Ascalon] unspeakable joy in all of Christendom."

To create this sense of common Christian identity had been one of the major goals in Urban II's crusade plan. Given the sense of triumph, celebrated throughout the European world in ceremonies and processions of thanksgiving, transcending the boundaries drawn during the continuing wars between pope and emperor, this aspect of his plan must be viewed as a success, but only a qualified one. The broader Christian world, Latin and Greek, was damaged, if not irreparably broken. Owing in no small part to ideas propagated in many crusade chronicles, the First Crusade engendered in certain learned circles an unrelenting hatred of the Greeks—an effeminate race, not only ungrateful for the military support that the Franks had given but also actively conspiring with the Turks against their fellow Christians. Rather than unite Western and Eastern churches, then, the crusade had only accentuated their differences. This sense of distinction turned out to be one of the crusade's most enduring legacies.[10]

There was now a fundamental series of oppositions between Latin and Greek and, more broadly, between West and East. The distinction is an old one, with roots in antiquity (Greeks and Persians, Romans and barbarians), but the crusade gave it new life and new detail. The opposition went beyond Christian and Saracen, beyond "Christendom" and "Pagandom," as Raymond of Aguilers put it. It was a question of two different worlds, an effeminate, flighty, unbelieving (schismatic or heretical) East that stood in sharp opposition to a virtuous Latin West. It is a dichotomy fundamental to the Franks' thought. As mentioned previously, Ralph of Caen could still recall how, while a child in Normandy, he had seen the skies turn a frightening shade of red the night after Mardi Gras in 1098. "Those in the West who saw it shouted out, 'The East fights!'" Or stated more succinctly, the English historian Henry of Huntingdon, thirty years after the conquest of Jerusalem, described the vision in which Christ appeared to Stephen of Valence and explained to him how the Christian army might yet prevail at Antioch. "You shall tell these things," he said, "to the sons of the West."[11]

The differences between East and West were on the surface religious, but the root cause was climatic. It is again an old idea, dating back to Hippocrates and Aristotle, but one that received new valorization because of the crusade. According to Guibert, the excessive heat in the East caused men's thoughts to be more transient, less stable, and unfixed. "The faith of Orientals has always been rather mutable," he wrote, and that is why most every major heresy originated in their world. William of Malmesbury mentioned the importance of climate in connection with the crusade on three separate occasions. Easterners, he observed, were dried up because of heat. They had less blood, which gave them more cunning minds, and they feared close combat because they had so little blood to spill. The heat also caused their blood to be less vital than the Franks', giving them a slavish character. For that reason alone—the inert blood of its people—the Persian Empire endured so long. The emperor's subjects lacked the vigor to rebel. The Franks, born in more temperate regions, were bold and savage and on several occasions shook themselves free of a single people's domination. The untamed ferocity of crusade warriors thus became, in William's analysis, a sign of cultural virtue.[12]

This emphasis on opposites, part of a style of thought that is fundamentally apocalyptic, was born of the oppositions with which by now we have become familiar: heaven and hell, the saved and the damned, God and Devil, Christ and Antichrist, Christian and Saracen. The vision of a West in perfect opposition to an East, the formation of a single people out of diverse tribes, the accomplishment of divine mission through an army of saints—all are apocalyptic ideas. The experience of a shared Apocalypse, one that did not disappear in a moment of sudden disillusionment in 1000, 1033, and 1065 but rather haunted the imagination for years, reified these ideas and transformed them into beliefs shared and celebrated in circles that extended beyond courtly and intellectual classes. When the crusade disappeared, these habits of thought, these imaginative bonds joining together disparate communities behind a label otherwise meaningless—"the West"—survived.

Some historians, and no doubt some readers, will be inclined to go further still, to see in the crusade not just the birth of the High Middle Ages but also the birth of the modern world, as we find ourselves living in a time again marred by religious strife and characterized by an instinctive division between East and West. Caution is necessary on this point. The word "crusade" has been used to distressing effect by all sides in recent global conflicts and never with anything resembling thoughtfulness or precision. It is surely ludicrous to draw one-to-one parallels across nine centuries of history. But at the same time, it is difficult to ignore the resonances between the eleventh-century story I have told and our own time: a Western army attacking a little-understood Eastern culture, earnestly believing itself to be a liberator of the cities it conquered, trusting that God was on its side and that to die in battle was to attain a martyr's death, both anxious and hopeful that its exertions would remake the world and create a peace so profound that history itself might draw to a close (with Christianity or liberal democracies covering the globe), only to discover that the sudden liberation of Jerusalem had led not to a new world but to an endless and endlessly dangerous occupation of enemy territory.

Whether that parallel will persist remains to be seen. In the Middle Ages, more than half a century was needed to sort out just which Apocalypse had happened, if any, and another half century still was required to iron out the various nuances of crusade doctrine. In the meantime the unintended consequences of that first great exercise in medieval holy war continued to pile up, one disaster atop another.

An event buried deeply in the past, with so many causes and effects between its day and ours, offers no clear lesson. But the First Crusade, as the original and perhaps the only Apocalypse fulfilled, does present a somber warning about the dangers of holy war once an army or the authority behind an army chooses to believe that its goals align with God's. The rivers of blood such a war unleashes run no less deep, specious though their otherworldly justifications may be.

At some point in the twelfth century, an unnamed scribe was just finishing a copy of Raymond of Aguilers's history of the First Crusade. He had a couple of blank pages at the end of the book. Not wanting to waste parchment, he filled them with a few details about Ida of Boulogne, Godfrey's saintly mother. In summing up her achievements and her life, he skipped naturally to July 15, 1099. Influenced by the general tenor of what he had just read in Raymond's book but not really recalling the details, he described the final entry of the Franks into Jerusalem. Godfrey and Tancred led the way. "At the point of attack where Godfrey was besieging Jerusalem, a white horseman came galloping down from the Mount of Olives. Godfrey and Tancred were the first to follow it." In the words of Apocalypse, "And I looked, and behold a white horse, and he who sat upon it held a bow, and a crown was given to him, and he went forth conquering, and to conquer. The armies who are in heaven were following him, on white horses, and they were clad in fine linen, white and pure."[13]

In such literary dark corners the apocalyptic First Crusade endures, where fallen knights like Galdemar Carpenel stand watch over a demonic foe, their spears raised toward Babylon in an unending war for the heavenly Jerusalem—a dream from which medieval men and women would one day awake, even if, like many a forgotten nightmare, the delirium of holy war would continue to haunt their psyches and shape their waking lives.

Acknowledgments

I n 1999, while attending a professional conference, I presented what I expected to be the first of three or four papers concerning the First Crusade. With luck, I hoped to turn these papers into a professional article. Twelve years later, I am finally able to publish this book, the first major contribution in an ongoing research project to which I would like to devote still more years. It has been, and remains, a long and rewarding journey. While undertaking it, I have benefited from the advice, friendship, and support of more people and institutions than I can possibly remember. But I will make a go of it here.

The serious work behind this book began thanks to the American Council of Learned Societies (ACLS), which in the academic year 2002–2003 enabled me to undertake research in and around Paris devoted to the First Crusade. I had very definite ideas about the crusade at this time—among them, that the First Crusade had almost nothing to do with the Apocalypse. Things changed. If I had not had this year to explore the literature and the manuscripts, this book would not have been possible.

In 2006–2007 I was fortunate enough to receive an ACLS Burkhardt Fellowship, which enabled me to spend a year at the American Academy in Rome, now with very different ideas about the crusade. The administrators of the American Academy, in particular the director at the time, Carmela Franklin, were incredibly supportive. The fellows of the Academy proved to be a welcoming and engaging community, whose questions, ideas, and enthusiasm for my research enriched this book immeasurably.

In the following year, 2007–2008, I returned to Paris, this time through the support of a fellowship from the National Endowment for the Humanities, where the first full version of this book began to take shape.

Without the support of these agencies (not to mention the generosity of my employer, the Department of History at the University of Tennessee, which allowed me to begin my career in Knoxville with a two-year leave), this book would certainly not have been possible. During the early months of my second year in Paris, I received a fellowship from the John D. and Catherine T. MacArthur Foundation. It has opened up whole new opportunities for research and writing, making it possible for me now to think of this book as the first chapter in a larger research project on the impact of the crusade movement in Europe.

In immediate connection with this book, I must thank my agent, Deborah Grosvenor, who guided my manuscript toward Basic Books and who has given me so much invaluable advice along the way. Lara Heimert at Basic Books strongly encouraged me to take the narrative approach in this book, retelling the events of the First Crusade through the prism of apocalyptic theory, and all of the editors and readers at Basic Books have done marvelous work turning a dense and difficult text into a far more accessible and effective story. Hats off especially to Brandon Proia, Melissa Veronesi, and Jan Kristiansson.

Will Fontanez and the University of Tennessee Cartographic Services Laboratory created this book's beautiful and beautifully clear maps, working well from my generally muddled requests and instruction. The UT History Department, the Marco Institute for Medieval Studies, and the UT Office of Research through the UT Exhibit, Performance, and Publication Expense Fund, generously contributed subventions to support the production of those maps as well as to pay for the many other illustrations that have enriched *Armies of Heaven*.

My colleagues and friends in medieval history have contributed enormously to this book in so many ways—through advice, through references, through reading and critiquing the many incarnations of its chapters, and through writing letters of support as I applied for a variety of different grants (many more than the ones listed here). I cannot imagine how I must have tried the patience of Sally Vaughn, Ed Peters, Sharon Farmer, Tim Graham, Philippe Buc, Jason Glenn, and Geoff Koziol. But they always came through with reference letters for me without fail. The people who wrote letters of endorsement for the MacArthur Fellowship were anonymous. I thank all of you, and I hope this book does not entirely disappoint.

The scholars who have given advice and encouragement are more numerous still. Thanks so much, in no particular order, to Dennis McCarthy, Helen Damico, Kevin Uhalde, Christopher MacEvitt, Peggy Brown, Bill North, Victoria Morse, Marina Rustow, Jerry Passannante, Tom Burman, Nick Paul, Clementine Oliver, Brett Whalen, Matthew Gabriele, Tom Madden, Mark Pegg, Benedicta Ward, Cecelia Gaposchkin, Dominique Barthélemy, Frédérique Lachaud, John Ott, Maura Lafferty, Jean-Charles Bédague, Richard Landes, and Karin Fuchs. A number of crusade scholars, whom I have either met only through e-mail or only in passing at academic conferences, have generously given advice, including Jonathan Riley-Smith, Marcus Bull, Jean Flori, John France, Nikolas Jaspert, and Luigi Russo. Finally, I thank all of the graduate and undergraduate students with whom I have been fortune enough to have worked, many of whom have suffered through my crusade class. In this category, at the University of Tennessee, I have to thank especially Meghan Worth and Geoff Martin. This list is woefully incomplete. To everyone else, please accept my apologies and gratitude.

My friends have borne patiently with this project as well. Many of them, who like me are part of the medieval history game, have been mentioned. Others who don't fall into that category (Tom Bissell, who traveled to Jerusalem with me in 2007; Joseph McAlhany, who traveled around Bohemond's homeland with me that same year; my parents, Gene and Marilyn Rubenstein; and John Randolph and Gary Barth, Chad Brumley and Steve Barrick, who are the best friends a person could ask for) have made equally important contributions.

On the same day that I began putting the final touches on this manuscript, two very good friends passed away. Tom Sizgorich taught me a lot about religious violence during the one year I was fortunate enough to walk the same hallways as he at the University of New Mexico. His contribution to the study of history was already extraordinary. The loss to the field at his early passing is incalculable; the loss to his friends is beyond expression.

Jim Powell also will not be able to see this book, in many ways the product of his encouragement. During the 1998–1999 academic year, when I was teaching at Syracuse, Jim treated me to many lunches, allowed me to raid his library, taught me so much about the crusades, and assured me that my small papers were saying something interesting about this well-worn historical topic of crusading. His friendship and support meant the world to me, and I will miss him sorely.

During the research and writing of this book, as is now apparent, I attended many conferences and spoke to many audiences. Most memorably, in the spring of 2008 I traveled from Paris to New York to participate in a conference at Fordham University. While there I went out to dinner with a magazine editor named Meredith McGroarty. About a year later, we were married. Because of her love and support, by the time I finished this book, I was a much happier person than I had been at the beginning—a transformation that enlivens even the darkest passages of this book. Because of her sharp advice and her editor's eye, *Armies of Heaven* tells a much better story than it would have done without her.

This book is for Meredith.

Abbreviations

Please note that in instances where both a Latin text and an English translation are listed here, it is always the Latin version that is cited in the text of this book. English translations are provided to enable curious nonspecialist readers to consult source material. Citations are made according to book and chapter, and in the case of Fulcher, sentences, as well as by page. Book and chapter citations should enable readers to locate the cited material quickly, whatever edition or printing or translation they are working from. Sources that are cited within a single chapter appear in full in the notes.

AA: Albert of Aachen, *Historia Ierosolimitana: History of the Journey to Jerusalem*, ed. and trans. Susan B. Edgington (Oxford, UK: Clarendon Press, 2007).

AASS: *Acta Sanctorum quotquot toto urbe coluntur*, ed. Johannes Ballandus et al., 70 vols. (Paris and Rome: Société des Bollandistes, 1863–).

Adso: Adso Dervensis, *De ortu et tempore Antichristi*, ed. D. Verhelst, CCCM 45 (Turnhout, Belgium: Brepols, 1976).

Alexiad: Anna Comnena, *The Alexiad*, trans. E. R. Sewter (London: Penguin Classics, 1969).

Alphandéry and Dupront: Paul Alphandéry and Alphonse Dupront, *La chrétienté et l'idée de croisade* (Paris: A. Michel, 1954–1959, repr. by A. Michel as a single volume, 1995).

Asbridge (2000): Thomas Asbridge, *The Creation of the Principality of Antioch, 1098–1130* (Woodbridge, UK: Boydell Press, 2000).

Asbridge (2004): Thomas Asbridge, *The First Crusade: A New History* (Oxford, UK: Oxford University Press, 2004).

Autour de la Croisade: Autour de la Première Croisade: Actes du Colloque de la Society for the Study of the Crusades and the Latin East (Clermont-Ferrand, 22–25 juin 1995), ed. M. Balard (Paris: Publications de la Sorbonne, 1996).

BB: Baudry of Bourgueil (aka, Baldric of Dol), *Historia Hierosolymitana*, RHC Oc. 4, 10–110.

BL: British Library.

BN: Bartolph of Nangis, *Gesta Francorum Iherusalem expugnantium*, RHC Oc. 3, 491–543.

BnF: Bibliothèque nationale de France.

BR: Bibliothèque Royale (Brussels).

Bull (1993): Marcus Bull, *Knightly Piety and the Lay Response to the First Crusade: The Limousin and Gascony, c. 970–c. 1130* (Oxford, UK: Clarendon Press, 1993).

Caffaro: Caffaro, *De liberatione civitatum orientis*, RHC Oc. 5, 47–73.

CCCM: Corpus Christianorum continuatio Mediaevalis.

CCSL: Corpus Christianorum series Latina.

CdA: *La Chanson d'Antioche*, ed. Suzanna Duparc-Quioc, 2 vols. (Paris: Paul Geuthner, 1977, 1978).

Chazan (1987): Robert Chazan, *European Jewry and the First Crusade* (Berkeley and Los Angeles: University of California Press, 1987).

Chroniques: Chroniques des comtes d'Anjou et des seigneurs d'Amboise, ed. Louis Halphen and René Poupardin (Paris: Auguste Picard, 1913).

Cohn (1957): Norman Cohn, *The Pursuit of the Millennium: Revolutionary Millenarians and Mystical Anarchists of the Middle Ages* (London: Secker and Warberg, 1957).

EA: Ekkehard of Aura, *Hierosolymita: De oppresione, liberatione ac restauratione Jerosolymitanae Ecclesiae*, RHC Oc., 5, 7–40.

École Française (1997): *Le Concile de Clermont de 1095 et l'appel à la Croisade* (Rome: École Française de Rome, 1997).

Erdmann, *Origin*: Carl Erdmann, *The Origin of the Idea of Crusade*, trans. Marshall W. Baldwin and Walter Goffart (Princeton, NJ: Princeton University Press, 1977).

FC: Fulcher of Chartres, *Historia Hierosolymitana*, ed. Heinrich Hagenmeyer (Heidelberg, Germany: Carl Winter's Universitätsbuchhandlung, 1913); trans. France Rita Ryan, *A History of the Expedition to Jerusalem, 1095–1127* (Knoxville: University of Tennessee Press, 1969).

Flori (1999): Jean Flori, *Pierre l'Ermite et la Première Croisade* (Paris: Fayard, 1999).

Flori (2007): Jean Flori, *L'Islam et la Fin des Temps: L'interprétation prophétique des invasions musulmanes dans la chrétienté médiévale* (Paris: Seuil, 2007).

France (1994): John France, *Victory in the East: A Military History of the First Crusade* (Cambridge, UK: Cambridge University Press, 1994).

France (2006): John France, "Two Types of Vision on the First Crusade: Stephen of Valence and Peter Bartholomew," *Crusades* 5 (2006): 1–20.

Frutolf: Frutolf of Michelsberg, *Frutolfs und Ekkhards Chroniken und die anonyme Kaiserchronik*, ed. and trans. Franz-Josef Schmale and Irene Schmale-Ott, Ausgenwählte Quellen zur deutschen Geschichte des Mittelalters, 15 (Darmstadt, Germany: Wissenschaftliche Buchgesellschaft, 1972).

Gabrieli: Francesco Gabrieli, *Arab Historians of the Crusades*, trans. E. J. Costello (Berkeley and Los Angeles: University of California Press, 1984).

GF: *Gesta Francorum et aliorum Hierosolimitanorum*, ed. Rosalind Hill (London: Nelson, 1962).

GN: Guibert of Nogent, *Dei gesta per Francos*, ed. R.B.C. Huygens,

CCCM 127A (Turnhout, Belgium: Brepols, 1996); trans. Robert Levine, *The Deeds of God Through the Franks: A Translation of Guibert de Nogent's Gesta Dei per Francos* (Woodbridge, UK: Boydell Press, 1997).

GP: Gilo of Paris, *Historia vie Hierosolimitane*, ed. and trans. C. W. Grocock and J. E. Siberry (Oxford, UK: Clarendon Press, 1997).

Hagenmeyer, *Chronologie*: Heinrich Hagenmeyer, *Chronologie de la Première Croisade, 1094–1100* (Hildesheim, Germany: Georg Olms, 1898–1901).

Hagenmeyer, *Epistulae*: Henrich Hagenmeyer, ed., *Epistulae et chartae ad primi belli sacri spectantes: Die Kreuzzugsbriefe aus den Jahren 1088–1100* (Hildesheim, Germany: Georg Olms, 1901).

HBS: *Historia belli sacri*, or *Historia peregrinorum euntium Jerusolymam*, RHC Oc. 3. 167–229.

Hill and Hill (1962): John Hugh Hill and Laurita L. Hill, *Raymond IV Count of Toulouse* (Syracuse, NY: Syracuse University Press, 1962).

Hillenbrand (1999): Carole Hillenbrand, *The Crusades: Islamic Perspectives* (Edinburgh: Edinburgh University Press, 1999).

Kedar (2004): Benjamin Z. Kedar, "The Jerusalem Massacres of July 1099 in the Western Historiography of the Crusades," *Crusades* 3 (2004): 15–76.

Landes (2000): Richard Landes, "The Fear of an Apocalyptic Year 1000: Augustinian Historiography, Medieval and Modern," *Speculum* 75 (2000): 97–145.

LF: Lambert of St. Omer, *Liber Floridus: Codex Autographus Bibliotheca Universitatis Gandavensis*, ed. A. Derolez and I. Strubbe (Ghent, Belgium: E. Story-Scientia, 1968); Ghent, MS Cod. 92 Universiteitsbibliotheek.

Matthew of Edessa: Ara Edmond Dostourian, trans., *Armenia and the Crusades, Tenth to Twelfth Centuries: The Chronicle of Matthew of Edessa* (New York: University Press of America, 1993).

Mayer, *Crusades*: Hans Eberhard Mayer, *The Crusades*, trans. John Gillingham, 2nd ed. (Oxford, UK: Oxford University Press, 1990).

MGH: *Monumenta Germaniae Historica*.

MGH in usum: MGH, *Scriptores rerum Germanicarum, in usum scholarum separatim editi*; (Hanover, Germany: Hahnsche Buchhandlung, 1871–).

MGH SRM: MGH *Scriptores rerum Merovingiarum*, ed. Bruno Krush and Wilhelm Levison, 7 vols. (Hanover, Germany: Hahnsche Buchhandlung, 1884–1920).

MGH SS: MGH *Scriptores*, ed. G. H. Pertz, et al., 38 vols. (Hanover, Germany: Hahnsche Buchhandlung, 1826–2006).

Monodies: Guibert of Nogent, *Monodiarum suarum libri tres*, ed. and trans. Edmond René Labande as *Autobiographie* (Paris: Belles Lettres, 1981); trans. Joseph McAlhany and Jay Rubenstein as *Monodies adn On the Relics of Saints* (London: Penguin Classics, 2011).

Morris (2005): Colin Morris, *The Sepulchre of Christ and the Medieval West: From the Beginning to 1600* (Oxford, UK: Oxford University Press, 2005).

OV: Orderic Vitalis, *Historia Ecclesiastica*, ed. M. Chibnall, 6 vols. (Oxford, UK: Clarendon Press, 1968–1980).

PL: Patrologia cursus completus, series Latina.

Poèmes: Baudry of Dol (Bourgueil), *Poèmes*, ed. and trans. Jean-Yves Tilliette, 2 vols. (Paris: Belles Lettres, 1998–2002).

PT: Peter Tudebode, *Historia de Hierosolymitano itinere*, ed. John Hugh Hill and Laurita Littleton Hill, trans. Philippe Wolff (Paris: Paul Geuthner, 1977); trans. John Hugh Hill and Laurita Littleton Hill (Philadelphia: American Philosophical Society, 1974).

Purkis (2008): William J. Purkis, *Crusading Spirituality in the Holy Land and Iberia, c. 1095–c.1187* (Woodbridge, UK: Boydell Press, 2008).

RA: Raymond of Aguilers, *Liber*, ed. John Hugh Hill and Laurita Littleton Hill, trans. Philippe Wolff (Paris: Paul Geuthner, 1969); trans. John Hugh Hill and Laurita Littleton Hill, *Historia Francorum Qui Ceperunt*

Iherusalem (Philadelphia: American Philosophical Society, 1968).

RC: Ralph of Caen, *Gesta Tancredi,* RHC *Oc.* 3, 587–710; trans. Bernard S. Bachrach and David S. Bachrach, *The Gesta Tancredi of Ralph of Caen: The Normans on the First Crusade* (Burlington, VT: Ashgate, 2005).

RHC Oc.: *Recueil des historiens des Croisades, Historiens occidentaux,* 5 vols. (Paris: Imprimerie Royale, 1844–1895).

RHC Or.: *Recueil des historiens des Croisades, Historiens orientaux,* 5 vols. (Paris: Imprimerie Royale, 1872–1906).

RHGF: *Recueil des historiens des Gaules et de la France,* ed. M. Bouquet et al., 24 vols. (Paris: Aux dépens des libraires, 1737–1904).

Riley-Smith (1977): Jonathan Riley-Smith, *What Were the Crusades?* (Totowa, NJ: Rowman and Littlefield, 1977).

Riley-Smith (1986): Jonathan Riley-Smith, *The First Crusade and the Idea of Crusading* (London: Athlone, 1986).

Riley-Smith (1997): Jonathan Riley-Smith, *The First Crusaders (1095–1131)* (Cambridge, UK: Cambridge University Press, 1997).

Ripoll Account: John France, ed., "The Text of the Account of the Capture of Jerusalem in the Ripoll Manuscript, Bibliothèque nationale (latin) 5132," *English Historical Review* 103 (1988): 640–657.

Rousset: Paul Rousset, *Les origines, et les caractères de la Première Croisade* (Neuchatel, Switzerland: à la Baconnerie, 1945).

RtM: Robert the Monk (aka Robert of Reims), *Historia Hierosolimitana,* RHC *Oc.* 3, 717–882; trans. Carol Sweetenham, *Robert the Monk's History of the First Crusade: Historia Hierosolimitana* (Burlington, VT: Ashgate, 2005).

Rubenstein (2002): Jay Rubenstein, *Guibert of Nogent: Portrait of a Medieval Mind* (New York: Routledge, 2002).

Rubenstein (2004): Jay Rubenstein, "What Is the *Gesta Francorum* and Who Is Peter Tudebode?" *Revue Mabillon* 16 (2004): 179–204.

Schein (2005): Sylvia Schein, *Gateway to the Heavenly City: Crusader Jerusalem and the Catholic West (1099–1187)* (Burlington, VT: Ashgate, 2005).

Sibyllinische Texte: *Sibyllinische Texte und Forschungen*, ed. Ernst Sackur (Halle, Germany: Max Niermeyer, 1898).

Somerville, *Councils*: Robert Somerville, *The Councils of Urban II* 1. *Decreta Claromontensia* (Amsterdam: Adolf M. Hakkert, 1972).

Suger: Suger, *Vita Ludovici Grossi*, ed. H. Waquet (Paris: Belles Lettres, 1964); trans. Richard Cusimano and John Moorhead, *The Deeds of Louis the Fat* (Washington, DC: Catholic University of America Press, 1992).

Tolan (2002): John V. Tolan, *Saracens: Islam in the Medieval European Imagination* (New York: Columbia University Press, 2002).

WM: William of Malmesbury, *Gesta Regum Anglorum*, ed. R. A. B. Mynors, R. M. Thomson, and M. Winterbottom, 2 vols. (Oxford, UK: Clarendon Press, 1998, 1999).

WP: William of Poitiers, *Gesta Guillelmi ducis Normannorum et regis Anglorum*, ed. R. H. C. Davis and M. Chibnall (Oxford, UK: Oxford University Press, 1998).

WT: William of Tyre, *Chronicon*, ed. R. B. C. Huygens. CCCM 63, 63a (Turnhout, Belgium: Brepols, 1986); trans. Emily Atwater Babcock and A. C. Krey, *A History of Deeds Done Beyond the Sea*, 2 vols. (New York: Columbia University Press, 1943).

A Note on Sources

One of the things that make the First Crusade an exciting and difficult topic for medieval historians is the unusual number of narrative sources it inspired. Within twenty years of the fall of Jerusalem, a dozen different authors composed detailed accounts of what had happened. For comparison, the Norman Conquest, just thirty years before the crusade, inspired only a single narrative history, and it survives in only one incomplete manuscript.

Three of the crusade narratives are especially important and for two reasons: Each was written soon after the events described, and each one appears to have been written independently from the other two. Of these three books, two were written by actual participants and were probably finished in the year 1101 at the latest. One of them, by an anonymous writer, is entitled *Gesta Francorum*, or *Deeds of the Franks*. It is likely a composite text—several stories assembled by a single writer during the course of the campaign. The second eyewitness account was written by a Provençal, or southern French, cleric named Raymond of Aguilers. At first he collaborated with a knight named Pons of Balazun, but Pons died in 1099, just a few months before the army arrived at Jerusalem, leaving Raymond to write the lion's share of the book by himself. The third important book in this category is not by an eyewitness, but its author, an otherwise unknown Lotharingian writer usually identified as Albert of Aachen, probably had access to a now-lost firsthand account of the crusade. He also spoke extensively with veterans of the campaign. The result of his research is a book full of original material and unique observations, every bit as valuable for the crusade historian as either the *Deeds of the Franks* or the book of Raymond. Part of the art of retelling the crusade story is to strike a balance among these three narratives.[1]

But in this book I have sought to incorporate as well other historical narratives that, at first glance, appear less valuable. These include four rewritten versions of the *Deeds of the Franks*, composed by three monks in the north of France named Guibert, Baudry, and Robert and by one anonymous monk probably working in the Italian monastery of Monte Cassino. All of these writers added new information to their source material, apparently, like Albert, based on the testimony of crusade veterans. This is even more true of the writer Ralph of Caen, who immigrated to the Middle East in 1107 and eventually wrote a biography of the crusading hero Tancred. Although Ralph's book, known as *The Deeds of Tancred*, was written later than most of the others, it was again based on eyewitness testimony, drawn mainly from crusaders who, like Ralph himself, chose to settle in the Middle East.

A few other books fall into a third category. The famous (among crusade scholars) Fulcher of Chartres was, like Raymond and the author of the *Deeds of the Franks,* a participant in the crusade, but he broke away from the main army long before it reached Jerusalem. Another writer, called Bartolph de Nangis (though I have not been able to find out where this name comes from), lightly revised an early draft of Fulcher's chronicle—one that preserves for us stories that either Fulcher did not include or that he eventually cut from later versions of his history. Finally, I ought to mention Peter Tudebode, a cleric from Poitou who accompanied the crusade all the way to Jerusalem and who, like the French and Italian monks just mentioned, revised the *Deeds of the Franks*. His revisions, however, are quite superficial. He adds a handful of facts to his source material, but his book is so close to the original that it barely merits being called a separate text.

What is most impressive about all of these texts (and some other sources that I have not mentioned here) is how close in spirit they are. And that spirit is, to return to the fundamental theme of this book, apocalyptic. That is to say, the war for Jerusalem was not just about an attempt by Europeans to capture a city in the Middle East. Nor was it a war fought solely in the name of personal piety. For those involved it had real implications on earth and in heaven. The crusaders who left for Jerusalem were fighting on behalf of God's plan for salvation, and in doing so, they fully expected to bring about, or else bring very near, the Last Days and the end of time.

In retelling the military narrative, I have attached the most significance to the first three sources mentioned: *Deeds of the Franks*, Raymond of Aguilers, and Albert of Aachen. When they contradict one another, I try to acknowledge those contradictions dutifully, often in the text, sometimes in endnotes only. Needless to say, in this process I have benefited greatly from recent work by other historians, most notably the brilliantly detailed military history of John France. Whenever I have disagreed with France or with other recent writers, or when I have advanced an entirely new interpretation of the facts, I have tried to acknowledge doing so, while explaining my reasons—sometimes in the text, more often in the endnotes.

In retelling the apocalyptic narrative, I have tended to attribute equal weight to all of the sources, which, as noted, are remarkably uniform in spirit. Eyewitness writers and their immediate twelfth-century successors did not dispute whether the First Crusade had apocalyptic significance. The only real debate was about what sort of Apocalypse the First Crusade had triggered—whether it was a millenarian Apocalypse or whether the Last World Emperor would appear in Jerusalem to inflict rough justice upon Antichrist. Readers who wish to follow up which writer related which sign can reconstruct these fine points from endnotes. I have also attempted to identify points in the endnotes when I have departed significantly from my historical predecessors' arguments. Most readers, I suspect, will have been content to do as the crusaders did—become immersed in an apocalyptic experience that for a time threatened to swallow up all humanity outside Jerusalem's walls.

Notes

Introduction

1. France (1994), pp. 22–42, sets the figure at 80,000, though acknowledging that 100,000 is not unreasonable. Two participants in the crusade estimated the army at 100,000 at the campaign's midpoint, presumably not based on any scientific method of calculation: Hagenmeyer, *Epistulae* 9, p. 147; and RA, p. 48. On the terminology for crusading, see Christopher Tyerman, "Were There Any Crusades in the Twelfth Century?" *English Historical Review* 110 (1995): 553–577. After some deliberation (and after I considered trying to avoid the terms "crusade" and "First Crusade" altogether), I have decided that the labels are too well attached and that avoiding them would serve no useful purpose. Chroniclers thought of the First Crusade as a unique phenomenon and something more than an ordinary pilgrimage. And by the end of the twelfth century—although the term "crusade" was just being coined—annalists were recognizing that three such movements had occurred, following the numbering conventions used in modern histories.

2. See, for example, the discussion in Riley-Smith (1977), pp. 15–17. On p. 16, after a discussion of just war, he observes, "The crusades, however, were expressions of another concept, that of Holy War, in which force of arms is regarded as being not merely justifiable and condoned by God, but positively sanctioned by him" and as "advanc[ing] his [God's] intentions for mankind." The observation is crucial and could be carried further, because to advance the intentions of God for mankind is to advance the progress of salvation history, which is by definition an apocalyptic act. Closer to the analysis here are the comments of Flori (1999), pp. 348–349.

Chapter 1

1. GF, p. 1. The opening epigraph is BB 1, 1, p. 11.

2. Charles Matson Odahl, *Constantine and the Christian Empire* (New York: Routledge, 2004), pp. 211–220; Morris (2005), pp. 16–40.

3. The Jerome passage appears in *Ep.* 58 to Paulinus of Nola, discussed in Morris (2005), pp. 47–49. I have discussed the four meanings of Jerusalem in Rubenstein (2002), pp. 26–27.

4. The bizarre stories of Khosrau and Heraclius can be found in Honorius Augustodunensis, *Speculum Ecclesiae*, PL 172, cols. 1004D–1006A. I have consulted a hagiographic account of Heraclius's war for the Cross in Vat. MS Reg. lat. 457, fols. 88r–89v. See also Morris (2005), pp. 90–94.

5. On pilgrimage, see Jonathan Sumption, *Pilgrimage: An Image of Medieaval Religion* (Totowa, NJ: Rowman and Littlefield, 1975), esp. pp. 114–136. See also Bull (1993), pp. 204–230.

6. The description of al-Hakim's war on Christians comes from the contemporary Muslim historian al-Qalansi, translated in F. E. Peters, *Jerusalem: The Holy City in the Eyes of Chroniclers, Visitors, Pilgrims, and Prophets from the Days of Abraham to the Beginning of Modern Times* (Princeton, NJ: Princeton University Press, 1985), pp. 258–260. See also Marina Rustow, *Heresy and the Politics of Community: The Jews of the Fatimid Caliphate* (Ithaca, NY: Cornell University Press, 2008), pp. 176–177; Morris (2005), pp. 135–139; Anis Obeid, *The Druze and Their Faith in Tawhid* (Syracuse, NY: Syracuse University Press, 2006), pp. 81–91; and Sadik A. Assad, *The Reign of al-Hakim bi Amr Allah (386/996–411/1021): A Political Study* (Beirut: Arab Institute for Research and Publishing, 1974), pp. 182–192.

7. Rodulfus Glaber, *Five Books of Histories*, ed. and trans. John France (Oxford, UK: Oxford University Press, 1989) 3, 7, 24, pp. 132–137. Glaber's contemporary Adémar of Chabannes depicts the French Jews as working in tandem with Spanish Muslims: Adémar de Chabannes, *Chronicon*, ed. R. Landes and P. Bourgain, *CCCM* 129 (Turnhout, Belgium: Brepols, 1999) 3, 47, pp. 166–167.

8. The details of the pogrom come from two sources: Glaber, *Histories* 3, 7, 24–25, pp. 134–137; and Adémar, *Chronicon*, 3, 47, pp. 166–167. Adémar mentions the suicides. He places the beginning of anti-Jewish violence at Limoges shortly before the destruction of the Holy Sepulcher, thus implying the Jews' mission to Egypt was retaliation for their persecution. See also Richard Landes, *Relics, Apocalypse, and the Deceits of History: Ademar of Chabannes, 989–1034* (Cambridge, MA: Harvard University Press, 1995), pp. 40–46.

9. John France, "The Destruction of Jerusalem and the First Crusade," *Journal of Ecclesiastical History* 47 (1996): 1–17, demonstrates how little mention the destruction of the Holy Sepulcher received in Western literature. Landes, *Relics, Apocalypse*, pp. 44–45, cites a twelfth-century chronicle that recalls apocalyptic fears in the year 1010. The historian ignorant of the Sepulcher's destruction is WM 3, 367, pp. 642–643. He does fear that Egyptians will try one day to destroy it: WM 3, 371, pp. 652–653.

10. The pilgrimage is described in Einar Joranson, "The Great German Pilgrimage of 1064–1065," in *The Crusades and Other Historical Essays, Presented to Dana C. Munro by His Former Students*, ed. Louis J. Paetow (New York: F. S. Crofts, 1928), pp. 3–56. See also Morris (2005), pp. 139–146; France, "Destruction," pp. 12–13; and Landes, *Relics, Apocalypse*, pp. 154–158, 320–327.

11. John France argues that the numbers are exaggerated, recalling that William of Normandy's army of 8,000 was enough to conquer England: John France, "Les origines de la Première Croisade: un nouvel examen," in *Autour de la Croisade*, pp. 43–56. To compare an army of professional soldiers gathered by a single lord and a mass assembly of pilgrims is, however, not entirely fair. On the bishops in the army, see Lambert of Hersfeld, *Annales*, ed. O. Holder-Egger, MGH in usum 38, an. 1064, p. 92. On the apocalyptic significance of 1065, see *Vita Altmanni Episcopi Pataviensis*, MGH SS 12, p. 230. See also Landes (2000), pp. 126–127; and Bernard McGinn, "*Iter Sancti Sepulchri*: The Piety of the First Crusaders," in *The Walter Prescott Webb Memorial Lectures: Essays on Medieval Civilization*, ed. Bede Karl Lackner and Kenneth Roy Philip (Austin: University of Texas Press, 1978), pp. 33–71 (p. 40).

12. On these details, see Lambert, *Annales*, an. 1065, pp. 94–95.

13. The *Vita Altmanni* 4, p. 230, relates the story of the abbess, not specifying when it happened, though it would make sense only as placed in the narrative here. On the date and the priests' counsel, see Lambert, *Annales*, an. 1065, p. 96.

14. Lambert, *Annales*, an. 1065, pp. 97–98; *Annales Altahenses maiores*, MGH SS 20, an. 1065, pp. 815–816.

15. *Vita Altmanni* 4, p. 230.

16. AA 1, 2–5, pp. 4–9. As another example of Peter as the originator of the crusade, the German author of the *Annales Brunwilarenses* (MGH SS 1, an. 1096, p. 100) writes simply, "In this year (1096) an expedition to the Holy Land was undertaken at the instigation of Peter the Hermit. The pilgrims captured Jerusalem, Antioch, Nicea, and other royal cities." Anna Comnena makes Peter the inventor of the crusade, too: *Alexiad* 10, 5, p. 309; as does the normally well-respected late-twelfth-century historian William of Tyre: WT 1, 13–14, pp. 129–130. See also HBS, "Prologue," pp. 169–170.

17. Peter's usual reputation is that of a demagogue who corrupted Urban's message and deceitfully claimed it as his own. See, for example, Riley-Smith (1986), pp. 34–35; and, more generally, Henrich Hagenmeyer, *Peter der Ermite* (Leipzig, Germany: O. Harrassowitz, 1879). There have been some attempts to rehabilitate him, notably Flori (1999); and E. O. Blake and Collin Morris, "A Hermit Goes to War: Peter and the Origins of the First Crusade," *Studies in Church History* 22 (1985): 79–107, who place Peter in the context of eleventh- and twelfth-century spirituality, particularly of better-respected figures like Norbert of Xanten and Robert of Arbrissel. The descriptions of Peter's appearance and his entourage here are taken from GN 2, 8, p. 171; and RtM 1, 5, p. 731.

18. *Annales Rosenveldenses*, MGH SS 16, an. 1096, pp. 101–102. On letters from heaven, see Alphandéry and Dupront, pp. 54–55. HBS, "Prologue," pp. 169–170, tells how shocked Peter was to see the Temple of the Lord turned into a Mahomerie. See also Luke 21:24.

19. *Monodies* 2, 5, pp. 246–249. It is unclear whether Peter himself preached an anti-Jewish message, though there appears to me no reason to think he did not. At the very least, the tenor of his message inspired listeners to anger against the Jews, as I have argued in "How, or How Much, to Reevaluate Peter the Hermit," in *The Medieval Crusade*, ed. Susan J. Ridyard (London: Boydell, 2004), pp. 22–41. *Annales Hildesheimnenses*, MGH SS 3, an. 1096, p. 106, draws a direct connection between the pogroms and the followers of Peter.

20. Frutolf, an. 1096, p. 106.

21. Thirty years later another German writer would use a similar turn of phrase, but for exactly the opposite end. In a German translation of the Book of Exodus, he would describe a plague of flies as being like "God's knights." In the 1090s supernatural plagues had been a way to describe the crusaders. By 1130 the crusade had become an image for making Old Testament plagues comprehensible. D. H. Green, *The Millstatter Exodus: A Crusading Epic* (Cambridge, UK: Cambridge University Press, 1966), pp. 273–279. The chronicle description of the flying worms appears in Frutolf, an. 1091, p. 104.

Chapter 2

1. The connections between crusading and the Gregorian reform movement have been treated extensively, most notably in the classic work of Erdmann, *Origin* (see esp. pp. 118–147). The events and personalities involved are examined in H. E. J. Cowdrey, *Pope Gregory VII* (Oxford, UK: Oxford University Press, 1999). FC 1, 7, 2–3, pp. 164–166, describes the situation in St. Peter's in 1096 and also calls Clement a blockhead.

2. Alfons Becker, "Le voyage d'Urbain II en France," in École Française (1997), pp. 127–140.

3. WT 1, 9, p. 121. Another less sensationalist account of the emperor's imprisonment appears in Michael Psellus, *Fourteen Byzantine Rulers*, trans. E. R. A. Sewter (London: Penguin Classics, 1966), pp. 357–358 and 365–366, on his blinding. Richard W. Southern gives a concise narrative of the schism in his *Western Church and Society in the Middle Ages* (Harmondsworth, UK: Penguin, 1970), pp. 67–72.

4. All these plans are outlined at Gregory VII, *Das Register Gregors VII, MGH Epistolae Selecta* 2, 2 vols., ed. Erich Caspar (Berlin: Weidmanschen Buchhandlung, 1920, 1923), 1, 46, pp. 69–71; 1, 49, pp. 75–76 (quote at p. 75); 2, 3, pp. 126–128; 2, 31, 166–168 (quote at pp. 166–167); and 2, 37, pp. 172–173.

5. Benzo of Alba, *Ad Heinricum IV. Imperatorem libri VII*, ed. Hans Seyffert, MGH in usum 65, 1, 15, p. 144. The verses in this quote (indicated here with italics) are Isa. 49:23 and Isa.11:10. The last verse is referenced by RtM 9, 9, p. 869.

6. On the military situation in Antatolia, see France (1994), pp. 152–155. On Piacenza, see Alfons Becker, *Der Papst, die griechische Christenheit und der Kreuzzug. Papst Urban II (1088–1099)*, 2 (Stuttgart, Germany: Anton Hiersemann, 1988), pp. 377–379; Erdmann, *Origin*, pp. 325–330; and Mayer, *Crusades*, p. 7. Only the Lotharingian Ekkehard of Aura mentions letters from Alexius to the pope appealing for aid, but without a direct mention of the council that year: EA 5, pp. 14–15. A monastic historian from Poitiers mentions the council of Piacenza and says that Urban II actually first proclaimed the crusade there, but the account fails to mention a Byzantine plea for help. The text is the *Historia monasterii novi Pictavensis*, excerpted by I. M. Watterich in *Pontificum Romanorum qui fuerunt inde ab exeunte saeculo IX usque ad finem seaculi XIII vitae ab aequalibus conscriptae*, 2 vols. (Leipzig, Germany: Wilhelm Engelmann, 1862) 1, pp. 597–598. Riley-Smith (1986) p. 13, n. 3, cites this passage as the only instance where an annalist noted a connection between Clermont and Piacenza. *Alexiad*, 7, 6, p. 229, and 7, 7, p. 232, describes the connections between Robert the elder and Alexius.

7. Erdmann argues that Urban II conceived of the crusade primarily as a way to help Byzantium and as part of a broader war against the Saracens. Jerusalem was at best peripheral to his message at Clermont: Erdmann, *Origin*, pp. 306–371 (e.g., Urban II's "interest in pilgrimages as such surely was as slight as his interest in the city of Jerusalem"; at p. 316). His somewhat counterintuitive arguments are occasionally still cited as authoritative (e.g., in Mayer, *Crusades*, pp. 8–10, where he argues that Urban preferred to stress the plight of Eastern Christians at Clermont, but that with the passage of time he gave in to public demand and started to talk about Jerusalem). The weight of scholarly opinion, however, has shifted so strongly against this proposition that there seems to me no reason to revisit Erdmann's argument in detail.

8. On Durand's death, see Hugh of Flavigny, *Chronicon,* ed. G. H. Pertz, MGH SS 8, p. 274, in an. 1095. The image of Durand's moldering body is in an aside in *Poèmes* 1, Poem 22, pp. 43–44. Poem 51 gives the day of Durand's death as the thirteenth before December. Depending on how one calculates dates, that would mean that he died either the day before the council began or else on November 18 itself, amid the opening ceremonies. The two epitaphs for Durand appear in *Poèmes* 1, 50–51, pp. 57–58 (the latter mentions the number of attendees at Clermont). Michel Aubrun gives a brief overview of Durand's career in his article "La Diocèse de Clermont, de la fin du XIe au début du XIIe siècle," in École Française (1997), pp. 24–32 (pp. 25–26).

9. BB 1, p. 15. Before the sermon begins, Baudry uses similarly vague terminology, saying that Urban spoke "a sermon of this sort": BB, p. 12. See also GN 2, 3, p. 111. RtM, "Apologeticus sermo," p. 721, comes closest to claiming authenticity for his sermon, saying that he chose to rewrite GF because it did not include any details of Clermont and because he himself had attended the council. FC, 1, 3, pp. 131–138,

appears to have based his report of Clermont on council decretals, though he famously fails to have Urban II mention Jerusalem.

10. Passages taken from BB 1, 2, and 4, pp. 11–14, and 4, 13, p. 101. The latter passage is a sermon credited to an anonymous preacher on the eve of the battle for Jerusalem that echoes the language from Urban's sermon. In addition to *instar*, which I have translated as "form of," the passage includes the more theologically loaded *forma*, which I have attempted to invest with equal theological baggage through the translation "image." There has been some scholarly dispute as to whether crusade preachers might have inadvertently or deliberately confused the heavenly and earthly Jerusalems in the minds of their listeners. See, for example, Cohn (1957), pp. 64–65. The confusion, however, was built into the actual theology. On these points, see also Schein (2005), pp. 141–157; and Daniel F. Callahan, "Jerusalem in the Monastic Imagination of the Early Eleventh Century," *Haskins Society Journal* 6 (1994): 119–127.

11. RtM 9, 26, p. 882. A fine introduction to the peace movement can be found in the essays edited by Thomas Head and Richard Landes, *The Peace of God: Social Violence and Religious Response in France Around the Year 1000* (Ithaca, NY: Cornell University Press, 1992).

12. The text of the indulgence reads, "*Quicumque pro sola devotione, non pro honoris vel pecunie adeptione, ad liberandam ecclesiam Dei Hierusalem profectus fuerit, iter illud pro omni penitentia ei reputetur*": Somerville, *Councils*, 2, p. 74. This passage is from a set of conciliar decrees collected by Bishop Lambert of Arras. It is one of sixty-one decrees, most of which deal with issues of church reform. On the place of knighthood and violence in the eleventh century, I am indebted to the work of Dominique Barthélemy. The best introduction in English to his approach is *The Serf, the Knight, and the Historian*, trans. Graham Robert Edwards (Ithaca, NY: Cornell University Press, 2009), esp. pp. 176–236. See also Dominique Barthélemy, *Chevaliers et miracles: La violence et la sacré dans la société féodale* (Paris: Armand Colin, 2004).

13. Such outbursts must have been fairly common at a church council. Earlier in the week, when the pope had proclaimed that anyone who attacked a bishop should no longer be allowed to carry weapons, he received an acclamation of "Let it happen! Let it happen!" Somerville, *Councils* 30, p. 81. The crowd did so perhaps because Bishop Lambert of Arras had been taken prisoner on his way to the council: Becker, "Le voyage d'Urbain II," in École Française (1997), p. 131. RtM 1, 2, p. 729, describes Urban's reaction to the chants. The argument presented here, about the combination of pilgrimage and warfare, is essentially that of Erdmann, *Origin*.

14. The most eloquent exponents of the role of penance in driving warriors to join the crusade are Bull (1993); and Riley-Smith (1997), pp. 60–72. Bull's work is especially important, based on a detailed analysis of monastic charters (grants of land made to churches by knights before they departed for Jerusalem). The charters purport to explain the thinking of knights as they hand over the property, usually emphasizing a desire to attain forgiveness for sins. That is, however, the usual jus-

tification for granting land to monasteries, regardless of whether the donor was going on crusade. Because most knights on crusade had to pay their own way, the need for financing more than for forgiveness was probably the most immediate grounds for donating land. The tendency to drift into caricature when writing of fearful and superstitious crusaders can mar even otherwise fine books, such as Thomas Asbridge, *The Crusades: The Authoritative History of the War for the Holy Land* (New York: HarperCollins, 2010), p. 38, in which he writes, "Bred upon a vision of religious faith that emphasised the overbearing threat of sin and damnation, the Latins of the West were enmeshed in a desperate, lifelong spiritual struggle to purge the taint of corruption from their souls." Such a description fails to do justice to the complexity of a Frankish warrior's worldview, not to mention his soul.

15. BB 1, 4, p. 14, and 1, 3, p. 12. In line with these arguments, Andrew Jotischky, "The Christians of Jerusalem, the Holy Sepulchre, and the Origins of the First Crusade," *Crusades* 7 (2008): 35–57, suggests that the sufferings of Christians and pilgrims in the East may have played a more direct role in inspiring the First Crusade than scholars have tended to acknowledge.

16. RtM, 1, 1, pp. 727–728. The italicized passage is from Ps. 78:8 (Vulgate 77:8).

17. The pun and the other charges (including "foully," *turpiter*) appear in BB 1, 4, p. 13.

18. The source for these charges is the letter attributed to Alexius Comnenus written to Count Robert of Flanders. It is probably a forgery or else a heavily redacted Latin translation of a Greek original, printed in Hagenmeyer, *Epistulae* 1, pp. 31–36. GN 1, 5, pp. 101–102, paraphrases the same letter. His phrase for violating the laws of humanity is *solutis humanitatum legibus*. As for violating the laws of nature, he argues that sodomy makes Saracens worse than beasts, because sex with women is at least within the course of nature.

19. Hagenmeyer, *Epistulae* 2, p. 136.

20. Otbert of Liège helped to finance the crusade of Godfrey of Bouillon. The reference appears in the edition of Urban's letters in PL 151, col. 396C, D. My thanks to Matthew Gabriele for calling my attention to this passage.

21. The writer of the apocalyptic sermon is GN 2, 4, pp. 113–114. The biblical passage concerning the conquest of three kings is Dan. 11:42–43: "And he will send his hand against the earth, the nation of Egypt shall not escape. And he will rule over the treasures of gold, silver, and all the valuable things of Egypt; through Libya and Ethiopia he will cross." Guibert has substituted "Africa" for "Libya."

22. The reconstruction of this scene follows BB 1, 5, pp. 15–16. It is notable that BB, before he begins describing this scene, mentions for the first time that he had attended the Council of Clermont. It is an important point: He does not vouch for the accuracy of his account of Urban's sermon, but he does claim that his account of these activities after the sermon is reliable. On Adhémar's career, see James A. Brundage, "Adhémar of Puy: The Bishop and His Critics," *Speculum* 34 (1959): 201–212, a response to John Hugh Hill and Laurita L. Hill, "Contemporary Accounts and the Later Reputation of Adhémar, Bishop of Le Puy," *Medievalia et Humanistica*

9 (1955): 30–38. See also Christian Lauranson-Rosaz, "Le Velay et la croisade," in École Française (1997), pp. 33–64 (pp. 50–51 and 61–62).

23. The Gospel reference is to Luke 14:27, long recognized as a key passage in crusade history and cited at the beginning of GF as the core of Urban II's message. The best introduction to Raymond's career (with some caution necessary about certain judgments) is Hill and Hill (1962); they discuss the rumor about the count's missing eye on p. 30. On the *fideles* of St. Peter, see Erdmann, *Origin*, pp. 206–224.

24. BB 1, 5, p. 16.

25. BB 1, 5–6, p. 16; RtM 1, 3, p. 730.

Chapter 3

1. Details taken from *Notitiae duae Lemovicenses de praedicatione crucis in Aquitania*, RHC Oc. 5, pp. 350–353 (p. 352).

2. *Chroniques*, pp. 234 and 237–238. George T. Beech, "Urban II, the Abbey of Saint-Florent of Saumur, and the First Crusade," in *Autour de la Croisade*, pp. 57–69, notes a similar failure of Urban's message. Riley-Smith (1997), p. 88.

3. Riley-Smith (1986), p. 43; Norman Housley, *Fighting for the Cross: Crusading to the Holy Land* (New Haven, CT: Yale University Press, 2008), pp. 162–170.

4. The only English-language biography of Bohemond is R. B. Yewdale, *Bohemond I, Prince of Antioch* (Princeton, NJ: Princeton University Press, 1924). There have been recent biographies in French and Italian: Jean Flori, *Bohémond d'Antioche, Chevalier d'Aventure* (Paris: Payot, 2007); and Luigi Russo, *Boemondo, Figilio del Guiscardo e principe di Antiochia* (Avellino, Italy: Elio Sellino, 2009). On these scenes, see Flori, *Bohémond*, pp. 61–78; and Russo, *Boemondo*, pp. 59–61. Flori suggests the likelihood that Bohemond knew of the crusade well before this near mythic encounter with Frankish soldiers. The description here is largely based on GF, pp. 7–8.

5. C. W. David, *Robert Curthose, Duke of Normandy*, Harvard Historical Studies 25 (Cambridge, MA: Harvard University Press, 1920), pp. 86–96; C. Warren Hollister, *Henry I* (New Haven, CT: Yale University Press, 2001), pp. 76–97; WM 3, 277, pp. 504–507.

6. Hagenmeyer, *Epistulae* 2, pp. 136–137 (the letter from Urban), and 7, pp. 142–143 (a charter issued from Robert's wife two years after his departure, where she speaks of rage against the Persians). Robert recalls his good works in a charter issued before his departure, published by Fernand Vercauteren, ed., *Actes des comtes de Flandre, 1071–1128* (Brussels: Palais des Académies, 1938), pp. 62–63. M. M. Knappen, "Robert II of Flanders in the First Crusade," in *The Crusades and Other Historical Essays, Presented to Dana C. Munro by His Former Students*, ed. Louis J. Paetow (New York: F. S. Crofts, 1928), pp. 79–100, verges on hagiography but is still useful.

7. Lampert of Hersfeld, *Annales* MGH SS, an. 1076, p. 243; H. E. J. Cowdrey, *Gregory VII, 1073–1085* (Oxford, UK: Clarendon Press, 1998), p. 142; John C. Andressohn, *The Ancestry and Life of Godfrey of Bouillon* (Bloomington: Indiana State University Press, 1947), pp. 16–20.

8. *Chronique de Saint-Hubert, dite Cantatorium*, ed. Karl Hanquet (Brussels: Librairie Kiessling, 1906), 19, pp. 48–50. The statement in Asbridge (2004), p. 62, that Godfrey had "no particular reputation for personal piety, being a known despoiler of Church land," is a bit of an overstatement.

9. *Chronique de Saint-Hubert*, 82–83, pp. 203–208; Andressohn, *The Ancestry and Life*, pp. 27–46. On the financing of Godfrey's army, see Alan V. Murray, "The Army of Godfrey of Bouillon, 1096–1099: Structure and Dynamics of a Contingent on the First Crusade," *Revue Belge de Philologie et d'histoire* 70 (1992): 301–329; and H. Dorchy, "Godefrois de Bouillon, duc de Basse-Lotharingie," *Revue Belge de Philologie et d'histoire* 26 (1948): 961–999 (p. 998).

10. Our one source for the Council of Paris is GN 2, 17, pp. 133–134, who seems to have been well informed on the early stages of the crusade in connection with the Capetian kings. He also mentions the French hopes that Hugh might become king of Jerusalem: GN 2, 14, p. 131. The figure of fifteen miles was not chosen at random. Philip warned his son, the future Louis VI, to be especially wary of the castle of Montlhéry, a place whose vile treachery had robbed Philip of his youth. Montlhéry was sixteen miles outside Paris: Suger, 8, p. 38. The verses cited are Apoc. 6:12–13 and Joel 2:30–32.

11. EA 10–11, pp. 18–19, and 2, p. 12. The chronology of these signs is unclear. Ekkehard saw the first comet on October 7, presumably 1096, though possibly 1095. The second sign occurred three years later, in March, probably 1099.

12. EA 10, p. 19; GN 7, 32, p. 330, discussed in Rubenstein (2002), p. 123.

13. "A viscous liquid was clearly seen to ooze from the violently cut line of the cross": GN 4, 17, p. 197. See also GN, 7, 32, p. 330, where he describes the green and red crosses more generally.

14. GN 7, 32, p. 331; AA 1, 30, pp. 58–59; EA 11, p. 19. Alphandéry and Dupront, pp. 55–56, give the goose a folkloric interpretation. For the Jewish report, see Chazan (1987), pp. 232–233.

15. Chazan (1987), pp. 56, 235, and, more generally, 232–240; *Annales Hildesheimnenses*, MGH SS 3, an. 1096, p. 106, which gives the figure of 1,014, although the annalist credits the deaths to Peter the Hermit. The quotation, surprisingly, is from AA 1, 27, pp. 52–53, whose use of the term "uncircumcised" elsewhere in this passage suggests that he had a remarkable ability to empathize with the Jews or else that he worked with a Jewish source or both.

16. Chazan (1987), p. 250; *Annales Pragenses* MGH SS 3, an. 1096, p. 120. The Norman massacre we know of thanks to *Monodies* 2, 5, pp. 246–249. It seems likely that Peter's followers were also responsible for anti-Jewish violence in Metz; see Chazan (1987), pp. 63 and 287.

17. Chazan (1987), pp. 95–97.

18. Chazan (1987), pp. 250–251. Chazan, pp. 65–66, downplays the apocalyptic overtones of this rhetoric. Matthew Gabriele, "Against the Enemies of Christ: The Role of Count Emicho in the Anti-Jewish Violence of the First Crusade," in *Christian Attitudes Toward Jews in the Middle Ages: A Casebook,* ed. Michael Frassetto (New York: Routledge, 2005), pp. 61–82. See also France (1994), p. 95; Flori, "Une ou plusieurs 'première croisade'? Le message d'Urbain II et les plus anciens pogroms d'Occident," *Revue Historique* 285 (1991): 3–27 (pp. 4–5).

19. *Annales Hildesheimnenses,* an. 1096, p. 106; *Annales Wirziburgenses,* an. 1096, p. 246; Sigebert, *Chronica,* MGH SS 6, an. 1096, p. 367. Benjamin Z. Kedar discusses the baptisms and canon law in "The Forcible Baptisms of 1096: History and Historiography," in *Forschungen zur Recihs-, Papst- und Landesgeschichte: Peter Herde zum 65. Geburtstag* 1 (Stuttgart, Germany: Anton Hiersemann, 1998), pp. 187–200.

20. The passage here is from the prophecy of the Tiburtine Sibyl, published in *Sibyllinische Texte,* p. 185. Adso, p. 28, states that two witnesses, foretold in Apoc. 11, will convert the remnant of the Jews. See also the version of Adso attributed to Methodius, which concludes with the conversion of the Jews: published in LF, fols. 108v–110r, pp. 220–223; and in Adso, pp. 146–152. See also the commentary of André Vauchez, "Les composante eschatologiques de l'idée de croisade," in École Française (1997), pp. 233–243 (p. 242).

21. EA 12, p. 20; *Gesta Andegavensium peregrinorum,* RHC Oc. 5, p. 346. Similarly reported by the later chronicler Richard of Poitou, monk of Cluny: *Chronicon,* in RHGF 12, pp. 411–412. On Godfrey's extortions, see Chazan (1987), pp. 53 and 86–88.

Chapter 4

1. OV 5, 9, pp. 28–29, says that the army included several eminent Frankish lords and 15,000 soldiers. AA 1, 6, pp. 8–9, says that there were only eight knights. Both writers draw the connection to Peter.

2. On Walter's name, see Edgington's n. 14 in AA, p. 9, and, more generally, AA 1, 6, pp. 8–13, our most detailed account of Walter's progress.

3. Philippopolis is in modern-day Bulgaria and is called Plovdiv. OV 5, 9, pp. 30–31, tells of Walter's death.

4. In this book I have mostly followed the dating in Hagenmeyer, *Chronologie.* But for Peter's army (and Godfrey's), I follow the revisions proposed by John W. Nesbitt, "The Rate of March of Crusading Armies in Europe: A Study and Computation," *Traditio* 19 (1963): 167–181. On this stage of Peter's march, see AA 1, 7, pp. 12–15. The verse cited is Gen. 22:17; see also 2 Sam. 17:11.

5. AA 1, 7, pp. 14–15; GN 2, 9, pp. 123 and 122. Guibert's account of these early stages of the crusade is admittedly compressed (though more substantial than the accounts of most of his peers). It is likely that he is conflating stories about Peter's

armies with stories about Emicho's (discussed later in the chapter). He says that many of Peter's followers returned after a battle with Hungarians at "Moysson," probably Coloman's castle Moson. See Edgington's n. 57 in AA p. 45.

6. AA 1, 7, pp. 14–17.

7. AA 1, 8, pp. 16–19.

8. AA 1, 9–12, pp. 18–27.

9. AA 1, 12–14, pp. 26–29.

10. AA 1, 14–15, pp. 28–29.

11. Folkmar is one of the shadowiest figures in the crusade narrative. Identified by Frutolf as a priest, the Magdeburg chronicler deliberately corrects this point to say that Folkmar was a layman who had once lived within monastic walls: Frutolf, an. 1096, p. 108; *Annales Magdeburgenses*, MGH 16, an. 1096, p. 179. EA 12, p. 20, gives the brief account of the destruction of Folkmar's army. Because Frutolf (and, following him, Ekkehard) describes Folkmar as traveling through Bohemia, he is usually connected with the pogrom there, described by Cosmas, *Chronicon Bohemorum*, MGH 9, an. 1096, p. 103.

12. AA 1, 23–24, pp. 44–49, is the most detailed account of Gottschalk's disastrous pilgrimage, which I have largely followed here. EA 12, p. 20, provides a much shorter account, saying that the pilgrims occupied a castle and that the locals attacked them and drove them out.

13. AA 1, 25, pp. 48–49; 1, 28, pp. 52–55; and 2, 1, pp. 60–61, where he mentions Drogo's presence in Emicho's army. There were other pogroms in Germany in Neuss on June 24, in Wevelinghovenon on June 25, in (possibly) Altenahr on June 26–27, in Xanten on June 27, and in Moers on June 29–July 1. See Chazan (1987), pp. 274–281 and pp. 347–348, n. 250. Not all of these persecutors were crusaders. But they were men motivated by the general atmosphere of apocalypse and revenge that surrounded the call to free Jerusalem. The other sources for Emicho's march are Frutolf, an. 1096, p. 108; and EA 12, pp. 20–21.

14. The details come mainly from AA 1, 29, pp. 54–59, largely confirmed by Frutolf and EA, as cited previously. We can place the survivors with Hugh because AA mentions the presence of Drogo and Clarembald with Hugh the Great in Constantinople in AA 2, 7, pp. 72–73.

15. FC 1, 6, 3, pp. 154–156; *Alexiad* 10, 7, pp. 313–314; GN 1, 19, p. 135. Anna says that almost all of Hugh's ships save his own were destroyed; Guibert describes the passage as "smooth sailing." The sources are more or less in agreement that Hugh was placed in captivity.

16. FC 1, 5, 12, p. 153, and 1, 6, 13, p. 163. The best introduction to Fulcher is Verena Epp, *Fulcher von Chartres: Studien zur Geschichtsscreibung des ersten Kreuzzuges* (Düsseldorf, Germany: Droste, 1990). Fulcher observes on 1, 6, 12, that the knights could expect a hundredfold return.

17. FC 1, 7, 1–3, pp. 163–166. The dates for the Franks' visit to Lucca and Rome as given in Hagenmeyer, *Chronologie* (October 25 and October 28) are highly speculative.

18. FC 1, 7, 4–5, pp. 166–168. Bohemond's sermon was discussed in Chapter 1. It is possible that Anna Comnena describes the capture of one of Robert's followers in *Alexiad* 10, 8, pp. 315–318. The name she gives is "Prebentzas." Anna uses the incident mainly to tell an amusing story about how belligerent Latin priests were. The translator's suggestion that Prebentzas was Richard of the Principate has little merit.

19. GF, pp. 7–9; HBS, 7–8, p. 177; AA 2, 14, pp. 82–83. France (1994), p. 107, estimates that Bohemond averaged around four kilometers a day, over one-half and in some cases almost one-third of what other leaders were able to achieve, even though Bohemond was traveling through territories with which he was well familiar.

20. The richest, and in many cases only, source for Godfrey's early activity is AA, in this case 2, 1–4, pp. 60–67.

21. AA 2, 5–10, pp. 68–77.

22. Hill and Hill (1962), pp. 33–40; Riley-Smith (1997), p. 119.

23. On the "celebrities" in Raymond's army, see Hill and Hill (1962), p. 35. Raymond mentions his ordination in RA, p. 108: "I was promoted to the priesthood during the journey of God."

24. RA, pp. 36–38. The number forty has obvious biblical connotations and should not be read too literally.

25. RA, pp. 39–41. Anna Comnena confirms that it was Alexius's policy to shadow the crusaders and occasionally skirmish with them: *Alexiad* 10, 5, pp. 310–311.

26. Frederic Duncalf, "The Peasants' Crusade," *American Historical Review* 26 (1921): 440–453 (which, despite the title, argues against the idea of the first wave of crusaders being a "popular" army); Riley-Smith (1986), pp. 50–52. See also the comments of France (1994), p. 95: "But if Peter's army was much more than a mere rabble of poor men, it also lacked leadership. . . . The failure of the People's Crusade was a failure of authority."

27. FC 1, 7, 1–5, p. 168–172.

Chapter 5

1. *Alexiad* 10, 5, pp. 308–309. Warren Treadgold gives a concise account of Alexius's career and character, and his response to the First Crusade, in *A History of the Byzantine State and Society* (Stanford, CA: Stanford University Press, 1997), pp. 612–637.

2. *Alexiad* 10, 5–6, pp. 309–312; 11, 6, p. 349; 10, 8, pp. 317–318.

3. AA 1, 15, pp. 28–31; GF, pp. 2–3; *Alexiad* 10, 6, p. 311.

4. The list of relics comes from the possibly spurious letter of Alexius to Count Robert discussed in the notes to Chapter 2. See Hagenmeyer, *Epistulae* 1, p. 134. The commentary on the pilgrims' behavior is GF, p. 3. AA 1, 15, pp. 30–31, does not mention any problematic behavior on the part of Peter's army, observing simply that

after five days it crossed the Straits of St. George. Flori (1999), pp. 285–286, following AA, suggests that Peter crossed the Bosphorus of his own accord, not under duress.

5. BB 1, 9, p. 18; Flori (1999), pp. 297–299; France (1994), p. 95.

6. The quotations are from BB 1, 9, p. 18, with details drawn from GF, pp. 2–4; and AA 1, 15–17, pp. 30–39. GF is more critical of the crusaders. AA notes neither the bad behavior nor the cultural conflicts within the army. He also says that the Franks and the Romans were making the raids and that the "Teutons" therefore decided to march inland. GF says that the Germans and the Italians (Alamanni and Lombards) broke away from the Franks because of the Franks' arrogance.

7. AA does not name the castle but says (1, 16, pp. 32–33) that it was three miles from Nicea. GF, p. 3, says that the pilgrims entered Nicea and marched for four days before attacking the castle called "Exrogorgos," which lay beyond Nicea. *Alexiad* 10, 6, pp. 311–312.

8. The anonymous source is, of course, GF, p. 4, who says as well that the leader of the Germans agreed to betray the city. AA does not specify the length of the siege; it is possible to read his account and conclude that it lasted only a day. AA 1, 18, pp. 36–37, also mentions Peter's motive for going to Constantinople. GF, p. 4, says that Peter left the army because he couldn't control it. The thirst imagery in GF, pp. 3–4, is very likely built from stock images of siege warfare since GF does not seem to have been terribly well informed about Peter's armies.

9. AA 1, 18–19, pp. 36–39. GF, p. 4, does not describe the Franks as organizing an attack; Kilij-Arslan's armies simply caught them unaware. *Alexiad* 10, 6, p. 312, tells the unlikely story (but no doubt highly entertaining for Anna's audience) that Kilij-Arslan dispatched spies into the Franks' camp to spread the rumor that the Germans had discovered great plunder; at the mention of the word "money," the Franks marched out of Civitot without a plan.

10. The description of Turkish battle tactics here is taken from a miracle story of St. Léonard of Noblat involving Bohemond: *Vita et miracula S. Leonardi*, in AASS, *Nov.* 6, 3, p. 161, supplemented by comments from FC 1, 11, 6, pp. 194–195. The miracle story was probably based on sermons preached by Bohemond in 1106: Nicholas L. Paul, "A Warlord's Wisdom: Literacy and Propaganda at the Time of the First Crusade," *Speculum* 85 (2010), 534–566 (pp. 557–558). The specifics of the battle come from AA 1, 20–21, pp. 40–43. I have attempted to be somewhat more sympathetic to the decisions of Walter and the rest of the army than most modern (and medieval accounts). For example, Asbridge (2004), p. 102, describes the pilgrims' action in attacking the Turks as "a perilously risky operation against a largely untested enemy, endangering the entire first wave of the crusade for little or no reason."

11. AA 1, 22, pp. 42–45. He estimates the number of pilgrims in the tower at 3,000. *Alexiad* 10, 6, pp. 312–313. GF, pp. 4–5, provides stock images of siege warfare, including the unlikely detail of a priest killed in the battle while performing mass.

12. *Alexiad* 6, 10, p. 313; GF, p. 5; AA 1, 22, pp. 42–45. AA 5, 3, pp. 342–343; and RA, p. 55, mention the rumors about the Turcopoles' lineage. The decapitated bodies in Nicomedia are noted by FC 1, 9, 5, p. 180, and will be discussed in the next chapter.

13. AA 2, 10, pp. 74–77; *Alexiad* 10, 9, pp. 320–323. Anna Comnena places these skirmishes during the Easter season. She also seems to conflate these battles with ones that occurred a little over two weeks after Christmas.

14. The analysis here is based on *Alexiad* 10, 6, p. 311. Anna Comnena states her belief there and at 10, 9, p. 319, that some of the crusaders, particularly Bohemond, were mainly interested in taking over Constantinople. The latter passage describes Alexius's attempt to break crusader communications.

15. AA 2, 13–14, pp. 78–83; *Alexiad* 10, 9, pp. 320–323, recalling that Anna appears to conflate several events here and moves these events, which happened January 13–19 to Easter. She also says that Godfrey gave in to Alexius's demands the next day and thus does not mention the subsequent plundering. GF, pp. 6–7, follows in general outline the events presented here.

16. AA 2, 14–15, pp. 82–85. AA suggests that Alexius learned of Bohemond's legation only after Bohemond's representatives had made their proposal to Godfrey.

17. AA 2, 16, pp. 84–87; *Alexiad* 10, 9–10, pp. 323–326. Anna associates the "peasant incident" with another army, but it is unclear which one she has in mind. She also places it after the soldiers have sworn the oaths. Given the degree of uncertainty, I have felt entitled to a little chronological freedom in my use of the anecdote.

18. *Alexiad* 10, 9, p. 323, and 10, 11, p. 328 (in reference to Bohemond's oath).

19. AA 2, 16, pp. 84–87; GF, pp. 11–12 (again, as in the previous note, in reference to Bohemond's oath); Hagenmeyer, *Epistulae* 4, p. 138. On the oaths, J. H. Pryor, "The Oath of the Leaders of the First Crusade to the Emperor Alexius Comnenus: Fealty, Homage," *Parergon* 2 (1984): 111–141, argues that the leaders took oaths of vassalage but not homage. Jonathan Shepard, "When Greek Meets Greek: Alexius Comnenus and Bohemond in 1097–8," *Byzantine and Modern Greek Studies* 12 (1988): 185–277 (pp. 227–237), suggests that Bohemond at least did perform liege homage to Alexius, accepting the emperor as his exclusive lord. Of course, we ought to be cautious in attributing too much precision to these ideas. The potential existed for cross-cultural miscommunication between Greeks and Latins, and ideas about vassalage and homage were very much in flux at this time in the Latin world. This was demonstrated famously by Susan Reynolds, *Fiefs and Vassals: The Medieval Evidence Reinterpreted* (Oxford, UK: Oxford University Press, 1994). Reynolds discusses Godfrey's oath on p. 405, though she treats the vocabulary with excessive caution since she mistakenly dates the composition of AA's history to 1119. See also the judicious comments by Flori (1999), pp. 109–112.

20. AA 2, 16–17, pp. 86–89.

21. *Alexiad*, 13, 10, p. 422. On Bohemond's facility with Greek, see Shepard, "When Greek Meets Greek," pp. 251–258.

22. *Alexiad* 10, 11, pp. 327–328.

23. *Alexiad* 10, 11, p. 329; GF, pp. 11–12; PT, p. 43, n. *v*, and p. 48; RC 10, p. 612. The Norman historiographical tradition on this point is extremely confused. I have previously attempted to sort out the details in Rubenstein (2004), pp. 194–196. The earliest version of the story, in brief, is likely the promise concerning lands "in Romania," as it appears in some manuscripts of the "Tudebode" chronicle and in RC. I am generally in accord with the analysis of Jean Flori, *Bohémond d'Antioche, Chevalier d'Aventure* (Paris: Payot, 2007), pp. 105–112. The arguments of Shepard, "When Greek Meets Greek," demonstrating that Bohemond struck an alliance with Alexius seem compelling, though, as already noted, I would be reluctant to frame an argument in terms of "liege homage."

24. GF, pp. 13–14; RC 11, p. 612.

25. RA, pp. 41–42, is the key source for these events. On the oaths, see Hill and Hill (1962), p. 51. More generally, on the character of oath-taking in Occitania, see Frederic L. Cheyette, *Ermengard of Narbonne and the World of the Troubadours* (Ithaca, NY: Cornell University Press, 2001), pp. 187–198. *Alexiad* 10, 11, pp. 329–330, describes the attention showered on Raymond by Alexius, though as noted elsewhere (Shepard, "When Greek Meets Greek," p. 205), Anna exaggerates the warmth of their relationship.

26. GN 3, 4, p. 143, presents a defense of why Bohemond took the oath. I have paraphrased it here.

Chapter 6

1. FC 1, 9, 1–3, pp. 176–179. The observation about the statues coming to life is from a crusade chronicle written one hundred years later by a knight named Robert of Clari, describing sculptures at the Hippodrome: Robert of Clari, *The Conquest of Constantinople*, trans. Edgar Holmes McNeal (New York: Columbia University Press, 1936), pp. 109–110.

2. FC 1, 9, 5, p. 180; BN 6, p. 494. BN clarifies that the bodies belonged to followers of Peter the Hermit. GF, pp. 13–14, describes the three-day stay at Nicomedia while the roads were cleared.

3. AA 2, 22, pp. 92–96; 2, 23, pp. 96–97; 2, 32, pp. 114–115 (the last passage being about the lake). The most detailed contemporary description of the city is RA, pp. 142–143. See also Hagenmeyer, *Epistulae* 4, p. 139. My description draws heavily from France (1994), pp. 143–144.

4. AA 2, 21, pp. 94–95, and 2, 25, pp. 102–103; France (1994), pp. 159–160.

5. *Alexiad* 11, 2, pp. 336–337; AA 25–26, pp. 103–107; GF, p. 15; GN 3, 8, p. 150 (part of a poem celebrating martyrdom).

6. See the diagram in France (1994), p. 123, and the description on pp. 160–161. The two essential accounts are RA, p. 43, who gives a fine sense of the chaos of the soldiers arriving at the city and then immediately entering into battle; and GF,

pp. 14–15. The sermon is in AA 2, 27, pp. 106–107. Anna's comment is at *Alexiad* 11, 1, p. 334.

7. Albert describes the gifts to the emperor and the catapulting of heads into the city at AA 2, 28, pp. 108–111. Other chroniclers confirm that the heads were used to frighten the enemy. See, for example, GF, p. 15, though the anonymous author observes only that the heads were cut from the dead, not from the wounded, too. Anselm of Ribemont says that the heads made a "happy spectacle" for the Christian army: Hagenmeyer, *Epistulae* 8, p. 144. See also *Alexiad* 11, 1, p. 334.

8. E.g., "These acts may appear to be utterly barbaric by modern standards, but they were a staple feature of medieval warfare and became a consistent theme of the siege of Antioch. In viewing such events, we must try to temper our instinctive judgment with an awareness that in the eleventh century war was governed by medieval, not modern, codes of practice. Within the context of a holy war, in which the Franks were conditioned to see their enemy as sub-human, Christian piety prompted not clemency but, rather, an atmosphere of extreme brutality and heightened savagery": Asbridge (2004), p. 168. The argument contradicts itself since it states, on the one hand, that these practices were typical of medieval war, and, on the other hand, that they were the peculiar products of holy war. The references to the Norman Conquest are in WP 2, 26, pp. 142–143, and 2, 25, pp. 140–141 (the latter concerning the burial of Harold's body).

9. AA 2, 30–33, pp. 112–119. I am privileging Albert's account over RA, p. 44, who credits the Provençal tortoise with bringing down the tower; and over GF, p. 15; and FC 1, 10, 6–9, pp. 185–188, whose accounts are somewhat vague. I am also in this case following Albert's analysis more than France's (1994), pp. 162–165, though as France observes, Albert's chronology is not always clear.

10. AA 2, 35–36, pp. 120–125, is the only source to mention the Lombard engineer. *Alexiad* 11, 1, p. 335, describes the same machine and attributes its construction to Count Raymond, as does RA, p. 44. AA makes this event the turning point in the siege.

11. The chronology of these events is admittedly vague. Most writers, as cited previously, place the destruction of the tower a few days before the arrival of the ships (if they deal with both incidents, which not all of them do). Albert places the arrival of the ships fairly early on in the siege. France (the best military historian of the crusade) states definitively that the placement of the ships on the lake was the turning point in the battle: France (1994), pp. 164–165, though the basis for his chronology is not altogether clear. Hagenmeyer's *Chronologie* dates the destruction of the tower to June 10, the arrival of the ships to June 17, and the surrender to June 19. The dating for most of these events, apart from the surrender, is therefore not at all certain—e.g., what AA divides into two attacks (the Provençal "tortoise" and the Lombard siege engine), Hagenmeyer conflates into one (no. 156 in the *Chronologie*). I have attempted to give equal weight in my narrative to the destruction of the tower and to the arrival of the ships, in part by having them occur almost simultaneously, a reading not confirmed with certainty by any one of the sources,

though an honest attempt to reconcile all of them. Readers, however, should take my arrangement of events in this instance with a grain of salt.

12. *Alexiad* 11, 2, p. 337.

13. Hagenmeyer, *Epistulae* 4, p. 140, and 8, p. 144. The letter from Stephen (4) describes the meeting place as "an island." See Hagenmeyer's n. 61 in *Epistulae*, pp. 235–236. RA, p. 44, curses Alexius. GN 3, 10, p. 153, notes the hostility among the commoners toward the princes. In doing so, he contradicts GF, p. 18, which observes that Alexius distributed bountiful charity to the poor pilgrims, raising the possibility that Guibert based this observation on conversations with crusade veterans. GF, p. 17, does, however, outline the conspiracy theory.

14. AA 2, 34, pp. 118–121.

15. FC 1, 10, 9–10, pp. 188–189; HBS 22, p. 181. The latter source is the only one to mention the sending of this delegation to Egypt, and it is an extremely problematic text. In this instance, however, its testimony has gained general acceptance: France (1994), pp. 165–166; Asbridge (2004), p. 132. RA, p. 110, mentions the distinctions between the two branches of Islam without using the proper names but noting correctly that the cause of the rift concerned the succession to the caliphate.

16. RC 17–18, pp. 618–620.

17. Albert gives all these reasons, adding that no one in the army knew why she had returned: AA 2, 37, pp. 126–129. Henry is mentioned departing with Godfrey in AA 2, 1, pp. 60–61. In assigning penance, clerics could have referred to Augustine's *City of God* 1, 16–19, the famous chapters where Augustine discusses nuns, and other women, who were raped by barbarians during the 410 Sack of Rome. Augustine argues that the women committed no sin because of the rape and that they were not obligated, as Roman women in the past had been, to commit suicide in order to preserve honor after a sexual assault.

18. Hagenmeyer, *Epistulae* 3, pp. 137–138, outlines Urban's restrictions on clerics joining the crusade.

Chapter 7

1. RC 29, p. 627. The passage refers to the battle of Dorylaeum, to be discussed in the next chapter. On the dating of *Roland*, see Luis Cortés, ed., *La Chanson de Roland*, trans. and introduction by Paulette Gabauda (Mayenne, France: Librarie Nizet, 1994), pp. 42–44. WM 3, 242, pp. 454–455, writing around 1120, says that William the Conqueror's army, in order to prepare itself for battle against the Anglo-Saxons in 1066, together struck up *The Song of Roland*—suggesting both the appeal of the *chanson* for a military audience and the popularity of the poem in the later eleventh century (even if, as seems likely, the Normans did no such thing at Hastings; WM believes they could have).

2. *The Song of Roland* is available in numerous translations. I tend to prefer the one by Robert Harrison (New York: New American Library, 1970), reprinted often

since. On the 112 characters, see Paul Aebischer, *Préhistoire et protohistoire du Roland d'Oxford* (Lausanne, Switzerland: Éditions Francke Berne, 1972), p. 287. About resonances between historical and literary treatments of Muslims in medieval texts, see Matthew Bennett, "First Crusaders' Images of Muslims: The Influence of Vernacular Poetry?" *Forum for Modern Language Studies* 22 (1986): 101–122.

3. Guibert of Nogent, *De pigneribus sanctorum*, ed. R. B. C. Huygens, CCCM 127 (Turnhout, Belgium: Brepols, 1993) 4, p. 170. See also the commentary of Norman Daniel, *Heroes and Saracens: An Interpretation of the* Chansons de Geste (Edinburgh: Edinburgh University Press, 1984), pp. 115–116: The Saracens are "just bogeys. . . . They are entirely imaginary, and their character as Saracens is a work of imagination too, not an interpretation of Islam."

4. The relevant texts are Gen. 16 (16:12, quoted here) and 21–22. The birth of Ishmael occurs before the Covenant, when Abraham and Sarah were still called Abram and Sarai, but for simplicity's sake I am using their later names. On this theme, S. Loutchitskaja, "*Barbarae nationes*: Les peuples musulmans dans les chroniques de la Première Croisade," in *Autour de la Croisade*, pp. 99–107, notes the tendency of crusade chroniclers to rely on ancient and biblical traditions for understanding Islam, rather than on firsthand knowledge or experience. Jerome, *Hebraicae quaestiones in libro Geneseos*, ed. P. Antin, CCSL 72 (Turnhout, Belgium: Brepols, 1959) 16, 12, pp. 20–21.

5. For an example of this commentary tradition, see Rupert of Deutz, *De sancta Trinitate et operibus suis*, ed. H. Haacke, CCCM 21 (Turnhout, Belgium: Brepols, 1971) 5, 26, pp. 358–359. Among crusade-era historians, see the popular chronicle by Hugh of Fleury: "This Muhammad, prince of the Saracens and Arabs and pseudo-prophet, was from the family of Ishmael, son of Abraham": "*Porro iste Muham et Sarracenorum et Arabum princeps. et pseudo propheta. fuit de genere Hismael filii Abrahe.*" Printed editions of Hugh's chronicle tend to be somewhat irregular, reflecting a confused manuscript tradition. I have transcribed this passage from the Vatican MS Reg. lat. 545, fol. 64r. The advice on the Agarenes appears in Adelphus, *Vita Machometi*, ed. B. Bischoff, as "Ein Leben Mohammeds (Adelphus?) (Zwölftes Jahrhundert)," *Anecdota Novissima: Texte des vierten bis sechzten Jahrhundert* (Stuttgart, Germany: A. Hiersemann, 1984), pp. 113–114, identifying his informant as a *greculus* who spoke Saracen and Latin (p. 113). The historical tradition behind this idea is a venerable one. The Merovingian Fredegar, writing in the seventh century, uses the terms synonymously, *Agarrini, qui et Saracini* (Hagarenes, who are also Saracens): *Chronica*, ed. Bruno Krusch, MGH SRM 2, 4, 66, p. 153. On this topic as well, Tolan (2002), pp. 10–11, notes that Isidore treats as synonymous Agarenes, Saracens, and Ishmaelites, as distinct from "Arabs," whereas other writers treat all four terms as identical. See also Tolan (2002), pp. 128–129 and 138.

6. GN 1, 3, p. 94. The verb that I have translated as "spell" is *exprimere*, meaning "to express" or to "force out," referring here, I think, to Guibert's attempts to spell a name he has only heard phonetically. I briefly discuss Guibert's life of Muhammad

in Rubenstein (2002), pp. 121–122. See also C. Meredith Jones, "The Conventional Saracen of the Songs of Geste," *Speculum* 17 (1942): 201–225 (p. 202).

7. *Sibyllinische Texte*, pp. 67–69. Gideon's career is described in the Book of Judges, Chapters 6–8. The war in question is against the Midianites, who were traditionally descendants of Midian, one of Abraham's sons by his second wife, Keturah; Gen. 25:1–2, though Judg. 8:22–24, indicates that they have assimilated with the Ishmaelites.

8. *Sibyllinische Texte*, pp. 80–82 and 84–86. All of these images, including the phrase *incontaminatum sacrificium*, are taken from Pseudo-Methodius, *Sibyllinische Texte*, pp. 84–86. An abridged version of the text circulating around the time of the crusade mentions Jerusalem filling with slaves: "*Replebitur Hierosolima de cunctis gentibus qui captivi ducuntur*" (taken from BnF MS lat. 7400A, fol. 146v.). Methodius says that Paul foretold some of these events in Rom. 1:26–27.

9. GN 1, 5, p. 101 (the opening point in Alexius's letter to Robert of Flanders, as Guibert paraphrases it).

10. The lives I am using here, in addition to Guibert's, are Adelphus, *Vita Machometi*; Walter of Compiègne, *Otia de Machomese*, ed. R. B. C. Huygens, in *Sacris Eruditi* 8 (1956): 287–328; Embrico of Mainz, *Historia de Mahumete*, in PL 171, cols. 1343–1366A; and a brief précis of the prophet's life in Sigebert of Gembloux's universal history, *Chronica*, MGH SS 6, p. 323, an. 630. Embrico's life is included in the bundle of crusade materials that is BR MS 9823–24, fols. 149r–156v.

11. GN 1, 4, pp. 94–95 and 98; Adelphus, *Vita Machometi*, pp. 114–15; John Victor Tolan, "Anti-hagiography: Embrico of Mainz's *Vita Mahumeti*," *Journal of Medieval History* 22 (1996): 25–41 (quotes at pp. 32–33 and 38).

12. Adelphus, *Vita Machometi*, p. 121; Sigebert, *Chronica*, p. 323: "*Gabrihelem archangelumm loquentem mecum contemplor. et non ferens splendorem vultus eius. utpote carnalis homo deficio: et cado*"; Hugh of Fleury, Vatican MS Reg. lat. 545, fol. 64v. Muhammad is attempting to placate his new wife, distressed at his disturbing condition. Guibert includes a similar anecdote, saying that Muhammad develops epilepsy from having too much sex and that the Alexandrian heretic offers this explanation: GN 1, 4, pp. 96–97.

13. Walter, *Otia de Machomese*, p. 327. Embrico says that Muhammad is developing new false doctrine when the seizure strikes: *Historia de Mahumete*, col. 1362D–1363A. See also GN 1, 4, p. 99. In Embrico's version, the Magus (who outlives his pupil) drives away the pigs and reclaims a now badly lacerated body. Adelphus simplifies the story by having wild pigs attack Muhammad while alone, leaving behind only the prophet's right arm: Adelphus, *Vita Machometi*, pp. 121–122.

14. John Victor Tolan describes this process as "anti-hagiography": Tolan, "Anti-hagiography," p. 30.

15. FC 1, 3, 6, p. 135; Ripoll Account, pp. 646–647. BB hints that the Saracens were Canaanites in a scene where the Turkish general Kerbogah explained to Peter the Hermit why his people's claim to the land was much older than that of the Franks': "We wonder at the greed with which you claim this land as your own. Our ancestors

possessed it before your superstitious Peter [who was patriarch of Antioch before he was bishop of Rome] did; but he turned them from the worship of their deity through his lies and seduced them through deception into your frivolous sect": BB 3, 15, p. 75. Thus, St. Peter convinced the original possessors of Antioch to turn away from the worship of a god whom Kerbogah viewed as legitimate, which would imply that their pre-Christian cult was Islam. Tolan (2002), pp. 73–74, shows how the seventh-century exegete and historian Bede similarly, though with more sophistication, attempted to fit the Saracens into the framework of Old Testament history. Cited here also are RtM 7, 8, p. 828; BB 4, 13, p. 101; and Adso, p. 149 (also LF, fol. 109v, p. 222). The commentary comes from Rupert of Deutz, *De sancta Trinitate*, 5, 25, p. 358, analyzing Gen. 16:6–9, where God sends Hagar back to Abraham and Sarah.

Chapter 8

1. Hagenmeyer, *Epistulae* 4, p. 140.

2. The descriptions of the battle here, drawn heavily on France (1994), pp. 170–185. AA 2, 38, pp. 128–129; and RtM 3, 7, p. 759, say that the division happened because of supply problems. GF, p. 18, says that the armies divided because of darkness. RC 20, pp. 620–621, mentions both possibilities. FC 1, 11, 5, pp. 193–194, admits that he simply doesn't know why it happened.

3. FC 1, 11, 1–5, pp. 189–194; GF, p. 20. The somewhat boastful cry for help is in GF, p. 19.

4. The name Dorylaeum is from *Alexiad* 11, 3, p. 341, named after an ancient nearby city. GF, pp. 18–19; AA, 2, 39, pp. 130–131; FC 1, 11, 6, pp. 194–195.

5. GF, pp. 19–20. See also GN, 3, 10, p. 154.

6. RtM 3, 10, p. 761; FC 1, 11, 8–10, pp. 195–197; GN 3, 10, p. 157. Fulcher places Adhémar at this scene of mass penance and confession—apparently an error since Adhémar was with Raymond and arrived at the second phase of the battle, as described in the next paragraph.

7. FC 1, 12, 2, pp. 197–198; Hagenmeyer *Epistulae* 8, p. 145, and (for the final quote) 12, p. 154; GF, pp. 19–20. RtM 3, 15, p. 764, gives a brief hint that not everyone in the army was sure that these dead qualified as martyrs. *Epistulae* 8 does as well.

8. RA, pp. 45–46; HBS 27, pp. 182–183; *Chronica monasterii Casinensis*, MGH SS 34, p. 480. FC 1, 12, 4, p. 198, says that the Turks fled for three days, with no one but God in pursuit. RA says that bodies were found for two days of the march, whereas HBS says it was for three days. See also Riley-Smith (1986), pp. 104–106, who notes that these saints were more closely associated with the East. Hence the crusaders probably learned to venerate them on the march. See also Erdmann, *Origin*, pp. 275–281; and Rousset, pp. 92–93.

9. The fantasy of Kilij-Arslan's retreat appears in GF, p. 22; most chroniclers follow GF's lead. The theological reading given here of Dorylaeum comes from RtM, 3, 14–15, pp. 763–764. In chap. 14 RtM imagines the Franks singing the same song

as the Israelites did upon crossing the Red Sea. In chap. 15 he gives an exegetical reading to the verses quoted here (Isa. 60:15–16).

10. BB 1, 17, p. 23, makes this observation about Saracens, Jews, and heretics. We know these eastern Christian groups and their role in the crusade story much better today thanks to the work of Christopher MacEvitt, *The Crusades and the Christian World of the East: Rough Tolerance* (Philadelphia: University of Pennsylvania Press, 2008). About the path of the army, including times and distances, see France (1994), pp. 185–190, who suggests important revisions to Hagenmeyer's *Chronologie*.

11. AA 3, 1–2, pp. 138–141; discussed more briefly in GF, p. 23.

12. AA 3, 4, pp. 142–145; GN 7, 12, pp. 286–287. GN says 15,000 men deserted his service. We must assume some significant exaggeration, as is usually the case with medieval chroniclers and their numbers, but the numbers must have been substantial. On the chronology of the attack, see the following the note.

13. RA, p. 46; GF, pp. 26–27. Hagenmeyer, in his *Chronologie*, places the bear attack and the illness around August 1 and 5, respectively, before the armies divide. I am following AA in placing the bear attack afterward. The date of Raymond's illness is nearly completely guesswork.

14. This account is based primarily on RC 34–36, pp. 630–632. See also the RC translation by Bachrach and Bachrach, p. 58, on the reconstruction of lost material from the manuscript.

15. Based primarily on AA 3, 8–10, pp. 150–155 (the source of the long quote); supplemented by RC 37–39, pp. 632–634; and GF, pp. 24–25. The best analysis of these events is MacEvitt, *Rough Tolerance*, pp. 55–58.

16. Matthew of Edessa 2, 110, pp. 164–165, and 2, 124, pp. 173–174. Matthew is the only source for this legend. It is worth remembering in this context that Edessa was the city where Baldwin would eventually rule as count, making him likely the original source for the legend. Matthew also mentions on p. 164 that Godfrey was a descendant of Roman emperors.

17. The Pirates were Belgian in the sense that they hailed from towns within the old Roman province of Gallia Belgica. AA 3, 11–13, pp. 154–159.

18. AA 3, 14, pp. 158–161.

19. AA 3, 15, pp. 160–163; RC 41–42, pp. 636–637. AA says that Tancred attacked the city, but RC, Tancred's biographer, seems better informed on this point.

20. AA 3, 16–17, pp. 162–167; RC, 44, p. 639. RC describes the peace as a *naenia*, which is a nursery song. The Latin reads *"Qui habet, habet; qui perdidit, perdidit,"* which means literally "He who has, has; he who lost, lost." My translation seems true to the spirit of the original. The list of castles conquered by Tancred appears in AA 3, 26, pp. 180–181; n. 58 notes previous attempts to identify these castles. To me they seem to preserve the echo of soldierly insults hurled at Tancred by AA's Lotharingian sources.

21. AA 3, 27, pp. 180–183. AA mentions that another knight died of the same disease in the same place.

22. FC 2, 12, 1, p. 416. AA 3, 17, pp. 164–167, tells how the Armenian Pakrad (or Bagrat) enticed Baldwin to Syria. FC 1, 16, 2–4, pp. 205–209, gives details of Baldwin's departure from the army. See also MacEvitt, *Rough Tolerance*, pp. 58–60.

23. RA, p. 46.

Chapter 9

1. AA 3, 32, pp. 190–191, describes the walls; on 3, 36, pp. 196–197, he says there were 360 towers. GF, p. 77, sets the figure at 450 and adds that the city contained 360 monasteries. Raymond's description of Antioch, which contains many of these details, at RA, p. 48, says that there were three mountains rather than four around Antioch. GF, pp. 76–77, sets the figure at four. See also FC, 1, 15, 2, p. 217; France (1994), pp. 222–225; and Asbridge (2004), pp. 158–160.

2. Acts 11:19–30 describes the founding of the church at Antioch.

3. GF, pp. 26–27. S. Loutchitskaja tries to identify the historical realities behind some of the exotic names used by Frankish chroniclers in crusade histories in "Barbarae Nationes: Les peoples musulmans dans les chroniques de la Première Croisade," in *Autour de la Croisade*, pp. 99–107. Following Ducange, Loutchitskaja (p. 105) identifies the *Publicani* as Paulicians, an early heresy that emphasized Christ's humanity over his divinity.

4. RA, pp. 46–47; AA 3, 35, pp. 192–195. GF, p. 28, observes simply that the Turks fell into panic and took flight, leaving much plunder for the Franks.

5. RA, pp. 48–49; Caffaro 3, pp. 49–50; GF, pp. 28–29 (who suggests that the Turks stayed in the city for two weeks out of simple fear). Caffaro places the port seventeen miles from Antioch. The best description of the Franks' implementation of their strategy is France (1994), pp. 197–267 (on the Bridge of Boats, p. 229).

6. The emotive language is from BB 2, 9, p. 41. See also GF, p. 29; and GN 4, 13, pp. 188–189.

7. Details of the conflict (and the expression "Christ's most powerful athlete") come from GF, p. 29; and RA, p. 41. GN 4, 3, p. 171, praises the cunning of the ambush. A similar strategy of false retreat and sudden ambush was employed most famously by William the Conqueror at Hastings. As already noted, it was a standard battle practice of the Turks, too.

8. GF, p. 29; RtM 4, 3, p. 777.

9. OV 2, 4, pp. 320–323, for Waltheof's execution. Orderic notes earlier (pp. 314–315) that beheading was the punishment in England for traitors. Chibnall adds (n. 1) that under Norman law forfeiture and imprisonment sufficed. When King William was presented with the head of another traitor, Earl Edwin of Mercia, he ordered the *proditores* (traitors) who brought it to him to leave the country: OV, 2, 4, pp. 258–259.

10. GN 4, 13, p. 189; FC 1, 15, 10, p. 221; HBS 54, p. 193.

11. BB 2, 9, p. 41. Robert's sunnier account of the decapitations appears at RtM 4, 2–3, pp. 776–777. He describes the woman's death at 4, 1, pp. 775–776. GN 4, 3, p. 172, discusses the same scenes and, like Baudry connects the woman's death to anger at the executions. GN describes Adhémar's offer at 7, 23, pp. 311–312.

12. WT 4, 23, pp. 266–267.

13. WM 4, 362, pp. 634–635. WM is the only historian to directly report cannibalism at Antioch, perhaps because cannibalism there was overshadowed by more spectacular and widespread examples from later in the crusade.

14. France (1994), pp. 229–232; GF, p. 30.

15. RA, p. 49 (and p. 55); RC 58, p. 649; FC 1, 15, 11–12, pp. 221–222, and 1, 16, 1–2, pp. 224–226; RtM 4, 4, p. 777.

16. FC 1, 15, 13–14, pp. 222–223, and 1, 16, 4, pp. 226–227; AA 3, 57, pp. 228–229.

17. RA, pp. 49 and 52; GF, pp. 31–32, though the story is preserved more fully in PT, pp. 66–67; AA 3, 51–52, pp. 218–221. Anselm of Ribemont says that Bohemond took 700 knights and "a few foot soldiers" and adds that they enjoyed a great victory over 12,000 Turks, led by "the king of Galipia," Hagenmeyer, *Epistulae*, 15, p. 158. RA, p. 49, says that Bohemond could raise only 150 knights. In this case as in most others, numbers are a matter of making educated guesses.

18. I am privileging here the account of RA, p. 51; to be compared to GF, p. 32.

19. RA, p. 54; FC 1, 15, 16, p. 224; Apoc. 6:12; Matthew of Edessa 2, 116, p. 168; RC 56, p. 648. RC places these celestial phenomena after the crusaders were victorious in another battle on February 9. But because no one else reports similar activity at this time, and because chronology was, for RC and many medieval observers, an inexact science, it is likely that he misremembers or misdates these events.

20. I am basing this account primarily on what RA reports (pp. 68–69, thus far). The earliest manuscript of Raymond's history begins this section in all capitals with the words THE DISCOVERY BEGINS and reads very much like a legal brief—a rough Latin translation of Peter's testimony (taken in June 1098) about his experiences with Andrew. It can be compared to GF, pp. 57–58/Tudebode, p. 101. The GF account is somewhat garbled, as I have discussed in Rubenstein (2004), pp. 192–193. The most detailed treatment of Peter's visions is France (2004).

21. The Andrew legend was already translated into many languages at the time of the crusade. See Robert Boening, ed. and trans., *The Acts of Andrew in the Country of the Cannibals: Translations from the Greek, Latin, and Old English* (New York: Routledge, 1991).

22. RA, pp. 69–70.

23. GF, p. 33; RA, p. 54. I am following the chronology of Hagenmeyer, *Chronologie,* here, though admittedly details are hazy.

24. GF, p. 34; PT, p. 69; BB, 2, 12, pp. 43–44; RtM 4, 12, pp. 781–782. The detail about the latrine comes from RC 60, pp. 650–651. RC's version of the desertion is markedly different. He does not mention Peter the Hermit. Instead, William plans to desert with Guy the Red, an important French noble. When Bohemond learns

of their plans, he threatens to convert their tents into latrines. I am taking some liberty in assuming that he did so. Flori (1999), pp. 482–492, suggests ingeniously that Peter never attempted to desert but rather that in circulating copies of GF later, Bohemond inserted Peter's name in place of Guy's out of fear of offending the Capetians, with whom Bohemond was negotiating a marriage on his own behalf. As Flori rightly points out, the sources describing Peter's desertion all grow from a single text, but I have elected to follow them (and presume that Guy deserted on another occasion). AA 4, 37, pp. 304–305, places William's final desertion much later in the siege.

25. GN 4, 8, pp. 179–180.

Chapter 10

1. The best primary source account of Baldwin's activity in Syria is AA (quoted here at 3, 18, pp. 166–167). FC 1, 14, 4–15, pp. 208–215, is very brief (despite being an eyewitness and a political player in these events). On this all-but-lost period of conquest, see Christopher MacEvitt, *The Crusades and the Christian World of the East: Rough Tolerance* (Philadelphia: University of Pennsylvania Press, 2008), pp. 58–63.

2. My overview of Edessan history owes its existence almost entirely to MacEvitt, *Rough Tolerance*, esp. pp. 65–68. On the economy of Edessa, see Monique Amouroux-Mourad, *Le Comté d'Edesse, 1098–1150* (Paris: Librairie Orientaliste Paul Geuthner, 1988), pp. 131–135. The terms of Toros's offer are not entirely clear: Compare AA 3, 19, 168–169, to FC 1, 14, 6, p. 210. Matthew of Edessa, 2, 117, pp. 168–169, is vague.

3. FC 1, 14, 7–11, pp. 210–212; AA 3, 19–20, pp. 168–171. AA uses the word "senator." Because he seems to have enjoyed especially good sources, I have elected to read his decision as growing out of the perceptions of Baldwin and his followers. AA also says that Baldwin had two hundred knights, not eighty. I am following FC here because, although laconic on most points, he is more trustworthy on such fine points of detail, having been present at these particular events.

4. FC 1, 14, 12, pp. 212–213; AA 3, 20–21, pp. 168–173.

5. The adoption ceremony is described at AA 3, 21, pp. 170–171; and GN 3, 14, pp. 163–164.

6. This is the version of AA 3, 22–24, pp. 172–174. FC 1, 14, 13, pp. 213–214, places the uprising two weeks after the adoption. A briefer but broadly similar version of this story appears in GN 3, 14, p. 164, which describes Toros's death as a noble sacrifice to save Baldwin.

7. Matthew of Edessa 2, 118, pp. 169–170; MacEvitt, *Rough Tolerance*, pp. 68–70.

8. FC 1, 13–14, pp. 213–215; AA 3, 24, pp. 176–177.

9. MacEvitt, *Rough Tolerance*, provides the best treatment of Baldwin's activity, esp. pp. 70–73. On the advantages brought to the crusade by Baldwin, see France (1994), pp. 132–133, 194–195, and 259–261.

Chapter 11

1. GF, pp. 34–35.

2. *Alexiad* 11, 4, p. 343. RA, pp. 55–56, tells of Tetigus's withdrawal and his offer of cities to Bohemond. On these maneuvers, see Jonathan Shepard, "When Greek Meets Greek: Alexius Comnenus and Bohemond in 1097–8," *Byzantine and Modern Greek Studies* 12 (1988): 262–275.

3. The story of Hilary appears only in HBS 47, p. 190, a text that, as I have argued elsewhere, preserves certain battlefield legend and campfire lore better than other apparently older chronicles like GF and PT. France (1994), pp. 198–199, nicely outlines the complexities of Syrian politics in 1096–1097.

4. GF, pp. 35–36; AA 3, 61, pp. 234–235; RA, pp. 56–57 (who says that the army looked almost three times bigger than it was). See also the commentary of France (1994), pp. 245–246.

5. RA, p. 57. GF, p. 36, describes the formation of six divisions. On the numbers of the army, see France (1994), p. 246. Although France's reconstruction of the details of the battle is, on the whole, superb, I cannot agree with his suggestion (pp. 247–248) that the Franks crossed the bridge before the battle. His argument overvalues the evidence of RC, 56, p. 648, written several years after the fact. RC did visit the battlefield when he was serving Tancred at Antioch, and he visited a grave near the Iron Bridge, but these facts make him no more able to reconstruct a battle narrative than anyone who visits a war site today. Based on the evidence of RA, who says that the knights traveled "two leagues" from camp before waiting to confront the Turks, and GF, p. 37, who says that the Franks eventually pursued the Turks all the way to the Iron Bridge, the reconstruction presented here seems more likely. It also seems unlikely that the seven hundred Frankish knights could have secretly crossed the Iron Bridge, even at night, unobserved.

6. In this description, I have followed the romanticizing instincts of GF, pp. 36–37, with detail from RA, p. 57.

7. HBS 50, p. 191.

8. RA, p. 58; AA 3, 62, pp. 236–239; GF, pp. 37–38; RC 56, p. 648.

9. BB 2, 17, p. 51; and RtM 4, 16, p. 784, both imply that the crusaders were trying to intimidate the Egyptians with the heads. AA 2, 28, pp. 108–111. About these Frankish-Egyptian negotiations, see Michael A Köhler, "Al-Afdal und Jerusalem— was versprach sich Ägypten vom ersten Kreuzzug?" *Saeculum* 37 (1986): 228–239.

10. RtM 5, 2, pp. 792–793. More coherent versions of the diplomatic missions appear in other sources listed in the next note. The wish to keep the purpose of these negotiations vague was equally true for both Christian and Muslim sides. See

Hillenbrand (1999), pp. 44–45 and 84–85, n. 29. See also France (1994), pp. 251–253.

11. See AA 3, 59, p. 230; GN 4, 13, p. 189, and 7, 3, pp. 271–272; Hagenmeyer, *Epistulae* 15, p. 160, and 10, pp. 149 and 151. See also GF, pp. 37–38; BB 2, 7, p. 51; RA, p. 58; HBS 48, pp. 189–190; and PT, p. 72.

12. These details come from RtM 5, 1, p. 791.

13. Asbridge (2004), p. 194, oddly translates "Mahomerie" as "Blessed Mary." I am presuming the Egyptian ambassadors accompanied Bohemond because as of May 9 they were at the port preparing to leave, as will become clear. On the decision to build the tower, see France (1994), pp. 231–232.

14. Based on AA 3, 63, pp. 238–41; and GF, p. 40. GF is, of course, the pro-Bohemond account; AA cannot resist the opportunity to criticize the Norman leader. RA, p. 59, puts the number of dead at three hundred.

15. RA, p. 60, provides the detail about the gates being locked. Yaghi-Siyan thus told his soldiers, "Conquer or die." In the 110th *laisse* of *Roland*, the poet observes that many mistake the moment of Roland's death for the beginning of the Last Judgment because of the great number of signs that accompany it.

16. BB 2, 17, pp. 50–51; GN 7, 11, p. 284; RtM 4, 20, pp. 786–787; AA 3, 65, pp. 244–245. It is notable that all of the writers who worked with GF report this incident, though GF does not. I have suggested elsewhere—Rubenstein (2004), p. 189, and nn. 53 and 54—that the story probably appeared in a now-lost rendition of GF.

17. GF, p. 41. The image of bodies not falling appears in RtM 4, 19, p. 786. The description brings to mind William of Poitiers's observation about the English at Hastings that their battle formation was so dense that there was hardly room for the dead to fall: WP 2, 19, p. 130. See also Sweetenham's note in her translation of RtM, p. 132, n. 42, about a similar image in Lucan. On the river battle more generally, see RtM 4, 21, pp. 787–788; RA, p. 61; and FC 1, 16, 8, p. 229. The reference made here is to Apoc. 16:4.

18. GF, p. 42; RtM 4, 21, p. 788; RA, p. 61. GF first tells the number of the dead and then reveals a few lines later the method used for counting them.

19. BB 2, 17, p. 51. GN, 4, 14, p. 193, comments on the tendency of the Saracens to bury their dead with treasure; as does RtM 4, 22, p. 788, where he also comments on the shame of the deed. It is possible that Robert means only that the Christians shamed the Saracens, but the other reading (that it was a shameful deed) seems more likely. See also GF, p. 42.

20. PT, pp. 79–81; HBS 56, p. 194. The dialogue here follows the HBS version of the story.

21. HBS 35, p. 186. See also HBS 60, p. 195.

22. AA 5, 1, pp. 338–339, is the only source to describe the patriarch being suspended over the walls. The patriarch's feet were not, as common folklore has it, beaten with iron rods while he hung there—e.g., Asbridge (2004), p. 168—the result of a mistranslation of AA, who says simply that the patriarch's feet were injured by

being placed in chains. AA does not specify at what point in the siege this torture occurred.

23. HBS 35, p. 186, and 60, p. 195, with the note about the floors in 61, p. 195. The "temples" he describes as *oracula*.

24. RA, p. 129; WT 6, 23, p. 339. He is elaborating on AA 5, 1, pp. 338–339, which also mentions the "blinding" of the painted figures. A similar passage appears in EA 3, p. 13.

25. HBS 61, p. 195.

Chapter 12

1. RtM 5, 5, p. 794. GP, whose poetic history closely follows Robert's, repeats this information in similar terms: GP 5 (2), ll. 411–460, pp. 126–129. Robert elsewhere describes Saracens simply as "rabid dogs" (*canes rabidos*): RtM 6, 8, p. 809. The lament occurs at RtM 5, 7, p. 795. See Riley-Smith (1997), pp. 88–89 and 224.

2. The second letter of Anselm of Ribemont, in Hagenmeyer, *Epistulae* 15, p. 159, written in July 1098, after the Franks defeated Kerbogah.

3. GN 7, 22, pp. 308–309.

4. On the three-week siege, see FC 1, 19, 2, pp. 242–243; and Matthew of Edessa 2, 119, p. 170.

5. RtM 4, 1, p. 775.

6. AA 4, 12–14, pp. 266–271, provides most of these details. His account is flawed because Bohemond belongs near the center of the story and one of AA's obvious historical goals is to downplay the Norman leader's contribution to the crusade. RA, p. 64, mentions some of the early desertions.

7. GF, pp. 44–45. The quip is from RtM 5, 10, p. 798.

8. GF, p. 45; AA 4, 15, pp. 270–271. The number 400,000 is used in a speech by Adhémar in RC 64, p. 653, as is the pronouncement about the dangers of abandoning Antioch. This incident is well served by two detailed recent treatments: Robert Levine, "The Pious Traitor: Rhetorical Reinventions of the Fall of Antioch," *Mittellateinishces Jahrbuch* 33 (1998): 59–80; and Rebecca L. Slitt, "Justifying Cross-Cultural Friendship: Bohemond, Firuz, and the Fall of Antioch," *Viator: Medieval and Renaissance Studies* 38 (2007): 339–349. I do not pretend here to resolve the question of whether Pirrus/Firuz was Armenian or Turkish, but see France (1994), pp. 257–264; Asbridge (2004), pp. 200–211; and Hillenbrand (1999), p. 57.

9. AA 4, 16, pp. 272–273, tells the hostage story; his information is somewhat garbled because he appears to confuse Pirrus with another Turkish convert who later took the name "Bohemond." RC 62, p. 652, tells of the harsh taxes (see also RC 57, p. 649). GF, p. 44, says bribery—the preferred explanation of GN 5, 2, p. 201.

10. BB 2, 19, pp. 53, and, more generally, 52–54. On this topic, see especially Slitt, "Justifying Cross-Cultural Friendship." GF, p. 44, speaks of the "closest friendship" between the two. See also RtM 5, 10, p. 798.

11. RtM 5, 8–9, pp. 796–798. The "jargon" necessary to interpret these visions grows out of the Eucharistic debate, still ongoing in the twelfth century. "Holy traitor" is the phrase of RC 66, p. 654. FC 1, 17, 1–5, pp. 230–232, also argues for a divine inspiration but more straightforwardly says that Jesus appeared three times to Pirrus and commanded him to hand over the city.

12. GF, pp. 45–46. On Stephen's departure, see GF, p. 63; RA, p. 77; and FC 1, 17, 5, pp. 232–233. See also France (1994), pp. 269–270.

13. AA 4, 16, pp. 272–275; GF, pp. 45–46.

14. AA 17–19, pp. 274–279; GF, p. 46; RA, p. 64.

15. AA 4, 21, pp. 278–280; GF, p. 47; RC 70, p. 657; RA, p. 65; GF, p. 46; BB 2, 20–21, pp. 56–57.

16. GF, pp. 46–47. That he writes this scene partly in the first person has traditionally formed a key component of the argument that the anonymous author was a warrior. It would not have been unexpected on the crusade, however, to find a cleric in the midst of battle.

17. FC 1, 17, 5, p. 233; BB 2, 21, pp. 56–57; AA 4, 23, pp. 282–283; GF, p. 47.

18. GF, pp. 47–48; RA, p. 65; AA 4, 23, pp. 282–283. FC observes that the commoners searched for goods but that the knights stayed focused on killing Turks: FC 1, 17, 7, pp. 234–235.

19. France (1994), pp. 264–265; AA 4, 22, pp. 280–281.

20. AA 4, 23, pp. 282–285; RtM 6, 2, p. 805.

21. GN 5, 6, p. 206, presents this argument, in the same place describing Adhémar's instructions about shaving; Caffaro 5, pp. 52–53.

22. RA, p. 66. For the description of Yaghi-Siyan's flight, I have drawn on Raymond as well as AA 4, 26, pp. 286–287; and GF, pp. 47–48.

Chapter 13

1. "Instituit nostro tempore prelia sancta deus, ut ordo equestris et vulgus oberrans, qui vetustae paganitatis exemplo in mutuas versabantur cedes, novum repperirent salutis promerendae genus": GN, preface, p. 87. See Chapter 3.

2. France (1994), pp. 355–356, makes essentially this case. He points toward the 1057 conquest of Melitene as an example of how the Turks lived according to similar rules. See also Kaspar Elm, "Die Eroberung Jerusalems in Jahre 1099. Ihre Darstellung, Beurteilung und Deutung in den Quellen zur Geschichte des Ersten Kreuzzugs," in *Jerusalem in Hoch-und Spätmittelalter: Konflikte und Konfliktbewältigung, Vorstellung and Vergegenwärtungen*, ed. Dieter Bauer, Klaus Herbers, and Nikolas Jaspert (Frankfurt, Germany: Campus, 2001), pp. 31–54. Kedar (2004) offers an effective critique of this argument, esp. pp. 67–72.

3. OV, 2, 3, pp. 92–93, following Chibnall's translation and Anglicized spelling.

4. William of Jumièges, *Gesta Normanorum*, 2, 5, 16, pp. 36–39. The Latin leaves unclear whether they burned it down deliberately after the battle or whether they

set fire to it during the course of the conflict. My thanks to Dominique Barthélemy for this reference.

5. These events are described in *Les miracles de saint Benoit écrits par Adrevald, Aimoin, André, Raoul Tortaire, et Hugues de Sainte Marie moines de Fleury,* ed. E. De Certain (Paris: Libraire de la Société de l'Histoire de France, 1858) 5, 1–4, pp. 192–198. Discussed in Thomas Head, "The Judgment of God: Andrew of Fleury's Account of the Peace League of Bourges," in *The Peace of God: Social Violence and Religious Response Around the Year 1000,* ed. Thomas Head and Richard Landes (Ithaca, NY: Cornell University Press, 1992), pp. 219–238; and Dominique Barthélemy, *L'An mil et la paix de Dieu: La France chrétienne et féodale, 980–1060* (Paris: Fayard, 1999), pp. 404–416.

6. *Les miracles de saint Benoit* 5, 4, pp. 197–198. Tomas Mastnak, *Crusading Peace: Christendom, the Muslim World, and Western Political Order* (Berkeley and Los Angeles: University of California Press, 2002), pp. 11–13.

7. Andrew makes the comparison in *Les miracles de Saint Benoit* 5, 4, p. 197. The incident occurs in Judg. 19–21. My description tends to downplay the true horror of the scene. After the concubine had been repeatedly raped throughout the night, her husband reclaimed her and then cut her body into twelve pieces, sending each piece to a different tribe and demanding justice for the crime.

8. BB 3, 26, p. 86, writing about the battle of Ma'arra at the end of 1098; and GN 5, 7, pp. 207–208, writing about the capture of Antioch in June 1098.

Chapter 14

1. On Kerbogah, see Hillenbrand (1999), pp. 56–58; France (1994), pp. 257–261, and 269–296; and Asbridge (2004), pp. 202–204. His name is also written as Kirbogah, Karbuqa, and Curbaram.

2. GN 6, 2, p. 234, and 5, 11, p. 214; BB 3, 2, pp. 61–62. The letter is in BB 3, 3, p. 62. The biographer of Saladin, the Muslim hero who would reconquer Jerusalem in 1187, reported a century later that his hero had proposed a similar war in Europe: Gabrieli, pp. 101–102.

3. GF, p. 50. PT, p. 90, uses slightly different language for the crucial oath that Sensadolus offered: "I will faithfully give my estates to you and then I will be made your man in connection with all of them, and in fidelity to you I will guard this citadel." I have discussed this scene and what it suggests about the composition of the early crusade sources in Rubenstein (2004), pp. 198–200.

4. The word choice "extort" (*extorquebat*) is Guibert's: GN 5, 8, p. 210.

5. GF, p. 51. Robert has him make the slightly sillier request that if the Franks win, he be allowed to run away: RtM, 6, 9, p. 810. The sequel to the story appears in HBS 66–67, pp. 198–199. See also France (1994), p. 269.

6. HBS 67, p. 198.

7. GF, pp. 53 and 51; GN 6, 3, p. 235. On the chains, see AA, 4, 45, pp. 318–319, and 4, 8, pp. 258–259. The last two boasts are AA 4, 5, pp. 254–255; and BB 3, 16, p. 76.

8. GF, p. 53, and, more generally, pp. 53–56. The scene with Kerbogha's mother is also described in PT, pp. 93–96; BB 3, 4, pp. 62–64; GN 5, 11–12, pp. 212–216; and RtM 6, 12, pp. 812–813. Natasha Hodgson analyzes this scene with a particular emphasis on gender in "The Role of Kerbogha's Mother in the *Gesta Francorum* and Selected Chronicles of the First Crusade," in *Gendering the Crusades*, ed. Susan B. Edgington and Sarah Lambert (New York: Columbia University Press, 2002), pp. 163–176.

9. GF, pp. 55–56, asking his mother whether Bohemond and Tancred were gods and whether the rumors were true that sometimes at a single sitting they could eat 2,000 cows and 4,000 pigs. RtM 8, 12, p. 813. Guibert uses a similar tactic: GN 5, 12, pp. 215–216.

10. AA 4, 28, pp. 288–291; RtM 6, 8, pp. 808–809.

11. AA 4, 33, pp. 296–299; GF, p. 56; RA, pp. 67–68.

12. RtM 6, 5–6, p. 807. I am translating *tormentum* as "missile" in the sense of a "bolt" fired from a catapult. Hugh is mentioned elsewhere at BB 3, 10, p. 68; GN 5, 10, p. 223; PT, p 102; and GF, p. 61, without discussion of the suicide.

13. BB 3, 10, p. 69; RC 77, p. 661.

14. AA 4, 34, pp. 300–301; RtM 6, 14, p. 815. The price list is PT, p. 104. The biblical passage is 2 Kings 6:25. Hagenmeyer, *Epistulae* 18, p. 169.

15. OV 5, 9, pp. 96–99; AA 4, 37, pp. 304–307.

16. AA 4, 38–39, pp. 306–309.

17. GF, pp. 57–58, says that the priest, who is not named, recognized Christ by his cross, mentioning as well the stench unto heaven. RA, pp. 72–74, describes the vision, adding the detail on p. 74 that Stephen recognized the cross behind Christ's head as a feature from *imagines* of the Lord. GN 5, 17, pp. 218–219, uses similar language. See also BB 3, 7, pp. 66–67; and RtM 7, 1, pp. 821–822.

18. RA, pp. 70–72. RA's account of Peter's story begins with the fifth vision (p. 68) and then relates the first four.

19. Peter contrasts *paupertatis mee abitum* (the garment of my poverty) with *vestram magnitudinem* (your splendor) while speaking with Adhémar and Count Raymond: RA, p. 70. Raymond says on the previous page that Andrew was not happy with Adhémar's preaching. The quotation about dreams is GN 5, 19, p. 221.

20. RA, pp. 95–96. France's commentary on this topic is judicious. "Holy poverty was a powerful idea with a wide appeal amongst Christian people which is not confined to the poor themselves": France (2006), p. 19. See also Alphandéry and Dupront, pp. 98–119.

21. On Adhémar's doubt and Raymond's belief, see RA, p. 72; and FC 1, 18, 2, pp. 236–237.

22. RA, pp. 74–75; GF, p. 62.

23. RA, p. 75. RA, p. 74, specifies twelve men digging. GF, p. 65, puts the number at thirteen, a figure that PT, p. 107, corrects to twelve.

24. FC 1, 20, 2, pp. 246–247; RA, p. 78.

25. GF, pp. 65–66; Flori (2007), pp. 165–166. Asbridge (2004), p. 229, suggests that Peter was selected as a "disgraced deserter and demagogue to the masses," though neither of those qualities would particularly recommend him as the person in whom the lives of the entire garrison ought to be entrusted. A more straightforward reading would be that Peter, as the long-standing eschatological conscience of the crusade, was now seen as the best, surest person to carry out a prophetically charged task.

26. RA p. 79; GF p. 66; BB 3, 15, p. 74; GN 6, 2, p. 234. The much later description is from CdA 345, p. 432, ll. 8768–8774. HBS 84, p. 206, reports that Bohemond sent Kerbogah's tent to Bari as a gift.

27. RtM 7, 5–6, pp. 825–826, mentions the offer of trial without bloodshed. FC 1, 21, 1, pp. 247–248, suggests an ordeal by combat involving ten, twenty, or one hundred men from either side. AA 4, 45, pp. 318–319, says that the ordeal would involve twenty men from each side. See also GF, p. 67; PT, p. 109; and RtM 7, 6, p. 826. On the Norman Conquest, see WP 2, 12, p. 120–123.

28. See the comments of Asbridge (2004), pp. 229–232, which are echoed in France (2006), p. 10 and n. 38. Asbridge, p. 232, argues that this version of the negotiations suggests "a subtly different species of crusader: one for whom spiritual devotion was still an extremely powerful motivating force, but perhaps not an all-conquering inspiration." To strengthen this case, Asbridge uses evidence from Matthew of Edessa 120, p. 171. Matthew says that the crusaders decided to surrender (as Asbridge quotes) but then decided against doing so as soon as the Lance was discovered (which he does not quote). Since the gist of Asbridge's argument is to downplay the impact of the Lance upon the morale of the army, this omission seems remarkable and worthy of mention.

29. AA 4, 46, pp. 320–321.

30. GF, pp. 67–68; RA, p. 78.

31. The game is mentioned by FC 1, 22, 5, p. 253. It is described as "checkers" (*scaccias*) by RA, p. 80; and as a "game" (*ludum*) by RC 86, p. 667. RA, p. 80, describes the Turkish advisor. RtM 7, 9, pp. 828–829, describes the heretic. On this battle in general, see France (1994), pp. 280–296.

32. RA p. 81; and FC 1, 22, 8, p. 254, both mention Kerbogah's last-second attempt to offer terms. Guibert describes a patient Kerbogah waiting to strike his enemy all at once: GN 6, 8, p. 238. In doing so, he agrees with Ibn al-Athir, reprinted in Gabrieli, p. 9.

33. RA, pp. 81–82; RC 87–89, pp. 668–669.

34. GF, p. 69; RA, pp. 70, 82, and 83.

35. FC 1, 23, 5, pp. 256–257. GF, p. 69, says that it was a signal to retreat. AA 4, 49–50, pp. 326–329, describes it as a battle tactic. RA, p. 81, says that it was a battle tactic to keep the Franks at bay rather than to aid the Saracens in their attack.

36. France (1994), pp. 281–282. AA 4, 28, pp. 290–291, puts the number of horses at around 150.

37. Ibn al-Athir's observation is recorded in Gabrieli, p. 7.

38. GF, pp. 70–71. GF, pp. 69–70, describes the grass fire. But see France (1994), p. 285, who says that this was a well-known tactic of Muslim armies.

Chapter 15

1. RA, p. 87; FC 1, 25, 10, pp. 271–274. FC observes that by April, when the armies finally did advance deliberately to Jerusalem, the Franks were able to live off the harvests.

2. The contradictory sources are GF, p. 72; and AA, 5, 3, pp. 340–343. RA, p. 83, describes Bohemond's expulsion of rival soldiers from his tower. Hugh's delegation, as cited here in AA, was apparently attacked by Turks or Turcopoles during the journey. By the time the group reached the comforts of Constantinople, his heart had likely wearied of the adventure.

3. AA 5, 1–2, pp. 338–341; Hagenmeyer, *Epistulae* 13, p. 155; RA, p. 87. James A. Brundage, "Adhémar of Puy: The Bishop and His Critics," *Speculum* 34 (1959): 201–212, attributes the appointment mainly to Adhémar (pp. 210–211), seeing it as part of a papal program of outreach to Byzantium. The evidence for this reading, however, is slight. It is a simpler and to my mind a more convincing reading of the sources that the Franks needed to restore order and make as many goodwill gestures as possible to a city whose Christian population they had brutalized a month earlier during the capture of Antioch.

4. RC 71, pp. 657–658; HBS 106, p. 216. The story in RC is problematic. In the text as we now have it, RC associates the miracle with the death of Bohemond's son, who died in 1130, although RC seems to have finished writing the book by 1118 (see RHC Oc. 3, preface, p. xxxix). As Tancred's biographer and as a member of Bohemond's entourage in 1107, RC was well informed about Norman affairs. Presuming that the candle story is part of his original narrative, and not a detail inserted by RC or another writer, he likely associated it, at the time of the book's original composition, with Bohemond's checkered rule of the city and the failure of his 1107 crusade.

5. GF, p. 74; GN 6, 13, p. 246. On Adhémar as the new Moses, see BB 1, 5, p. 16; and RC 95, pp. 673–674. Baudry also has Urban II as Moses: BB 1, 4, p. 14. On Adhémar's death more generally, see RA, p. 84; and AA 5, 4, pp. 342–345. Why AA diverges so sharply from other accounts is difficult to say. He hears report of a ship from Regensburg arriving at Saint-Simeon, whose passengers all died of plague. He may simply connect this story to Adhémar's death and a few other pilgrims who died of illness, and from there he concludes that what was on the crusade normal mortality for six months was a great plague in which countless men and women

(AA outrageously says more than 100,000) died. On the ship from Regensburg, see AA 5, 23, pp. 364–367.

6. RA, pp. 84–85.

7. RA, pp. 86–88.

8. FC 1, 24, 14, p. 264; Hagenmeyer, *Epistulae* 16, pp. 164–165. Riley-Smith (1986), p. 164, reads this passage as the crusaders saying that they were making an internal "monastic" pilgrimage as well as an external pilgrimage, a spiritual reading that seems to me far less likely than the anagogical one proposed here.

9. GF, pp. 73–74. See also France (1994), pp. 311–312. The observation that the city was densely populated is based on the fact that when it was conquered, Arab historians remembered the slaughter as the greatest massacre of the crusade.

10. GF, p. 72; RA, pp. 84, and 88–89 (the latter, a brief account of the affair at Azaz). RA says that Godfrey told Count Raymond that the defenders of Azaz had been seen making the sign of the cross. AA 5, 5–12, pp. 344–355, gives the whole affair a chivalric veneer, attributing Godfrey's intervention to a Christian woman who had gained influence at Omar's court. See also Asbridge (2000), p. 28.

11. AA 5, 15–17, pp. 356–361; GN 3, 14, pp. 164–165.

12. RA, pp. 90–91. Peter says that Raymond had offered the first candle five days earlier on St. Faith's Day, which falls on October 6—hence my date for the vision on October 10. Accepting this date would mean that Raymond's expedition to Albara would have to be pushed back later than c. September 25, the date to which Hagenmeyer assigns it in his *Chronologie*.

13. On this phase of the crusade, see Thomas Asbridge, "The Principality of Antioch and the Jabal as-Summaq," in *The First Crusade: Origins and Impact*, ed. Jonathan Philips (Manchester, UK: Manchester University Press, 1997), pp. 142–152.

14. GF, p. 75; RA, pp. 91–92. GN 6, 14, p. 247, writes of settling *colonis* there.

15. GF, pp. 75–76. RA, pp. 92–93, tells of Godfrey's exploits and describes the council on pp. 93–94, saying that a date for departure had been agreed upon.

16. GF, pp. 77–78; RA, pp. 94–95.

17. RA, pp. 94–96 and 98.

18. FC 1, 25, 2, pp. 266–267; RC 97, p. 675 (the recent translation of RC, p. 116, n. 157, says, somewhat inexplicably, that this passage refers not to actual cannibalism but to scarcity); RA, p. 101.

19. AA 5, 29, pp. 374–375; GN 7, 23, pp. 310–311; GF, p. 80. The Bible verses are Isa. 49:26, Mic. 3:3, Apoc. 19:17–18, and 1 Kings 14:11.

20. The best battle accounts are RA, p. 97; and GF, pp. 78–80. See also RtM 8, 6, p. 847; and GP 8, ll. 198–202, pp. 208–209, where the dog image appears.

21. The Arab historian Ibn al-Athir places the number of dead at 100,000: Gabrieli, p. 9. The *Damascus Chronicle* of Ibn al-Qalanisi, published as Roger le Tourneau, trans., *Damas de 1075 à 1154* (Damascus: Institut Français de Damas, 1952), pp. 42–43, refers to Frankish treachery, the Franks killing of citizens of Ma'arra after promising them safety. See also the Aleppo chronicle in RHC *Or.* 3, p. 579; RA, pp. 97–98; and GF, pp. 79–80.

22. RA, p. 99.

23. RA, p. 101; GF, pp. 80–81.

24. RA, pp. 100–101. RA acknowledges the existence of cannibalism in the midst of his story about tearing down the walls.

25. RA, p. 102; GF, p. 81.

Chapter 16

1. RA, pp. 103–104; GF, pp. 81–83.

2. RtM 8, 11, p. 853; RA, pp. 106–107; GF, p. 83.

3. RA, pp. 106–107. France (1994), pp. 317–324, provides a convincing analysis of this phase of the crusade, though somewhat different from the one here.

4. AA 5, 28, pp. 372–373.

5. RtM 8, 15, p. 855; AA 5, 33, pp. 380–381; GF, p. 84.

6. AA uses the technical verb *exfestucavit*, indicating a formal, ceremonial rupture with Count Raymond, at 5, 35, pp. 382–385; RA, p. 110 and (less sympathetic toward Tancred), p. 112; GF, p. 84.

7. RA, p. 108. Raymond, p. 107, discusses how greed drove the decision to attack the castle. On Pons's death, see RA, p. 107. On Anselm of Ribemont, see Riley-Smith (1986), p. 68, and pp. 117–118; Hagenmeyer, *Epistulae*, 8, pp. 144–146, and 15, pp. 156–160; RA, p. 109; and RC 106, p. 681.

8. RA, pp. 112–116. See also France (2006), p. 17. Hill and Hill (1962), p. 112, n. 2, compare the dreams to visions in the Book of Daniel 7 and 8. Raymond likely would have had the comparison in mind as he wrote.

9. RA, p. 113. Hill and Hill (1962), p. 93, in their translation, render *cum aliis submerses esse*, as "You were almost overwhelmed by sin like the others," though the Latin does not justify that metaphorical reading.

10. RA, p. 106, where he writes of simple *pauperes*, of *pedites pauperes*, and of *milites plebei*.

11. RA, p. 114. I cannot agree with the suggestion of France (2006), p. 17, that the five *ordines* here are the five cultural groups within the army at Arqa, led by Raymond, Robert of Normandy, Robert of Flanders, Godfrey, and Tancred, respectively.

12. RA, p. 115. See also p. 86, where Andrew speaks to Peter of those "who go by the right path or who love God."

13. As Christ enunciates to Peter at RA, p. 114.

14. RA, pp. 115–116. See also Conor Kostick, *Social Structure of the First Crusade* (Leiden, the Netherlands: Brill, 2008), pp. 143–146. The Latin word translated here as "sovereign" is *potestas*: RA, p. 115. The word does not necessarily refer to the count but rather to the authority in the army more generally, including, presumably, the judges.

15. RA, pp. 113–114. The Bible verse is Apoc. 20:4–5. A similar analysis of this vision appears in Philippe Buc, "Martyrdom in the West: Vengeance, Purge, Salvation and History," in Nils Holger Petersen, Andreas Bücker, and Eyolf Oestrem, eds.,

Resonances: Historical Essays on Continuity and Change (Turnhout, Belgium: Brepols 2010), 21–56, esp. pp. 45–48.

16. See RC 100, p. 677, and 102, p. 678. RC had also known him in Normandy before the crusade and dedicated his book to him. Alphandéry and Dupront, p. 117, speak of Ralph's *rationalisme normand*, marshaled in the name of defending Bohemond's claims to Antioch.

17. The other chronicler is PT, p. 101.

18. RC 102, p. 678. Ralph references in this context James 1:17, that the victory was "from above, coming down from the Father of lights." Among modern historians, France (2006), p. 20, argues, "In the end [Peter Bartholomew's] association with Count Raymond and his Provençal patriotism exposed him to attack, and that was his undoing." See also Colin Morris, "Policy and Visions: The Case of the Holy Lance at Antioch," in *War and Government in the Middle Ages: Essays in Honour of J. O. Prwestwich*, ed. J. Gillingham and J. C. Holt (Woodbridge, UK: Boydell Press, 1984), pp. 33–45 (pp. 44–45).

19. RC 102, p. 678.

20. These visions occur in rapid succession: RA, pp. 116–120.

21. RA, pp. 116 and 120.

22. RA, pp. 120–121. It is highly likely that Raymond was involved in the pyre's construction. One manuscript of Peter Tudebode (London BL MS Harley 3904) confirms that the woodpiles were thirteen feet long and adds that they were three and one-half feet high; see the Hills's edition of PT, p. 131. The quotation is from Robert Bartlett, *Trial by Fire and Water: The Medieval Judicial Ordeal* (Oxford, UK: Clarendon Press, 1986), p. 1.

23. RA, p. 121. The manuscript is BL MS Harley 3904.

24. RA, p. 123. The other two accounts are FC 1, 18, 4, pp. 238–240; and GN 6, 22, p. 263.

25. "Guillelmus Maluspuer" and "Guillelmus Bonofilius"; RA, pp. 121–122.

26. RA, pp. 123–124. Fulcher gives the date of his death: FC, 1, 18, 4, pp. 238–240. RC, anxious to undermine Peter's reputation as much as possible, places his death *postridie*, which is to say, the day after the ordeal: RC 108, p. 682. GN 6, 22, p. 263, independently of Raymond's book, offers the same explanation for Peter's death (that the crowd crushed him in the midst of celebration).

Chapter 17

1. Gog and Magog, or rather "Gog of the land of Magog," are mentioned in prophecy in Ezek. 38:2. They were believed to have been imprisoned by Alexander the Great.

2. On Augustine and millenarianism, see Paula Fredriksen, "Tyconius and Augustine on the Apocalypse," in *The Apocalypse in the Middle Ages*, ed. Richard K. Emmerson and Bernard McGinn (Ithaca, NY: Cornell University Press, 1992), pp. 20–37. As for other signs, the prophecies of "pseudo-Methodius" remained

immensely popular throughout the Middle Ages, despite being built on an explicitly millenarian model. The regularity with which exegetes and theologians condemned millenarianism was in itself a sign that people continued to read the Apocalypse in this fashion. In general, modern historians, enamored of St. Augustine, have attributed more potency to his words than seems plausible.

3. These passages, the so-called Little Apocalypse, appear in Matt. 24, Mark 13, and Luke 21.

4. Adso, p. 26. The prophet pseudo-Methodius describes the moment more generally as the end to all earthly rule: *Sibyllinische Texte*, p. 93. The best study on the interplay between crusade thought and these prophetic texts remains Carl Erdmann, "Endkaiserglaube und Kreuzzugsgedanke im 11. Jahrhundert," *Zeitschrift für Kirchengeschichte* 51 (1932): 384–414.

5. RA, p. 111, describes the distribution of tithes. If Peter the Hermit was at Arqa before Godfrey and Robert of Flanders arrived, my presumption is that he was traveling with Robert of Normandy's contingent. His appointment to responsible ecclesiastical office indicates, moreover, that he would have won the trust of Arnulf.

6. RA, pp. 127–128.

7. RA, pp. 125–126, and p. 110. Alexius proposed to arrive on the Feast of John, which is July 25.

8. RA, pp. 109–110. RA places these negotiations just before his account of Peter Bartholomew's ordeal. Hagenmeyer's *Chronologie* places the negotiations around May 1, based on evidence from HBS 108, pp. 216–217. Other historians have followed his lead. I place this encounter in the general period of mid-April to early May but have kept the exact date vague because the evidence is uncertain. For example, HBS 102, pp. 214–215, does say that the Frankish ambassadors spent Easter (April 10, 1099) in Jerusalem with al-Afdal. France (1994), p. 325, based on this evidence, observes that the Franks were "obviously on friendly terms with their hosts." The story in fact says that al-Afdal threatened to kill them in Jerusalem and that they were saved only by a miracle—again, we must treat the evidence with caution.

9. RA, pp. 124–125; GF, pp. 84–85.

10. RC 110, p. 683; RA, pp. 130–131.

Chapter 18

1. AA 5, 38, pp. 388–389; RA, pp. 134–135; France (1994), pp. 325–330.

2. AA 5, 39–40, pp. 390–395.

3. Luke 24:13–27; RC 111, p. 683; HBS 109, p. 217; AA 5, 44, pp. 400–401; FC 1, 25, 14–15, pp. 278–280. I am translating the expression *communem domum* at RA, p. 143, as "town hall." Literally, it means "common house." On the objections, see RA, p. 137. I have reconstructed pilgrimage details from Saewulf, *Peregrinationes tres*, ed. R. B. C. Huygens CCCM 139 (Turnhout, Belgium: Brepols, 1994), p. 73; and FC, 1, 25, 16, p. 280.

4. RC 111–112, pp. 683–85; HBS 110, p. 217. I have elected to follow Tancred's biographer rather than AA 5, 45, pp. 400–401, who says that Tancred rejoined the army on the main road to Jerusalem.

5. RC 113–114, pp. 685–686; HBS 111, p. 217.

6. BB 4, 9, pp. 96–97; RtM 9, 1, p. 863, marginal note; AA, 5, 45, pp. 402–403. AA estimates the number of survivors at this point at 60,000; France (1994), 141–142, estimates 20,000.

7. GN 7, preface, p. 266; 7, 2, pp. 269–270; 7, 5–6, p. 275.

8. GN 7, 9, p. 282; RC 123, p. 691. On Jerusalem syndrome, see, for example, Yair Bar-El, Rimona Durst, Gregory Katz, Josef Zislin, Ziva Strauss, and Haim Y. Knobler, "Jerusalem Syndrome," *British Journal of Psychiatry* 176 (2000): 86–90. As this article points out, Jerusalem syndrome has not been conclusively demonstrated as a disorder affecting mentally well-balanced visitors to the Holy Land (i.e., apparent sufferers may have gone to the Holy Land already susceptible to such extreme psychological reactions). After the physical and emotional hardships of the crusade, however, many of the Franks would likely have been prone to similar reactions. Aryeh Graboïs, *Le pèlerin occidental en Terre sainte au Moyen Âge* (Brussels: De Boeck Université, 1998), argues similarly that medieval pilgrims experienced the historical/biblical Jerusalem rather than the Jerusalem of current events when they visited the Holy Land.

9. RA, p. 139; RC 118, p. 688. France (1994), p. 345, argues that even without the hermit, it is likely the crusaders would have settled upon an early attack.

10. HBS 115, p. 219; AA 6, 1, pp. 406–407. FC, 1, 27, 1, pp. 292–293, indicates that there were multiple ladders but is probably not to be trusted here. RA, pp. 137 and 139. Baudry observes that they all would have walked barefoot, except for fear of an enemy attack: BB, 4, 9, p. 97.

11. RA, pp. 139–141. See also, among others, GF, p. 89; AA 6, 6, pp. 410–413; and BB 4, 12, pp. 99–100. On the physical conditions of the march generally, Riley-Smith (1986), pp. 60–73, is particularly eloquent.

12. RC, 120, p. 689, places this discovery after the first attack, rather than before, as in Asbridge (2004), p. 303. On the ships, see France (1994), pp. 336–337; GF, pp. 88–89; and RA, pp. 141–142 and 146.

13. RA, p. 138, mentions the resistance to the move. See also France (1994), pp. 338–339 and 344–345; and Adrian J. Boas, *Jerusalem in the Time of the Crusades* (New York: Routledge, 2001), p. 43.

14. GF, p. 91. On the presence of women among those carrying out this difficult task, see Ripoll Account, p. 645.

15. GF pp. 67–68; AA 6, 7, pp. 412–413. This is the first time Albert mentions the hermit; he thus does not associate him with the failed attack of June 13. On processions, see France (1994), p. 347; and Riley-Smith (1986), pp. 82–85. In a letter from the future patriarch of Jerusalem, Daimbert (written, or ghostwritten, by Raymond of Aguilers) says that "the Lord was placated by this humility": Hagenmeyer, *Epistulae*, 18, p. 171.

16. RA, pp. 144–145.

17. Josh. 6:1–21. GN 7, 6, pp. 276–277, draws the connection explicitly. See also PT, pp. 137–138.

18. BN 34, p. 513; PT, p. 137; RA p. 145; AA 6, 8–9, pp. 414–415.

19. RA, p. 145; AA 6, 8, pp. 412–415. PT, p. 138, attributes the sermon to Arnulf.

20. He does not state explicitly that the sermon occurred during the procession, but he does note that all the bishops and priests were present, in full vestment, and that one man set in a higher place spoke to the people: BB 4, 13, p. 100.

21. BB 4, 13, pp. 100–101. The editors of the RHC suggest that this last passage is a paraphrase of Virgil, *Ecl*. 3.16. This entire elegant structure grows out of a meditation in Eph. 6:10–20, the famous Pauline passage about putting on the armor of God.

22. BB 4, 13, p. 101, and 1, 17, p. 23.

23. GP 9, 5, p. 244, ll. 271–272; CdA 11, p. 26, ll. 171–178.

24. RA, p. 147. GF, p. 90, says the towers were moved four days before, on July 9. RA, p. 147, places the move on the night before the battle, apparently July 13: "On the eve of when the combat had been ordered" (*"Instante autem iusse obpugnationis die"*), despite the Hills's note to the contrary (n. 1). Historical tradition tends to favor GF in all things (e.g., France [1994], pp. 347–348). In this case I would—like Asbridge (2004), p. 310—follow Raymond since moving the tower and equipment four days earlier would seem to undercut significantly the element of surprise. RC, 122–124, pp. 690–692, agrees with Raymond. AA 6, 9, pp. 414–415, agrees with GF, placing the maneuver just after the procession. The other towers are mentioned in HBS 121, p. 221.

25. AA 6, 9–11, pp. 414–419; RC 124, pp. 691–692; FC 1, 27, 8, pp. 297–298.

26. AA 6, 15, pp. 422–423; RA pp. 148–149.

27. BB 4, 14, p. 101; AA 6, 16, pp. 422–423; RtM 9, 7, p. 866, and 8, 14, p. 855; HBS 121, p. 221; RA, p. 149.

28. RA, p. 149; PT, pp. 140–141; Ripoll Account, p. 649; Apoc. 19:12. See also France's commentary on the historical significance of the sermon (as well as the author's possible eyewitness status): "An Unknown Account of the Capture of Jerusalem," *English Historical Review* 87 (1972): 772–783. The rider on the white horse is first mentioned in Apoc. 6:2. See also Don Denny, "A Romanesque Fresco in Auxerre Cathedral," *Gesta* 25 (1986): 197–202. RA, p. 150.

29. On the first person over the wall: Lethold was the consensus candidate— mentioned in GF, pp. 90–91; PT, p. 91; GN 7, 7, p. 278 (predicting Lethold will be celebrated for generations); BB 4, 14, p. 102; and RtM 9, 7, p. 867 (adding that a certain Guicher followed Lethold). AA 6, 19, pp. 428–429, has the brothers climbing onto the walls together. HBS 122, p. 221, says that Bernard was the first, followed by Lethold and Engelbert, RA, pp. 150 and 151, says at first that Tancred and Godfrey were first but then notes a little later that several people saw Adhémar lead the way. On the battle details: AA 6, 18–19, pp. 426–429 (who mentions that local Christians warned the Franks about this fire); and RC 125, p. 693. RA, p. 150, describes

Godfrey's dramatic entry onto Jerusalem's walls. See also France (1994), pp. 351–353. AA 7, 3, pp. 488–491, elaborates on the mechanics of Greek Fire in a battle fought by Godfrey as king of Jerusalem.

30. GN 7, 7, p. 279, and 7, 10, p. 283; BN 35, p. 515; HBS 126, p. 223; RtM 9, 8, p. 868; RA, p. 150.

31. GF, p. 91; GN 7, 7, p. 279, and 7, 8, p. 280; BB 4, 14, p. 102; BN 35, p. 515; RtM 9, 8, p. 868.

32. RA, p. 150. Raymond would use a similar description in a letter written in September 1099 on behalf of Archbishop Daimbert of Pisa, later patriarch of Jerusalem, saying that the horses in Jerusalem rode through blood up to their knees: Hagenmeyer, *Epistulae* 18, p. 171. EA 17, p. 24, borrows this language. See also Kedar (2004), p. 65.

33. RC 129, pp. 695–696; AA 6, 23–25, pp. 430–437. FC 1, 26, 9, p. 290, mentions in the Temple of the Lord, or Dome of the Rock, an "idol named Muhammad."

34. AA 6, 26, pp. 436–439; BB 4, 14, p. 103; FC 1, 29, 2, pp. 304–305; RA, p. 151. Isa. 11:10, in the Vulgate, reads *"Et erit sepulchrum eius gloriosum."* Robert discusses this verse as it applies to the crusaders: RtM 9, 9, p. 869. See also Riley-Smith (1986), pp. 142–143.

Chapter 19

1. RA, p. 150.

2. FC 1, 28, 1, pp. 301–302; HBS 123, p. 222.

3. AA 6, 28, pp. 438–439. Albert says here as well that Raymond received a huge amount of money in exchange for their release. See also RA, p. 151; GF, p. 92; and PT, p. 141.

4. AA 6, 28–29, pp. 438–441; GF, pp. 91–92. PT, p. 141, unusually, says that Tancred ordered the killing himself.

5. AA 6, 29, pp. 440–441.

6. AA 6, 30, pp. 440–443 (I am closely following Edgington's translation).

7. GF, p. 92; FC 1, 33, 19, pp. 332–333, and note b. See also n. 51 on the same page; and Kedar (2004), p. 20, and n. 8. EA 20, p. 26, also comments on the stench around Jerusalem.

8. RA, p. 143.

9. RA, p. 152; AA 6, 33, pp. 444–446; GN 7, 11, p. 284.

10. FC 1, 30, 1, p. 308.

11. GN 7, 25, p. 318; HBS 130, p. 225. The epitaph reads, *"Rex licet electus. rex noluit intitulari. Nec dyademari. sed sub christo famulari."*; recorded in Brussels BR MS 9823–9824, fol. 138v. I discuss the origins of the "advocate" myth later in the chapter.

12. AA 2, 16, pp. 84–87; EA 11, p. 19.

13. AA 6, 34–35, pp. 446–449. Alphandéry and Dupront, p. 131, suggest that this story and the ones to follow were probably retrospective inventions made after Godfrey had become king, but there is no particular reason to see them as such. They are just as likely examples of the evidence mustered to support Godfrey's claim to leadership.

14. AA 6, 26–27, pp. 436–439. Albert refers briefly to Stabelo's activity during Baldwin I's reign: AA 9, 4, pp. 640–643.

15. AA 6, 36–37, pp. 448–451.

16. *Vita beatae Idea* [in AASS Apr. 2] 4, p. 142, with the vision of the sun mentioned at 3, p. 142. The later version is published in RHC *Oc.* 5, pp. 307–309; and is appended to a collection of crusade chronicles in Paris BnF Arsenal MS 1101, fol. 101v. See also WT 9, 6, p. 427.

17. RA, pp. 152–153.

18. RA, p. 71.

19. RA, p. 153.

20. Hagenmeyer, *Epistulae* 18, pp. 167–174. Specifically in the preamble (p. 168), Godfrey is described as "by the grace of God now advocate of the church of the Holy Sepulcher." On the composition of the letter, see Hagenmeyer's notes in *Epistulae*, pp. 108–110; John France, "The Election and Title of Godfrey de Bouillon," *Canadian Journal of History* 18 (1983): 321–329 (pp. 326–327); and Alan V. Murray, "The Title of Godfrey of Bouillon as Ruler of Jerusalem," *Collegium Medievale* 3 (1990): 163–178 (pp. 163–164).

Chapter 20

1. GF, p. 93, says that Tancred and Eustace captured Nablus and then received a summons from Godfrey to return because of an impending battle at Ascalon. Within a few lines, the author reported that while returning, Tancred learned of an Egyptian army massing at Ascalon and sent warning to Godfrey. AA 6, 42, p. 456, has Godfrey carrying out reconnaissance work with Tancred and Robert of Flanders because of the rumored attack and learning himself of the army at Ascalon. Other potentially independent sources, such as FC 1, 31, 1–2, pp. 311–312, and RC 138, p. 703, are vague on the details of who discovered the army.

2. RA, p. 154.

3. The discovery of the True Cross is described in several places: RA, pp. 154–155; FC 1, 30, 4, pp. 309–310; BN 37, p. 516; EA 29, pp. 33–34; and AA 6, 38, 450–453.

4. GF, p. 94. AA 6, 41, pp. 456–457, says that Peter traveled to Ascalon with the army. In either case Peter was playing a remarkably prominent role. See the analysis of Flori (1999), pp. 457–461.

5. GF, p. 94.

6. RA, pp. 156–158; GF, pp. 94–95; FC 1, 31, 5–6, pp. 313–315; AA 6, 42, pp. 458–459, and 6, 44, pp. 460–463; GN 7, 17, p. 296. AA and GN are the only writers to argue that it was a deliberate ruse on the part of the Egyptians.

7. The herds are described at GF, p. 94; and RA, pp. 155–156. PT, p. 145, alone mentions the dueling sermons with Lance and Cross. AA 6, 42, pp. 456–457, observes that Raymond refused at first to go because of petulance, but relented owing to external pressures.

8. AA 6, 43–44, pp. 458–461.

9. RA, p. 157–158; GF, p. 96; BB 4, 20, p. 109; RtM 9, 16, p. 873.

10. GF, pp. 95; RtM 9, 19, p. 875, and 9, 23, p. 879; GN 7, 20, p. 299; BB 4, 20, p. 109. See also France (1994), pp. 362–366. Guibert specifies that Robert had not captured the standard himself but had instead bought it from another soldier—still, a sign of the duke's marvelous generosity.

11. BN 39, p. 518. The German writer is Frutolf, p. 116. BB 4, 20–21, pp. 109–110; RtM 9, 21, p. 878. One of Baudry's earliest copyists spotted the potential embarrassment from this passage (given that wars with Egypt continued unabated) and excised it from the text. It appears to survive in only two manuscripts (of the fourteen that I have examined). See Apoc. 8:7, where at the sound of the first trumpet, fire and hail mixed with blood rain down from heaven.

12. FC 1, 31, 10, pp. 316–317.

13. BN 71, p. 541; FC 2, 35, 2, p. 507. More generally, FC 2, 34–35, pp. 503–509. BN is either a lightly revised version of FC's chronicle or (in my opinion the more likely case) a copy of the first draft of FC's chronicle, finished in 1106, preserving elements of that draft that have since been lost.

Conclusion

1. This anecdote about Galdemar was published as a continuation to Raymond's chronicle (henceforth, "Continuation") in RHC *Oc.* 5, pp. 307–308. The author only specifies Greek and Armenian; I am presuming the Latin. At one point Galdemar started to leave Hugh, but the archbishop ordered him by the oath he had made to him in life to return. See also Riley-Smith (1997), p. 75.

2. "Continuation," p. 308.

3. The treaty appears in Fernand Vercauteren, ed., *Actes des comtes de Flandre, 1071–1128* (Brussels: Palais des Académies, 1938), pp. 90–91.

4. CdA 233, pp. 284–285, for example; OV 5, 10, pp. 324–325; GN 5, 25, p. 228.

5. The literature on this topic is vast, but to hit the highlights: R. N. Swanson, *The Twelfth-Century Renaissance* (Manchester, UK: Manchester University Press, 1999); R. W. Southern, *Medieval Humanism and Other Studies* (Oxford, UK: Blackwell, 1970); Colin Morris, *The Discovery of the Individual, 1050–1200* (New York: Harper and Row, 1972). The most important recent foray into the topic is Rachel Fulton, *From Judgment to Passion: Devotion to Christ and the Virgin Mary, 800–1200*

(New York: Columbia University Press, 2002), which considers the question of the development of empathy in the twelfth century.

6. On Raimbold Croton, see Riley-Smith (1997), pp. 155–156.

7. GN 5, 11, p. 214; BN 35, p. 515; I Sam. 15:3.

8. BB 1, 4, p. 14. Robert uses the image frequently: RtM 2, 16, p. 747; 3, 14, p. 763; 6, 12, p. 812. See also RC 125, p. 693.

9. In particular, GN 2, 1, p. 109. On this theme generally, see Anthony D. Smith, *Chosen Peoples: Sacred Sources of National Identity* (Oxford, UK: Oxford University Press, 2003), esp. pp. 44–65, 120–123, and 137–141; and Mary Garrison, "The Franks as the New Israel? Education for an Identity from Pippin to Charlemagne," in *Uses of the Past in the Early Middle Ages*, ed. Yitzhak Hen and Matthew Innes (Cambridge, UK: Cambridge University Press, 2002), pp. 114–161. Matthew Gabriele's book is titled *An Empire of Memory: The Legend of Charlemagne, the Franks, and Jerusalem Before the First Crusade*. (Oxford, UK: Oxford University Press, 2011).

10. Brett Edward Whalen, *Dominion of God: Christendom and Apocalypse in the Middle Ages* (Cambridge, MA: Harvard University Press, 2009). On the definition of *Christianitas*, Rousset, pp. 102–103, makes this point. Denis Hay, *Europe: The Emergence of an Idea* (New York: Harper and Row, 1957), pp. 22–23 and 27–28, notes the word's ambiguities but draws too sharp a distinction between *Christianitas* as "the faithful" and *Christianismus* as the "faith," which was not a universally understood distinction. See also BB prologue, p. 9; 1, 11, p. 20; 2, 3, pp. 35–36; 2, 7, p. 39; 2, 16, p. 49; 4, 21, p. 110; and RA, p. 110.

11. RA, p. 151; RC 57, p. 648; Henry of Huntingdon, *Historia Anglorum*, ed. and trans. Diana Greenway (Oxford, UK: Clarendon Press, 1996), 7, 14, pp. 436–437. See the recent study by Suzanne Conklin Akbari, *Idols in the East: European Representations of Islam and the Orient, 1100–1450* (Ithaca, NY: Cornell University Press, 2009). I most certainly attribute more influence to the First Crusade for the propagation of these ideas than does Akbari.

12. GN 1, 2, p. 89, and, more generally, pp. 89–90; WM, 347, pp. 602–603, and 360, pp. 632–635. See also WM, 372, pp. 654–655, where he says it was a miracle that so many men, accustomed to cold weather, would willingly travel East. See the comments of Hay, *Europe*, pp. 3–5 and 32–33.

13. Paris BnF MS Arsenal 1101, fol. 101v, printed in the "Continuation," p. 309. See also Ripoll Account, p. 649. The biblical passage here conflates Apoc. 6:2 and 19:14.

A Note on Sources

1. *Deeds of the Franks*, or GF, has long enjoyed a reputation for being the most important of the crusade sources. I have presented a detailed interpretation of it in Rubenstein (2004). Historians, by contrast, have tended to discount the value of Raymond's book, seeing it as a revised version of GF, when in fact all evidence

points to the two books being composed at the same time (and it is indeed likely that the two writers would have known of each other's work during the crusade itself, perhaps helping to explain the similarities). Historians have only recently begun to appreciate the value of Albert of Aachen's chronicle (AA), thanks to the work of his most recent editor, Susan Edgington. I have disagreed with Edgington here by saying that Albert made use of a now-lost source (and am currently preparing an article to make this case more forcefully).

Index

Abraham, 121, 162

Acre, 274

Adela of Blois (wife of Stephen of
Blois), 93–94, 127, 176, 315–316

Adhémar (bishop of le Puy), 28–30, 74,
76, 97, 142, 247
and Antioch, 146, 153, 192
battle orations of, 107
cross of, 267–268, 270
death of, 155, 231–232
and decapitation, 151
and Dorylaeum, 130
and Holy Lance, 232
and Holy Lance, excavation of, 218
and Kerbogah, defeat of, 223, 227
and Nicea, 106–107
and nun from Trier, 114
and Peter Bartholomew, visions of,
157–158, 216, 217, 232–233, 258,
259, 267–268
and Peter Desiderius, visions of,
258, 270, 283
and Stephen of Valence, visions of,
214, 215
and Urban II, 36

Adultery, 153–154

Aelia Capitolina, 2

Agarenes, 121. *See also* Muslims;
Saracens

Agatha (saint), 268

Ahmad ibn-Marwan, 207–208, 223,
226–227

Aimo (archbishop of Bourges), 201–202

Al-Afdal, 176, 308, 309, 310

Al-Aqsa Mosque, 27

Albara, 238

Albert of Aachen, 12, 14, 59, 62, 64,
65–66, 66–67
and Adhémar, death of, 231–232
and Antioch, 133, 195–196
and Ascalon, 307, 308
and Bohemond, 136–137, 250
and cannibalism, 241
and Civitot, 88
and Godfrey of Bouillon, 71, 91, 92,
93, 300
and Jerusalem, massacre at, 295–296
and Nicea, 104, 106, 107
and nun from Trier, 114–115
and procession of penance and
humility, 284
and Sidon, 274